AF411966

NEW PATHWAYS IN
MICROSIMULATION

New Pathways in Microsimulation *is an extremely useful reference for those involved in the design and the evaluation of tax-benefit systems. Beyond methodological advances, it contains valuable examples from different policy domains, for example from the very timely field of pension reform in light of demographic and budgetary pressures. The authors demonstrate the substantial added value of microsimulations over purely aggregate or representative agent models.*

Alain Jousten, University of Liège, Belgium and Maastricht University, Holland

This volume illustrates the powerful approach of microsimulation in policy evaluation and design. There is a broad review of current applications including the effectiveness of tax-benefit policy, the analysis of poverty, health status, population ageing and the spatial effects of VAT-increases on household expenditures. Those interested in pension issues will for instance benefit from an analysis of the impact of the financial crisis on old-age poverty in Sweden using a model, which allows an interaction between the pension system, the labour market and an endogenous tax policy. Also recommended is a chapter on a stylized model of the pension system in Belgium, which brings out a number of basic properties of the system. However, a comparison demonstrates the advantages of a fully developed microsimulation model. Model builders will for instance enjoy contemplating how far the ideas of estimating block recursive models, and validating models by backwards simulation of a historical period will take us. This book is highly recommended to policy analysts, model builders and readers with a general interest in economics and social science.

Anders Klevmarken, Professor Emeritus, Uppsala University, Finland

*This book is dedicated to the memory of Reinhold Hatzinger and
Thomas Lindh; contributors to this book who never saw it being published.*

New Pathways in Microsimulation

Edited by

GIJS DEKKERS
*Federal Planning Bureau and KU Leuven, Belgium and
CEPS/INSTEAD, Luxembourg*

MARCIA KEEGAN
University of Canberra, Australia

CATHAL O'DONOGHUE
The Irish Agriculture and Food Development Authority, Ireland

ASHGATE

Published by
Ashgate Publishing Limited
Wey Court East
Union Road
Farnham
Surrey, GU9 7PT
England

Ashgate Publishing Company
110 Cherry Street
Suite 3-1
Burlington, VT 05401-3818
USA

www.ashgate.com

British Library Cataloguing in Publication Data
A catalogue record for this book is available from the British Library

The Library of Congress has cataloged the printed edition as follows:
Dekkers, Gijs.
  New pathways in microsimulation / by Gijs Dekkers, Marcia Keegan and Cathal O'Donoghue.
    pages cm
  Includes bibliographical references and index.
   ISBN 978-1-4094-6931-5 (hardback)—ISBN 978-1-4094-6932-2 (ebook)—ISBN 978-1-4094-6933-9 (epub) 1. Social sciences—Simulation methods. 2. Economics—Simulation methods. 3. Econometric models. I. Title.
   H61.25.D45 2014
   300.1'1—dc23

2013025917

ISBN 9781409469315 (hbk)
ISBN 9781409469322 (ebk – PDF)
ISBN 9781409469339 (ebk – ePUB)

Printed in the United Kingdom by Henry Ling Limited, at the Dorset Press, Dorchester, DT1 1HD

Contents

List of Figures

List of Tables

Editors' Biographies

Dr Gijsbrecht 'Gijs' Dekkers is Senior Researcher at the Directorate General of the Federal Planning Bureau, Belgium. He is also an Affiliated Research Associate at the Centre for Sociological Research CESO, Katholieke Universiteit Leuven, Belgium, and Affiliated Senior Researcher at CEPS/INSTEAD in Luxembourg. Finally, he is external lecturer 'chargé de cours' at the IUP Gestion du Patrimoine, Université Paris-Dauphine, France. Gijs is chief editor of the *International Journal of Microsimulation.*

Besides doing applied and academic research involving dynamic microsimulation, his main activity is developing and extending the model MIDAS and applying it for policy assessment in Belgium. He is also the initiator of a team of researchers that develop and test the open-source toolbox LIAM2 (http://liam2.plan.be), designed for the development of dynamic microsimulation models.

Gijs holds an MA in Economics (cum laude) from the University of Maastricht, and a doctorate in Social Sciences from Tilburg University, both in the Netherlands.

Dr Marcia Keegan is a Research Fellow at the National Centre for Social and Economic Modelling (NATSEM) at the University of Canberra. After completing a Bachelor of Economics (Honours) at the University of Western Australia and a Bachelor of Laws at the Australian National University, she undertook a PhD at NATSEM in dynamic microsimulation modelling. Since then her main area of research has been the accumulation and drawdown of wealth over the life course, in particular superannuation. She also undertakes research on tax-transfer modelling, labour force participation, earnings and life satisfaction. Marcia is Vice-President of the International Microsimulation Association, Treasurer of the ACT Economic Society and President of the ACT Young Economists' Network.

Prof Dr Cathal O'Donoghue, PhD in Economics (London School of Economics and Political Science), is Professorial Research Fellow at Maastricht University and heads the Rural Economy and Development Programme at Teagasc, in Ireland. Cathal is President of the International Microsimulation Association. He is an expert in microsimulation modelling and developed, among others, the LIAM and SMILE frameworks. He also helped develop EUROMOD and has published over 100 articles in peer-reviewed scientific journals and book chapters. He worked on a number of projects financed by the European Commission and provided advice to ministries in Ireland and the UK, the OECD, UNDP and UNICEF.

List of Contributors

Marta Adiego, Instituto de Estudios Fiscales, Spain
Ben Anderson, University of Southampton, United Kingdom
Luis Ayala, Universidad Rey Juan Carlos, Spain
Muriel Barlet, Ministère des Affaires sociales et de la Santé, France
Elisa Baroni, Swedish Pensions Agency, Sweden
Mark Birkin, University of Leeds, United Kingdom
Lisa Brouwers, KTH Royal Institute of Technology, Sweden
Olga Cantó, Universidad de Alcalá, Spain
Marie Cavillon, Ministère des Affaires sociales et de la Santé, France
Richard Cumpston, Australian National University, Australia
Paola De Agostini, University of Essex, United Kingdom
Gijs Dekkers, Federal Planning Bureau, Belgium
Anders Ekholm, Ministry of Health and Social Affairs, Sweden
Lina Maria Ellegård, Lund University, Sweden
Dennis Fredriksen, Statistics Norway
Hege Marie Gjefsen, Statistics Norway
Reinhold Hatzinger, Vienna University of Economics and Business, Austria
Seiichi Inagaki, Hitotsubashi University, Japan
Nils Janlöv, Swedish Agency for Health Care Services Analysis, Sweden
Pontus Johansson, Ministry of Health and Social Affairs, Sweden
Marcia Keegan, University of Canberra, Australia
Tony Lawson, University of Essex, United Kingdom
Roberto Leombruni, University of Turin, Italy
Horacio Levy, OECD, France
Philippe Liégeois, CEPS/INSTEAD, Luxembourg
Jinjing Li, University of Canberra, Australia
Thomas Lindh, Institute for Futures Studies, Sweden
Jason Loughrey, Teagasc Rural Economy and Development Programme, Ireland
Nicolas Malleson, University of Leeds, United Kingdom
Karyn Morrissey, University of Liverpool, Ireland
Michele Mosca, University of Turin, Italy
Karin Mossler, Ministry of Health and Social Affairs, Sweden
Georg P. Mueller, University of Fribourg, Switzerland
Gustav Öberg, Institute for Futures Studies, Sweden
Cathal O'Donoghue, Teagasc Rural Economy and Development Programme, Ireland
Milagros Paniagua, Instituto de Estudios Fiscales, Spain

Nils Martin Stølen, Statistics Norway
Robert Tanton, University of Canberra, Australia
Eveline van Leeuwen, VU University Amsterdam, the Netherlands
Quoc Ngu Vu, Department of Education, Employment and Workplace Relations, Australia
Marcus Wurzer, Vienna University of Economics and Business, Austria

Chapter 1

Introduction

Gijs Dekkers, Cathal O'Donoghue and Marcia Keegan

Introduction

In June 2011, the International Microsimulation Association held its third General Conference in Stockholm, Sweden, hosted by Statistics Sweden and the Swedish Ministry of Finance. It was attended by over 200 microsimulation modellers, researchers, academics and policymakers from around the world. Models from over 40 nations and all six inhabited continents were presented, discussed and analysed. The conference's main focus was on socioeconomic microsimulation; that is, the simulation of demographics, labour supply, pensions, health and inequality, and the impact of government policy in these areas. There was also a strong focus on methodology: new methods of microsimulation, validation of existing techniques and new applications of familiar methods.

After the first two conferences, in Vienna in 2007 and Ottawa in 2009, this conference was yet another key step in the development of the field of microsimulation. After the pioneering work of Guy Orcutt in the 1950s, and in line with his vision where microsimulation models should be used for the assessment of governmental actions (Wolfson 2009: 23), microsimulation models in the 1990s had become a field in which models in many countries were used 'routinely within government' (Harding 1996: 1) to assess the immediate redistributive impact of policy. This commitment to policy relevance is still the case today (Williamson et al. 2009: 32).

However, Harding also concluded that it was a field where 'slow progress' (op. cit.) was being made. This, fortunately, is less the case today, even though progress seems more to be the case in increasing coverage of microsimulation models of countries than in methodological development as such. The model with the broadest coverage is EUROMOD, which currently covers all 27 EU countries and has been adapted to South Africa, Serbia, Australia, Turkey and Russia. This has led to a boost in comparative research (see Lelkes and Sutherland 2009, Figari and Tasseva 2013). The UNU WIDER project that covers 10 African countries is another example, and recently a static tax-transfer modelling project was developed and applied to five Latin American countries (Urzúa 2012). In dynamic modelling, there have been a number of international modelling projects including those based upon MODGEN.[1] A slower, considerably less visible

---

1   See an application of this framework in Rowe and Gribble (2007).

but potentially interesting development pertains to the developments of LIAM and LIAM2. These are generic simulation modelling packages designed for the development of dynamic microsimulation models (de Menten et al. 2012). This allowed the Irish model LIAM to be the basis for the MIDAS models for Belgium, Germany and Italy. The first of these then stood at the basis of Luxembourg and Hungarian models that are currently under development. The last was developed and expanded into T-DYMM in Italy.

But also beyond that 'traditional' progress in increased country coverage, the pace of progress in other aspects of microsimulation also seems to be increasing. This includes the exchange of best practices, methodological developments and new applications of existing methods. Harding and Gupta (2007) identified three factors that contributed to the spread of microsimulation since the 1990s: the availability of microdata which forms the basis of most microsimulation models; the complexity of tax-transfer systems in developed economies, and growing concern about social and economic impacts of population ageing. It has further been helped by forever growing computer power, allowing the computation of larger datasets, more complex models and varied user interfaces. Partly as a result of these factors, microsimulation is spreading out from its traditional areas of health, population ageing and tax-transfer modelling into new areas. For example, papers at the 2011 IMA conference discussed models relating to a very wide range of topics – from smoking to financial planning; from farming to language development in multilingual regions to the spread of disease; from childcare to student success in college.

What started as a niche area of modelling has become much more widespread, as more and more researchers and policymakers learn of new developments and applications for this powerful tool. It is our belief that the consecutive international IMA conferences have had a significant role in this, not in the least because of the *International Journal of Microsimulation* it hosts. All in all, this makes the IMA an indispensable factor for microsimulation modelling to achieve 'the scientific status it deserves' (Wolfson 2009: 29).

This book hopes to add to this development by presenting a selection of chapters based on presentations held during the 2011 IMA conference in Stockholm. The selection of chapters was based not just on availability, but on whether the editors felt that the contributions opened new territories or made original contributions to traditional domains in microsimulation. These may in the future turn out to be dead ends (we of course hope they are not) but most of the chapters collected in this book aim to bring microsimulation further in some way and as such they stand for the new dynamism that characterizes our field.

The Structure of the Book

The contributions are grouped in five sections. These are austerity, health, pensions, poverty and methodology. Of course, the choice of what section to put a specific chapter in is sometimes ambiguous. For example, a chapter such as

Seiichi Inagaki's, which evaluates the impact of pension reform on poverty risk, could easily fit in the pensions or poverty sections. In this case, it was put in the former, because the problem definition in the paper is on pension (reform) while the assessment of reforms is one on the basis of poverty as well as on other indicators of pension adequacy and sustainability. But in other cases, the choice was not obvious. The chapter by Georg P. Mueller, for example, could just as well have been put in the 'methodology' section of the book, and the grouping in sections sometimes caused some debate among the editors.

Before turning to a more detailed discussion of the sections of the book, note that some chapters have some extensive appendices. In order to limit the size of the book, some of these appendices have been put online at http://www. microsimulation.org/resource-centre/new-pathways/.

Austerity

The first two chapters illustrate how microsimulation models are being used to assess the redistributive impacts of recent austerity measures taken in the UK and Ireland. The global financial crisis, the recession it caused and the stimulus measures undertaken to mitigate it, have forced governments of developed nations to take a long, hard look at their budgets. When economic times are poor, the problems associated with frequent budget deficits become more apparent and costly. However, reducing budget deficits by increasing taxes and cutting spending – commonly known as austerity measures – are likely to exacerbate poverty and hardship caused by recession.

Microsimulation modelling of austerity measures is essential to ensuring that the burden of spending cuts and tax increases is spread fairly across the population and not concentrated in any particular socioeconomic demographic or group, especially among the poor.

The research by Ben Anderson, Paola De Agostini and Tony Lawson focuses on the impacts of austerity in the United Kingdom using dynamic microsimulation, this time focusing on the spatial effects of the increase in Value Added Tax (VAT) from 17.5 per cent to 20 per cent. It projects the population out to 2021, and uses spatial microsimulation to project the impact of the increase in VAT on household expenditure on transport and telecommunications.

The chapter by Cathal O'Donoghue, Karyn Morrissey and Jason Loughrey focuses on the impact of the global economic crisis on labour force participation, income distribution and income inequality in Ireland. It uses microsimulation modelling to simulate income inequality where sufficient data do not exist. It uses an Irish labour market model to simulate income distribution, then a static tax-transfer model to simulate incomes, taxation and benefits for the Irish population to 2011, and finds that earnings movements and policy changes have had a reasonably progressive effect.

Health

The use of microsimulation models in health and healthcare is a relatively recent phenomena, as Wolfson (2009: 28) points out. Although living longer is a goal most individuals aspire to, it tends to be treated as a dilemma by public policymakers when accomplished by populations as a whole. Developed nations, whose citizens' average life expectancy has been increasing for decades, generally have publicly-funded support systems in place so that the elderly do not need to work for income and their healthcare is provided inexpensively or free of charge. When the proportion of the population relying on these support systems increases, the sustainability of these systems comes into question. Older people are more likely to suffer from disease, which adds to healthcare costs, and more working-age people are needed to care for the elderly. This book includes three chapters on health.

The first chapter in this section describes how a classic dynamic microsimulation model was adapted to simulate the consumption of healthcare and elderly care in Sweden. Lisa Brouwers, Anders Ekholm, Nils Janlöv, Pontus Johansson and Karin Mossler use an adaptation of Sweden's long-standing dynamic microsimulation model SESIM-LEV, which projects the health of the Swedish population and the demand for health and aged care. Their chapter describes the operation of SESIM-LEV, and simulates a number of scenarios relating to the future mortality and morbidity of the Swedish people.

Richard Cumpston describes how a dynamic microsimulation model was adapted to simulate the development of disease in Australia. It applies models of 123 diseases developed by the Australian Institute for Health and Welfare to a microsimulation projection of Australia's population. The chapter considers the effectiveness of the model to simulate incidence of disease, death rates from disease and need for aged care as a result of disease, pointing to a way for disease incidence to be projected onto an ageing population.

Muriel Barlet and Marie Cavillon use a spatial dynamic microsimulation to project the supply of nurses in France. It simulates the number of working nurses out to 2030 by age, gender, region and mode of practice; by modelling new nursing graduates, entry into the workforce (including region and form of employment), workforce transitions and retirement. Through also projecting the distribution of the general French population, the model projects density of nurses by region in France, allowing policymakers to predict future health workforce shortages.

Pensions

The assessment and analysis of the redistributive impact of the pension system is one of the more traditional fields in which microsimulation has proven its worth. See Li and O'Donoghue, Section 2 for a discussion. This book includes three chapters that take a novel approach in this traditional field. Dennis Fredriksen and

Nils Martin Stølen use the dynamic microsimulation model MOSART to analyse the impact of recent reform in the Norwegian pension system on both annual and life-cycle redistribution to gender. This reform reinforces the link between earnings and the accrual of pension entitlements, and therefore reduces the annual distributional effects of the new pension system. On the contrary, the reform does not have an important impact on the life cycle of the redistribution between men and women via the pension system.

Roberto Leombruni and Michele Mosca report on the redistributive features of the pension system currently in place in Italy. Their question is fairly simple: was the PAYG regime really progressive? Somewhat surprisingly, the answer is negative. One of their conclusions is that the Italian pension system is redistributing income from the poor to the rich.

The work by Seiichi Inagaki uses the dynamic model INAHSIM to evaluate the effect of the proposals for public pension reform on the projected income level of the elderly in Japan, as well as on their additional budgetary costs. He concludes that, contrary to what one might believe in a society that is ageing as fast as the Japanese, the percentage of the elderly with very low pensions will not increase. Instead, primarily changes in the co-resident families of the elderly, such as the increase in the number of people living alone, may cause the poverty risk of the elderly to increase.

Poverty

This section of the book contains three chapters and focuses on utilizing microsimulation models for assessing the impact of public policy on poverty. Microsimulation models are useful analytical tools for assessing the impact of policy on poverty as they contain representative samples of the population and analytical tools that enable the simulation of policy.

While microsimulation models have been used to consider these issues for many years, this section adds value in a number of dimensions. These include methodological developments:

- Creating early warning indicators of old-age poverty, which can be used as stress-tests of the analysed welfare regimes;
- Using agent-based models combined with a microsimulation model to assess the impact of the old-age crisis; and
- The extension of the European tax-benefit model, EUROMOD, to look at sub-national issues, in this case child benefit reforms in different Autonomous Communities in Spain.

Georg P. Mueller's chapter assesses current and future poverty by old-age retirement under different welfare regimes, like those of Sweden, Switzerland, Germany and the United Kingdom. On the basis of secondary statistical analyses of personal interviews available in the European Social Survey (ESS), the chapter first identifies the social groups which are most vulnerable to poverty by retirement. On the grounds of this knowledge, the study simulates the effects of retirement on the income of future generations of pensioners. This kind of microsimulation allows the construction of early warning indicators of old-age poverty, which can be used as stress-tests of the analysed welfare regimes. Countries with constant or decreasing values of vulnerability by old-age poverty stand the test, whereas others with increasing vulnerability-indicators are likely to face additional poverty problems in the future and may have to consider reforms of their retirement systems.

Pensions are both directly and indirectly affected by financial crises. The reform of the Swedish pension system into a notional defined contribution system with a minor funded part has attracted international attention for its solutions to ensure fiscal sustainability. As the financial crisis devalued the buffer funds this released the automatic balancing mechanism that is designed to decrease pension liabilities. The pension system is, however, still in transition and the long-term consequences in a fully mature system cannot be deduced from this incident. Elisa Baroni, Gustav Öberg and Thomas Lindh use an agent-based model approach to study how the mature Swedish pension system may react to a financial crisis. First of all, the funded parts of both the public and the occupational pension system will be directly affected. Through the automatic balancing mechanism, the buffer funds may release an automatic cut in pension rights. They try to establish what the effects on poverty rates are for birth cohorts who are at different stages in their life course when the financial crisis hits. Results indicate that cohorts just on the verge of retirement will be hit hardest. In another dimension men are harder hit than women, partly but not entirely due to the fact that only females in the model are allowed to vary labour supply.

In recent years, child-related policies in Spain have experienced several changes implemented at different government levels. The central government implemented a new universal child benefit at birth and reformed some of the most relevant policies for children living in low-income households. Also, many regional governments (Comunidades Autónomas) have implemented their own policies to support families with children with different schemes in terms of design and generosity. All these policies have increased social protection expenditure aimed at families and children in the country as a whole over the last decade (one of the lowest in the EU). So far, however, little is known about their impact on child poverty in Spain. Making use of the tax-benefit model for the European Union – EUROMOD – a chapter by Olga Cantó, Marta Adiego, Luis Ayala, Horacio Levy and Milagros Paniagua simulates the eligibility and receipt of most of the existing monetary child-related policies at all government levels and assesses their real (for central government policies) or potential (for regional policies) effect on the reduction of child poverty in Spain.

Methodology

As stated in the Introduction, the choice of chapters included in this book was primarily based on our feeling that they in some way added to the scientific character of our field. It therefore may come as no surprise that the methodology section is by far the largest section of the book. It contains no less than eight chapters that focus on methodology in the broadest sense of the word, and therefore less on the (discussion of) simulation results of microsimulation models.

The contribution by Philippe Liégeois and Gijs Dekkers discusses issues and pitfalls when embedding a static microsimulation model – in this case EUROMOD – in the Luxembourg dynamic microsimulation model MIDAS_LU. A first conclusion is that the combination of the two models is indeed possible, thanks also to the setup of LIAM, and that the two models are sufficiently complementary. EUROMOD by definition can deal with the immediate impact of changes in the tax-benefit system. On the other hand, MIDAS_LU includes demographic developments, policy hypotheses and evolutions, and behavioural reactions. A problem that arises is that the dynamic model does not provide all the variables that EUROMOD requires. So either the former has to be developed further, or the latter has to be 'toned down'. Furthermore, there are issues regarding the difference between households and families or nuclear households and the use of weights in the dynamic model.

Jinjing Li and Cathal O'Donoghue return to an older yet very interesting discussion in dynamic microsimulation, namely that of alignment. The (non-)sense of alignment is often discussed, but the various alignment methods are rarely, if ever, evaluated vis-à-vis one another. The authors develop a set of theoretical and statistical criteria proposed in the earlier literature and use them to evaluate six of the most common alignment techniques. They conclude that there is no single best method for all simulation scenarios. Instead, the choice of alignment method might need to be adapted to the assumptions and requirements in a specific project.

When detailed information is poor or only available for a small sample, microsimulation can be used to make it more reliable through matching and benchmarking techniques. Eveline van Leeuwen presents the results of a project in which a two-step microsimulation procedure has been used to overcome the data problems associated with getting a detailed picture of all residents of the Cairngorms National Park, Scotland, with characteristics related to shopping and employment.

The contribution by Robert Tanton, Marcia Keegan and Quoc Ngu Vu is special because it approaches the notion of 'methodology' from an unusual angle. Rather than presenting simulation results from a specific model or research project, in this case a model designed to simulate the New South Wales electricity tariff rules, this chapter describes the development process of such a model and the design choices made, given the constraints imposed by the client's requirements. It shows how a complex microsimulation model can be implemented in a powerful programming language, but then presented to the end-user in a simple Excel spreadsheet.

Marcus Wurzer and Reinhold Hatzinger start their chapter by introducing Graphical Modelling and argue its usefulness in microsimulation modelling. Next, they present and apply the Cox-Wermuth selection strategy that can be used to fit Graphical Models, and explain its use in two illustrative examples.

The approach by Hege Marie Gjefsen is more traditional in that it describes a recently developed part of an existing model, in this case the Norwegian model MOSART. It is however original in that it represents a relatively new development, which is that some microsimulation models now also include detailed modelling of the in- and outflow in education and training, something which other models, often due to a lack of data, tend to treat in a more superficial manner. MOSART is a clear example of the former group. It projects numbers of students distributed over fields and levels. The model also produces projections for level of education, of both the population as a whole and the labour force. This information is thereafter vital for the simulation of earnings, and also for assessing future public expenditure on education and uncovering possible future education 'mismatches' in the labour market.

One of the problems that microsimulation faces in receiving full scientific credibility is that many models, especially the dynamic ones, are seen as 'black boxes': one sees what goes in and comes out, but what happens in between remains a mystery. The chapter by Gijs Dekkers makes a first attempt to shine some light in the black box. Starting from the observation that the discussion of trends in simulation results on income inequality tend to be based on only a few fundamental conceptual parameters, a simple stylized model describing these fundamental relations is developed to capture these trends. The chapter then continues by proposing this approach as a possible strategy to validate dynamic microsimulation models. It illustrates this point by comparing the output from a stylized model with those of the dynamic microsimulation model MIDAS for Belgium.

Finally, Mark Birkin and Nicolas Malleson consider a novel method of validation of a spatial population model of Leeds, UK. Their chapter describes a method called *backsim* – running a dynamic microsimulation model to project a future event, then taking the results of the model and running them backwards through the model. If the simulated results are close to the original data, this suggests the model is substantially reflecting the factors affecting the development of the population.

Conclusions

In summary, this book provides a snapshot of primarily applied and methodological developments in microsimulation in the first decade of the twenty-first century. The breadth of chapters reflects the broadening scope built around the simulation of social and economic or policy change at the micro level. The applications reflect the need for speedy, useful evidence for decision makers during a time of rapid economic change. The chapters emphasize the continued and increasing relevance of the field in this time of uncertainty.

Sadly for their colleagues, co-authors and for the microsimulation community in general, we lost two valuable persons in the course of producing this book. Thomas Lindh (05/11/1952–17/01/2013) contributed to Chapter 11. He was head of the economic research project Demographics and Economics at the Institute for Fiscal Studies and Professor of Economics at Linneus University (Växjö). His co-authors and colleagues are deeply grateful to him for his invaluable supervision under all their years as research students and for all he has taught. Reinhold Hatzinger (22/06/1953–17/07/2012) contributed to Chapter 17 of this book. He worked at the Institute for Statistics and Mathematics of the Department of Finance, Accounting and Statistics at the Vienna University of Economics and Business, and was head of the Competence Centre for Empirical Research Methods at this university. He was known for his work on item response theory models, preference models and graphical models, and with his accommodating and friendly manner, he was a great educator for everyone who studied or worked with him. This book is dedicated to their memory.

References

De Menten, G., Dekkers, G., Desmet, R., Bryon, G., Liègeois, P., Wagener, R. and O'Donoghue, C. 2012. *LIAM 2: a new open source development tool for the development of discrete-time dynamic microsimulation models*. Paper presented at the séminaire scientifique international, Caisse des Dépôts, Bordeaux, France, 15 November, 2012.

Figari, F. and Tasseva, I. 2013. Editorial Special Issue EUROMOD. *International Journal of Microsimulation*, 6(1), 1–3.

Harding, A. 1996. Introduction, in *Microsimulation and Public Policy. Contributions to Economic Analysis*, edited by A. Harding. Bingley: Emerald, 1–22.

Harding, A. and Gupta, A. 2007. Introduction and Overview, in *Modelling Our Future: Population Ageing, Social Security and Taxation*, edited by A. Gupta and A. Harding. International Symposia in Economic Theory and Econometrics, Amsterdam: Elsevier BV, 1–32.

Lelkes, Orsolya and Holly Sutherland (eds) 2009. *Tax and Benefit Policies in the Enlarged Europe: Assessing the Impact with Microsimulation Models*. Farnham: Ashgate.

Rowe, G. and Gribble, S. 2007. Lifepaths Model, in *Modelling Our Future: Population Ageing, Health and Aged Care*, 449–52, edited by A. Gupta and A. Harding. International Symposia in Economic Theory and Econometrics, Amsterdam: Elsevier BV.

Urzúa, C.M. 2012. *Fiscal Inclusive Development: Microsimulation Models for Latin America*, Tecnológico de Monterrey, Campus Ciudad de México, http://EconPapers.repec.org/RePEc:ega:libros:201202 [23/09/2013].

Williamson, P., Zaidi, A. and Harding, A. 2009. New Frontiers in Microsimulation Modelling: Introduction, in *New Frontiers in Microsimulation Modelling*, 31–50, edited by A. Zaidi, A. Harding and P. Williamson. Farnham/Vienna: European Centre Vienna and Ashgate.

Wolfson, M. 2009. Preface – Orcutt's vision 50 years on, in *New Frontiers in Microsimulation Modelling*, 21–30, edited by A. Zaidi, A. Harding and P. Williamson. Farnham/Vienna: European Centre Vienna and Ashgate.

Chapter 2

Estimating the Small Area Effects of Austerity Measures in the UK

Ben Anderson, Paola De Agostini and Tony Lawson

Introduction

In response to recent economic and financial difficulties, governments across Europe and beyond have implemented a range of cost-cutting and income-generating programmes in order to re-balance their fiscal budgets following substantial investments in stabilizing domestic financial institutions in 2008 and 2009. One approach has been to increase tax rates such as the increase in Value Added Tax (VAT) in the United Kingdom (UK) from 17.5 per cent to 20 per cent from 1 January 2011.

Whilst analyses of changes to tax rates are relatively common and microsimulation of their effects is now relatively well known (Zaidi et al. 2009, Mitton et al. 2000, Hancock et al. 1992) we are not aware of substantial exploration of the small area effects of such changes despite indications of its value in analysing the potential small area effects of tax and benefit rate changes (Clarke 1996, Ballas and Clarke 2001, Chin et al. 2005, Tanton et al. 2009). In addition, as far as we are aware there has been no attempt to model, at the small area level, not just the impact of tax-rate changes on income or on expenditure on specific consumption items, but the effect on a system of household expenditure into the future.

In this chapter we combine a number of research methods to explore the differential spatial impact of the UK VAT rise on household expenditure on public and private transport and communication technology from 2006 to 2016. We do this by combining three elements: an agent-based dynamic population microsimulation model that produces projected snapshots of the UK population in 2006, 2011 and 2016; an expenditure system model based on the familiar Quadratic Almost Ideal Demand System approach; and synthetic small area census tables produced by projecting historical UK census data.

Taken together these elements provide a toolkit for assessing the potential spatial impact of rising taxes or prices (or both) using a spatial microsimulation approach and we use them to compare small area projections of household expenditure under two scenarios. The first is a 'no intervention' scenario where prices and income align to UK government inflation forecasts and the second is a one-off non-reversed 2.5 per cent increase in VAT on goods and services rated at 17.5 per cent on 1 January 2011. We present results for different areas (rural versus urban/deprived versus affluent) and for different income groups within them and discuss their substantive and methodological implications.

Projection and Estimation Methods

Our approach to projecting small area estimates of household expenditure comprises three main strands. The first is the projection of small area statistics for specific household attributes using historical census tables. The second is the projection of a household population sample together with their household attributes, income and expenditure patterns and the third is the development of a demand system model linking household expenditures to each other, to household attributes and to time. These are then combined using a spatial microsimulation approach to produce small area estimates of future household expenditures over time.

As we discuss below each of these strands presents a range of challenges but when in place they provide a set of tools for modelling the small area consequences of, for example, changes in prices, in area-level demographic change and, as here, changes in indirect consumption tax rates. A preliminary version of this approach was presented in previous work (Anderson et al. 2009) and in this chapter we discuss extensions to that work which bases the small area projections on Census data from 1971, 1981, 1991 and 2001 (rather than just 1981/1991 and 2001); which uses an agent-based dynamic population projection model (Lawson 2009) to produce synthetic households (rather than the autoregressive method) and which uses an improved system demand model to estimate future expenditures for the dynamically projected households.

Data

As in previous work we use the UK's Expenditure and Food Survey for 2001/2 to 2005/6 (EFS 2006) as our consumption survey data and the UK Census small area tables for 1971, 1981, 1991 and 2001. In addition, we have conducted extensive analysis of the longitudinal British Household Panel Study (1991–2006) (BHPS 2010) as part of the development of transition probabilities for the dynamic agent-based population model.

Spatial Projection

Our approach to the projection of small area statistics follows our earlier work (Anderson et al. 2009) in re-zoning UK census small areas (wards) to form consistent geographical zones over time (Gregory and Ell 2005, Norman et al. 2003). In this work we have switched to the UK Office for National Statistics' Lower Layer Super Output Area (LSOA) level using Enumeration District (ED) data for the 1971/1981/1991 Censuses and Output Area (OA) level data for the

2001 Census. Our rationale for moving to the LSOA level includes the availability of substantial local area data at the LSOA level, such as updates of the English Indices of Multiple Deprivation.

As discussed in more detail elsewhere (Anderson et al. 2013), a postcode-based aerial interpolation approach was used to re-weight the historical census data and allocate the weighted values to fragments of historical zones before the fragments (and available historical data) were re-aggregated to Census 2001 LSOAs. A review of the census data suggested that variables available over time were the socio-economic/employment status of household representative person (HRP); the number of cars in the household; number of dependent children; the number of persons per household; number of rooms and type of tenure.

Following Ballas et al. (2005), we then used the Holt-Winters non-seasonal smoothing algorithm to smooth the LSOA level proportions of households in the observed census variable categories for 1971 to 2001 and a gravitational model to project constraint proportions and total household numbers forwards at LSOA level to 2011 and 2021. Household projections from the UK Government at Local Authority level[1] were used to normalize household numbers and the projected proportions were converted to projected household counts using these normalized total household counts. The method projected 1-n constraint proportions and then calculated the last constraint as the residual. Any negative proportions were changed to the most recent positive proportion and any zero value to a small non-zero number to prevent errors in any future spatial microsimulation process where division by 0 would cause a failure. Finally proportions were re-scaled so that they summed to 1 (100 per cent) for each constraint. Following this correction step the projected constraint counts were then calculated using the projected total household counts that had been normalized to the most recent official Local Authority level estimates. Due to the processing requirements of this method the projections were limited to the 3,550 LSOAs in the East of England.

Overall the projected trends appeared relatively plausible given that they are contingent on historical trends. In some cases, such as the proportion of households with 2+ cars or the reduction in the proportion of those who are social/council renters an earlier asymptote might have been expected as socio-economic limits are reached (see Anderson et al. 2013). However, considerably more complex dynamic projection modelling would be required to address this issue and it is outside the scope of this chapter.

Demographic Projection

With the spatial projections in place, we now turn to the projection of a sample survey population as a basis for the microsimulation of the 2011 tax increase

---

1   https://www.gov.uk/government/organisations/department-for-communities-and-local-government/series/household-projections (last accessed 17 September 2013).

using an agent-based dynamic population projection model. This model aged a sample population (EFS 2005/6, n = 11,204 persons in 4,732 households) through the application of a range of dynamic demographic projection modules (Lawson 2009, Lawson 2011). These modules included a partnership formation module which selected a number of individuals from the population each year to either marry or cohabit whilst a mortality module selected which individuals were to be removed from the population. Additional modules were added to represent single people leaving and returning to the parental home and were run sequentially for each simulated year. Each transition between states was controlled by transition probabilities estimated mainly from BHPS-derived logistic regression models although additional probabilities were taken from the SAGE Technical Notes (Scott 2003).

Once the modelling framework (transition probabilities and module processes) was in place, the BHPS survey sample was replaced by the EFS survey sample in order to then project the EFS sample 'forwards' in time to 2006, 2011 and 2016. The agent-based model was used to project household income; number of persons in different age groups in each household; number of children in household; household composition (married/partnered couple, single parent, single person, other); employment status of the Household Response Person (NS-SEC 1, NS-SEC 2, NS-SEC 3, Inactive (including unemployed), Retired); the number of persons per household and the age of Household Response Person. These variables form the basis for the demand system model used to estimate future household expenditures (see below) and also included most of the variables found in the projected small area Census data (see above).

One absence from the dynamic population projection was housing tenure which was imputed for the projected EFS survey data using a multinomial regression model based on income, number of children, number of persons, composition and employment status. The resulting coefficients were then used to predict the probability that a projected household was of a given tenure type and households were selected into tenure type if their probability of being in that type was greater than the median predicted probability (see Anderson et al. 2013).

Demand System Model

As in previous work (Anderson et al. 2009) a Quadratic Almost Ideal Demand System model (Banks et al. 1997) was used to project consumers' behaviours into the future by estimating a system of n share equations using the EFS data from 2001/02 to 2005/06 based on prices, household income and other household characteristics where n is the number of goods or services being considered.

The model focused on a 'communication demand system' by including household expenditures on communications technologies (landline, mobile and internet), transport (car fuel and public transports) and as the residual, all other expenditures net of housing costs. Expenditures were converted to December 2007 prices using the UK Retail Price Index (RPI) provided by the ONS. Comparisons over time, therefore, refer to real-terms changes.

Although there may be many other factors affecting households' spending decisions, for simplicity the demographic characteristics that were included in the agent-based population and which could therefore be used to calculate expenditure estimates for 2006, 2011 and 2016 were used as model co-variates. The demand system was estimated using STATA 10 (Poi 2008, Poi 2002) and full results are shown in Table 2.1. In addition, we developed a separate regression model (not shown) which predicted total household expenditure as a function of household income and the same socio-demographic variables for use in estimating future expenditure in money-value terms.

With these results to hand we were then in a position to estimate the share of expenditure on the household consumption categories using both the observed sample data for 2001/02 to 2005/06 and the 2006/2011/2016 synthetic population sample produced by the agent-based approach. We did this by using the QAIDS model coefficients (Table 2.1) to calculate the expected share of total expenditure for each item for each projected household in each year. This estimated budget share was then converted to a £ value using the estimated household expenditure values to provide the baseline projection of expenditures under a 'no price change' scenario but allowing for compositional change of the household population through the agent-based dynamic projection.

To calculate the estimated expenditures under the scenario condition of a 2.5 per cent rise in VAT on 1 January 2011 price elasticities were calculated for each item using the QAIDS model results (see Table 2.2).

Own-price elasticities are reported in bold on the main diagonal of Table 2.2 and as we would expect these were all negative, indicating that an increase in the price of a good led to a decrease in the demand for that good. Own-price elasticity for car fuel was smaller than −1 (−0.57) showing that demand decreased more slowly than price increased – people found it hard to reduce car fuel expenditure.

Cross price elasticities are the off-diagonal values and are of less critical importance here although they do help to explain some of the subsequent modelling results. For example, a price increase in car fuel leads to an increase in demand of ICTs (landline, mobile and internet). This may suggest that when private transport becomes more expensive, people use/spend more on telecommunication and public transport. This appears to be 'paid for' out of other expenditure suggesting that as (if) fuel prices rise substantially, revenue from consumer-based telecommunications will rise at the expense of other expenditures. The relatively small size of the variation suggests that this response was uniform across the sample.

Table 2.1 Estimated QAIDS model using EFS 2001/02–2005/06 (n. of observations 30,774)

		Landline		Mobile		Internet		Car Fuel		Public Transport		Other	
alpha[1]		0.029	*(0.87)*	0.029	*(6.00)*	0.010	*(0.87)*	0.124	*(5.01)*	0.038	*(1.61)*	0.770	*(11.85)*
gamma[2]	Landline	−0.005	*−(0.90)*	0.000	*−(0.77)*	0.004	*(1.72)*	0.001	*(0.28)*	0.002	*(0.78)*	−0.002	*−(0.22)*
	Mobile	(omitted)[3]										0.000	*(1.44)*
	Internet	0.004	*(1.72)*	0.000	*(0.46)*	−0.002	*−(0.93)*	0.001	*(0.56)*	0.000	*−(0.32)*	−0.002	*−(0.60)*
	Car fuel	0.001	*(0.28)*	0.000	*−(2.17)*	0.001	*(0.56)*	0.020	*(4.10)*	0.004	*(1.25)*	−0.026	*−(3.94)*
	Public transport	0.002	*(0.78)*	0.000	*−(1.83)*	0.000	*−(0.32)*	0.004	*(1.25)*	−0.001	*−(0.26)*	−0.005	*−(0.80)*
	Others	−0.002	*−(0.22)*	0.000	*(1.44)*	−0.002	*−(0.60)*	−0.026	*−(3.94)*	−0.005	*−(0.80)*	0.035	*(2.00)*
beta[4]		−0.014	*−(25.70)*	−0.004	*−(5.49)*	−0.001	*−(4.76)*	−0.002	*−(2.02)*	−0.004	*−(5.24)*	0.024	*(15.77)*
Lambda		0.005	*(43.38)*	−0.001	*−(5.07)*	−0.001	*−(19.63)*	−0.007	*−(28.78)*	−0.001	*−(4.06)*	0.004	*(12.61)*
rho[5]		−0.003	*−(4.78)*	−0.003	*−(3.88)*	−0.002	*−(12.33)*	−0.012	*−(9.35)*	−0.004	*−(4.46)*	0.023	*(13.73)*
Time (in years)		−0.001	*−(11.82)*	0.002	*(13.37)*	0.000	*(10.72)*	0.001	*(6.33)*	0.000	*(0.11)*	−0.002	*−(6.58)*
Age of HRP (16–24)	25–34	0.005	*(5.46)*	−0.015	*−(14.18)*	0.002	*(5.50)*	0.007	*(3.47)*	−0.005	*−(3.80)*	0.007	*(2.72)*
	35–44	0.005	*(5.78)*	−0.024	*−(22.42)*	0.002	*(6.43)*	0.007	*(3.56)*	−0.008	*−(6.47)*	0.019	*(7.19)*
	45–54	0.007	*(6.56)*	−0.032	*−(23.57)*	0.001	*(3.75)*	0.008	*(3.52)*	−0.009	*−(5.64)*	0.023	*(7.33)*
	55–64	0.007	*(5.87)*	−0.039	*−(27.78)*	0.000	*(0.05)*	0.008	*(3.24)*	−0.011	*−(6.67)*	0.035	*(10.46)*
	65–74	0.007	*(4.66)*	−0.043	*−(25.07)*	−0.001	*−(1.32)*	0.010	*(3.37)*	−0.011	*−(5.82)*	0.038	*(9.40)*
	75+	0.003	*(2.09)*	−0.047	*−(26.36)*	−0.001	*−(2.58)*	0.005	*(1.58)*	−0.012	*−(6.00)*	0.052	*(12.38)*
Employment status of HRP (1 – Managerial and professional occupations)	Intermediate occ.	0.001	*(2.00)*	0.002	*(3.45)*	0.000	*−(2.45)*	0.002	*(2.03)*	−0.004	*−(6.32)*	−0.001	*−(0.35)*
	Routine and manual occ.	0.000	*−(0.67)*	0.006	*(10.03)*	−0.001	*−(6.94)*	0.002	*(2.12)*	−0.009	*−(12.23)*	0.002	*(1.06)*
	Inactive (Never worked, long term unemp)	0.002	*(2.30)*	0.005	*(6.55)*	0.000	*−(2.03)*	−0.007	*−(4.64)*	−0.007	*−(7.19)*	0.007	*(3.54)*
	Retired	0.001	*(1.51)*	0.000	*−(0.30)*	−0.003	*−(9.96)*	−0.012	*−(6.07)*	−0.009	*−(7.33)*	0.023	*(8.72)*

N. of children (none)	One child	0.002	*(2.09)*	−0.001	*−(1.18)*	0.000	*(1.04)*	−0.001	*−(0.58)*	−0.003	*−(2.96)*	0.004	*(1.50)*
	Two or more	0.002	*(1.37)*	−0.003	*−(1.70)*	0.000	*(0.26)*	0.000	*(0.02)*	−0.006	*−(2.67)*	0.007	*(1.47)*
N. of persons by age	0–4	0.000	*(0.30)*	−0.004	*−(5.24)*	−0.001	*−(4.54)*	−0.001	*−(0.90)*	−0.003	*−(2.80)*	0.009	*(4.62)*
	5–17	0.000	*(0.55)*	0.000	*(0.43)*	0.000	*−(1.42)*	−0.002	*−(1.39)*	0.001	*(1.51)*	0.000	*(0.09)*
	18–44	0.000	*(0.29)*	0.003	*(2.95)*	0.000	*−(0.93)*	0.004	*(2.41)*	0.004	*(4.07)*	−0.011	*−(4.97)*
	45–64	0.000	*−(0.15)*	0.004	*(3.98)*	0.000	*−(1.18)*	0.004	*(2.21)*	0.003	*(2.24)*	−0.010	*−(4.20)*
	65+	−0.001	*−(1.20)*	0.005	*(4.12)*	0.000	*−(1.07)*	0.003	*(1.43)*	0.002	*(1.54)*	−0.008	*−(3.00)*
N. of people in the household (single person)	2	−0.001	*−(0.52)*	−0.004	*−(1.43)*	0.000	*(0.49)*	0.003	*(0.53)*	−0.002	*−(0.64)*	0.004	*(0.64)*
	3	0.000	*(0.16)*	−0.002	*−(1.02)*	0.001	*(1.11)*	0.001	*(0.30)*	−0.001	*−(0.43)*	0.001	*(0.23)*
	4	−0.001	*−(0.71)*	−0.002	*−(1.73)*	0.000	*(0.39)*	0.000	*(0.09)*	−0.001	*−(0.83)*	0.004	*(1.26)*
	4+	(omitted)		(omitted)		(omitted)		(omitted)		(omitted)		(omitted)	
Composition (married/ partnered)	Single parent	0.000	*(0.66)*	0.004	*(6.76)*	0.000	*−(1.27)*	−0.005	*−(5.64)*	0.002	*(3.17)*	0.000	*−(0.28)*
	Single person	−0.001	*−(0.40)*	0.005	*(1.19)*	0.001	*(0.89)*	−0.001	*−(0.09)*	0.003	*(0.58)*	−0.006	*−(0.67)*
	Others	0.002	*(3.01)*	0.013	*(19.53)*	0.000	*−(2.49)*	−0.013	*−(10.66)*	0.013	*(16.27)*	−0.014	*−(8.87)*

Figures in italics are z values

[1] Alpha = constant term

[2] Gamma: the effect of price on demand

[3] Omitted in all but 'Other' as it is collinear with the price of landline (there is no way to distinguish between landline and mobile prices in the RPI provided by the ONS, thus the price for telecommunications in general was attributed to both landline and mobiles)

[4] Beta and Lambda together represent the effect of income (proxied by total expenditure)

[5] Rho = term to control for system endogeneity

Table 2.2   Mean own- and cross-price elasticity

		Variation of 1% in price					
		Landline	Mobile	Internet	Car fuel	Pub. tran.	Others
	Landline	**−1.20**	0.02	0.66	0.07	0.22	0.02
		(0.36)	*(0.12)*	*(7.18)*	*(0.55)*	*(2.82)*	*(0.01)*
	Mobile	0.00	**−1.00**	0.00	0.00	0.00	0.00
		(0.00)	*(0.02)*	*(0.03)*	*(0.00)*	*(0.04)*	*(0.00)*
	Internet subscription	0.16	0.00	**−1.34**	0.01	−0.03	0.00
		(0.26)	*(0.00)*	*(3.90)*	*(0.04)*	*(0.40)*	*(0.00)*
% Variation in quantity	Car fuel	0.03	−0.01	0.09	**−0.57**	0.31	−0.04
		(0.07)	*(0.02)*	*(1.25)*	*(2.04)*	*(4.76)*	*(0.01)*
	Public transport	0.11	0.00	−0.06	0.10	**−1.09**	0.00
		(0.18)	*(0.03)*	*(0.69)*	*(0.50)*	*(1.29)*	*(0.00)*
	Others	−0.10	−0.01	−0.35	−0.62	−0.41	**−0.98**
		(0.16)	*(0.16)*	*(3.86)*	*(3.12)*	*(5.92)*	*(0.00)*

Note: Figures in parentheses are standard deviations and indicate the degree of heterogeneity of response.

Finally, car fuel and public transport were also substitutes (positive cross price elasticity) although the rise in public transport's fares had a stronger effect on the use of cars than the other way around – those who use cars were more likely to stick with them whilst those who used public transport were more likely to switch to cars when public transport prices rise. The difference in the level of heterogeneity of response was also relevant – car fuel demand responses to rises in the cost of public transport were much more varied (4.76) than the inverse (0.5).

The own-price elasticities were then used to estimate the mean weekly expenditure on each of these items following a price rise of 2.08 per cent corresponding to a VAT increase from 17.5 per cent to 20 per cent. The full results are discussed elsewhere (Anderson et al. 2013) but in summary they suggest that, on average, raising general prices by 2.5 per cent in January 2011 does not strongly affect estimated household spending on the items modelled. In particular, given the inelastic[2] demand of some of the goods considered, a decrease in demand does not offset the price rise resulting in a more noticeable increase of expenditures on mobile and car fuel compared to the baseline forecast. However, it should be noted that a much more important impact of a recession would be to increase unemployment and reduce earnings, which would reduce household income and make it much harder to maintain current consumption levels for those who become unemployed. To allow for this we would need to use the agent-based population projection model with time-varying employment risk rates to produce a new projected population. Such a model has been implemented (Lawson 2009) but the results were not used here.

---

2   Price elasticity close to zero.

Spatial Microsimulation

With these results and data to hand it was possible to combine the projected small area Census tables with the projected households to produce small area projections of future expenditures under the baseline and scenario conditions.

This was achieved using a spatial microsimulation method (Birkin and Clarke 1989, Smith et al. 2009, Ballas et al. 2005, Ballas and Clarke 2001) to iteratively re-weight the projected survey data to fit into each Census area on the basis of common constraints. The choice and ordering of the potential constraints was determined using a stepwise regression process (Anderson 2012). Unsurprisingly given the limited constraints available there is very little variation between the models in terms of the ordering of the constraints and none were rejected (see Anderson et al. 2013).

An iterative proportional fitting spatial microsimulation method (Anderson 2012, Simpson and Tranmer 2005, Wong 1992) was then used to generate 'snapshot' small area estimates of household expenditure on the five items in 2001–02 and 2006 and for both the baseline and +2.5 per cent VAT scenario for 2011 and 2016 in the East of England.

Results

In this section we describe the results of this spatial microsimulation process and whilst the full set of results are discussed elsewhere (Anderson et al. 2013), we concentrate here on the car fuel results as an explicative exemplar of a policy-relevant semi-commodity. In these discussions we refer to the 'Difference' statistic – the numerical difference between the baseline and 2.5 per cent VAT scenario percentage change over 2006–16 rather than a simple numerical difference in mean expenditure for any given year which may be instructive for a given year but gives no sense of change over time.

We present the results as maps at the LSOA level for the East of England and also as charts making use of the income deprivation sub-score of the most recent LSOA level Indices of Multiple Deprivation (McLennan et al. 2010) to illustrate the relationships between expenditure change and levels of income deprivation. We have coded the income score into deciles for ease of analysis and we also make use of the DEFRA/ONS 2004 rural/urban classification scheme for LSOAs.[3]

The projected estimated expenditures on car fuel suggest that whilst the spatial distribution of the effects of the 2.5 per cent increase appear relatively evenly distributed (Figure 2.1), the IMD income deprivation decile and rural/urban chart (Figure 2.2) suggests that the biggest 'losers' will tend to be some (but not exclusively) deprived urban areas perhaps reflecting the elasticity results reported above where we found that lower income households were less sensitive

---

3   http://www.ons.gov.uk/ons/guide-method/geography/products/area-classifications/ns-area-classifications/index/overview/index.html (last accessed 17 September 2013).

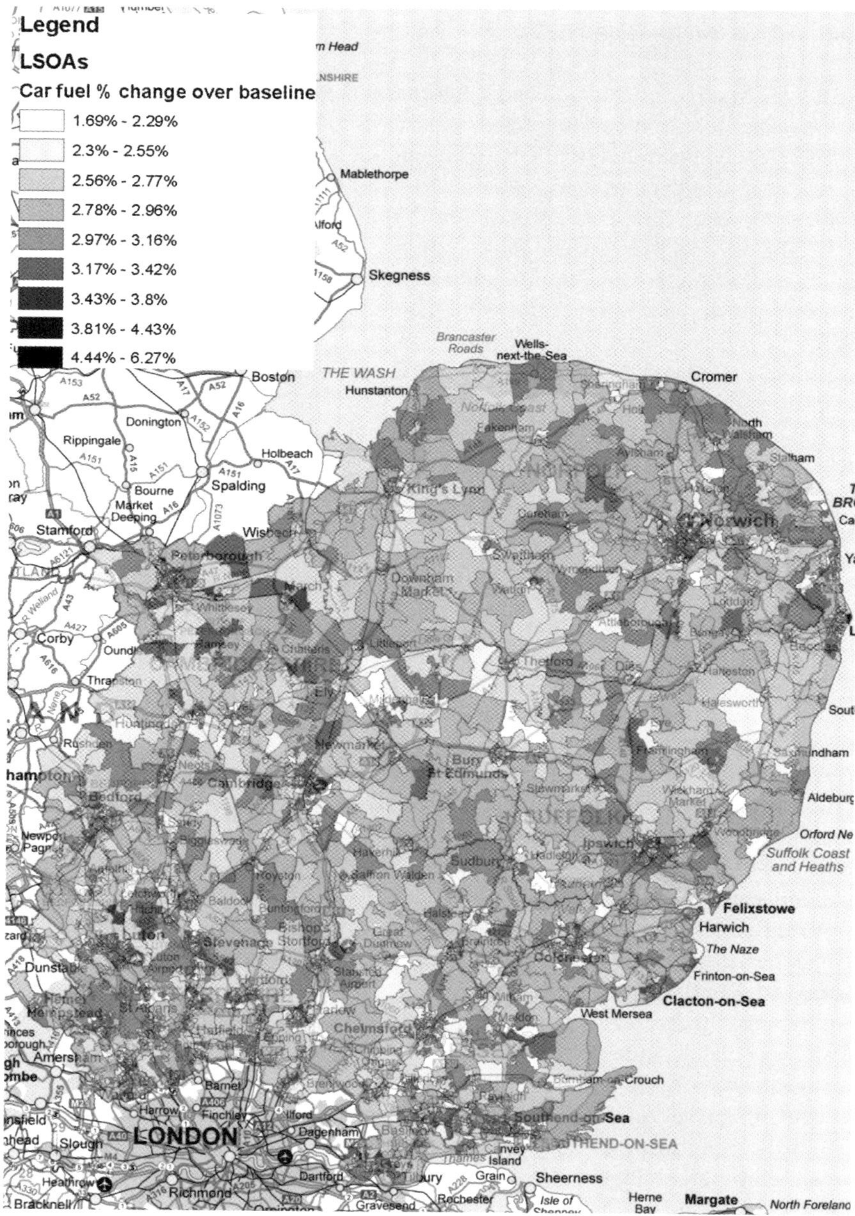

Figure 2.1   **Difference between the car fuel baseline and 2.5 per cent VAT scenario percentage change over 2006–16 at the LSOA level for the East of England (spatial microsimulation, projected EFS, projected Census 2006–16)**

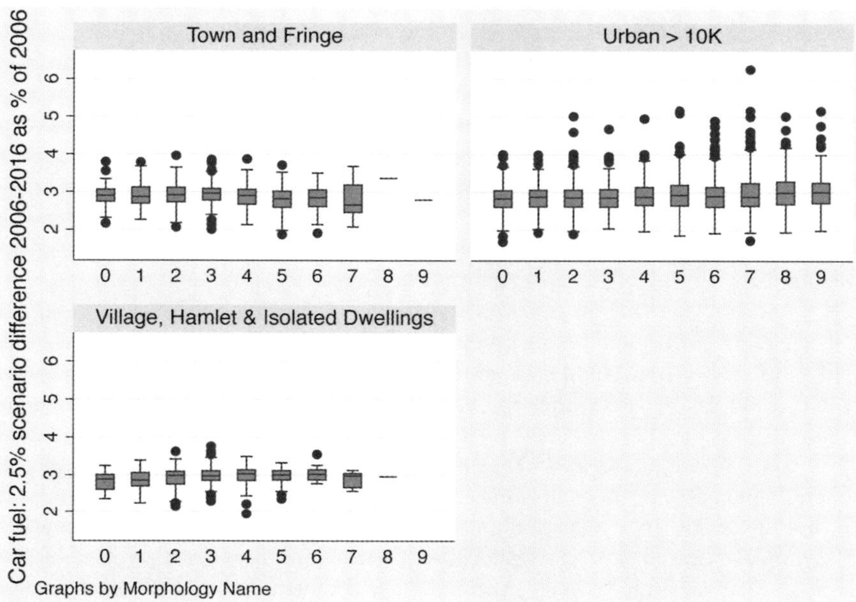

Figure 2.2   Difference between the car fuel baseline and 2.5 per cent VAT scenario percentage change over 2006–16 by rural/urban classification and IMD 2010 income deprivation decile

to car fuel price increases than were higher income households. Thus when car fuel prices rise, lower income households either choose or are forced to pay the higher prices whereas higher income households appear to substitute for other modes of transport or even for less travel, perhaps through, for example, changes to commuting practices.

In this regard we might expect the biggest 'losers' to be households in rural areas where we would assume there to be poorer public transport infrastructure and therefore an inability to switch from car use. The fact that we do not see this effect suggests that these factors are not adequately captured by the microsimulation model and that this modelling approach performs less well where expenditures rely on an unevenly distributed infrastructure such as public transport, which is not reflected in the socio-demographic distributions of the constraint variables used.

This was more explicitly tested by correlating the baseline estimated weekly expenditure on car fuel for 2011 with the 'Geographical Barriers'[4] sub-domain score of the IMD 2010. This showed a weak positive correlation between

---

4   Components: road distance to a GP surgery; road distance to a food shop; road distance to a primary school; road distance to a Post Office. Mclennan, D., Barnes, H., Noble, M., Davies, J., Garratt, E. and Dibben, C. (2010). The English Indices of Deprivation 2010. London, Department for Communities and Local Government.

geographical barriers and baseline 2011 car fuel expenditure (r = 0.2626) and an even weaker (positive) relationship with expenditure on public transport (r = 0.1494). This is to some extent expected given that for those in rural areas who (can) use it, the costs are likely to be higher but we would have expected a stronger correlation between car fuel expenditure and geographical barriers if the spatial microsimulation model adequately captured this aspect.

Discussion

This chapter has brought together a number of modelling strands to produce small area estimates of household expenditures for the East of England to 2016 under baseline and 2.5 per cent price increase scenarios using the approach set out in Figure 2.3.

Overall, the method appears feasible in that each strand of the model produced generally plausible results with some exceptions that we have noted above and will discuss further below. The modelled responses to price rises for different kinds of households appeared to produce plausible spatial distributions and revealed effects in places that would have been expected given the demand system model results. With some amendments such as the estimation of area level totals rather than means, the total reduction/increase in expenditure under the different scenarios could be calculated. As an exercise in evaluating a socio-spatial policy relevant modelling approach it can therefore be seen as a success.

More specifically, as we have noted only a few of the own and cross price effects in the model turned out to be statistically significant. Whilst it could be argued that this may simply reflect non-response to price increases it is also possible that there is unmeasured variation (heterogeneity) caused by missing demographic and expenditure variables that could be included in the model and, if this were done, the price effects may become clearer.

Further, with only four constraint variables available of which one was imputed it is possible that the spatial microsimulation process is unable to sufficiently re-weight the households appropriately. This is more obviously the case where the constraints we have are relatively poor predictors of the expenditure variables (see Anderson et al. 2013). In this case the estimation process is unlikely to produce sufficient differentiation between areas due to missing constraint variables. Of course, the number of constraints that can be projected using the methods described here are restricted to those available from the UK Census over time and which are also included in the dynamic population projection.

Of course, the use of the QUAIDS model to estimate future expenditures relies on the use of coefficients (relationships) between variables that were true for the observed data period (2001/02 to 2005/06). We therefore make the assumption that these relationships, essentially the component 'value' of the goods and their relationship to socio-demographics as well as their elasticities remain constant

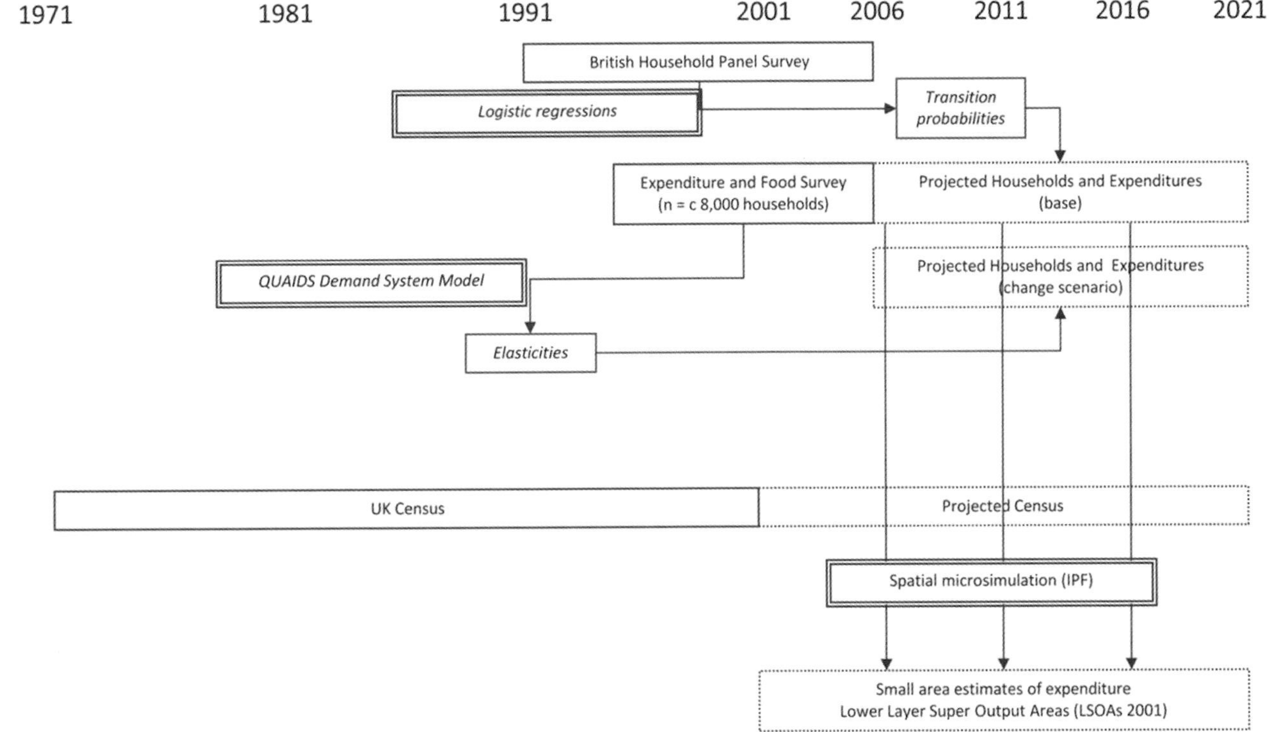

Figure 2.3   Summary of contributing models

over time. This is an unlikely situation since the values applied to different goods and services may vary over time.

In addition the discussion of the results for car fuel illustrate the difficulty of estimating expenditure which is linked to a highly uneven infrastructure distribution when that distribution is very unlikely to be captured by the distribution of the available constraint variables. The case in point here is public transport availability, which is unlikely to be predicted by particular distributions of the number of persons per household, household response person employment status, tenure or number of children per household and yet has a role to play in substituting for private transport (cf. Table 2.2).

Finally, as will have become clear from the foregoing discussions, there are multiple layers of potential error in these estimates. These include 'error' in the QUAIDS modelling process caused by unmeasured household characteristics, sampling bias and excluded variables; 'error' in the dynamic population modelling caused by assumptions about constancy of transition probabilities and fertility rates; and 'error' in the census projection caused by the re-zoning process, the smoothing process and the projection approach. There is also potential error in the spatial microsimulation process caused by the reduced number of constraints available and the relatively low predictive power that these constraints have for some of the expenditure variables as well as the inability to adequately account for 'patchy' infrastructure.

Whilst there are recognized ways of modelling and characterizing 'error' in econometric models such as QUAIDS (such as through t-values and confidence intervals), in dynamic projection models (such as through sensitivity tests) and in spatial microsimulation (through the SAE and other approaches (Smith et al. 2009, Edwards et al. 2011)) there is currently no accepted way to bring together these aspects of error in such a way as to express some form of 'robustness' about the results for a given small area.

Conclusion

Overall, whilst the work summarized in this chapter provides an exploration of the value of using a combination of methods to estimate small area household expenditure levels into the future for the East of England it has also raised a range of potential issues that should be addressed in future research.

These might include the expansion of the demand system model to include additional related budget shares and/or socio-demographic variables although one should be mindful of the additional estimation time/computing resources required. Attention should also be given to the extent to which 'patchy' infrastructures can be modelled using 'constraints' based on characteristics of survey cases and geo-coded infrastructure data.

As others have noted (Birkin and Clarke 2011), perhaps most important of all is the need for the development of conceptual and methodological approaches to the characterization of multiple sources and levels of error in small area microsimulation models, drawing perhaps on recent developments in the analysis of multiple levels of survey error (Weisberg 2005).

Acknowledgements

The research reported in this chapter was supported by BT and the Department of Communities and Local Government.

The Expenditure and Food Survey was collected by the Office for National Statistics, sponsored by the Office for National Statistics and the Department for Environment, Food and Rural Affairs, and distributed by the UK Data Archive, University of Essex, Colchester. The data is copyright and is reproduced with the permission of the Controller of HMSO and the Queen's Printer for Scotland.

Census data were created and funded by the Office for National Statistics and distributed by the Census Dissemination Unit, MIMAS (University of Manchester). Output is Crown copyright and is reproduced with the permission of the Controller of HMSO and the Queen's Printer for Scotland.

The British Household Panel Survey was collected by GfK NOP, Office for National Statistics and the Northern Ireland Statistics and Research Agency, sponsored by the Economic and Social Research Council and distributed by the UK Data Archive, University of Essex, Colchester. The data is copyright of the Institute for Social and Economic Research.

This chapter uses data provided through EDINA UKBORDERS with the support of the ESRC and JISC and uses boundary material which is copyright of the Crown.

References

Anderson, B. (2012) Estimating Small Area Income Deprivation: An Iterative Proportional Fitting Approach, in Edwards, K. and Tanton, R. (eds), *Spatial Microsimulation: A Reference Guide for Users*. London: Springer.

Anderson, B., De Agostini, P., Laidoudi, S., Weston, A. and Zong, P. (2009) Time and Money in Space: Estimating Household Expenditure and Time Use at the Small Area Level in Great Britain, in Zaidi, A., Harding, A. and Williamson, P. (eds), *New Frontiers in Microsimulation Modelling: Public Policy and Social Welfare Vol. 36*. Aldershot: Ashgate.

Anderson, B., De Agostini, P. and Lawson, T. (2013) Estimating the small area effects of austerity measures in the UK. *Centre for Research in Economic Sociology and Innovation (CRESI) Working Paper*. Colchester, University of Essex. Available at: http://repository.essex.ac.uk/5107/ (last accessed 17 September 2013).

Ballas, D. and Clarke, G. (2001) Modelling the local impacts of national social policies: a spatial microsimulation approach. *Environment and Planning C: Government and Policy*, 19, 587–606.

Ballas, D., Clarke, G., Dorling, D., Eyre, H., Thomas, B. and Rossiter, D. (2005) SimBritain: A Spatial Microsimulation Approach to Population Dynamics. *Population, Space and Place*, 11, 13–34.

Banks, J., Blundell, R. and Lewbel, A. (1997) Quadratic engel curves and consumer demand. *The Review of Economics and Statistics*, 79, 527–39.

BHPS (2010) British Household Panel Survey: Waves 1–18, 1991–2009 [computer file] 7th Edition Colchester, University of Essex. Institute for Social and Economic Research.

Birkin, M. and Clarke, G. (1989) The generation of individual and household incomes at the small area level using Synthesis. *Regional Studies*, 23, 535–48.

Birkin, M. and Clarke, M. (2011) Spatial Microsimulation Models: A Review and a Glimpse into the Future, in Stillwell, J. and Clarke, M. (eds), *Population Dynamics and Projection Methods*. London: Springer.

Chin, S.-F., Harding, A., Lloyd, R., Mc Namara, J., Phillips, B. and Ngu Vu, Q. (2005) Spatial Microsimulation Using Synthetic Small-Area Estimates of Income, Tax and Social Security Benefits. *Australasian Journal of Regional Studies*, 11, 303–35.

Clarke, G.P. (1996) *Microsimulation for urban and regional policy analysis*. London, Pion.

Edwards, K., Clarke, G., Thomas, J. and Forman, D. (2011) Internal and External Validation of Spatial Microsimulation Models: Small Area Estimates of Adult Obesity. *Applied Spatial Analysis and Policy*, 1–20.

EFS (2006) Expenditure and Food Survey, 2006 [computer file]. 3rd edition. Colchester, Essex: UK Data Archive [distributor], July 2009. SN: 5986. Colchester, Office for National Statistics and Department for Environment, Food and Rural Affairs.

Gregory, I.N. and Ell, P.S. (2005) Breaking the boundaries: geographical approaches to integrating 200 years of the census. *Journal- Royal Statistical Society Series A*, 168, 419–37.

Hancock, R., Sutherland, H. and Suntory-Toyota International Centre for Economics and Related Disciplines (1992) *Microsimulation models for public policy analysis: new frontiers*, London, Suntory-Toyota International Centre for Economics and Related Disciplines.

Lawson, T. (2009) A Demographic Microsimulation Model Using Netlogo. *Centre for Research in Economic Sociology and Innovation (CRESI) Working Paper 2009–02*. Colchester, University of Essex.

Lawson, T. (2011) An Agent-Based Model of Household Spending Based on a Random Assignment Scheme. *IMA 2011 – Microsimulation and Policy Design, June 8th to 10th, 2011*. Sweden: Stockholm.

Mclennan, D., Barnes, H., Noble, M., Davies, J., Garratt, E. and Dibben, C. (2010) The English Indices of Deprivation 2010. London, Department for Communities and Local Government.

Mitton, L., Sutherland, H. and Weeks, M.J. (2000) *Microsimulation modelling for policy analysis: challenges and innovations.* Cambridge: Cambridge University Press.

Norman, P., Rees, P. and Boyle, P. (2003) Achieving Data Compatibility Over Space and Time: Creating Consistent Geographical Zones. *International Journal of Population Geography*, 9, 365–86.

Poi, B.P. (2002) From the Help Desk: Demand System Estimation. *The Stata Journal*, 2, 403–10.

Poi, B.P. (2008) Stata Tip 58: nl is not just for non-linear models. *The Stata Journal*, 8, 139–41.

Scott, A. (2003) Implementation of demographic transitions in the SAGE Model. *SAGE Technical Note.* London, London School of Economics and Political Science.

Simpson, L. and Tranmer, M. (2005) Combining sample and census data in small area estimates: Iterative Proportional Fitting with standard software. *The Professional Geographer*, 57, 222–34.

Smith, D., Clarke, G. and Harland, K. (2009) Improving the synthetic data generation process in spatial microsimulation models. *Environment and Planning A*, 41, 1251–68.

Tanton, R., Vidyattama, Y., Mcnamara, J., Vu, Q.N. and Harding, A. (2009) Old, Single and Poor: Using Microsimulation and Microdata to Analyse Poverty and the Impact of Policy Change among Older Australians. *Economic Papers: A journal of applied economics and policy*, 28, 102–20.

Weisberg, H. (2005) *The Total Survey Error Approach: A Guide to The New Science of Survey Research*. Chicago: University of Chicago Press.

Wong, D. (1992) The Reliability of Using the Iterative Proportional Fitting Procedure. *Professional Geographer*, 44, 340–48.

Zaidi, A., Harding, A. and Williamson, P. (eds) (2009) *New Frontiers in Microsimulation Modelling. Public Policy and Social Welfare Vol. 36.* Aldershot: Ashgate.

Chapter 3

Microsimulation Estimates of the Inequality Impact of the Economic Crisis in Ireland

Cathal O'Donoghue,[1] Jason Loughrey and Karyn Morrissey

Introduction

Ireland's economic crisis is well documented. After a very high growth period from the mid-1990s until the mid-2000s, growing from 115 per cent of EU GDP per capita, just below the EU15 average in 1997, to a high point of 148 per cent in 2007, 32 per cent above the EU15 average,[2] Ireland faced an unprecedented economic decline from late 2007. GDP fell by 11.5 per cent from its peak in quarter 4 2007 to quarter 4 2009; and GNP fell 15.6 per cent from its peak in quarter 4 2007 to its floor in quarter 1 2011. At this point, real GDP was equivalent to the value in quarter 4 2005.

Whelan (2010) discusses some of the reasons for and implications of the economic crisis. Firstly, as a small open economy, it was inevitable that Ireland would be significantly affected by the global economic and financial crisis. The construction boom that characterized the last years of the boom period saw the share of the labour force working in construction reach an unsustainable 13.7 per cent of the work force in 2007, fully 5 percentage points higher than most other EU countries. In addition, demographic changes were no longer contributing to economic growth as the size of the labour force peaked. Productivity growth had also slowed. In parallel, lending by financial institutions to property developers tripled or quadrupled over the period 2004–07 as the banks concentrated on the property sector.

The period of economic growth had also seen the composition of fiscal policy change from income taxes to property capital gains taxes and VAT, which were largely related to the property boom. The ending of the property bubble saw construction employment decline from 270,000 in early 2007 to 126,000 at the end of 2009. Government tax revenues saw a sharp decline of nearly 18 per cent as a result of this unemployment and also lost the tax revenues associated with construction, while public expenditure on transfers increased from €18.7 billion in 2007 to €23.5 billion in 2009. The collapse of the property bubble left most of

---

1   The authors are grateful for helpful comments provided at the IZA-OECD conference in Paris and from two anonymous referees.

2   See EUROSTAT, GDP per capita in Purchasing Power Standards (PPS) 1997–2008.

the Irish banks in precarious positions as a result of the fall in property values of around 40 per cent, resulting in the state stepping in to guarantee the banks.

The economic crisis manifested itself in changes both to the labour market, wages, prices (including housing costs) and public policy changes to tax, transfer and public sector pay costs. Each of these changes has quite heterogeneous impacts on the population and it is difficult to understand *a priori* who is impacted most by these changes. It is quite important from a public policy perspective to understand the distributional impacts of these changes.

The impact of this decline can be felt in the household sector in a number of dimensions. Public sector wages have been reduced via a number of policy changes which Callan and Nolan (2010) found to be progressive. Callan and Nolan (2010) examined the tax increases and welfare rate reductions between 2009 and 2010, again finding these policy changes to be progressive. As the crisis progressed, combined with increases in mortgage interest rates, households with high mortgages have faced pressures in meeting payments. McCarthy and McQuinn (2010) have considered the distributional characteristics of the ratio of mortgage interest to income ratio, finding quite significant heterogeneity. Counterbalancing falls in income 2009 and 2010 saw falls in the CPI with differential changes across commodity groups. Loughrey and O'Donoghue (2011) examined the distributional impact of these price changes.

Nolan et al. (2011) used the EU-SILC to understand changes in inequality over time around the crisis. However, comparing the income distribution of one year with another using micro-data, we have a confounding effect of labour market and population change on the one hand and policy change on the other. To decompose this effect, we would like to compare the counterfactual effect of differences due to tax-benefit changes alone. Microsimulation analysis is particularly useful methodology for counterfactual simulation, which can help to explain the functioning of the tax-benefit system relative to alternatives.

Microsimulation modelling is a simulation-based method using micro-data that is frequently used to assess the impact of policy changes. In Ireland, the SWITCH model (Callan et al. 1994) has been used for 20 years to assess the impact of policy change on inequality (Callan et al. 2001). They utilize a special version of the EU-SILC dataset available for Ireland for 2008. Callan et al. (2011) assessed the impact of budgetary policy relative to a base population in 2008 adjusted for population and labour market change using reweighting and updating.

First we describe the tax-benefit microsimulation methodology used in this chapter. The next section describes the data used, while the following section describes the welfare impact of labour market and tax-benefit changes. The final section concludes and summarizes the results.

Methodology – Tax Benefit Microsimulation

Changes in income inequality depend not only upon changes in market income, but also changes in tax-benefit policy. The Irish tax-benefit system falls within the

Anglo-liberal category of welfare states, social transfers have primarily a poverty reduction focus based around flat rate insurance benefits, or means tested benefits.[3] In this section, we describe the structure of the Irish tax-benefit system and the modelling requirements for the system.

There are no earnings related components of the benefit system. Income taxation has a schedule with two rates and has an optional joint filing system with partial transfer of bands and credits. The 2000s have seen a move away from allowances to credits payable at the standard rate. Social insurance contributions are flat rate with a floor and a ceiling on payments. Increases in the value of credits has seen a gradual erosion of the tax-payer base over time, with 650,000 of 1.9 million tax-payers exempt in 2005 and 40 per cent in 2007.

Disposable income, defined as income after direct taxation and social benefits is calculated through the use of a static tax-benefit microsimulation model, programmed in Stata. The model simulates the main direct tax and transfer instruments:

- Income Taxation;
- Social Insurance Contributions (Employee, Self-Employed and Employer);
- Income and Pension Levies;
- Family Benefits;
- Social Assistance Benefits; and
- Social Insurance Benefits.

Using the tax-benefit model, the level of payment of social insurance benefits are modelled, with eligibility being assumed to depend upon receipt in the data, within this chapter. The tax-benefit system is stylized, focusing on the main instruments, but ignoring some tax-credits and housing related benefits.

O'Donoghue et al. (2013) describe the functioning of the tax-benefit system, simulating this system in 2005 for a hypothetical family with single earner married couple with two children simulated using the tax-benefit microsimulation model used in this paper. The main earner has a wage rate of two thirds of the average wage rate per hour, with hours varying from zero hours (and seeking work) through to 80 hours per week.

Disposable income is comprised of net market income, equal to gross market income minus income taxation, social insurance contributions and income levies. Unemployment assistance is paid at zero hours and gradually tapered away with a 60 per cent withdrawal rate up until 20 hours per week is worked. Once this 20-hour limit is reached, a family income supplement (FIS), an in-work cash benefit for low-income families, is paid. Child-related benefits, including child benefits and from 2006 a child-care subsidy for young children, are also included.

They reported trends in the overall budget constraint over the period of respectively 2003–07, the period up to the crash, and for 2007 to 2012, the period

---

3   For a broad description of the structure of the Irish tax-benefit system, see O'Donoghue (2004).

after the crash, reflecting the disposable income associated with different hours worked at the averages, deflating by the CPI to account for changes to purchasing power.

Most changes to the structure of the tax-benefit system over the period were parametric, with some structural changes to 'income levies' or additional taxes, social insurance contributions and the introduction and abolition of a childcare supplement. Some of the changes applied to part years. In order to incorporate this, looking at annual incomes, we apply a proportion of each set of policy parameters to the appropriate number of months.

In the period to 2007, the overall budget constraint flattened, with the ratio of disposable income for 40 hours to zero hours decreasing from 1.70 in 2003 to 1.45 in 2007. It also continues to fall in 2009 at 1.39, before rising again. The period to 2007 had a steady rise in the level of the budget constraint as the purchasing power for all parts of the budget constraint rose as wage and benefit growth outstripped inflation. In 2008, the budget declined slightly at the top. In 2009, the purchasing power of the bottom of the distribution rose slightly, but fell at the top, with the reverse occurring in 2010. In 2011, purchasing power fell for most groups, with the bottom falling slightly more. Purchasing power continued to fall across all income levels in 2012. However, in 2013 the system became more regressive, with purchasing power rising at the top as we make the assumption that earnings will grow at the same rate as the previous year, the same assumption that is made for CPI.

Changes in the values of sectoral wage rates, CPI, tax credits and benefit levels drove some changes. CPI rose to 2008, but then fell as Ireland experienced deflation to 2010, before prices rose again to 2012. Working age unemployment benefits rose the most relative to CPI, even with a nominal cut in 2009 and 2010.[4] As old-age benefits incurred no nominal cut, by the end of the period, even with no nominal rise since 2009 purchasing power increased for this group. Tax credits initially rose at a rate close to CPI, but then nominal cuts relative to rising CPI saw the index dip below CPI, thus leading to fiscal drag. The financial sector, given the banking collapse, has seen the largest fall relative to CPI, with the industrial, largely export-based sector having wage growth exceeding CPI.

Data

In order to simulate taxes or benefits, we require data with the following characteristics:

- A dataset representative of the household population with appropriate weights, with sufficient sample size for sub-groups to undertake disaggregated analysis;
- Data that has incomes before the application of incomes (gross incomes);

---

4   There were much more significant cuts for young people.

- The period of analysis may vary from instrument to instrument too, with income taxes typically assessed over a year (which may or may not align with the calendar year), while some benefits may have a period of analysis of a month. Sometimes the period of analysis for payment of a benefit (current month), may differ from the period of analysis of the means for assessment (e.g. previous year). However, very few datasets allow for such heterogeneity.

Understanding the impact of changes in labour market, incomes and policy measures required data with sufficient detail. SILC is a dataset that has been collected in Ireland since 2003 and is the successor to the earlier European Community Household Panel Survey. The SILC dataset collects information on incomes, labour market characteristics, demographics and living conditions and is used to undertake analyses on poverty, inequality and deprivation.

The EU-SILC is collected at the national level, with a harmonized version supplied to Eurostat, which is then processed and provided to researchers as a harmonized User Database (UDB). We utilize the Irish component of the EU-SILC (UDB) in which to model the income distribution. Data are provided gross of taxes and contributions.The Irish component uses partially survey and partially register data. Eighty per cent of respondents allowed their national social security number to be used to access administrative data in relation to their benefit entitlement (Callan et al. 2010).

There are a number of challenges to utilizing the EU-SILC for microsimulation modelling. A challenge in the use of the EU-SILC rests in the difference between the period of analysis for the income variables, which typically are the previous year, and the personal characteristics which typically relate to the time of interview. Thus one may observe people made unemployed in the interview year but with employment income in the data. Thus there may be inconsistencies between both. Ireland has a slightly different definition as the reference period spans two tax years; as the 'income reference period' is '12 months prior the date of interview', the end of income reference period is the date of the interview. Approximately 25 per cent of the sample is collected in each quarter.

As both tax-benefit models and the EU-SILC aim to measure household disposable income, by and large, the EU-SILC has the appropriate variables required for tax-benefit modelling. However, there are a number of issues. Firstly, there are some missing variables such as capital gains and wealth or property values. However, this is typical of most income surveys and so most tax-benefit microsimulation models utilize a definition of disposable income that does not incorporate taxes based upon these measures. It would be reasonable therefore for an EU-SILC based model to make a similar assumption.

A particular challenge to microsimulation modelling is that some of the variables are not easily attributable to the appropriate unit of analysis. For example some of the income variables that are received by individuals such as capital income, rental income, private transfers and young person's income, are only recorded at the household level. Thus, in practice, these variables will be assigned to the head of household, which in a progressive tax system, may over-estimate the amount of taxation if some of these incomes were incident on others in the household. This is also the case with family benefits, which may be incident at the nuclear family level but are only recorded at the household level. Where these instruments are taxable, this too may bias the results.

One of the most serious challenges to using the EU-SILC for microsimulation modelling is the aggregation of benefits. Within the EU-SILC, social benefits are aggregated into six benefits recorded at the individual level (unemployment, old-age, survivor, sickness, disability and education) plus three recorded at the household level (family, social exclusion and housing benefits). If it were possible to utilize other data to model all benefits, then this aggregation would not be an issue, as we could replace the data recorded benefits with the simulated benefits. However, while in practice we model most benefits in Ireland as there are no earnings related benefits, we model the value for most benefits. The Irish social science data archive makes available a variant of the SILC for Ireland with disaggregated benefits. However, this dataset is not suitable for tax-benefit microsimulation modelling as incomes are aggregated to the household level and some variables such as age have been banded.

As we do not know the contributory conditions used for social insurance benefits, we would like to utilize benefit receipt to model the level of these benefits. For most social assistance and family benefits, we have sufficient information to model the benefit. Callan et al. (2010) have access to a special research version of the 2008 EU-SILC which does not suffer from these aggregation issues. O'Donoghue et al. (2013) describe a methodology for correcting the EU-SILC of these issues, utilizing equations estimated on other data to impute disaggregated benefits.

It should be noted, however, that even where we can fully model an instrument, because of benefit take-up issues, we would still like to know the value and presence of the benefit so that take-up can be modelled; although many models assume 100 per cent take-up, requiring the modelling of take-up to bridge the gap (see O'Donoghue et al. 2013).

A similar issue to benefit take-up is the use of survey data to make inferences about mis-calculation of taxes and social insurance contributions. Ideally, therefore, taxes and social contributions would be available separately at the most appropriate unit of analysis. However, within the EU-SILC, they are reported at an aggregated level in terms of the instruments being reported in a single variable and at an aggregate level in terms of being reported at the household level. However, this is not a major issue as many income datasets do not have separate income tax and social insurance contribution data.

Results: Distributional Impact of Downturn

In this section we report the results of our analysis based upon our model. We firstly track mean incomes: market income, gross income (market plus benefits) and disposable income (gross minus taxes and contributions). We have deflated by CPI to report the change in purchasing power. Each measure exhibits the same trend, rising to 2007 and then falling to 2010. We note that average market income is lower in real terms in 2010 than in 2004. However, both mean gross income and disposable income are at levels equivalent to 2005. We note for each measure the ratio of actual data to simulated data. Gross income is slightly lower reflecting issues associated with take-up and issues associated with the length of benefit receipt in a year. The ratio remains relatively constant over time.

Table 3.1   Mean equivalized household incomes (actual and simulated)

Market Income	2004	2005	2006	2007	2008	2009	2010
Simulated	20972.05	21781.42	22991.5	24883.61	23496.18	21961.61	19628.753
Data	20861.85	21670.41	22891.81	24739.57	23360.41	21803.77	19496.665
Ratio	0.99	0.99	1.00	0.99	0.99	0.99	0.99
Gross Income	**2004**	**2005**	**2006**	**2007**	**2008**	**2009**	**2010**
Simulated	25738	26933	28659	31177	30402	29115	27127
Data	24720	25916	27595	29975	28995	27613	25500
Ratio	0.96	0.96	0.96	0.96	0.95	0.95	0.94
Disposable Income	**2004**	**2005**	**2006**	**2007**	**2008**	**2009**	**2010**
Simulated	21059	21927	23235	25170	24666	23182	21518
Data	21007	21601	22970	25091	24401	22994	21434
Ratio	0.99	0.99	0.99	1.00	0.99	0.99	1.00

Notes:
1. Equivalence scale used is the modified OECD scale.
2. For validation purposes, we have not used weights in this table.

Inequality

In Figure 3.1, we report the trend in the inequality of equivalized household disposable income over time. We note that inequality fell from 2004 to 2009 and then rose significantly in 2010. Thus the initial impact of the crisis in 2008 and 2009 was inequality reducing, while inequality increased rapidly in 2010.

We validate the microsimulation model by comparing actual and simulated Gini coefficients. The data years in the Irish EU-SILC span two years as incomes apply to the 12 months before the interview date, with interviews conducted more or less equally across the year. As a result we model the simulated year as the weighted average of the current and lagged year as a function of the quarter of data collection. We also report the simulation of tax-benefit systems in the current and lagged year. We note firstly due to reasons such as benefit non-take up and specification issues in the simulation of taxation such as the inability to model specific allowances, as well as tax evasion and avoidance, that there is a gap between the level of the Gini coefficient for simulated and actual equivalized disposable income. This is not surprising and is consistent with other microsimulation analyses. For the period to 2009, there is not much difference in the trend between the different assumptions, with a correlation of about 0.98. However, the trend shifts in 2010, with the current system matching the trend much more closely, resulting in a correlation over the whole period of 0.95. Meanwhile, the lagged system has a different trends (rising, but at a lower rate), with a correlation of 0.68, resulting in the weighted average also growing at a relatively lower rate between the two measures, with a correlation of 0.88. We would therefore conclude that the current tax-benefit system is a better predictor of the trend than the lagged or weighted average.

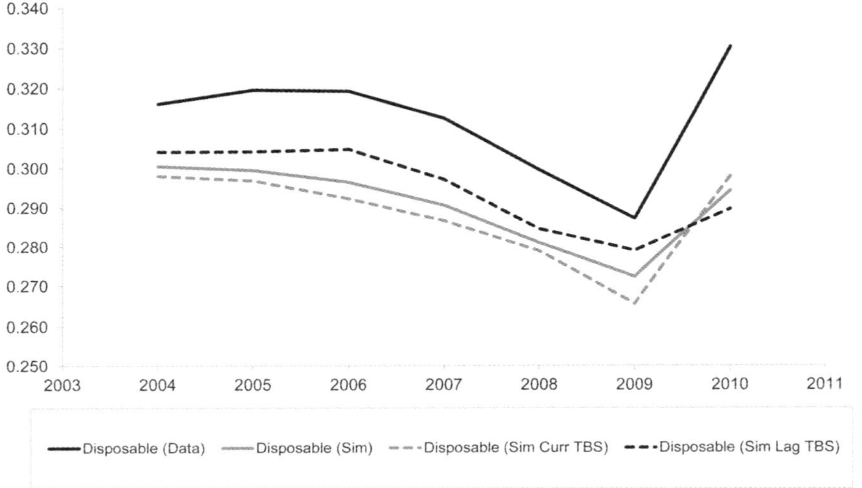

Figure 3.1   Distribution of disposable income, simulated and actual

Note: Equivalence scale used is the modified OECD scale.

We now try to understand the differences in the levels between the actual and simulated data as a result of the assumptions made. We focus first on the assumptions made in relation to the benefits system. We consider three alternatives, modelling:

- Non take-up with the weighted average of current and lagged systems;
- Non take-up and an estimate of months of benefit receipt with the weighted average of current and lagged systems;
- Non take-up and an estimate of months of benefit receipt with the current system.

We model take-up at the level of the benefit unit level. The coefficients follow the usual signs, with the higher the potential benefit receipt, the higher the take-up. Higher other sources of household income is associated with lower take-up. Similarly, being in employment increases take-up, while farmers have a lower take-up than other groups. Separated or divorced persons are less likely to take-up benefits than other groups. Interestingly, prior to the boom, those with higher education had a lower propensity to take-up social benefits, while after the crash, this effect was no longer significant.

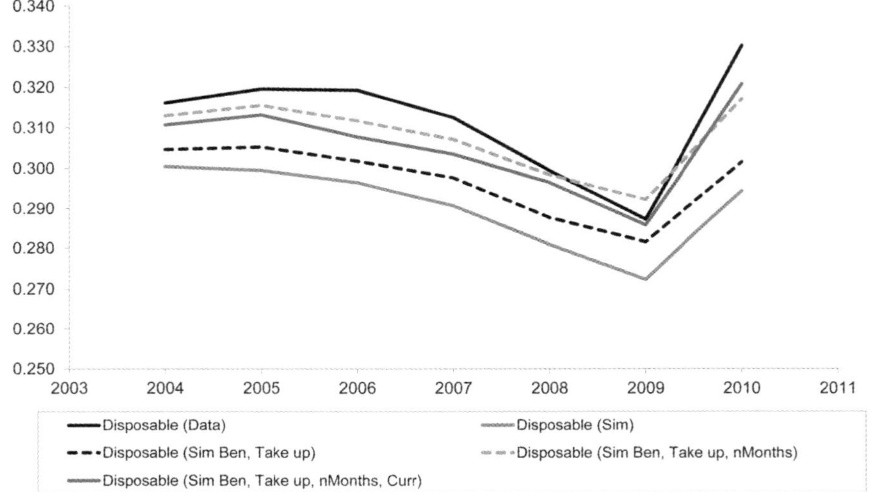

Figure 3.2   Distribution of disposable income, simulated and actual with different benefit assumptions

Note: Equivalence scale used is the modified OECD scale.

Modelling benefit non-take-up at the family level, we see that the inequality trend over time remains the same, with the curve shifting so that about a quarter to a half of the gap is closed. As noted above, part of the reason for the over-simulation of benefits is that it is not possible to identify receipt of benefits of less than a year in the EU-SILC data. Imputing the number of months received on the basis of the difference between actual and simulated benefits, we see that much of the remaining gap is closed in Figure 3.2. In 2009, this over-compensates pushing inequality over 100 per cent. However, this is as a result of utilizing the weighted average of the two years. Utilizing only the rules of the current year, we see that inequality tracks but is always lower than the actual data. This is consistent with the fact that we have not modelled misspecification in modelling taxes and contributions.

We now consider the impact of misspecification in the modelling of taxes and contributions. We do this by replacing the simulated value for taxes and contributions with the variable supplied in the data. We note in Figure 3.3 that prior to 2009, replacing simulated taxes and contributions (based upon a weighted average of two years) with the actual value had quite a varied effect, reducing the gap by between 10 per cent and 50 per cent. This effect is much more consistent, however, at 30–40 per cent when one looks at the change in the gap between actual and simulated based upon the current tax-benefit year. We note, however, that the gap is reduced by a greater degree by improvements in the benefit assumptions.

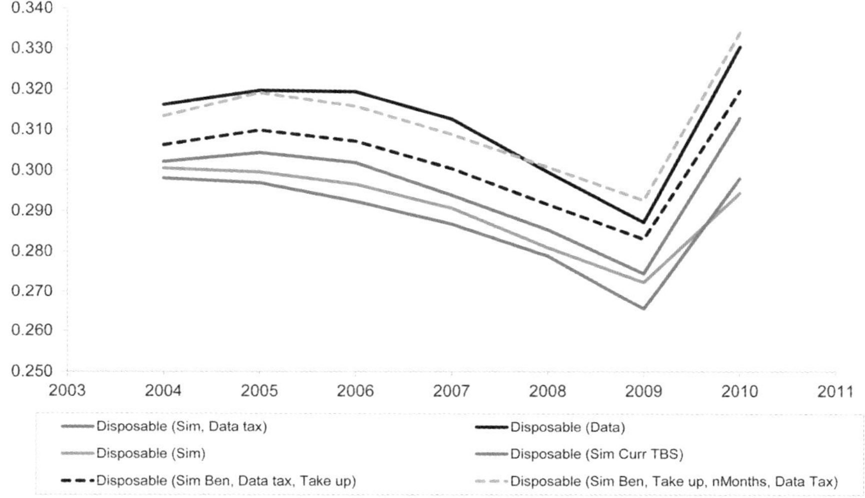

Figure 3.3   Distribution of disposable income, simulated and actual with different tax assumptions

Note: Equivalence scale used is the modified OECD scale.

Conclusions

In this chapter we attempted to chart the impact of the early part of Ireland's economic crisis from 2008–10 on the distribution of income. In order to decompose the impact of components of income, we utilized a microsimulation methodology. We undertook a detailed validation of the methodology, finding that the methodology was reasonably effective, subject to the usual consequences of assumptions using microsimulation such as 100 per cent benefit take-up and under-estimating the impact of non-modellable allowances, full year of receipt for benefits and tax avoidance/evasion in the tax system. Overall, we found that the simulated and data based approaches generated a similar trend, albeit with lower levels of inequality for these reasons. Modelling benefit take-up, and partial year receipt, we were able to bridge much of the gap between the two approaches, giving us confidence in our methodology.

We utilized the framework to model changes to the level of income inequality from the period just before the crisis in 2004 to after the crisis in 2010. In terms of the impact of the economic crisis, we found that the income inequality fell in the early part of the crisis, but rose steadily and then rapidly. Much of this change was due to rising inequality of market incomes (even when discounting unemployment). O'Donoghue et al. (2013) showed that this was due to the differential effect of the downturn on different sectors where some sectors such as the construction and public sectors were significantly hit, while the international traded sectors have been relatively immune from the downturn and have seen continued growth. The impact of the tax-benefit system has been to mitigate this upward pressure, with a gradual rise in the redistributive effect of the tax-benefit system driven by an increase in demand on the benefits side and increased progressivity on the tax side.

References

Callan, T., Keane, C., Walsh, J.R. and Lane, M. 2010. From Data to Policy Analysis: Tax-Benefit Modelling using SILC 2008. *Journal of the Statistical and Social Inquiry Society of Ireland* XL.

Callan T., Keeney, M.J., Nolan, B. and Walsh, J.R. 2001. Reforming Tax and Welfare ESRI Policy Research Series 42. Dublin: Economic and Social Research Institute.

Callan, T. and Nolan, B. 2010. Inequality and the Crisis: The Distributional Impact of Tax Increases and Welfare and Public Sector Pay Cuts. *The Economic and Social Review*, 41(4), 461–71.

Callan T., O'Donoghue, C. and O'Neill, C. 1994. Analysis of Basic Income Schemes for Ireland, Dublin: ESRI Policy Research Series Paper No. 21.

CSO. 2006. EU Survey on Income and Living Conditions. Dublin: the Stationary Office.

Francesco, F., Levy, H. and Sutherland, H. 2007. Using the EU-SILC for Policy Simulation: Prospects, Some Limitations and Suggestions. EUROMOD Working Paper No. EM1/07.

Hancock, R., Pudney, S., Barker, G., Hernandez, M. and Sutherland, H. 2004. The Take-Up of Multiple Means-Tested Benefits by British Pensioners: Evidence from the Family Resources Survey. *Fiscal Studies*, 25(3), 279–303.

Immervoll, H., O'Donoghue, C. and Sutherland, H. 1999. An Introduction to EUROMOD. *EUROMOD Working Paper* no. 0/99.

Levy, H. and Mercader-Prats, M. 2003. EUROMOD Country Report SPAIN. http://www.iser.essex.ac.uk/msu/emod/countries/spain/cr01sp0903.pdf, last accessed 2 January 2013.

Levy, L. and Mercador-Prats, M. 2002. Simplifying the personal income tax system: lessons from the 1998 Spanish reform. *Fiscal Studies*, 23(3), 419–43.

Loughrey, J. and O'Donoghue C. 2012. The Welfare Impact of Price Changes on Household Welfare and Inequality 1999–2010. *Economic and Social Review*, 43(1) (Spring), 31–66.

McCarthy, Y. and McQuinn, K. 2011. How are Irish Households Coping with their Mortgage Repayments? Information from the Survey on Income and Living Conditions. *The Economic and Social Review*, 42(1), 71–94.

Matsaganis, M. and Flevotomou, M. 2010. Distributional Implications of Tax Evasion in Greece, GreeSE – Hellenic Observatory Papers on Greece and Southeast Europe, Hellenic Observatory, LSE, Paper No. 31.

Nolan, B. 2004. Long-Term Trends in Top Incomes in Ireland, mimeo., ESRI: Dublin.

Nolan, B. and Smeeding, T.M. 2005. Ireland's income distribution in a Comparative Perspective. *Review of Income and Wealth*, Blackwell Publishing, 51(4), 537–60.

Nolan, Maitre. 2000. A Comparative Perspective on Trends in Income Inequality in Ireland. *The Economic and Social Review*, 31(4), 329–50.

O'Donoghue, C. 2004. Redistributive Forces in the Irish Tax-Benefit System. *Journal of the Statistical and Social Inquiry Society of Ireland.*

O'Donoghue, C., Loughrey, J. and Morrissey, K. 2013. Using the EU-SILC to Model the Impact of the Economic Crisis on Inequality. *IZA Discussion Paper.*

Pudney, S., Hancock, R. and Sutherland, H. 2006. Simulating the Reform of Means-tested Benefits with Endogenous Take-up and Claim Costs. *Oxford Bulletin of Economics and Statistics*, 68(2), 135–66.

Whelan, K. 2010. Policy Lessons from Ireland's Latest Depression. *The Economic and Social Review*, 41(2), 225–54.

Chapter 4

Simulating the Need for Health- and Elderly Care in Sweden – A Model Description of SESIM-LEV

Lisa Brouwers,[1] Lina Maria Ellegård, Nils Janlöv,
Pontus Johansson, Karin Mossler and Anders Ekholm

Background

Life expectancy has increased in Sweden as in most countries over the last century, and so has the number of people reaching an old age. According to forecasts from Statistics Sweden the proportion of the elderly is expected to increase by 30 per cent between 2010 and 2050, meaning that a quarter of the population will be 65 years old or more by the year 2050. Increasing life expectancy also means that the number of very old people will grow quickly. The number of people aged 95 or more is expected to increase by a factor of three, from 17,000 in 2010 to 45,000 in 2050.[2]

This is a positive trend, but since elderly people need care in terms of home help services or special housing, as well as more healthcare than younger people do, society must adapt to the increased demand. From the point of view of healthcare, the demographic pressure will be at its greatest around 2020; and for elderly care, from 2025–30.

The Ministry of Health and Social Affairs has simulated how demographics, health, morbidity and mortality may develop over the next 40 years, and what impact this has on the need for health and elderly care up to year 2050. This chapter summarizes the development of the model within the LEV project, which was initiated in 2006/07. Further details on the simulation results are available in the report 'The future need for care' (Ministry of Health and Social Affairs 2010).

---

1   The authors wish to thank Björn Lindgren (Lund University/University of Gothenburg/National Bureau of Economic Research, Cambridge) and Mårten Lagergren (Ageing Research Council) for substantial contributions in the SESIM-LEV project.

2   Statistics Sweden population forecasts from 15/04/2010. The model projections are based on the 2006 forecast.

The Simulation Model

The SESIM (2007) model was originally developed by the Swedish Ministry of Finance. SESIM is a typical dynamic microsimulation model, i.e. events and individual variables are updated sequentially every year. The model population consists of a representative sample of the Swedish population in 1999, geographically distributed over nine fictive geographical regions.[3] From the year 2000, all model individuals are annually exposed to a probability of changing their attributes as a result of events such as marrying, having children, becoming employed or entering retirement. Only events relevant to the public welfare systems are modelled. Figure 4.1 presents an overview of the model structure.

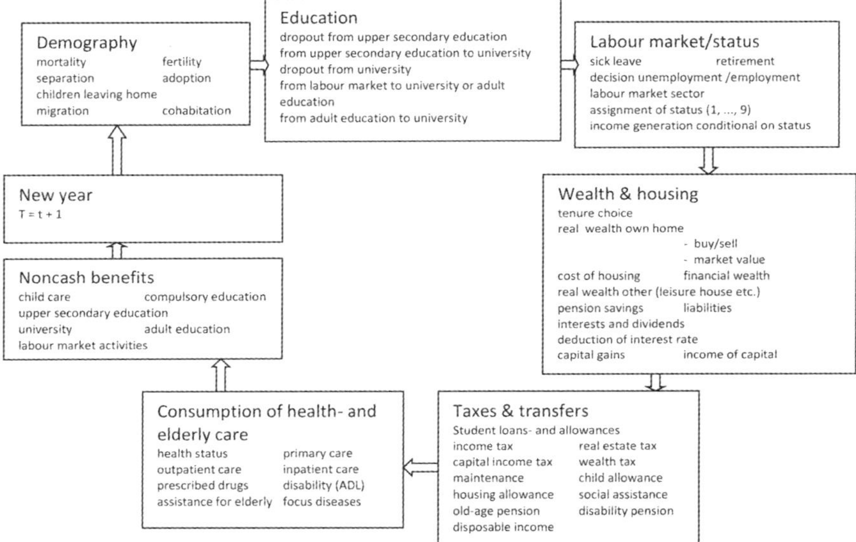

Figure 4.1   Conceptual description of the flows in the SESIM-LEV model

SESIM is programmed in Visual Basic, version 6. The typical projection period is 51 years, from 1999 to 2050. One such simulation typically takes 30 minutes.

Contributions of the LEV Project

SESIM has previously been used for studying the effects of an ageing population on inpatient care and elderly care. This work, called the BabyBoom project, is described by Klevmarken and Lindgren (2008). The LEV project built on the

---

3   Stockholm, Gothenburg, Malmoe/Lund, Urban South, Urban Mid, Urban North, Rural South, Rural Mid and Rural North.

BabyBoom work, and extended the SESIM model into what we here refer to as SESIM-LEV. The LEV project developed SESIM in a number of important areas:

- New parts were added to the health consumption module, including primary care, specialized outpatient care and prescribed outpatient drugs.
- Existing modules for consumption of elderly care and inpatient care were updated.
- Healthcare consumption and specific death risks for four important disease groups were added: cancer, cardiovascular diseases, dementia and diabetes.
- A link was introduced between individual health status and death risk.
- A conversion between the persons health status and quality adjusted life years (QALYs) was introduced to enable quantification of the population's health.

Data Sources

The primary data source from which the model population was collected is LINDA (2012), a longitudinal database containing approximately 3.5 per cent of the Swedish population. The family members of these individuals were then added, resulting in a data set consisting of 786,000 individuals. By sampling families from this data set, a base population comprising 318,500 persons was constructed. Besides forming the base population, LINDA was used for the estimation of most statistical models used in the different modules. Other important data sources used in the LEV-project were HINK/HEK (Statistics Sweden 2013), HILDA/ULF (Statistics Sweden 2011), the National Patient Register (Socialstyrelsen 2011), SHARE (2012),[4] and the Kungsholmen project (SNAC-K 2012).

HINK/HEK is a yearly national survey on households' economy. HILDA (Health and Individuals Longitudinal Data Analysis) is an individual-level database from Lund University, which links data from the Survey on Living Conditions (ULF) to data from several other registers, for example the National Patient Register, which records all inpatients at public hospitals, specialized outpatient visits, and (from 2005) prescribed outpatient drugs. SHARE (Survey of Health, Ageing and Retirement in Europe) is a European panel database on health, socio-economic status, social and other networks in which only persons aged 50 or more

---

4   SHARE: This chapter uses data from SHARE Waves 1 & 2, as of December 2008. SHARE data collection in 2004–2007 was primarily funded by the European Commission through its 5th and 6th framework programs (project numbers QLK6-CT-2001-00360; RII-CT-2006-062193; CIT5-CT-2005-028857). Additional funding by the US National Institute on Aging (grant numbers U01 AG09740-13S2; P01 AG005842; P01 AG08291; P30 AG12815; Y1-AG-4553-01; OGHA 04-064; R21 AG025169) as well as by various national sources is gratefully acknowledged (see http://www.share-project.org for a full list of funding institutions).

are included. The Kungsholmen project is a longitudinal population-based study on ageing and dementia carried out in the district Kungsholmen in Stockholm

In order to preserve data confidentiality, the personal identifier, which makes it possible to link different data registers, was removed from all data records by Statistics Sweden before data delivery. Access to micro-data is restricted to a limited group of persons at the Ministry of Finance and the Ministry of Health and Social Affairs at the government offices. Program development and simulations are run on specific stand-alone computers to minimize the risk of unauthorized access.

Imputation and Updating of Health- and Elderly Care Consumption

The base population in SESIM held no information on health- or elderly care consumption. They were therefore assigned an initial consumption in the first year of the simulation. Similarly, initial consumption was imputed for all persons that entered the model population via births or in-migration, or that reached the age of inclusion in a certain risk population. The imputation was based on statistical estimates of healthcare consumption as a function of different background factors available in SESIM (e.g. age and sex, see below). These estimations were performed on data that held information on both the individual's consumption and the background variables. Similar estimates governed the annual update of individual care consumption; the update models are however *dynamic*, i.e. care consumption also depends on care consumption in the previous year.

Health Status

Individual health status is perhaps the most important determinant of healthcare consumption, but this was lacking from the base population. Therefore, health status was imputed for the model population; using estimates from ULF/HILDA, during the BabyBoom project (see Klevmarken and Lindgren 2008). Briefly, health is described by an index taking values 1 (severe illness), 2 (some illness), 3 (not full health) or 4 (full health). The survey questions underlying the index capture self-assessed health, mobility, chronic illness and capacity for work. The health distribution in the Swedish population follows what is expected, with a distinct age-profile; the higher the age the larger the fraction of people in illness. In general women tend to have better health than men.

The LEV project made no changes to the health module. However, to increase policy relevance of the simulation results, we converted simulated increases in life-length into Quality-Adjusted Life Years (QALYs). Specifically, we calculated the Euro-QoL weight for each individual in the ULF survey and then used the mean weight of each health index level (Burström 2003).

Healthcare Module: Update and Extension

As mentioned, the LEV project updated the model for inpatient care and extended the healthcare module to cover also outpatient care and consumption of prescribed drugs. Since the first year in the SESIM-LEV is 1999 it was possible to validate model generated care consumption against real data. The statistical models were estimated on ULF/HILDA. Acknowledging that most individuals in HILDA do not consume healthcare at all during a year, we used the negative binomial (NB) and the zero-inflated negative binomial (ZINB) models in the estimation of outpatient visits and days spent in hospital, and a two-part model (logit + GLM) to estimate pharmaceutical consumption. Table 4.1 shows the applied econometric model, the number of observations and the McFadden R2 of each estimation. Unsurprisingly, given the skewness of healthcare consumption, the models were only able to account for a small share of the total variation; however, out-of-sample predictions as well as comparisons of simulated and actual healthcare consumption showed that the models predicted care consumption satisfactorily.

The choice of background variables in the econometric models was largely governed by the variables used in the BabyBoom version of the inpatient care module; there was no threshold confidence level for inclusion into the final model. The background variables are presented briefly in the next paragraphs and in Table A1 in the Appendix.

Table 4.1   Econometric models used in estimations of healthcare consumption

Dependent variable (type of consumption)	Population at risk	Econometric model	
		Static estimation	Dynamic estimation
Primary care	60+	**NB** N = 1,862, McFadden R2 = 0.16	**NB** N = 1,122, McFadden R2 = 0.23
Specialized outpatient care	16–59	**NB** N = 15,398, McFadden R2 = 0.05	**NB** N = 15,398, McFadden R2 = 0.08
	60+	**NB** N = 7,156, McFadden R2 = 0.05	**ZINB** N = 7,156, McFadden R2 = 0.10
Inpatient care	16–59	**ZINB** N = 15,398, McFadden R2 = 0.16	**ZINB** N = 15,398, McFadden R2 = 0.16
	60+	**ZINB** N = 7,156, McFadden R2 = 0.12	**ZINB** N = 7,156, McFadden R2 = 0.12

Dependent variable (type of consumption)	Population at risk	Econometric model	
		Static estimation	Dynamic estimation
Prescribed drugs	16–59	**Logit + GLM (log link, gamma family)** *Pr(drugs), female:* N = 3,493, McFadden R2 = 0.10 *Pr(drugs), male:* N = 3,532, McFadden R2 = 0.16 *Total costs, all (GLM):* N = 4,592, McFadden R2 = 0.07	–
	60+	**Logit + GLM (log link, gamma family)** *Pr(drugs), female:* N = 1,581, McFadden R2 = 0.21 *Total costs, female (GLM):* N = 1,409, McFadden R2 = 0.02 *Pr(drugs), male:* N = 1,275, McFadden R2 = 0.24 *Total costs, male (GLM):* N = 1,076, McFadden R2 = 0.02	–
Mortality	60+ with no elderly care and ADL/DEM = 0	**Logit** N = 5,859, McFadden R2 = 0.25	–

As already explained, care consumption in the previous year was added as an explanatory variable in the dynamic models. The extension of the healthcare module further allowed us to let care consumption of one type, e.g. outpatient care, be an explanatory variable for care consumption of another type, e.g. inpatient care. Figure 4.2 illustrates the modelled dependencies (note that care consumption also influenced individual death risk). For instance, inpatient care (IP) was affected by the same year's outpatient care and by last year's inpatient care.

To give a brief overview of the results, we discuss the dynamic models for specialized outpatient care and for inpatient care. The fitted coefficients for all models are available in an online appendix to this chapter.[5] Table 4.2 lists the most important variables for *out- and inpatient care* consumption. There is a relationship

***

5   See http://www.microsimulation.org/resource-centre/new-pathways/ (last accessed 3 October 2013).

with health status for both age groups. Persons with health status 1 (worse) make more visits than those with status 2, etc. Previous outpatient care consumption is also an important predictor: exactly one visit last year implies 0.5 more visits on average, while at least two visits last year implies 1.2–1.7 more visits on average.

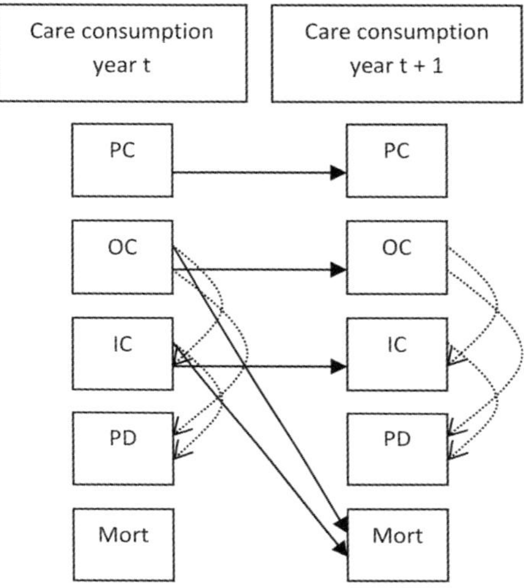

Figure 4.2　　Care consumption and the influence within or between years

PC = primary care, OC = outpatient care, IC = inpatient care, PD = prescribed drugs, MORT = mortality.

Table 4.2　　Variables affecting out- and inpatient care

Variable	Model	Direction
Health status	Outpatient care	(bad → more)
Last year's # of outpatient visits	Outpatient care	(many → more)
Education [60+]	Outpatient care	(university → more)
Type of residential area [60+]	Outpatient care	(city → more)
Health status	Inpatient care	(bad → more)
Current year's outpatient visits	Inpatient care	(many → more)
Last year's inpatient days [60+]	Inpatient care	(many → more)
Baby [women 16–59]	Inpatient care	(yes → more)
Country of birth [16–59]	Inpatient care	(Sweden → more)
Sex [60+]	Inpatient care	(women → more)
Relative income [60+]	Inpatient care	(high → more)
Cohabiting [60+]	Inpatient care	(yes → fewer)
Country of birth [60+]	Inpatient care	(Sweden → fewer)

The estimated relations between *inpatient care* and health status, outpatient visits and previous inpatient care consumption also followed the expected pattern. Conditional on health status, the larger inpatient care consumption of richer individuals may be explained by more articulated demand by this group.

Healthcare Consumption for People with a Focus Disease

Several studies have shown that a large proportion of the consumption and the cost for healthcare are tied to a few, extremely care demanding, diagnoses. A few diagnoses, affecting 5 per cent of the population, together consume 60 per cent of healthcare resources.[6] In the LEV work we included the following focus diseases; cancer (breast, prostate, rectum, lung and other forms of cancer), AMI, stroke and diabetes. The yearly prevalence for these disease groups were 6.2 per cent[7] in the Swedish population above 16.[8] For these focus diseases, the LEV project collected data on incidence, prevalence and care consumption from the national patient registers, aggregated by sex and five-year age classes.

Instead of determining the care consumption of people with cancer, AMI or stroke by the regular healthcare module, we used the disease-specific care consumption during a six-year period (unless the person died during this period). The death risks were also replaced by disease- and age-specific risks. The pattern of consumption and death risk changed over time; for instance, the number of inpatient days as well as the death risk was higher the first year than in the fifth year. After the six-year period, the individuals were not considered affected by the focus disease any longer and so their healthcare consumption and death risks were again determined by the normal estimation models. For diabetes, disease-specific care consumption and death risk were used until the person died, as it is a chronic disease.

Elderly Care, Dementia and Disability Module: Update and Extension

A module for the demand for elderly care was part of the previous version of SESIM. The new version, SESIM-LEV, differed in that it included dementia explicitly. The estimations were based on material from the Kungsholmen study together with material from ULF/HILDA. The following five estimations were made:

- Presence of dementia (initial, binary)
- Disability /ADL[9]-dependence (initial, 4 levels)
- Elderly care/assistance (initial, 3 levels)
- Elderly care/assistance (dynamic, 3 levels)
- ADL/DEM (dynamic, 4 levels. Combination of dementia and ADL)

---

6   SOU 2003: 88.
7   According to data from the Patient Registers, National Board of Health and Welfare.
8   Data from Region Skåne, 2004.
9   Activity in Daily Living dependence.

The individuals' elderly care was divided into home care services (level 1) and special housing with 24-hour care services (level 2). Table 4.3 describes the estimated models; logit models were used in most cases, except for the dynamic disability estimations, in which a proportional odds model was used. The background variables that were included in the different models are presented in Appendix Table A2. Note that the two variables capturing ADL-dependence and presence of dementia were combined into a new variable, called ADL/DEM. It may be noted that in the Kungsholmen study, the objects were interviewed every third year, which is why the dynamic estimations based on this study relate to changes taking place during a three-year period rather than to annual changes.

Table 4.3   Models used in estimations of elderly care, ADL and dementia

Dependent variable	Population at risk	Econometric model	
		Static estimation	**Dynamic estimation**
Dementia	65+	N = 1,612 Logit (binary)	– (see ADL/DEM)
ADL-dependence	65+	N = 2,421 Proportional odds model (ordinal logistic regression)	– (see ADL/DEM)
Elderly care (assistance)	75+	Step 1 N = 1,611 Step 2 N = 585 Logit (binary) in 2 steps: 1. assistance? (1 = yes/0 = no) 2. level? (1 = home service, 2 = special housing)	Step 1 N = 785 Step 2 N = 216 Logit (multinomial). Two models: one for persons with level 0 and one for level 1. Level 3 is irreversible.
ADL/DEM	65+ (last ADL/DEM = 0 or 2)	ADL / Dementia / ADL/DEM No / No / 0 No / Yes / 1 Yes / No / 2 Yes / Yes / 3	ADL/DEM = 0, N = 785 ADL/DEM = 2, N = 216 Logit (multinomial). Possible outcomes 0–3
	65+ (last ADL/DEM = 1)	Last year's ADL and dementia values were combined to an ADL/DEM index	N = 109 Logit (binary). Possible outcomes: 1 and 3
Mortality	Elderly care > 0 and/or ADL/DEM > 0	–	Without, N = 5,123 With, N = 1,569 Proportional hazard

We next briefly describe the estimation results, which are available in the online appendix to this chapter.[10] For *dementia*, we found the expected positive relationship between dementia and ADL-dependence. Other important explanatory variables were age, cohabitation and level of education (see Table 4.4).

Table 4.4   Variables affecting the risk of dementia

Variable	Model	Direction
ADL-dependence	Dementia	(yes → more)
Age	Dementia	(high → more)
Cohabiting	Dementia	(yes → lower)
Education	Dementia	(high → lower)

Before turning to the estimation results for ADL-dependence, it may be noted that the simulation of a person's ADL-dependence took place *after* the estimation of the level of assistance (elderly care). This was to allow for level of assistance as an explanatory variable, acknowledging that persons living in their own homes tend to deteriorate in health more slowly than persons in special housing with 24-hour care. For ADL-dependence, seven different transition models were estimated:

- If Assistance > 0 (home assistance or special housing) and ADL/DEM = 0 or ADL/DEM = 2
  - transition to ADL/DEM = 0
  - transition to ADL/DEM = 1
  - transition to ADL/DEM = 2
- If Assistance = 0 (no assistance or special housing) and ADL/DEM = 0 or ADL/DEM = 2
  - transition to ADL/DEM = 0
  - transition to ADL/DEM = 1
  - transition to ADL/DEM = 2
- If ADL/DEM = 1
  - transmission to ADL/DEM = 1
  - transmission to ADL/DEM = 3.
- Dementia (ADL/DEM = 3) was considered irreversible – no transitions possible.

Not very surprisingly, an ADL/DEM level = 0 increased the chance to stay in ADL/DEM = 0. Living in special housing sharply increased the probability for

---

10   See http://www.microsimulation.org/resource-centre/new-pathways/ (last accessed 3 October 2013).

an increased level of ADL/DEM, and high age tended to lower the probability of keeping or reverting to a state of non-dependence (ADL/DEM = 0).

Regarding *elderly care* (assistance), the dynamic estimations were based on two different models: one for persons who had no assistance three years ago, and another for persons with home services. Living in special housing (level 2) was considered irrevocable.

In the estimations of transition from no assistance (level 0) to assistance (level 1), significant positive correlations were noted for ADL/DEM and age. Other explanatory variables were sex, cohabitation and level of education. For transition from level 0 to level 2, only ADL/DEM = 1 and ADL/DEM = 3 were significant (dementia was present in both states). A reasonable explanation is that transitions directly from no assistance to living in special housing are often associated with having experienced a trauma, e.g. a stroke. Such events could not be considered, since the lagged ADL/DEM value describes the person's situation three years earlier while the trauma probably happened more recently. ADL/DEM = 2 (no dementia) did not increase the probability so much. All other things held constant, the probability for assistance increased with age.

Mortality Module: Linking Health Status and Mortality

Before the LEV project, SESIM had no explicit connection between the individual's health status and death risk. This made too many unhealthy people survive and too many healthy people die. To correct this problem, we introduced mortality model(s) explicitly taking the health status and the care consumption into account. The main mortality model was estimated on all individuals above 60 years of age in HILDA, using a logit model (see Tables 4.1 and A1).[11] Quite soon, however, we saw that healthcare consumption was not a very good predictor of mortality for old persons receiving elderly care (assistance > 0), therefore we made a separate mortality model for this group. ADL dependency and presence of dementia turned out to be pivotal background variables for the mortality of people receiving assistance. Another strong predictor for mortality was, not surprisingly, living in special housing (rather than receiving home care services).

Modelling: Validation, Calibration and Scenarios

Validation

We verified that every statistical estimation model was correctly implemented in the SESIM model by running the SESIM model in debug mode and comparing the computer generated outcomes – number of outpatient visits for example – against

---

11   The model included control variables for the focus diseases.

manually calculated outcomes for 5–10 individuals.[12] After implementation we did static and dynamic analysis of the outcomes. The static analysis consisted in studying the distribution, of inpatient days for example, in a given year by age group, gender and other individual characteristics. Consumption of care was compared with empirical care consumption data from 2005–08 from the Swedish Association of Local Authorities and Regions (SALAR) and from a large Swedish County Council, Region Skåne. Dynamic analysis meant that we looked into the development over time, making sure that the model produced both the expected levels of consumption and that the distribution of health- and elderly care consumption was realistic within the age-groups.

Calibration

When the SESIM-LEV model population was simulated until 2050 it grew larger, but not as much as projected in the forecasts from Statistics Sweden (SCB). The forecasts from Statistics Sweden can to some extent be considered 'black boxes', a continuation of current trends. We did not believe that the forecasts produced by the LEV model were more correct than the one from Statistics Sweden. It merely told us that the simulated structural changes of the population, higher level of education for instance, were not enough to explain the increase projected by SCB. We decided to align the SESIM model to the demographic forecasts by Statistics Sweden by calibrating the death-risks.

Longevity Scenarios: Filling the Gap

The gap between the SESIM-LEV forecast and the Statistics Sweden forecast must be filled with something to make explicit the assumptions that are made to reach the increased life expectancy in 2050. There are three competing influential hypotheses about how the increased life expectancy will affect the demand for healthcare and elderly care:

- **Dynamic equilibrium**: according to this view, the care need is postponed equally as much as life expectancy increases. The greatest demand for care arises during a person's last years, before death. According to this hypothesis a longer life does not entail an increased demand for care.
- **Compression of morbidity**: this view claims that the period with illness in the last years is reduced, that is, the numbers of years in good health increase more than life expectancy.
- **Expansion of morbidity**: a more pessimistic view, stating that the period with bad health increases almost as much as the increase in life expectancy, since people will survive longer in bad health.

12　Based on the estimations, using Excel.

Figure 4.3 below depicts the division between healthy and unhealthy years in 2050 in the different scenarios in a stylized way.

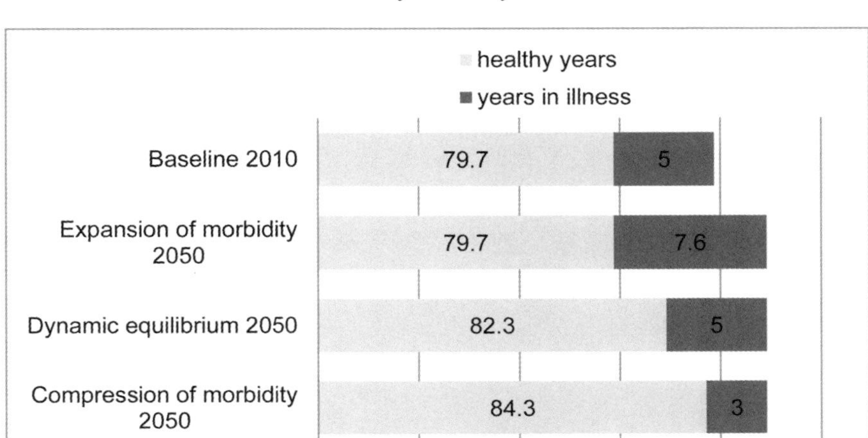

Figure 4.3　　Three scenarios describing different hypotheses regarding health and ageing

We chose to implement the three scenarios described above to investigate their effect on the future care demand. All scenarios had a demographic development consistent with the forecasts from Statistics Sweden – i.e., the model generated approximately the same number of persons in the population and assumed an increased average longevity of 2.6 years.

The scenarios' dynamic equilibrium and compression of morbidity were created by rejuvenating the model individuals when updating their health status. In practice this meant that all persons between 60 and 90 were assigned a temporary age, a shadow age, lower than their real age. This shadow age was used when the new health status was estimated. The size of the rejuvenation varied over the years, over the ages and between the sexes with the goal of producing a population consistent with the forecasts not only in numbers but also having a realistic composition in terms of age, sex, health, prevalence of dementia and level of assistance. The rejuvenation was generally larger later on in the simulation and persons in the ages 70–79 lost most years, as many as eight from year 2025. Rejuvenation was larger for men (Figure 4.4) than for women where it affected the group aged 65–69 years most and had the size six years.

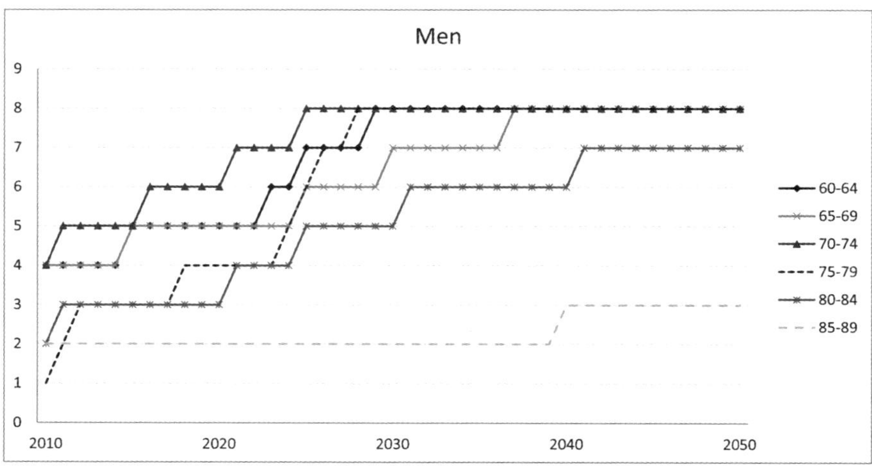

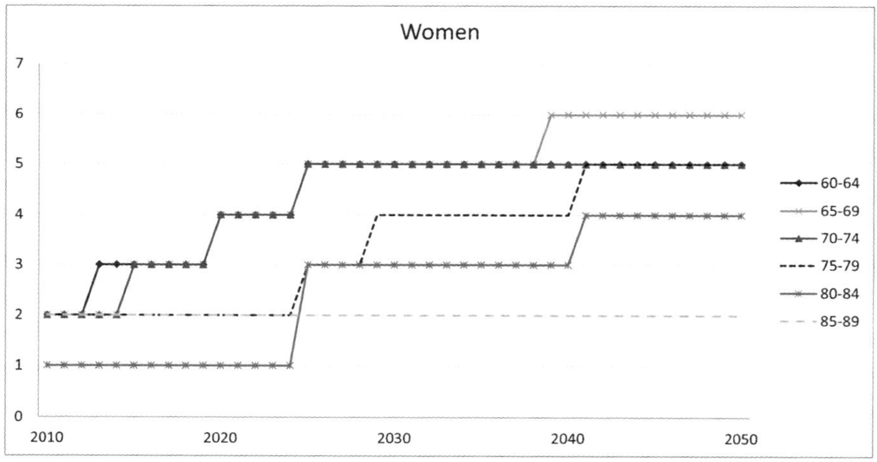

Figure 4.4   Rejuvenation of men (top) and women (bottom) in the scenario compression of morbidity

Beside the three scenarios described above, we implemented a scenario with an alternative demographic development, called the Lancet scenario (see Figure 4.5). Here it was assumed that 50 per cent of persons born today would experience their one hundredth birthday – see Table 1 in Christensen et al. (2009).

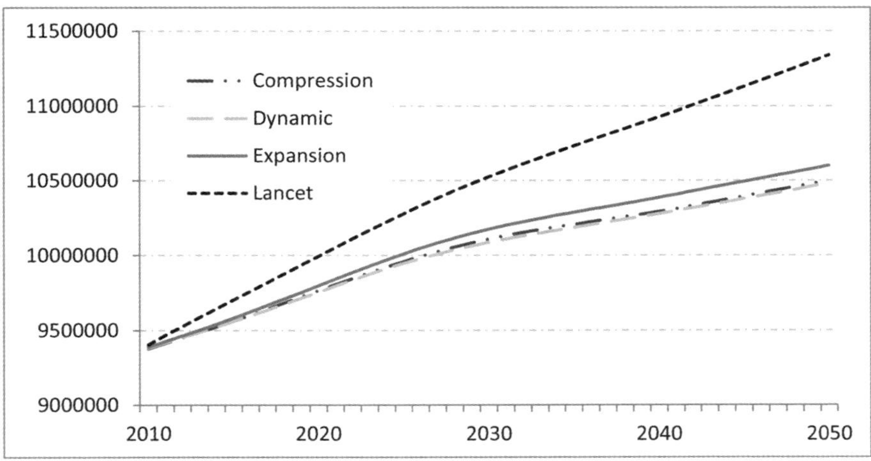

Figure 4.5   Four demographic developments. The three simulated scenarios close together (from bottom): compression of morbidity, dynamic equilibrium, and expansion of morbidity. The upper line shows the Lancet scenario. Population in millions at y-axis.

Focus Disease Scenarios

We also set up a number of scenarios for the focus diseases, called '*heaven*' and '*hell*'. The continuation of current risks was called '*baseline*', see Figures 4.6 and 4.7 for examples. The *heaven* scenario implemented a hypothetical situation where a cure against the focus disease under study was broadly introduced in 2020. The new 'pill' would not cure the already ill, but would prevent all new cases of the disease. The *hell* scenario, implementing a worst case scenario, doubled the incidence of the focus diseases starting from 2020.

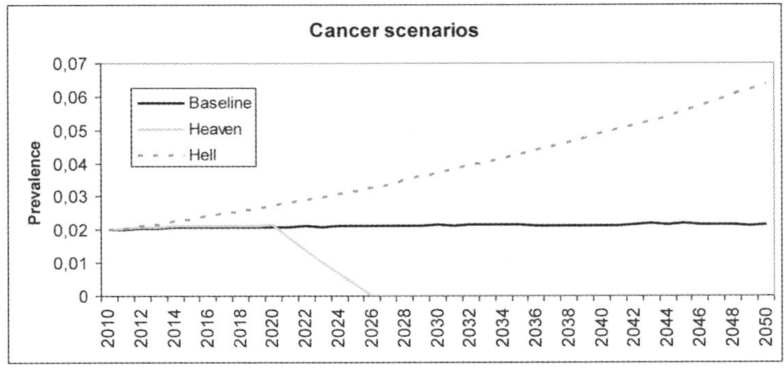

Figure 4.6   Cancer scenarios; baseline, heaven and hell

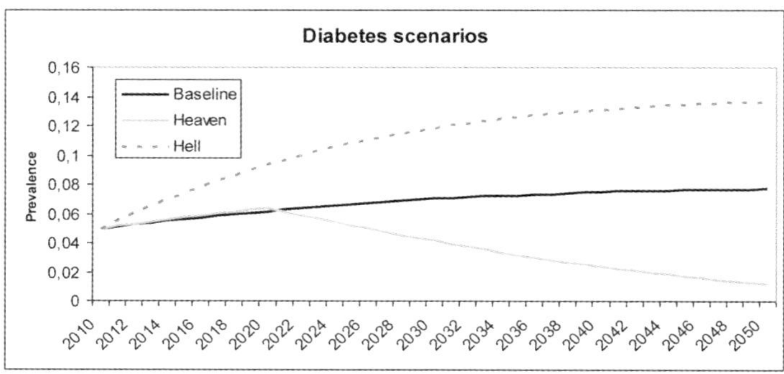

Figure 4.7   Diabetes scenarios; baseline, heaven and hell

Results and Policy Implications

Results from the project, along with policy implications, are presented in the report titled *The Future Need for Care – Results from the LEV project* (Ministry of Health and Social Affairs 2010). The simulations in the LEV-project show that an ageing population poses a challenge for the health- and elderly care in 2050, but that there is time to change. By increasing the number of hours worked, there will be less pressure on the public finances. It is possible to influence morbidity and disability and reduce their obstructive impact. There is, lastly, a great potential for efficiency improvements in health- and elderly care. Anders Ekholm, chief analyst at the Ministry for Health and Social Affairs, has presented the SESIM-LEV results to approximately 6,000 persons since 2010; politicians, civil servants, administrators and professionals within health- and elderly care. Evidence of the impact of the SESIM-LEV project, according to Mr Ekholm, is that increased productivity in elderly care is now on the political agenda. A recent addition to the SESIM-LEV model is tobacco smoking, making it possible to analyse the effect of tobacco interventions. We plan to extend the model with other lifestyle factors explaining health, for instance exercise and alcohol consumption.

References

Burström, K. 2003. *Population health and inequalities in health – measurement of health-related quality of life and changes in QALYs over time in Sweden.* Dissertation, Karolinska Institutet.
Christensen, K., Doblhammer, G., Rau, R. and Vaupel, J. 2009. Ageing populations: the challenges ahead. *Lancet*, 374(9696): 1196–208.

Klevmarken, A. and Lindgren, B. 2008. Simulating an Ageing Population. A microsimulation approach applied to Sweden. *Contributions to Economic Analysis*, vol. 285. Emerald.

LINDA. 2012. LINDA database. [Online] Available at: http://linda.nek.uu.se/ (last accessed 3 October 2013).

Ministry of Health and Social Affairs. 2010. *The Future Need for Care – Results from the LEV project, S2010.021.* [Online] Available at: http://www.government.se/sb/d/574/a/153657 (last accessed 3 October 2013).

SESIM. 2007. [Online] Available at: http://www.sesim.org (last accessed 3 October 2013).

SHARE. 2012. Survey of Health, Ageing and Retirement in Europe. [Online] Available at: http://www.share-project.org (last accessed 3 October 2013).

SNAC-K. 2012. The Swedish National study on Aging and Care in Kungsholmen (the Kungsholm study) [Online] Available at: http://www.snac-k.se/index.htm (last accessed 3 October 2013).

Socialstyrelsen. 2011. The National Patient Register. [Online] Available at: http://www.socialstyrelsen.se/register/halsodataregister/patientregistret/inenglish (last accessed 3 October 2013).

Statistics Sweden. 2011. Undersökningarna av levnadsförhållanden (ULF/SILC). [Online] Available at: http://www.scb.se/Pages/Product____12199.aspx (last accessed 3 October 2013).

Statistics Sweden. 2013. Hushållens ekonomi (HEK). [Online] Available at: http://www.scb.se/Pages/List____257684.aspx (last accessed 3 October 2013).

Appendix

Table A1   List of variables in estimations of healthcare consumption

Variable	Description	Primary care	Spec. outpatient care	Inpatient care	Prescribed drugs	Mortality
Male	1 if male, 0 else	Yes	Yes	Yes	Yes	Yes
Age	age at time for interview	Yes	Yes	Yes	Yes	Yes
Health 1	1 if health status = 1, 0 else Reference.	Yes	Yes	Yes	Yes	Yes
Health 2	1 if health status = 2, 0 else	Yes	Yes	Yes	Yes	Yes
Health 3	1 if health status = 3, 0 else	Yes	Yes	Yes	Yes	Yes
Health 4	1 if health status = 4, 0 else	Yes	Yes	Yes	Yes	Yes
Co-habiting	1 if co-habiting, 0 else	Yes	Yes	Yes	Yes	Yes

Variable	Description	Primary care	Spec. outpatient care	Inpatient care	Prescribed drugs	Mortality
Baby	1 if woman and having child under age 1, 0 else	No	Yes (<60)	Yes (<60)	No	No
Child	1 if there are children under age 6 in household, 0 else	No	No	No	Yes (<60)	No
Rel. income	Own taxable income/average income	Yes	Yes	Yes	Yes	No
Secondary education	1 if secondary education is highest level of education, 0 else	Yes	Yes	Yes	Yes	Yes
University	1 if university education, 0 else	Yes	Yes	Yes	Yes (*male under 60)	Yes
City	1 if living in Stockholm, Gothenburg of Malmoe, 0 else	No	Yes	Yes	Yes	No
Small town	1 if living in other urban area, 0 else	No	Yes	Yes	Yes	No
Born in Sweden	1 if born in Sweden, 0 else	Yes	Yes	Yes	Yes	No
# prim. last year	No. of visits in primary care last year	Yes (dynamic)	No	No	No	No
1 outp. visit this year	1 if exactly 1 visit in spec. outpatient care within 1 year from interview, 0 else	No	No	Yes	Yes	Yes
> 1 outp. visit this year	1 if ≥ 2 spec. outpatient care visits within 1 year from interview, 0 else	No	No	Yes	Yes	Yes

Table A2   List of variables present in estimations of elderly care including dementia and ADL

Variable	Description	Elderly care			
		ADL	Dementia	ADL/ DEM	Elderly care (assistance)
Woman	1 if woman, 0 else	Yes	No	Yes (static)	No
Sex	man = 1, woman = 2	No	No	Yes (dynamic)	Yes

Age	age at interview	Yes (10-year classes)	Yes	Yes (dynamic)	Yes
Cohabiting	1 if cohabiting, 0 else	No	Yes	Yes (dynamic)	Yes
ADL1	ADL > 1 this year	No	Yes	Yes (static)	No
Assistance2	1 if assistance = 2, 0 else	No	No	Yes (dynamic)	No
Dem	1 if dementia = 1, 0 else	No	No	Yes (static)	No
Adl/dem_1	1 if Adl/dem this year = 1, 0 else	No	No	No	Yes (static)
Adl/dem _2	1 if Adl/dem this year = 2, 0 else	No	No	No	Yes (static)
Adl/dem _3	1 if Adl/dem this year = 3, 0 else	No	No	No	Yes (static)
Adl/dem 3_1	1 if Adl/dem 3 years ago = 1, 0 else	No	No	No	Yes (dynamic)
Adl/dem 3_2	1 if Adl/dem 3 years ago = 2, 0 else	No	No	No	Yes (dynamic)
Adl/dem 3_3	1 if Adl/dem 3 years ago = 3, 0 else	No	No	No	Yes (dynamic)
Adl/Dem3_0	1 if Adl/dem 3 years ago = 0, 0 else	No	No	Yes (dynamic)	No
Health 1	1 if Health = 1, 0 else.	Yes	No	No	No
Health 2	1 if Health = 2, 0 else	Yes	No	No	No
Health 3	1 if Health = 3, 0 else	Yes	No	No	No
Health 4	1 if Health = 4, 0 else	Yes	No	No	No
Secondary education	1 if secondary education is highest level of education, 0 else	No	Yes	Yes (dynamic)	Yes
University	1 if university education is highest level of education, 0 else	No	Yes	Yes (dynamic)	Yes

Chapter 5

An Australian Disease and Long-term Care Microsimulation Model

Richard Cumpston

Background

With an ageing population, Australia needs to plan ahead for the medical and care requirements of older persons. For example, the Australian Department of Health and Ageing has issued licences for aged care facilities, using deterministic population projections for about 1,300 statistical local areas. Private developers of aged care facilities need good local projections of potential residents, taking into account their financial capacity to pay charges. Probabilities of admission to aged care depend on specific diseases such as dementia, which may also affect the type of facility required. The need for detailed disease simulations with fine geographic subdivisions suggested that a large household microsimulation model might be useful.

This chapter describes:

- The household microsimulation model used to test disease microsimulation;
- The simulation of diseases, using AIHW disease models;
- Retrospective imputation of baseline diseases;
- Probability-weighted imputation of baseline diseases;
- Comparisons between actual and simulated deaths;
- Models of the probability of being in aged care;
- Comparisons between simulated and actual persons in aged care; and
- The feasibility of simulations with many more persons and areas.

The Australian Institute of Health and Welfare (AIHW) has published models of the incidence and development of 176 diseases (Mathers, Vos and Stevenson 1999), without geographic subdivisions. Leaving aside diseases unlikely to cause death or permanent disability, 123 of these disease models were added to an existing household microsimulation model with 57 geographic subdivisions. This chapter describes the model, disease data sources, modelling techniques and validations, and notes that the model is currently being expanded to 22 million persons and 2,200 geographic subdivisions.

Household Microsimulation Model

The model was based on a 1 per cent sample of Australian households from the 2001 census (Australian Bureau of Statistics 2003). After removing incomplete households, an unweighted sample file of 175,044 persons remained, equivalent to about a 0.9 per cent sample. The households were located within 57 statistical divisions. The model simulates births, deaths, emigrants, immigrants, household membership changes and moves, education, work, superannuation and housing forward for 50 years, within simulation cycles between one year and one day. Sampling with loaded probabilities (Cumpston 2012), and best of n matching (Cumpston 2010) are used to reduce runtimes.

The Australian Institute of Health and Welfare (AIHW) has published models of the incidence and development of 176 diseases (Mathers, Vos and Stevenson 1999). Leaving aside diseases unlikely to cause death or permanent disability, 123 of these disease models were added to the model. Mortality assumptions were included for each disease. Diseases for each person in the baseline population were retrospectively imputed, assuming stable incidence, development and mortality rates. Aged care residents in the baseline population were imputed, based on diseases and marital status.

Simulation of Diseases and Disease Stages, Using AIHW Models

Many of the 123 AIHW disease models are subdivided by type or development stage. For example, Table 5.1 shows that the breast cancer model includes three types of breast cancer, each with four development stages:

Table 5.1   Breast cancer types and stages

Type	Stage no.	Stage	Force of mortality	Force of recovery	Force of transition
Tumour < 2 cm	1	Diagnosis & primary treatment			4.62
Tumour < 2 cm	2	Remission		0.29	0.10
Tumour < 2 cm	3	Disseminated cancer			0.57
Tumour < 2 cm	4	Terminal stage	12		
Tumour 2–5 cm	1	Diagnosis & primary treatment			2.83
Tumour 2–5 cm	2	Remission		0.28	0.23
Tumour 2–5 cm	3	Disseminated cancer			0.57
Tumour 2–5 cm	4	Terminal stage	12		
Tumour > 5 cm	1	Diagnosis & primary treatment			1.50
Tumour > 5 cm	2	Remission		0.23	0.55
Tumour > 5 cm	3	Disseminated cancer			0.57
Tumour > 5 cm	4	Terminal stage	12		

The only pathways assumed from each disease stage are death, recovery and transition to the next stage of the disease. Forces of mortality, recovery and transition are assumed to be constants depending only on sex and age. If $f(x)$ is the probability of being in a particular disease stage at time x, given the person is in that state at time 0, then

$$df(x)/dx = - (\lambda m + \lambda r + \lambda t)\ f(x) \tag{1}$$

where λm is the force of mortality, λr the force of recovery and λt the force of transition.

Integrating and setting $f(0) = 0$ gives

$$f(x) = \exp[- (\lambda m + \lambda r + \lambda t)\ x\ ] \tag{2}$$

Forces of mortality, recovery and transition were estimated from a range of information in the spreadsheets available with Mathers, Vos and Stevenson (1999), including average stage durations, relative mortality rates and five-year survival rates.

In all, 123 of the 169 diseases were chosen for simulation, with the omitted diseases being those with durations under six months or very low disability weights. These 123 selected diseases were identified as having a total of 584 stages. For all but one of these stages, disability weights and recovery, transition and mortality parameters were estimated from the spreadsheets. The exception was a one-stage disease called 'back problems', where the spreadsheet assumed high incidences, each with an average duration of 0.011 years. Incidence rates for chronic back pain, assuming no recovery or extra mortality, were estimated from the unit record data for the Survey of Disability and Carers 2003 (ABS 2005).

Some of the average durations for disease stages are very short. For example, the average duration assumed for the terminal stages of most cancers is one month. To allow for short durations without excessive calculation times, continuous time simulation is used for disease events within projection periods. From equation 2, the time x since entering a disease state is

$$x = - \ln(f(x)) / (\lambda m + \lambda r + \lambda t) \tag{3}$$

For example, a person in remission from breast cancer with tumours under 2 cm has a recovery time constant of 0.29, and a transition time constant of 0.10. The mortality constant is zero, as no deaths from cancer are assumed until the terminal stage. The time until either remission or transition occurs is simulated by selecting a random number r between 0 and 1, and calculating the time as $- \ln(r) / 0.39$. If this simulated time is less than the time remaining to the end of the simulation period, an event is assumed to occur. If more than one type of event is possible, then the choice between event types is made by selecting another random number, and choosing in proportion to the time constants of the possible events.

Retrospective Imputation of Baseline Diseases Using AIHW Disease Models

The initial diseases and disease stages for each of the 175,044 persons in the baseline data at 30/06/01 were simulated by an iterative process:

- For persons born in Australia, the occurrence of a congenital or birth-related defect was simulated.
- Stepping forward a year at a time from each person's birth or immigration date, the occurrence of new diseases, and the development of existing diseases, was simulated.
- Each year, death from each disease was simulated, taking into account only the extra risks of death from disease.
- If death from disease occurred, the process was restarted at the birth or immigration date.

If no allowance had been made for deaths, the baseline population might (for example) have contained far too many persons in terminal stages of cancer. It is not clear, however, whether this process gives a realistic distribution of persons with life-threatening diseases. The imputation process assumes that the age-specific incidence, recovery, transition and mortality risks from each disease have remained unchanged up to 2001. The Australian Bureau of Statistics (2004: 3) noted that there was 'little change in the disability rate between 1998 (20.1%) and 2003 (20.0%)'. Begg et al. (2007: 33–4) noted the considerable increase in the incidence of type 2 diabetes, and the lack of any data suggesting trends in mental health, hearing loss, vision loss and musculoskeletal disorders. The process also assumes that immigrants come to Australia with no diseases. Kennedy, McDonald and Biddle (2007) provide evidence of the 'healthy immigrant effect' in the US, Canada, UK and Australia. For Australia, they show that the incidence of chronic conditions is substantially lower for all immigrant regions, self-assessed health generally better, and obesity and smoking rates lower. Chronic hepatitis B prevalence rates are however higher in some immigrants, particularly those from the Asia-Pacific region (Butler, Korda, Watson and Watson 2009: 11). More exact allowances for immigration effects could be included in the above process.

Table 5.2 compares the numbers of each disability estimated from the unit records from the 2003 Survey of Disability Ageing and Carers (ABS 2004) with those simulated as at 2001, and then projected forward two years allowing for births, deaths, immigration and emigration, and for disease incidence and development. The main condition for each simulated person was taken as the disease with the highest AIHW disability weight. The simulated numbers were multiplied by 19.719/0.178 (the ratio of the Australian population at 30/06/03 to the simulated numbers of persons at 30/06/03).

Table 5.2   Observed and simulated numbers of persons with each main condition

ICD10 Chapter	Description of main condition	Simulated m	SDAC m
I	Infectious & parasitic diseases	0.015	0.030
II	Neoplasms	0.182	0.103
III	Diseases of the blood & blood-forming organs	0.426	0.018
IV	Endocrine, nutritional & metabolic diseases	0.294	0.471
V	Mental & behaviourial disorders	3.547	0.912
VI	Diseases of the nervous system	0.145	0.521
VII	Diseases of the eye & adnexa	0.216	0.108
VIII	Diseases of the ear & mastoid process	0.725	0.454
IX	Diseases of the circulatory system	0.195	1.010
X	Diseases of the respiratory system	0.809	1.068
XI	Diseases of the digestive system	0.054	0.159
XII	Diseases of the skin & subcutaneous tissue	0.321	0.067
XIII	Musculoskeletal	1.226	2.348
XIV	Diseases of the genitourinary system	0.198	0.072
XVI	Certain conditions originating in the perinatal period	0.010	0.003
XVII	Congenital malformations	0.017	0.049
XVIII	Symptoms, signs and abnormal findings, nec	0.000	0.182
XX	External causes of morbidity & mortality	0.999	0.512
Total		9.380	8.087

There are many reasons to expect differences between the survey and simulated numbers:

- Random variations, both in the simulations and the survey data;
- Surveyed persons with multiple diseases reporting a different main condition to the disease with the highest disability weight;
- Some persons may not have reported certain conditions because of the sensitive nature of the condition – e.g. alcohol and drug-related conditions, schizophrenia, mental retardation or mental degeneration (ABS 2004: 60);
- Some conditions may be episodic or seasonal – e.g. asthma, epilepsy;
- Lack of awareness of the presence of a condition, such as mild diabetes;
- Lack of comprehensive medical information kept by cared-accommodation establishments, who completed survey returns on behalf of their residents;
- The simulations rest on incidence, recovery, transition and mortality assumptions separately derived for each of 123 diseases, together with the assumption that these rates have not changed in the past.

The differences between simulated and survey numbers are large for most disease chapters, and the reasons for the differences are likely to depend on the disease. The imputation process assumes that existing diseases are uncorrelated with a person's employment and socioeconomic status. In practice, however, persons with severe disabilities are less likely to be employed, less likely to be in partnerships and more likely to be in areas of low socio-economic status.

Probability-Weighted Imputation of Baseline Diseases

A more direct method of imputing baseline disease is suggested, to give better matching with prevalence data, and to help allow for the effects of employment and socioeconomic status. Using the best available survey data and prevalence estimates, the numbers of persons in each age group with each disease are estimated, separately for males and females. If the data permits, these estimates are subdivided by broad geographic regions. The numbers of persons with a particular disease in a sex and age group within a broad region are then used to select the persons with that disease in the region, using probability-weighted selection. The relative probability of each person of that sex and age group in having the disease is estimated, using any relevant information available. For example, if the probabilities of having a disease increase within an age group, linearly increasing relative probabilities might be assumed. Allowance could be made for any employment, partnership and socio-economic correlations known for the disease. The relative probabilities for each person are added, and a random number between 0 and the probability total selected. The person matching the random number is selected to have the disease, and the process repeated until the required number of persons with the disease have been selected. This imputation procedure is being implemented in the current version of the model.

Simulated and Actual Deaths in 2002

The main causes of death in 2002 were estimated by projecting for two years from 30/06/01. These gave 2,618 deaths, and this low number means that there are substantial uncertainties in the simulated numbers of deaths, particularly for the less common causes. Table 5.3 compares their composition with the main causes of death reported for Australia in 2002 (Australian Bureau of Statistics 2008). Some of the possible causes of the differences between simulated and actual deaths are:

- Random variations in the simulations;
- Uncertainty about the mortality assumptions for some diseases in the Australian Institute of Health and Welfare disease models;
- Reluctance by medical practitioners to show dementia as the main cause of death in death certificates;
- Deficiencies in the imputed baseline population at 30/06/01.

Table 5.3   Simulated causes of death in 2002, compared with actual

ICD10 Chapter	Description of main cause of death	Simulated deaths	Actual deaths
I	Infectious & parasitic diseases	1.10%	1.30%
II	Neoplasms	25.60%	28.70%
III	Diseases of the blood & blood-forming organs	0.10%	0.30%
IV	Endocrine, nutritional & metabolic diseases	6.70%	3.50%
V	Mental & behaviourial disorders	1.30%	2.40%
VI	Diseases of the nervous system	18.00%	3.50%
VII	Diseases of the eye & adnexa	0.00%	0.00%
VIII	Diseases of the ear & mastoid process	0.00%	0.00%
IX	Diseases of the circulatory system	31.40%	37.60%
X	Diseases of the respiratory system	7.90%	8.70%
XI	Diseases of the digestive system	0.70%	3.30%
XII	Diseases of the skin & subcutaneous tissue	0.00%	0.20%
XIII	Musculoskeletal	0.30%	0.80%
XIV	Diseases of the genitourinary system	1.00%	2.20%
XV	Pregnancy, childbirth & the puerperium	0.00%	0.00%
XVI	Certain conditions originating in the perinatal period	0.10%	0.50%
XVII	Congenital malformations	0.00%	0.40%
XVIII	Symptoms, signs and abnormal findings, nec	0.00%	0.60%
XX	External causes of morbidity & mortality	5.90%	5.80%
Total		100.00%	100.00%

Models of the Probability of Being in Aged Care

The logistic models in Table 5.4 were fitted to 39,086 persons without dementia, and 2,147 persons with dementia, in the unit records for SDAC 2003 (ABS 2004). The models were fitted by weighted stepwise backwards regression, omitting variables with a significance probability of 10 per cent or more. The log likelihood reduction was 0.538 for the without dementia model, but only 0.105 for the with dementia model. The population at risk for the model of persons without dementia is persons of any age, excluding those with dementia. The population at risk for persons with dementia is all persons with dementia. The variable 'sex' is 1 for males and 2 for females.

Dementia is a key determinant of the probability of being in aged care – 0.4 per cent of persons without dementia are in aged care, and 64 per cent of those with dementia are in aged care. The probability of being in aged care increases linearly with age. Married persons have a much lower probability of being in aged care, regardless of their sex. This presumably reflects the ability of many partners to care for persons who would otherwise require aged care. For persons without dementia, cerebral palsy, depression, epilepsy, multiple sclerosis, paralysis,

Parkinson's disease, retardation and schizophrenia are all strongly associated with aged care. For those with dementia, only epilepsy, paralysis, Parkinson's disease and schizophrenia are strongly associated.

Table 5.4   Logistic models of the probability of being in aged care

Variable	Without dementia Coefficient	Without dementia SE	With dementia Coefficient	With dementia SE
Age	0.143	0.004	0.058	0.014
Cerebral palsy	2.854	0.669		
Congenital	1.527	0.369		
Depression	2.145	0.142		
Diabetes	0.416	0.116		
Epilepsy	1.632	0.337	1.422	0.449
Head injury			0.814	0.280
Heart	0.755	0.105	0.603	0.246
Married	−1.693	0.100	−0.647	0.220
Multiple sclerosis	4.963	0.476		
Neoplasm	0.686	0.175	0.623	0.373
Paralysis	3.727	0.380	3.130	1.098
Parkinson	2.737	0.299	1.480	0.411
Retardation	2.099	0.385		
Schizophrenia	3.508	0.355	1.642	0.532
Sex			0.417	0.215
Stroke	0.875	0.118		
Urinary	1.204	0.312		
Constant	−15.119	0.346	−5.129	1.202
N		39086		2147
Log likelihood reduction		0.528		0.105
Adjustment to constant	−0.8		−0.2	

Simulated and Actual Persons in Aged Care in 2003

In the absence of longitudinal data on aged care residence, probabilities of admission to aged care were estimated from the models in Table 5.4, adjusting the regression constants by the amounts in the last line of the table. These adjustments were chosen so as to simulate approximately correct numbers of persons in aged care in 2003, separately for persons without and with dementia. Given the data limitations, the results in Table 5.5 seem broadly reasonable.

Table 5.5   Characteristics of simulated and actual persons in care in 2003

Personal characteristics	Simulated	Actual	Source
Average age of persons in care	85.6	83.4	AIHW 2004 table 2.2
% of all persons in care	0.71%	0.72%	AIHW 2004 table 2.2
% in care who are male	33.40%	27.80%	AIHW 2004 table 2.2
% in care with dementia	42.60%	44.50%	SDAC 2003
Admissions to care pa, as % of those in care	34.60%	37.00%	AIHW 2004 table 3.2
Deaths in care pa, as % of those in care	29.50%	28.70%	AIHW 2004 table 3.5

Feasibility of Simulations with Many More Persons and Areas

A 50-year projection starting with 175,000 persons took about a minute. Apart from assumption input, all the process times should be linearly dependent on the numbers of persons. Education, work, superannuation and disease development are all done by sequential processing of the person file, and their process times do not depend on area numbers. Household changes, such as partnership selection, are done by selecting a search area, randomly selecting a small number of prospects, and choosing the best prospect. More complex criteria for selecting search areas may be needed with increased numbers of areas, but this should have little or no effect on runtimes.

For example, baseline data of all Australians in 2011 would be about 22.7m persons, and might take about four hours to project 2,200 regions for 50 years. Parallel processing, as used by Fredricksen, Knudsen and Stolen (2011) in the MOSART model of Norway, could reduce this runtime substantially. Births, diseases, education, superannuation and work accounted for about 60 per cent of total time. All these are processes which only affect individuals, and could be done by parallel processing. A total runtime of about two hours might be feasible. A model with 22 million persons and 2,200 regions is due for completion in February 2013.

Glossary

ABS   Australian Bureau of Statistics
AIHW   Australian Institute of Health and Welfare
SDAC   Survey of Disability Ageing and Carers

References

Australian Bureau of Statistics. 2003. *2037.0 – Census of Population and Housing: Household Sample File Technical Paper, 2001.* Available at: http://www.abs. gov.au/AUSSTATS/abs@.nsf/allprimarymainfeatures/EC42CE6B39433DFA CA2574C10015B126?opendocument [accessed 26/11/12].

Australian Bureau of Statistics. 2004. 4430.0.00.001. *Information Paper: Disability, Ageing and Carers, Basic CURF, Australia (Reissue), 2003.* Available at: http:// www.abs.gov.au/AUSSTATS/abs@.nsf/DetailsPage/4430.0.00.0012003?Open Document [accessed 26/11/12].

Australian Bureau of Statistics. 2008. *3303.0 – Causes of Death, Australia, 2006.* Available at: http://www.abs.gov.au/AUSSTATS/abs@.nsf/allprimarymainfe atures/4D3E7129BC863F0ECA25757C00137471?opendocument [accessed 26/11/12].

Australian Institute of Health and Welfare. 2004. *Residential aged care in Australia 2002–03 – a statistical overview.* Canberra.

Begg, S., Vos, T., Barker, B., Stevenson, C, Stanley, L. and Lopez, A. 2007. *The burden of disease and injury in Australia 2003.* Canberra: Australian Institute of Health and Welfare.

Butler, J., Korda, R., Watson, K. and Watson, D. 2009. *The impact of chronic hepatitis B in Australia: Projecting mortality, morbidity and economic impact.* Australian Centre for Economic Research on Health Research report no 7.

Cumpston, J.R. 2010. Alignment and matching in multi-purpose household microsimulations. *International Journal of Microsimulation*, 3(2), 34–45.

Cumpston, J.R. 2012. A more efficient sampling procedure, using loaded probabilities. *International Journal of Microsimulation*, 5(1), 21–30.

Fredricksen, D., Knudsen, P. and Stolen, N.M. 2011. *The dynamic cross-sectional microsimulation model MOSART.* Paper presented to the third general conference of the International Microsimulation Association, Stockholm, June 8–10, available at: http://www.scb.se/Grupp/Produkter_Tjanster/Kurser/_Dok ument/IMA/Stoelen_MOSART_IMA%202011.pdf [accessed 26/11/12].

Kennedy, S., McDonald, J.T. and Biddle, N. 2007. Health Assimilation Patterns Amongst Australian Immigrants. *Economic Record*, 83(260), 16–30.

Mathers, C., Vos, T. and Stevenson, C. 1999. *The burden of injury and disease in Australia.* Canberra: Australian Institute of Health and Welfare.

Chapter 6

Projection of the Supply of Nurses in France: A Microsimulation Model

Muriel Barlet and Marie Cavillon

Introduction

With close to 520,000 nurses working in France as of 1 January 2010, the nursing profession is the premiere healthcare profession in terms of workforce, surpassing doctors (212,000), pharmacists (75,000) and physiotherapists (71,000). This is a historic high, whether the nursing workforce or the density of working nurses per inhabitant is considered. According to the Adeli directory[1] (répertoire Adeli), the nursing workforce has increased by 2.8 per cent per year over the past 20 years. This increase has recently accelerated, as between 1990 and 1999, the annual rate of growth was 2.1 per cent whereas it has been 3.2 per cent since 2000. The density of nurses has thus gone from 633 nurses under 65 years of age per 100,000 inhabitants in 2000 to 809 in 2010. Besides, the spatial distribution of nurses is particularly unequal; especially for the independent nurses that are more concentrated across the French territory than general practitioners, dentists, pharmacists and physiotherapists (Barlet and Collin 2010).

In the years to come, two scope phenomena may reinforce the need for nurses. On the one hand, the ageing of the population (Blanpain and Chardon 2010) and on the other, the anticipated 10 per cent decrease in the number of doctors over the next ten years (Attal-Toubert and Vanderschelden 2009).

Projection models are one of the tools that can be used to shed light upon the tendencies and stakes in the demography of nurses. At regular intervals, the Direction of Research, Studies, Evaluation and Statistics of the French Ministry of Health (DREES) carries out such exercises. They are not predictions, but rather an attempt at making models for and quantifying different scenarios to enable the government to make enlightened decisions. The projection exercise whose main results will be presented in this chapter consisted in simulating different scenarios, each of which were based on different hypotheses. It is a spatial dynamic microsimulation model. The nurses are classified by age, gender, the region in which they practice and the mode of practice (independent, employed by

---

1   The Adeli directory lists the health professionals who have a legal authorization to practice their profession. All health professionals have indeed the obligation to register their diploma with the agency's regional health of their place of residence professional.

public hospitals, employed by private hospitals, employed by retirement homes or employed in non-hospital establishments). It uses data from the 2006 census as an initial base and covers nurses between the ages of 18 and 65 residing in and practicing in France.

The baseline scenario is based on the hypothesis of constant behaviour. We thus made the hypothesis that the behaviour of nurses observed in the recent past and the government's regulatory measures will remain unchanged for the entire projection period. Other scenarios, called variants, are also anticipated. Each variant only differs from the baseline scenario by one hypothesis, which enables us to isolate the effect of the behavioural evolution or the implementation of a measure corresponding to this hypothesis and to measure the probable impact on the size of the workforce. Thus, the hypothesis concerning the national quota, the proportion of salaried employee nurses working in public hospitals who choose to change to category A and that concerning ceasing activity were modified so as to measure the impact of the statutory reform[2] of nurses employed by public hospitals or retirement reform,[3] which are not yet fully implemented, on the evolution of the number of nurses in the workforce.

Nursing Supply Model

General Description

The model gives, for each year in the projection period going from 2006 to 2030, the number of working nurses on the French territory by age, gender, region and mode of practice (independent, employed by public hospitals, employed by private hospitals, employed by an establishment for the elderly, employed by another non-hospital establishment). It draws mainly upon the projection model created

---

2　Decree 2010-1139 of 29 September 2010 regulating the special status of the general nursing corps and specialists in public hospitals stipulates that, starting in 2012, all recently graduated nurses will be in Category A and cannot, de facto, retire before age 60 (the current retirement age is 55). However, those nurses already practicing before this date can either continue their career in Category B maintaining their position in the employed category and could, de facto, retire from age 55, or they can integrate Category A, which has a longer career length, and a more interesting remuneration grid. Nurses have until the end of March 2011 to make their choice, which will be final and binding, between these two options, i.e. six months from the date this decree was published.

3　Law 2010-1330 of 9 November 2010 pertaining to the retirement reform anticipates a progressive shift (due to an annual four-month period) of the legal age for full-benefit retirement. Thus, the legal retirement age will go from 60 to 62 in 2018 and the age for full-benefit retirement from 65 to 67 in 2023. For the nurses employed by public hospitals, the age for retirement benefits goes from 55 to 57 for those nurses who choose to remain in Category B, remains at 60 (and not 62) for nurses who choose to change to Category A, and goes from 60 to 62 for newly graduated nurses (beginning in 2012).

for doctors in 2008 (Attal-Toubert and Vanderschelden 2009). The last nursing workforce projections were carry out by the Direction of Research, Studies, Evaluation and Statistics of the French Ministry of Health (DREES) in 2004. It was a projection model on a national scale. Moreover, this model is the first to present the nursing workforce at the regional scale.

A study of the profession's demographic situation (Barlet and Cavillon 2010) prior to conducting this study shed light upon different behaviour in each region: from training that attracts people more or less to different regions (Île-de-France, Loire Valley, Picardy and Nord-Pas-de-Calais regions have the biggest gap between their quota and the number of entries in the first year of training), choosing the region in which to practice (for example, 63 per cent of the nurses who have obtained their diploma within less than five years in the Poitou-Charentes region are still practicing in the region while the national average is 76 per cent), and also the changes in the mode of practice and location over the course of a career. The spatial distribution of nurses is particularly unequal, especially for the independent nurses that are less spread across the French territory than general practitioners, dentists, pharmacists and physiotherapists (Barlet and Collin 2010). Thus, we observe a strong North-South discrepancy for the independent nurses, which is more pronounced than the one observed for dentists or physiotherapists. In addition, although regional migrations are infrequent, they are always in favour (or against) particular regions, i.e. southern regions benefit from these flows. Therefore, it is important to take into account the different nurses' behaviour among each region and to project the nursing workforce both at a national and at a regional level. The regional level led us to favour a microsimulation model, as it is much more flexible than a cell-based macro model and it enable more detailed declension of the total nursing workforce.

This study is mainly based upon the 2006 census (Appendix 1) since the age structure and the distribution by mode of exercise are doubtlessly more reliable than those in the Adeli directory. Thus, the projection period begins in 2006 (census year for which we possess the totality of variables used for the projection). Other sources were used to estimate the model's parameters: school surveys (Enquêtes Écoles), annual declarations of social data (Déclarations annuelles de données sociales), the CNAMTS (French National Health Insurance Agency for Wage Earners) data, and the data from Cereq's Enquête Génération 98 (Generation 98 Survey).

The sample field used is the nurses working in France who also reside in France and are between 18 and 65 years of age. Therefore, nurses working in France who live abroad are not taken into consideration in this model. Moreover, the model does not take foreign nurses entering France into account.

The model takes into account four major components: (1) modelling the number of new graduates, (2) modelling the entry into working life (the delay between the year in which a diploma was obtained and the year the nurse entered the workforce, the choice of region for activity and the mode of practice), (3) modelling the mid-career changes (the changes of region or mode of practice), and (4) modelling the retirement. For better accuracy, we estimate parameters using, for each event, the most appropriate database (professional directory, specific surveys, annual declarations of social data).

Figure 6.1 contains a diagram of our projection model. The population of nurses at time t+i results from the changes that affected the population since time t. In the model used, an individual can decide to practice in a region which differs from the region in which he received his diploma, choose his mode of practice, move to another region, change his mode of practice, cease working.

The model starts by determining, for a given year in the projection period, the number of graduates by age, sex and region in which they obtained their diplomas, using the parameters defined in the Training Module [① Component Training, Appendix 2].

The number of individual nurses who will exercise at least one day on French territory are then determined using microsimulation by simulating the following events: 'escape rate', 'set up delay', 'region of practice' and 'choice of mode of practice'. After this step, we have an individual database of graduates who will practice on French territory either during the year in which their diploma was obtained or the following year. For these nurses entering the workforce, we also have information on their gender, age, region in which they obtained their diploma, region in which they first practiced, category and mode of practice (for employees of public hospitals). Nurses entering the workforce the year in which they graduated are not immediately added to the initial stock of working nurses. Before adding them to the database which contains nurses in activity at time t+1, we simulate retirements and the mid-career changes of nurses who are active in time t [② Component Entry into Working Life].

Nurses ceasing to work are randomly selected and removed from the initial database (working nurses) [③ Component Ceasing Work]. At this stage, we have an individual database that contains nurses who work two consecutive years (during the current year of the projection period and during the following year).

Then we successively simulated on this field, changes of region and mode of practice. The region and the mode of practice of the nurses who would have experienced one of these events are updated. The calculation of probabilities of mid-career changes (region or mode of practice) requires that the order of each event is predefined. Thus, we decided to simulate the change of region before, so as to determine the nurses who change mode of practice. We estimate the probability for a nurse of working the year N+1 in the region R2 knowing that during the year t+1, they work in the region R1 in two stages: first, we estimate the probability of changing region (respectively mode of practice) between two consecutive years, then we estimate the probability of choosing the region R2 on the field of nurses who changed regions between the two years. The change of category for salaried nurses in public hospitals is also simulated. Those who decide to be employees of a public hospital will be classified in the category A starting in 2011 [④ Component Mid-career Changes].

Nurses entering the workforce in the current year of the projection period, as well as last year's nursing graduates (after having been aged one year) are then added to the database of practicing nurses [⑤].

The last step consists in incrementing the counters of the model: the age of the working nurses and the year of the projection period [⑥].

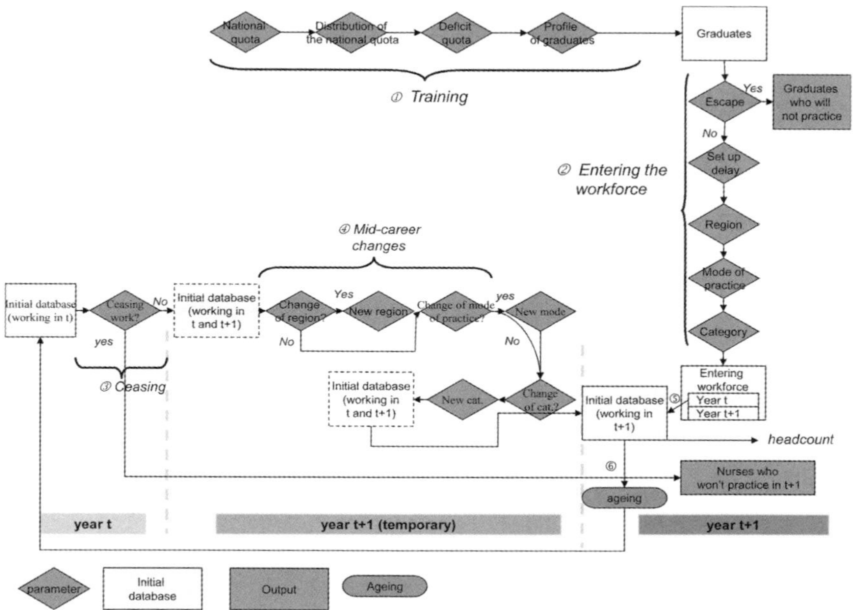

Figure 6.1   Schematic representation of the nursing supply microsimulation model

The Baseline Scenario Assumptions

The current trends scenario (or baseline scenario) is based upon the assumptions of the nurses' constant behaviour. For the years included in the projection period prior to 2010, the values of the parameters relative to training are observed values.

The assumptions related to training are:

- The national quota fixing the number of places available in IFSI (Institut de Formation en Soins Infirmiers – French Institute of Nursing Training) corresponds to the most recent national quota observed (that of 2010) starting in 2011.
- The regional distribution of the national quota is assumed to be identical to that observed in 2010.

- The deficit between the number of graduates and the quota in each region is assumed to be identical as of 2009 to the average deficit for each region in 2006, 2007 and 2008.
- The profile of the nurses holding a state diploma in each region (gender, age) is identical, as of 2008, to that observed in 2005, 2006 and 2007.

The assumptions related to entering the workforce:

- The escape rate, that is, the percentage of nurses who graduated in France but who will never practice in the French territory, is fixed at 2 per cent for the entire projection period. This hypothesis is drawn from Cereq's Enquête Génération 98. This survey is done for studying the entry into working life.
- The set up delay, which corresponds to the delay between the year in which a diploma was obtained and the year the nurse entered the workforce, is identical over the entire projection period: 99 per cent of newly graduated nurses enter the workforce the same year that they receive their diplomas, 1 per cent do so the following year. Like for the escape rate, the hypothesis relative to the set up delay is based on the data from Cereq's Enquête Génération 98.
- The distribution by the region in which nurses, having received diplomas in a given region, practice is assumed to be constant throughout the projection period and also to correspond to the average observed in 2008, 2009 and 2010 for diplomas received less than five years ago. This hypothesis is drawn from the Adeli directory, which is the only database to record for each health professional the region in which they have received their diploma and their region of practice. Even if nurses do not systematically register in the directory just after graduation, we assume that within five years after graduation, all graduates are registered.
- The distribution by the mode of practice of nurses entering the workforce is constant throughout the projection period and corresponds to the average observed in 2008, 2009 and 2010 for diplomas received less than two years ago (forcing the ratio of independent nurses to be 0 per cent due to the fact that nurses wishing to work independently are obliged to have worked in a hospital for two years under the authority of a healthcare manager). This estimation is based on the Adeli directory for the years 2008, 2009 and 2010. The distribution by mode of practice depends on the region of practice and the gender.

The assumptions related to the course of the career:

- The portion of nurses changing regions or mode of practice between two consecutive years is assumed to be constant throughout the projection period and to correspond to the average observed in the last few years.

- The choice of a new region in which to practice and a new mode of practice for nurses having either changed their region or mode of practice is assumed to be constant throughout the projection period and to be equal to the average distribution observed in 2005/06, 2006/07 and 2008/09.

These two parameters are estimated from the Adeli directory.

- The choice of a region in which independent nurses practice is not taken into account in the model with the additional clause 1 of the national nursing convention for independent nurses adopted on 4 September 2008[4] as this clause applies to the infra regional level.

The assumptions related to ceasing work:

- For independent nurses: the probability of ceasing to work at each age is estimated for the 2005–08 period using data from the CNAMTS.
- For nurses employed by public and private hospitals, the probability of ceasing work is estimated using statistical information from the 2007 and 2008 DADS.
- For nurses employed by non-hospital establishments: the probability of ceasing work corresponds to that estimated for private hospital employees.
- Finally, we assume that the ensemble of nurses, regardless of their mode of practice, will not work after age 65.

Main Results of the Baseline Projection

The Number of Working Nurses will Continue to Rise but at a Less Sustained Rate

If the future behaviour of nurses remains constant with the behaviour observed over the past few years, in 2030, France will have 657,800 working nurses, i.e. 37 per cent more than in 2006. Thus, the number of working nurses will increase, on average, by 1.3 per cent per year (Figure 6.2). We presume, for the current trends scenario, that the national quota will remain at the same level as the quota observed in 2010 for the entire projection period. The number of working nurses

---

4   The latter, approved by the ministerial decree of 17 October 2008, defines the measures aiming to regulate both nursing and home nursing care. The territory is thus divided into five zones (very over-manned, over-manned, intermediately manned, under-manned, very under-manned). This division is accompanied by measures aiming to incite nurses to set up (or remain) in 'very under-manned' zones. Moreover, in the 'very over-manned' zones, approval by the French health service is only granted upon the definitive work cessation of a nurse in the zone considered.

will, therefore, continue to increase. However, this progression should be less and less sustained. In fact, although the number of working nurses should continue to increase by 1.6 per cent between 2010 and 2011, the annual rate of growth should be inferior to 1 per cent from 2026 on.

The average age of working nurses will remain relatively stable over the entire projection period going from 40.2 years in 2006 to 40.9 in 2030, even though the age structure will probably be modified. Thus, after having slightly increased between 2006 and 2009, the number of nurses under 30 should continue to decrease over the entire projection period (going from 20 per cent of the workforce in 2009 to 17 per cent in 2030). The number of nurses over 50 should, after having increased until 2011, progressively decrease until 2022 (22 per cent) due to an increase in nurses ceasing work. The number should, following this, progressively increase, until it surpasses 23 per cent in 2030.

Moreover, so as to fully appreciate the demographic situation of nurses at a given point in time, we must compare it to the population's healthcare needs. Although the model's goal is not to measure the evolution in the healthcare demand, it can be approximated, firstly, by the population. Between 2006 and 2030, the French population should grow by 12 per cent.[5] The density of nurses, that is, the number of working nurses per 100,000 inhabitants, should thus go from 760 in 2006 to 929 in 2030, i.e. an increase of 22 per cent. The growth in density will thus be the result of a greater increase in working nurses than in the French population.

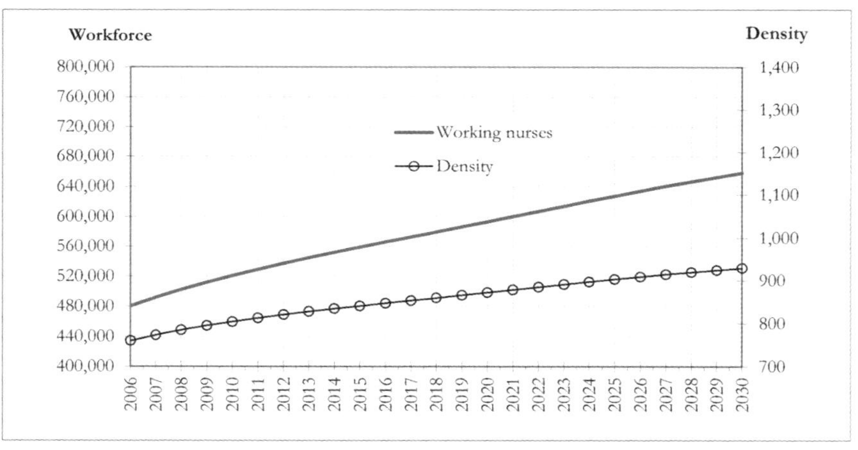

Figure 6.2   Evolution of the number of and the density of working nurses according to the baseline scenario

Field: Working nurses between 18 and 65 years of age, all of France.
Sources: INSEE – 2006 Census, INSEE – Population projections, DREES projections.

---

5   Source: population projection, INSEE, 2010.

In 2030, the Majority of Nurses Will Still Work in Public Hospitals

The distribution of nurses by mode of practice depends not only upon the nurses' preferences, but also on the number of paid positions available. Consequently, in the past as in the future, the nurses' choice of mode of practice are choices made within constraints. The hypothesis on constant behaviour on which the baseline scenario is based thus implies that the nurses' preferences in mode of practice will remain identical for the entire projection period. In addition, no constraints were integrated as to an evolution in the offering of salaried positions or an evolution in the financial capabilities thereof: the mode of practice projections do not integrate questions regarding the solvency of nursing job offers.

The number of independent nurses should increase the most. In fact, the numbers thereof should increase by 2.9 per cent per year, going from 57,800 in 2006 to 116,100 in 2030, i.e. doubling in 25 years. This increase is the result of the evolution of the nurses' age structure throughout the projection period. On the one hand, there will be more independent nurses, who, on average, retire later than those who are salaried employees, nearing retirement age than there are today. On the other hand, nurses under 35 years of age are currently relatively numerous. Yet, transitions from being a salaried employee to being an independent worker are more frequent in the beginning of careers. The number of nurses working in public and private sector hospitals will rise 1.5 per cent and 2.0 per cent respectively per year. The number of nurses employed in non-hospital establishments for the elderly should increase by 1.4 per cent per year. However, the number of nurses employed by other types of non-hospital establishments should decrease by 1.4 per cent on average throughout the projection period.[6]

In 2030, independent nurses will thus make up 18 per cent of the nursing workforce, as compared to 12 per cent in 2006. The portion of nurses working in public hospitals should remain relatively stable at around 50 per cent. The portion of nurses employed by private hospitals should go from 14 per cent in 2006 to 16 per cent in 2030. Thus, the majority of nurses will still be employed by public hospitals. Nurses working in establishments for the elderly will make up 4 per cent of the nursing workforce, which was already the case in 2006. On the other hand, nurses employed by non-hospital establishments (other than establishments for the elderly) will make up 11 per cent of the nursing workforce in 2030, i.e. 10 points less than in 2006.

---

6   Nevertheless, the Adeli directory, from which the transition probabilities between the different modes of practice were calculated, underestimates the number of nurses employed by non-hospital establishments; it is therefore possible that transitions to this sector are also underestimated. Due to this, the model therefore probably underestimates the decrease in the number of nurses employed by non-hospital establishments.

The Density of Nurses Should Increase in All of the Regions in France

The number of working nurses should increase in all of the regions in France. However, the evolution of the number of nurses is not the same in every region (Table 6.1). Reunion, the Antilles-Guiana regions, Lorraine, Franche-Comté, the Loire Valley and Languedoc-Roussillon are the regions that should have the greatest increase in the number of working nurses between 2006 and 2030 (more than 20 per cent greater than the national growth), as opposed to the regions of Île-de-France and Auvergne (growth of 20 per cent less than the national growth rate). Nevertheless, the evolution of the number of nurses is not sufficient to measure the adequacy between the offer of nursing care of which a region has and the demand of its population. In fact, the evolution of the number of working nurses in a given region must be reconciled with the growth of its population. The regions in the east of France (Champagne-Ardenne, Lorraine, Alsace and Bourgogne) will thus owe the great growth in their density not only to the great increase in the number of working nurses, but also to a lesser increase, or even a decrease in their number of residents. Thus, the number of working nurses in Lorraine should increase by 49.3 per cent (as compared to an average of 37.0 per cent), whereas the number of residents in the region should only increase by 2.3 per cent (as compared to an average of 12.1 per cent).

As for the Midi-Pyrénées region, its density should move closer to the national average due to a great increase in its population (21.8 per cent as compared to an average of 12.1 per cent). Thus, the projected evolution of some regional populations between 2006 and 2030 should amplify (or limit, or even nullify) the effect of the increase in the number of working nurses.

The regions that had the least amount of nursing personnel relative to their population in 2006 (Central France, Upper-Normandy, Île-de-France, Antilles-Guiana, Reunion) should remain so in 2030. However, the regions in Southern France (with the exception of the Provence-Alpes-Côte d'Azur region) will have higher densities. Thus, the density of nurses should only increase by 7.9 per cent in the Midi-Pyrénées region, 18.9 per cent in the Languedoc-Roussillon region and by 16.7 per cent in Corsica, i.e. a progression over 15 per cent lower than the growth rate of the national density. On the other hand, Limousin and Brittany should remain the regions with the highest density and in 2030, should respectively have 1,295 and 1,089 nurses per 100,000 inhabitants in 2030.

The Regional Distribution of Independent Nurses Could Become Less Unequal

The regional distribution of employed nurses is closely linked to the number of inhabitants in the region and the proportion of older people (see the next subsection); that of independent nurses is much more unequal. Indeed, regional densities vary in 2006 between 1 and 5.

However, gaps between the highest and lowest regional densities for independent nurses should, according to the constant behaviour hypothesis, be

Table 6.1　**Number and density of working nurses per region in 2006 and 2030, as per the current trends scenario**

	Number of nurses		Population (in thousands)		Number of nurses (per 100,000)		Evolution (in %) from 2006 to 2030		
	2006	2030	2006	2030	2006	2030	Of the number of nurses	Of the population	Of the density
Île-de-France	75,553	87,788	11,532	12,491	655	703	16.2	8.3	7.3
Champagne-Ardenne	9,376	12,895	1,339	1,326	700	973	37.5	–1.0	38.9
Picardy	13,488	19,049	1,894	2,013	712	946	41.2	6.2	32.9
Upper-Normandy	12,070	16,033	1,811	1,921	666	835	32.8	6.1	25.2
Central France	17,392	22,666	2,520	2,737	690	828	30.3	8.6	20.0
Lower Normandy	11,447	16,185	1,457	1,550	786	1,044	41.4	6.4	32.9
Burgundy	12,354	17,920	1,629	1,704	758	1,051	45.0	4.6	38.6
Nord-Pas-de-Calais	29,095	38,785	4,019	4,135	724	938	33.3	2.9	29.5
Lorraine	18,789	28,055	2,336	2,390	804	1,174	49.3	2.3	45.9
Alsace	14,908	20,971	1,815	1,986	821	1,056	40.7	9.4	28.6
Franche-Comté	9,629	14,114	1,151	1,246	837	1,133	46.6	8.3	35.4
Loire Valley	24,801	36,282	3,450	4,147	719	875	46.3	20.2	21.7
Brittany	27,696	40,024	3,095	3,674	895	1,089	44.5	18.7	21.7
Poitou-Charentes	12,129	17,054	1,724	1,979	703	862	40.6	14.8	22.5
Aquitaine	25,499	36,015	3,120	3,688	817	976	41.2	18.2	19.5
Midi-Pyrénées	24,737	32,528	2,777	3,383	891	961	31.5	21.8	7.9
Limousin	7,119	10,238	731	791	974	1,295	43.8	8.2	32.9
Rhône-Alpes	47,172	66,783	6,021	7,094	783	941	41.6	17.8	20.2
Auvergne	11,778	14,679	1,336	1,421	882	1,033	24.6	6.4	17.2
Languedoc-Roussillon	22,277	32,443	2,534	3,105	879	1,045	45.6	22.5	18.9
PACA	39,790	55,374	4,815	5,412	826	1,023	39.2	12.4	23.8
Corsica	2,598	3,500	294	339	883	1,031	34.7	15.4	16.7
Antilles-Guiana	6,424	9,886	1,004	1,274	640	776	53.9	26.9	21.3
Reunion	4,087	8,575	782	997	523	860	109.8	27.5	64.5
All of France	480,207	657,841	63,186	70,803	760	929	37.0	12.1	22.3

Field: Working nurses 18 to 65 years of age, all of France.

Sources: INSEE – 2006 Census, INSEE – Population projections, DREES projections.

reduced during the projection period. In fact, while the regional densities in 2006 varied between 1 and 5, they should vary no more than 1 to 2 at the end of the projection period. Thus, the regional distribution of independent nurses should become less and less unequal. The territorial inequalities should greatly go down during the projection period. In fact, the Gini coefficient[7] should be cut in half between 2006 and 2030, going from 0.26 to 0.12.

The whole of the French regions should have an increase in the density of independent nurses between 2006 and 2030. In 2030, Limousin, the Languedoc-Roussillon region, Brittany, Corsica and the Midi-Pyrénées region should be the regions with the most independent nurses relative to their populations. Thus, in 2030, Limousin should have 236 independent nurses per 100,000 inhabitants (Figure 6.3). On the contrary, Île-de-France, Upper Normandy, Picardy, Central France and the Champagne-Ardenne region, Antilles-Guiana and the Poitou-Charentes region should have lower densities than the national average (over 5 per cent less) in 2030. With the exception of the Antilles-Guiana region, these regions already showed a deficit in 2006, nevertheless, the gaps in densities in relation to the national density should be rectified. Thus, the deficit observed in 2006 between the Northern and Southern regions could be rectified between 2006 and 2030. The reduction in the gaps can be explained again by the concurrent evolution in the number of independent nurses working in the region and the number of residents in the region. The Lorraine and Franche-Comté regions, which already showed deficits in 2006, should have densities over 12 per cent superior to the national density in 2030, which could be explained by an increase in the number of nurses working in their regions or by a lower increase in their populations. The Southern regions should still have high densities in 2030, nevertheless, the gaps with the national density should be rectified due to a lesser increase in the number of independent nurses working in the region, and also (for the Midi-Pyrénées and Languedoc-Roussillon regions) a large increase in their populations.

However, these projections are based on the constant behaviour assumptions, in particular concerning inter-regional migration. But, it is highly probable that the disruption that the current trends evolution could augur will modify nurses' behaviour. In particular, the fact that certain Southern regions, reputed for being attractive, are currently very well-manned and thus their markets are probably saturated could, as they come closer to the national average, create a magnet effect, thus intensifying migration to these regions. The projections illustrate the fact that demographic perspectives make it possible to restore the job offer balance for independent nurses between the different regions if the government implements adapted measures for those newly arrived.

---

7 This is a coefficient that measures inequalities in the spatial distribution of the nurses relative to the population. It varies between 0 and 1. It is equal to 0 if the nurses are distributed as is the population. It is equal to 1 if all of the nurses are concentrated in one geographic zone.

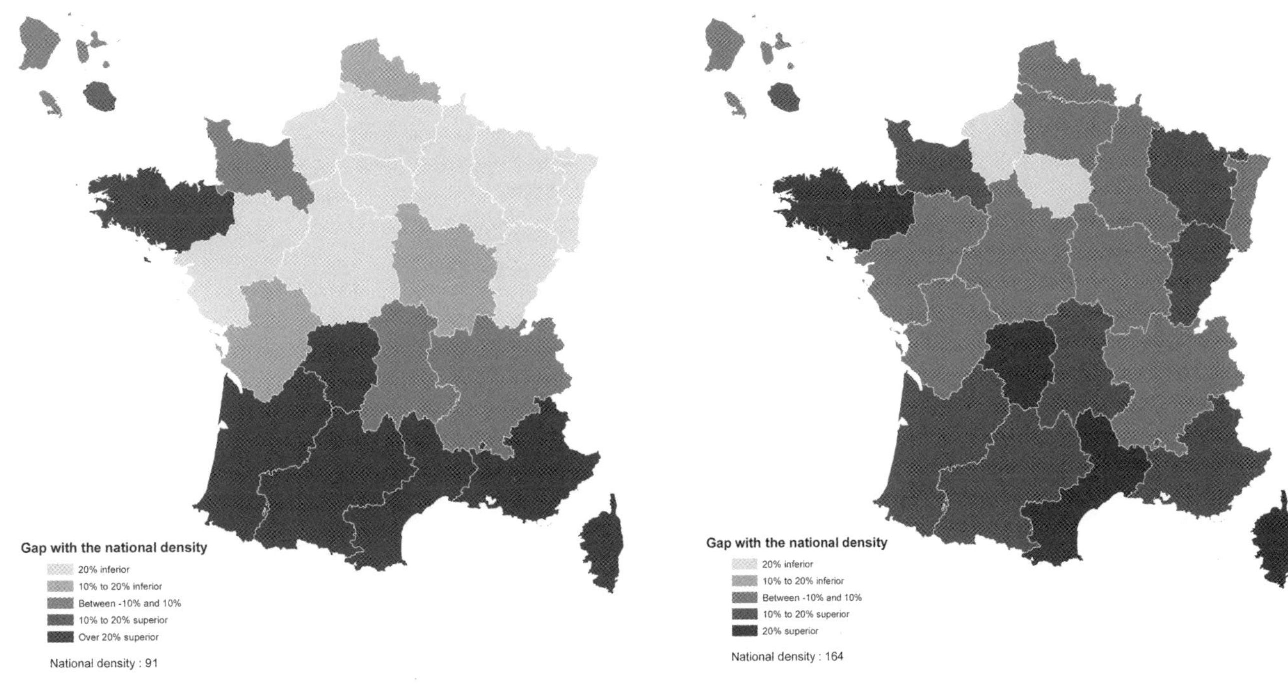

Figure 6.3   Density of independent nurses in 2006 and 2030, according to the baseline scenario

© IGN – DREES 2011

Field: Working nurses 18 to 65 years of age, all of France.

Sources: INSEE – 2006 Census, INSEE – population projections, DREES projections.

Another Econometric Approach to Estimating the Number of Salaried Employee Nurses Working in Each Region

An econometric estimate, determined outside of the model, reveals that the number of employees working in a given region positively depends upon the number of inhabitants in the region and the age structure of the region's population. This inter-dependent relationship was estimated using the number of nurses employed in each region observed in the 2006 census and the total population in each region also using information from the census. A linear multiplicative model was thus estimated:

$$\text{Log}(\text{Eff\_sal\_Reg}_i) = 8,35 + 1,03 \times \text{Log}(\text{nb\_million\_Hbts\_Reg}_i) + 0,05 \times \text{Part\_over\_75\_Reg}_i$$

where:
Eff_sal_Reg$_i$ is the number of employees working in the region i,
Nb_million_Hbts_Reg$_i$ is the number of inhabitants (in million) in the region *i*
and Part_over_75_Reg$_i$ is the percentage of people aged over 75 years in the region *i*.

This model explains 99 per cent of the gaps between regions.

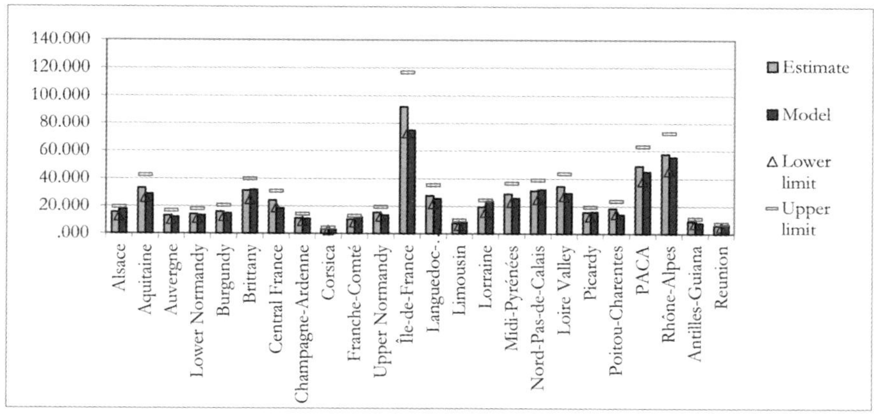

Figure 6.4   Estimate of the number of salaried employee nurses working in each region in 2030

Field: Working nurses 18 to 65 years of age, all of France.
Sources: INSEE – 2006 Census, Population projections, DREES estimates.
Note: 95 per cent confidence intervals.

In order to estimate the number of salaried employee nurses that will be working in each region in 2030, we suppose the inter-dependent relationship observed in 2006 will still exist in 2030. Thus, using the INSEE's regional population projections, we can make a projection of the number of salaried employee nurses there will be in 2030, with a confidence interval. This econometric approach, which differs greatly from that proposed by the projection model, reveals that the nursing workforce numbers, for the ensemble of the regions, given by the projection model fall within the estimate's confidence interval (Figure 6.4). Thus, the projections do not contradict the estimate model's findings. They maintain the link between the number of salaried employee nurses working in a region, the regional population and the region's age structure observed today.

Alternative Scenarios: Simulating the Impact of Reforms and Regulatory Measures

Each of the three scenarios presented below aim to evaluate the effect of a single regulatory measure or behavioural evolution. Thus, each scenario differs from the current trends scenario merely by a single hypothesis, which enables us to isolate the effect of behavioural evolution or the implementation of a measure corresponding to that hypothesis and to measure its probable impact on the number of nurses in the workforce.

Changing the Categories of Nurses in Public Hospitals

The statutory reform concerning salaried employee nurses in public hospitals could have been integrated into the current trends scenario insofar as it has actually been implemented. Nonetheless, at the time this chapter was written, the nurses had not yet expressed their choice to remain in category B or to change to category A. Due to this, it is necessary to hypothesize as to the nurses' behaviour in relation to choosing a category. In addition, the impact of the category on the age at which work is ceased cannot be observed and thus must also be formed into a hypothesis. This is why it seemed better to construct a variant to make a model for this reform. This variant differs from the baseline scenario by the hypotheses made on the proportion of salaried employee nurses working in public hospitals who choose, in 2011, to change to category A and on the probabilities of departure (ceasing work or death) at each age. In fact, it is possible that the oldest nurses will be more inclined to remain in category B and retire at age 55.

We suppose that in 2011, the ensemble of salaried employee nurses under 40 working in public hospitals will choose to change to category A and that the portion of nurses choosing category A will drop by 10 points per year between the ages of 40 and 49. Thus, the salaried employee nurses aged 50 and up working in public hospitals will all choose to remain in category B. Moreover, starting in 2011, the nurses changing their mode of practice to become salaried employees of public hospitals will also automatically be in category A. For nurses in category A, the probability of departure at each age is delayed by five years in relation to the estimates in the current trends scenario. However, this delay is only in effect for nurses who are potentially near the end of their careers, i.e. over 54 years of age. Before this age, we suppose that the probability of their departure will remain identical to that in the current trends scenario.

Under these new hypotheses, there would be 684,100 working nurses in 2030, i.e. 4 per cent more than in the current trends scenario . Relative to the baseline scenario, there would be 7.3 per cent more salaried employee nurses working for public hospitals in 2030. The average age of working nurses should increase slightly (41.6 years of age in 2030 as compared to 40.9 years in the current trends scenario). The increase in the portion of nurses aged 50 and over observed starting in 2022 in the current trends scenario would begin in 2020 and would be much more marked (+ 3 points between 2020 and 2030). The average age of departure (ceasing activity or death) of salaried employee nurses working in public hospitals would thus increase by 2.6 years. In 2030, the salaried employee nurses working in public hospitals would cease working, on average, at age 58.

The 2010 Retirement Reform

Added to the reform changing the status of nurses working in the public hospitals is another reform, the retirement reform. The 2010 French retirement reform (Law No. 2010-1330 of 9 November 2010) progressively raises (at the rate of four months each year) the minimum age for retirement from 60 to 62 in 2018. Besides, the age at which workers who have not made full contributions can receive a pension without penalties would rise from 65 in 2018 to 67 in 2023.

For nurses working in public hospitals and who will choose to stay in category 'active',[8] the minimum age for retirement would rise from 55 to 57. For those who will choose to change to category A it would remain at 60 (not 62). For newly graduated nurses it would rise from 60 to 62 (from 2012).

As the reform was adopted in 2010, there is insufficient hindsight with which to predict nurses' behaviour with regards to retirement. Moreover, this reform could modify the behaviour of nurses working in public hospitals in terms of category choice. Indeed, nurses close to retirement who might have wanted to remain in category B might now find it more interesting to opt for category A, due to having two additional years before retirement (57 instead of 55). For these reasons, we preferred not to take the retirement reform into account for the baseline scenario.

The retirement reform variant differs from the baseline scenario through the hypothesis made on the probabilities of departure (ceasing work or death) at each age for all the nurses. Thus, we have delayed the probability of retirement progressively, at the rate of one year in 2014 and one year in 2017. However, this delay is only in effect for nurses who are potentially near the end of their careers, i.e. over 54 years of age for employees of public hospitals and 58 for the

---

8   Occupations classified as category 'active' (as opposed to the sedentary category) are exposed to particular risks or unusual tiredness.

others. Before this age, we suppose that the probability of their departure remains identical to that in the current trends scenario.

The age for full benefit retirement is equally progressively delayed, at the rate of one year in 2019 and one year in 2022. We thus suppose that beginning in 2022, the ensemble of nurses will cease working entirely after 67 years of age. This scenario does not take into account the suppression of the possibility of retiring after 15 years for parents of three or more children who work as civil servants. We felt it was too delicate to make a model of this measure using the available data.

Postponing retirement age for two years should increase the number of working nurses by 3.5 per cent in 2030 relative to the current trends scenario. Thus, in 2030, there should be 681,000 working nurses under 67 years of age. The number of nurses in the workforce will not be the same depending upon the mode of practice. In 2030, the number of independent nurses should be 5 per cent greater than the current trends scenario, whereas the number of nurses employed in private sector hospitals will only be 1.9 per cent relative to the current trends scenario. The retirement reform should have the same effect as the statutory reform on the average age of working nurses. The portion of those aged 50 and over would remain relatively stable between 2010 and 2021, whereas it would decrease according to the hypothesis of the current trends scenario. Furthermore, the retirement reform would shift the average age of nurses ceasing work in 2030 by 1.5 years relative to the current trends scenario. Thus, nurses would, on average, cease working at 59 years of age.

Until 2024, the number of nurses per 100,000 inhabitants should be close to that which it would be if the national nursing quota were raised by 10 per cent. After 2025, the density of nurses would be as high as it would be under the hypothesis underlying the statutory reform (less than a 1 per cent gap). Nevertheless, the effect on the profession's age structure is not the same. Indeed, a 10 per cent rise in the quota would lead to a lesser drop in the portion of nurses under 30 years of age and would have no effect on the portion of the nurses over 50 which would remain close to that in the current trends scenario.

Conclusion

The evolution in the number of practicing nurses depends upon the nurses' professional choices as well as decisions made by the government. The projections presented here allow us to illustrate, under certain assumptions, the probable effects of regulatory measures and of behavioural changes in the evolution of the number of nurses in the workforce.

According to the hypotheses of the scenario of reference, maintaining constant in nurses' behaviour and in governmental decisions, the number of nurses in the workforce should continue to increase until 2030, albeit at a less sustained rate. The breakdown of nurses according to mode of practice will hardly be modified, with public hospitals remaining the most frequent mode of practice (approximately

50 per cent of nurses will continue to work in them). The regional distribution of independent nurses should improve.

Models were created for two other scenarios so as to simulate the impact of the retirement reform and of the statutory reform concerning nurses employed in public hospitals. The retirement reform, like the statutory reform, would lead to a 4 per cent increase in the number of working nurses in 2030. This increase would be distributed evenly through all sectors of activity regarding the retirement reform, but would concern almost exclusively the nurses employed by public hospitals as regards the statutory reform. This increase in the workforce is similar to the increase that would be produced by an increase comprised between 5 per cent and 10 per cent annually in the national quota starting in 2011.

In summary, the nursing supply model is a powerful tool for projecting nurses' supply under alternative sets of assumptions. Thus, it permits us to investigate trends in medical demography and to test the impact of different public policies on the dynamics of health professionals. Lastly, we approximate a region's demand of care by its population; to be more precise, it would be better to develop a specific nursing demand model.

References

Attal-Toubert, K. and Vanderschelden, M. 2009. *La démographie médicale à l'horizon 2030: de nouvelles projections nationales et régionales détaillées*, DREES, Dossiers Solidarité et Santé, no. 12.

Barlet, M. and Cavillon, M. 2010. La profession infirmière: Situation démographique et trajectoires professionnelles, DREES, *Work document Études et Recherche Series*, no. 101.

Barlet, M. and Collin, C. 2010. Localisation des professionnels de santé libéraux, DREES, Comptes nationaux de la Santé 2009.

Bélanger, A. Caron Malenfant, Martel, L. and Gélinas, R. 2007. Projecting ethno-cultural diversity of the Canadian population using a microsimulation approach, *Work session on demographic projections* – Bucharest, 10–12 October.

Blanpain, N. and Chardon, O. 2010. Projections de population à l'horizon 2060, INSEE première no. 1320.

INSEE, division 'Redistribution et politiques sociales', 1999, 'Le modèle de microsimulation dynamique DESTINIE', Série des documents de travail de la Direction des Études et Synthèses Économiques.

Legendre, F., Lorgnet, J.P. and Thibault, F. Les modèles socio-économiques de microsimulation: Panorama et état des lieux pour la France: Évaluer les politiques familiales et sociales, Recherches et Prévisions.

U.S. Department of Health and Human Services. 2004. What is Behind HRSA's Projected Supply, Demand, and Shortage of Registered Nurses?, September.

U.S. Department of Health and Human Services. 2007. Projected Supply, Demand, and Shortages of Registered Nurses: 2000 to 2020, *International*

Microsimulation Conference on Population Ageing, Health and the Health Workforce, December.

Appendix 1   Data Sources Used in the Projection Model

The Adeli directory lists the health professionals who have a legal authorization to practice their profession. All health professionals have the obligation to register their diploma. This directory is the only exhaustive database about nurses practicing in France which is continually updated. It is the only source that allows study of the changes of region or mode of practice. However, despite the legal obligation to register, the directory has some weaknesses. First of all, nurses are not encouraged to unsubscribe (because of free registration) when they cease their activity temporarily or definitively. In addition, nurses seem to register their diploma with some delay. Thus, the Adeli directory underestimates the number of young nurses. Finally, the non-hospital employed nurses do not seem to be all registered: they appear under-represented in the directory relative to the census.

The population census (2006) identifies people who declare themselves nurses. It is a declarative source, contrary to the Adeli directory. Nevertheless, this profession is probably well identified. The census takes place at residents' homes, so nurses working in France and living abroad are not recorded. However, the census records nurses living in France and working abroad (these nurses are not considered in this study). It distinguishes the employees of the public hospital from those of the private sector. A comparison of different sources available showed that the structure by age and mode of practice is probably more reliable in the 2006 census than in the Adeli directory. For this reason the initial database of our projection model is the 2006 census.

Other databases have been used to estimate the different parameters of our model:

- The schools survey (Enquêtes Écoles) is an annual survey which identifies training centres for health professionals. This survey also allows us to count the students for each profession and to know their characteristics.
- The Generation 98 CEREQ survey aims to collect data necessary for the study of the careers of the 742,000 young people who left initial training in 1998. It describes month by month the situation of the young graduates from their graduation to the time of the survey (employment, unemployment, inactivity, national service, training or studies). Contrary to the Adeli directory, this survey is more reliable to study the entry into working life. In fact, the new graduates are slow to register their diploma into the Adeli directory. Nevertheless, the number of nurses in the survey doesn't allow analysis of the choice of the region of practice according to the region in which they have obtained their diploma.

- Since 2007, the annual declaration of social data (déclarations annuelles de données sociales) reliably identifies nurses employed by public hospitals thanks to the nomenclature of hospital jobs (NEH), and the employees of the private hospitals thanks to the variable 'professionals category (PCS)'. In fact, due to the non-systematic deregistration of nurses who have ceased their activity, the Adeli directory is not a sufficiently reliable source to study cessation of activity. Also, to study the age at which nurses leave public hospitals, we used data from 2007 and 2008 and calculated, for a given age A, the percentage of nurses still present the following year at the age A+1. The estimation of the probability of ceasing work is based on the assumptions that before the age of 40 no nurses cease their activity and that all nurses cease all activity after 65 years of age. Those assumptions seem realistic to the extent that, on the one hand, we observed that the probability of ceasing work before 40 years is under 3 per cent or negative (when the entries are greater than departures) and there are few employed nurses aged over 66 years who are still working.
- The French National Health Insurance Agency for Wage Earners (CNAMTS) records the activity of all independent nurses (except remplaçantes nurses). We used the same methodology for nurses employed by hospitals to estimate the probability of retirement. Thus, the retirement rates include both retirements, but also changes in mode of practice and deaths. Nevertheless, the transitions between modes of practice are limited, especially after 45 years. As well as hospital nurses, we assume that all nurses cease to work before age 66 and none cease before age 40.

Appendix 2   Description of the Different Parameters of the Model

Components	Description	Parameters	Shape	Data
Training	Modelling the number of new graduates	National quota	year	Health Ministry
		Regional distribution of the national quota	year * region	Health Ministry
		Deficit quota	year * region	School surveys and Health Ministry
		Profile of graduates	year * region * gender * age	School surveys and Health Ministry
Entering the workforce	Modelling the entry into working life	Escape	region	Generation 98 Survey
		Set up delay	region * delay	Generation 98 Survey
		Region	region of diploma * region for activity	Adeli directory
		Mode of practice	year * region of practice * gender * age group * mode of practice	Adeli directory

Mid-career changes	Modelling the changes of region or mode of practice	Change of region	year * age group * region of practice	Adeli directory
		New region	year * old region * new region	Adeli directory
		Change of mode of practice	year * gender * mode of practice * change of region	Adeli directory
		New mode of practice	year * gender * old mode of practice * new mode of practice	Adeli directory
		Change of category	year * mode of practice	Decree
		New category	year * mode of practice * age * category	Authors' hypothesis
Ceasing	Modelling the retirement	Probability of ceasing work	year * mode of practice * gender * age * category	DADS and Cnamts

Chapter 7

Gender Aspects of the Norwegian Pension System

Dennis Fredriksen and Nils Martin Stølen

Introduction

Compared to a market based system females are favoured in the National Insurance Scheme of Norway like in most other Western countries. The major distributional effect is caused by gender neutral financing and benefits in combination with considerably higher life expectancy for women than for men. These important characteristics are not much affected by the reform of the public pension system in Norway that started to be implemented from 2011.

In 2011 life expectancy at the age of 62 (which is the lowest possible retirement age for old-age pensions with the new system) was estimated to be 20.5 years for men and 23.8 years for women. According to the medium alternative in the population projections from Statistics Norway in 2012 the corresponding figures in 2050 may reach 24.8 and 27.7. Remaining life-expectancy at the age of 62 is thus expected to increase slightly more for men than for women in the coming decades. Females also benefit from gender neutral financing and benefits in the disability part of the system as the share of women getting disabled is somewhat higher than for men. Disability pension is a very common exit route from labour market participation in Norway. Before being transferred to an old-age pension at the age of 67 an average Norwegian woman now is expected to receive disability pension for 5.2 years while the corresponding figure for men is 3.9.

Because of lower lifetime earnings than for men, women also benefit from minimum pension benefits and a ceiling on accrual of entitlements from yearly incomes. Although these elements are somewhat modified with the new Norwegian pension system, the main characteristics remain. Pension entitlements from unpaid home care are somewhat improved with the new system. More favourable entitlements for unpaid care are introduced to counteract a possible adverse effect on female pension benefits from shifting from entitlements based on the 20 best years of incomes in the old pension system towards incomes from every working year in the new. Survivors' pensions also favour women because a majority of them outlive their husbands, and this element is going to be adjusted to the new system. Because of increasing labour market participation rates and incomes for women compared to men, the importance of survivors' pensions is expected to decrease in the next decades.

A traditional approach to analysing distributional aspects of tax and pension systems is to calculate taxes paid and benefits received for persons with different characteristics. However, analyses of pension replacement rates are often based on simplified assumptions cf. a report on Pension Adequacy from the European Union (2012). In real life incomes vary, and due to non-linearity in most tax and benefit systems it can be discussed how representative the chosen assumptions are.

Although the gender dimension of pension systems is discussed in a relevant way in several papers and reports cf. James et al. (2003), Ståhlberg et al. (2006), James et al. (2008), James (2013) and Fajnzylber (2013), the empirical analyses of distributional effects by gender are rather weak. Commonly the discussion is worked out without use of any tax-benefit model, or alternatively calculations based on very simplifying assumptions. As advocated by Orcutt et al. (1986) a microsimulation approach may be highly beneficial in policy analyses of effects from non-linear tax and benefit systems where different parts of the population may face different rules. In such a situation there may be substantial problems of aggregation in calculating the total effects on government budgets and the corresponding effects on distribution of incomes. The main strength of microsimulation is to represent a socioeconomic system by a sample of decision units and then model different events which these units may be exposed to. Contrary to what is possible in a macroeconomic approach, detailed and complicated tax and benefit rules may be exactly reproduced. Aggregated numbers are obtained by multiplying the variable of interest for each unit with its sample weight and the summing up across the sample. Budget effects and distributional effects may also be analysed in a consistent way.

In analysing gender aspects of the Norwegian pension system we use the dynamic microsimulation model MOSART documented in Fredriksen (1998). By utilizing this kind of model it is possible to comply with the arguments from Creedy (1990) that 'for many purposes the measurement of inequality should be based on income measured over a longer period than a single year'. The main focus of the chapter is on old-age pensions in the Norwegian National Insurance Scheme, and MOSART has been intensively used in analysing the effects from the reform that started to be implemented from 1 January 2011.

Design of the Norwegian Pension System

Public Old-Age Pensions

The former system for public old-age pensions in Norway was based on defined benefits and financed pay-as-you-go. If this system had been maintained the expenditures for old-age pensions, and thereby the financial burden, would have doubled from 2010 to 2050 because of a strong growth in the number of old-age pensioners caused by increasing life expectancy and large cohorts born after The Second World War replacing small cohorts born in the previous decades. Heavy work on reforming the system has thus taken place for more than a decade, and the implementation of the new pension system started in January 2011. The main change was to make the public old-age pension system more actuarial. Based on the pension entitlements accumulated over the working period, the annual benefits are made dependent on the age of retiring and remaining life expectancy. Compared to the former system this design is expected to reduce growth in pension expenditures and postpone retirement when life expectancy increases.

To make the system more actuarial, a closer connection between pension entitlements and former labour incomes is also introduced. Between ages 13 and 75 entitlements for old-age pensions in the new system are accumulated by 18.1 per cent of annual labour incomes up to a ceiling of 7.1 times the basic pension unit (BPU). BPU is a measurement unit in the National Insurance Scheme and amounted to NOK 78,024 as a yearly average for 2011 corresponding to about 1/6 of the average annual wage level for a full time employee. The ceiling thus corresponds to approximately 115 per cent of the average wage level.

The main changes to obtain greater correspondence between pension entitlements and former labour incomes compared to the old system are:

- Accumulation of entitlements from the first income earned against 1 BPU with the old system;
- A maximum of 40 years of entitlements in the old system is abolished;
- A rule for accumulation of entitlements based on the 20 years with highest incomes is also abolished;
- Compared to the ceiling of 7.1 BPU for earning of entitlements with the new system, full accumulation of entitlements in the old system took place up to 6 BPU with a slanting roof of 1/3 between 6 and 12 BPU.

For persons with unpaid homecare yearly entitlements are increased from 4 BPU in the old system to 4.5 BPU in the new. These entitlements are means-tested 100 per cent against labour incomes.

A guarantee pension of 2 BPU for singles and 1.85 BPU per person for couples secures a minimum level of benefits for pensioners with low labour incomes. The guarantee pension is means-tested with 80 per cent against income entitlements, and even persons with small incomes will obtain a level of pension benefits somewhat higher than the minimum level as shown in Figure 7.1. In this figure the connection between annual pension benefits and former labour incomes is shown with the new and the old system for a single person with constant labour incomes during a period of 40 years. The annual benefits are shown before taking life expectancy adjustments into account, and thus represent the system for accumulation of entitlements. A ceiling on annual incomes for full accumulation of entitlements at 7.1 BPU in the new system compared to 6 BPU in the old means that especially persons in this interval gain from the change in the accumulation model. However, for persons with annual incomes between 7.1 and 12 BPU the connection between former labour incomes and accumulation of entitlements is weakened.

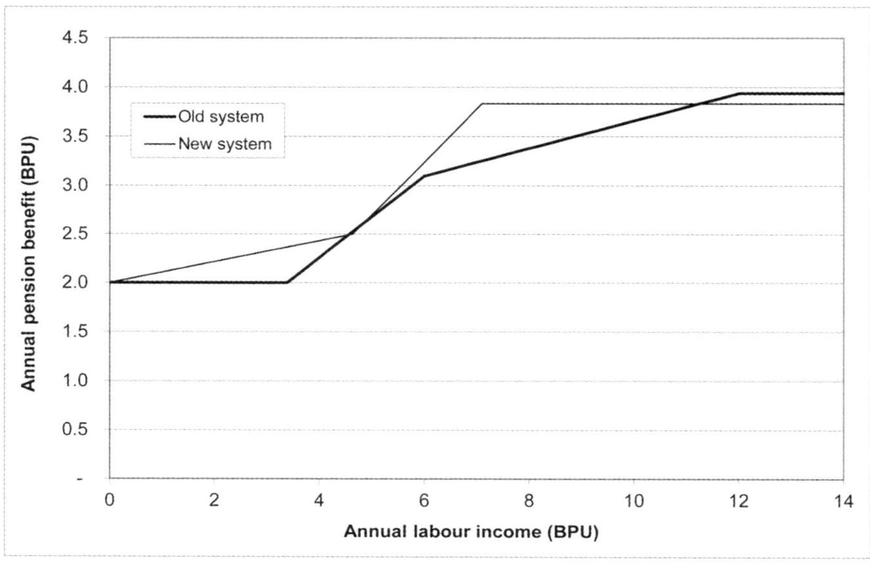

Figure 7.1   Connection between annual labour incomes and annual pension benefits with old and new pension system

The actuarial design with adjustments for changes in life expectancy in combination with flexible retirement over the interval 62–75 years is introduced from 2011. This means that old-age pension benefits may be drawn partly or completely from the age of 62, and work and pensions may be freely combined without any earnings test. From accumulated entitlements at retirement age A, W_A, annual pension benefits for a cohort K retiring at that age are calculated by dividing by *divisors* $\Phi_{K,A}$ reflecting remaining life expectancy at that age.

(1) $B_{K,A} = W_A / \Phi_{K,A}$

Here
$B_{K,A}$ = Annual pension benefits for persons from cohort K, retiring at age A
W_A = Accumulated entitlements at age A, and
$\Phi_{K,A}$ = Divisors for persons from cohort K retiring at age A

The actuarial design reflected in (1) says that accumulated entitlements are divided by expected years as retired. Early retirement leads to lower annual benefits because accumulated entitlements have to be divided by more years. This is also the case when life expectancy increases for a given retirement age. Lower benefits when life expectancy increases may be counteracted by postponing retirement.

In the new system pension entitlements in the accumulation phase are indexed to wage growth. After retirement the income pension in payment is indexed to wages, but subtracted a fixed factor of 0.75 per cent per year. The level of the guaranteed pension will be adjusted by growth in wages, but reduced with higher life expectancy. In the demographic projections from Statistics Norway life expectancy at the age of 67 is assumed to increase by 0.5 per cent a year in the long run. Then the indexation of minimum pensions usually will be higher than price indexation.

Persons born in 1953 or earlier will earn their pension entitlements only according to the old system. In the group born from 1954 to 1962 pension entitlements will partly be calculated from the old system and partly from the new with a gradually increasing share. People born in 1963 or later will earn their pension entitlements completely according to the new system.

Disability Pensions and Old-Age Pensions for Former Disabled

Under the old system the disability pension and the old-age pension were interconnected, and disability pensioners usually kept their pensions unchanged when they were transferred to the old-age pension at age 67. About 11 per cent of the population aged 18–67 is on disability pension. Because disability pensions partly have been used as an early retirement scheme for older workers facing difficulties in the labour market, at age 67 about 40 per cent of the new old-age pensioners have been former disabled. As a part of the pension reform the Government in 2011 proposed a new disability scheme and a new model for calculating old-age pensions for the earlier disabled. The new disability scheme will be introduced from 2015. With the new scheme the disability pension will be determined more as short term benefit with a replacement rate of 66 per cent and taxed like earnings.

As in the old system, disability pensioners will be transferred to old-age pensions at the age of 67. Because persons receiving disability benefits are not allowed to work after this age to counteract higher life expectancy, the reduction in yearly benefits at age 67 for a new disabled is only the half of the reduction implemented for the former non-disabled retiring at this age. By 2018 the life expectancy adjustment of the old-age pension for earlier disabled is to be evaluated in light of whether the non-disabled compensate for the life expectancy adjustment by working longer.

Survivors' Pensions

Survivors' pensions are also interconnected to the old system for old-age pensions. Given some conditions about own incomes and common children, a surviving spouse may get extra pension benefits dependent on the accumulated entitlements of the deceased spouse. If the surviving spouse receives old-age benefits, she may also get a supplementary survivor's pension means-tested against her own entitlements for supplementary/income dependent pension. A majority of the surviving spouses are women, and normally their pension entitlements are significantly lower than the corresponding entitlements of their husbands.

The Dynamic Microsimulation Model MOSART

The analyses in this chapter are based on Statistics Norway's dynamic microsimulation model MOSART documented in Fredriksen (1998). In this model, projections for demographic development and labour supply are combined with different rules for accumulation of pension entitlements, an actuarial design and adjustments for increasing life expectancy. In addition to the direct effects from the reform of the Norwegian public pension system, plausible labour supply assumptions are implemented exogenously in the model. These assumptions are particularly important to understanding retirement behaviour effects.

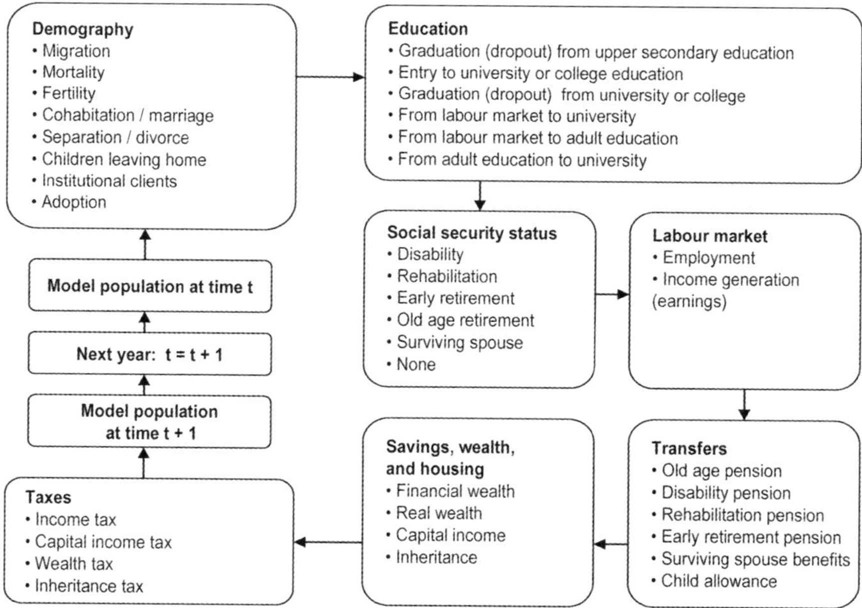

Figure 7.2   Structure of the dynamic microsimulation model MOSART

The main structure of the MOSART model is presented in Figure 7.2. The calculations with the model presented in this chapter are based on information from administrative registers for the entire Norwegian population from 2008 calibrated up to 2011. From 2008 the model simulates the further life course for every person in the country. The life course is simulated by possible transitions from one state to another, given by transition probabilities depending on each person's characteristics. The transition probabilities are estimated from observed transitions in a recent period. Events included in the simulation are migration, deaths, births, marriages, divorces, educational activities, retirements and labour force participation. Public pension benefits are calculated from labour market earnings and other characteristics included in the simulation. Old-age pensions, disability pensions, survival pensions, rehabilitation pensions and early retirement pensions are included in the model.

The demographic assumptions are based on the medium alternative of Statistics Norway's demographic projections from June 2012. A total fertility rate of 1.87 and net immigration shrinking from the present level of more than 40,000 persons towards 10–15,000 persons per year in the long run imply a continual growth in the younger part of the population in the first decades. But especially the number of elderly will show a significant growth in the first decades as a result of the larger cohorts born after the Second World War and expected growth in remaining life expectancy at the age of 62 of about four years from 2011 to 2050.

Probable labour supply effects that may arise as a result of the Norwegian pension reform are discussed in further detail in Christensen et al. (2012). Labour supply is expected to be affected in two ways:

- A clearer connection between earlier labour incomes and accumulation of entitlements means an implicit reduction of marginal tax rates. This may stimulate persons of working age to work more.
- The actuarial design of the new system means a closer link between private incentives and the social costs of early retirement. People are stimulated to postpone retirement when life expectancy increases.

In correspondence with central findings in the labour market literature, as pointed out by Blundell and MaCurdy (1999), the effects tend to be strongest for retirement decisions. Based on simulations with the MOSART model we find that the reform may reduce implicit marginal tax rates on labour incomes for those in work by about 5 percentage points. Combined with estimates for the marginal compensated labour supply elasticity of about 0.5, this yields a rough estimate on the supply of persons-hours as a result of the reform of 2.5 per cent.

With the old system most people in Norway who did not exit earlier to achieve disability pension or early retirement pension commonly retired at age 67. Therefore it has only been possible to make simple estimates of how retirement age may be affected by a shift towards a more actuarial system. Because early retirement had no negative consequences for future pension benefits under the old scheme, early retirement was favoured as shown in different empirical analyses. The new actuarial system is thus expected to have a considerable effect on participation rates for elderly workers. Increasing life expectancy is expected to increase the effect further. To maintain yearly pension benefits relative to wages it seems necessary to postpone retirement by eight months for each year life expectancy increases. By 2050 we thus estimate labour supply to increase by 4 per cent as a result of postponed retirement. Unemployment is not taken into consideration because of assumptions of a low and constant unemployment rate in Norway. Unemployment benefits are also included in the income base for accumulation of old-age pension benefits.

Gender Effects from Minimum Pensions

At present all old-age pension entitlements for public pensions are based on the rules from the old pension system. This system was implemented in 1967, but because of the need for 40 years of accumulation to obtain maximum benefits, the effect on pension expenditures has not matured yet for those who retired some years ago. Labour supply among women has increased significantly during the past decades, but because of the long period of maturing still a large part of women in Norway receives minimum pensions. A strengthening of the minimum pension benefit level in the years 2008 to 2010 also increased the share of minimum pensioners over this period.

As a consequence of increasing participation rates and increasing labour market earnings for women during the past decades, the share of minimum pensioners is decreasing as shown in Figure 7.3. This will be strengthened with the new system as the guarantee pension is means-tested at the rate of 80 per cent against the income pension (cf. Figure 7.1). With the new system the main remaining part of minimum pensioners will consist of immigrated persons with a too short period of work in Norway to receive more than a minimum pension. In fact due to curtailment for a short period of living their old-age pension may be less than the standard minimum pension for Norwegians having stayed most of their working life in Norway. For these persons, only those with almost no labour incomes will become minimum pensioners in the future based on entitlements from the new system. As most of the immigrants working in Norway for only a short time are men, the share of minimum pensioners will increase more for men than for women.

After 2020 an increasing part of the pensioners partly will receive some guarantee supplements with the new system. In addition to an increasing share of immigrants with a relatively short period of working in Norway, this is partly caused by the fact that the earlier disabled will be transferred to old-age pensions at the age of 67. Although the life-expectancy adjustment for former disabled is only the half of the adjustment for the former non-disabled, their old-age pension benefit will decrease relative to old-age pensions for non-disabled when life expectancy increases.

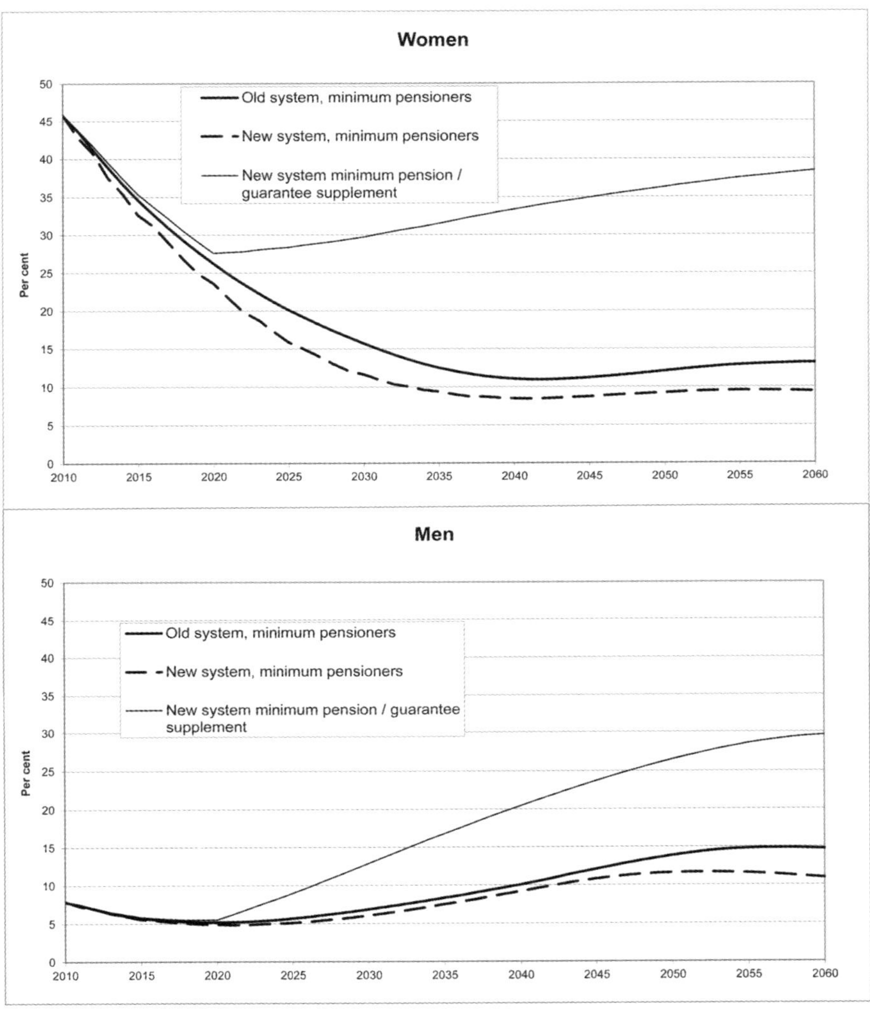

Figure 7.3　**Share of old-age pensioners receiving minimum/guarantee pension with new and old pension system. Per cent**

Unpaid Homecare

Specific rules for accumulation of pension entitlements for people taking care of children and elderly were introduced in the old system with effect from 1992. Annual entitlements for unpaid home-care are given as a floor for persons with low labour incomes. The floor was increased from 4 BPU in the old system to 4.5 in the new, corresponding to 75 per cent of an average full-time wage. For people taking care of children, entitlements for unpaid work may be given for children younger than six. Both the mother and the father of a child may receive such entitlements, but only one of the parents in any given year. Normally women benefit most because of lower labour incomes than for men. People with children under the age of six earning more than 75 per cent of the average wage level will not receive any extra pension entitlements for unpaid care at all.

The main purpose of the specific rules is to compensate for lost labour incomes. Because of the abolishment of the '20 best years count rule' as a part of the pension reform, the effect of the specific rules will be larger with the new system than with the old. To prevent large arbitrary differences in pension benefits due to entitlements for unpaid homecare from one cohort to the next, the Norwegian Parliament has decided to allow retroactive entitlements for unpaid home-care before 1992 back to the 1954-cohort who is the first cohort partly affected by the new rules for accumulation of entitlements with the new system. However, the fiscal effect of this retroactive shift in a more favourable direction is only of minor importance.

Figure 7.4 shows the average old-age pension benefit for women with the new pension system inclusive and exclusive entitlements for unpaid homecare. It is evident that a long period of maturing causes the effects from accumulated entitlements from unpaid home-care on average old-age pension benefits for women not to become significant before 2020. From 2050 average benefits for women (relative to total average wages) are increased by about 3 per cent as a result of these entitlements.

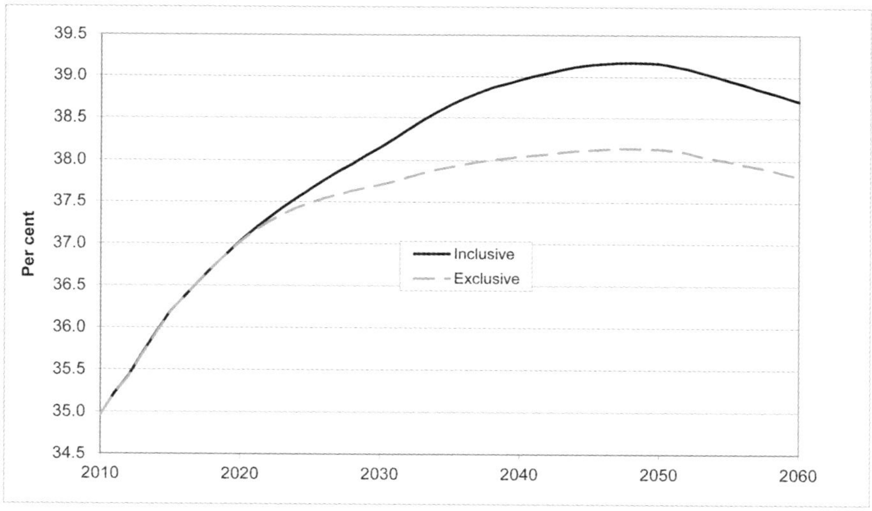

Figure 7.4   **Average old-age pension benefit for women with the new pension system inclusive and exclusive entitlements for unpaid homecare. Measured in per cent of total average wages**

Overall Horizontal Effects from the Pension Reform

A common approach when analysing distributional effects from tax and pension reforms is to illustrate distributional effects by simplified assumptions for typical households as in Figure 7.1. There are two main shortcomings with this figure. Firstly, no one experiences constant earnings during their working period of life, and pension rules for couples differ somewhat from rules for singles. Thus, it may be discussed how 'typical' the illustration is. Secondly, it is impossible to include all elements of the pension system in the figure. 'The 20 best years count' rule in the old system and entitlements from unpaid homecare are typical examples of elements not included in the illustration.

By using a microsimulation model like MOSART it is possible to represent all relevant rules in a correct way as well as taking the heterogeneity of the population into account. Wage profiles over the life cycle for each individual dependent on age, gender, education and former labour market experience, in addition to stochastic variability, are included in the model. It is thus possible to obtain a more accurate description of the distributional consequences of the pension reform, and the model may be used to show the effects before and after including behavioural effects. But even with a microsimulation model, analyses of distributional effects from a pension reform have to be built on some simplifying assumptions. In the first stage we want to concentrate on the horizontal effects in a specific year (2050) that is so far ahead that the main effects are exhausted. Later we return to the dynamic effects over the life-cycle including behavioural effects.

In most countries with funded or Nonfinancial Defined Contribution (NDC) systems there is a close connection between pension premiums paid and benefits received. Although this also was the intension when the National Insurance System in Norway was established in 1967, this link gradually vanished when the systems for taxes (including pension premiums) and pensions were changed. Old-age pensions in Norway are fully integrated into the general tax revenues and expenditures of the government budget. When analysing the distributional effects from the pension reform in Norway it is thus convenient to restrict the analysis to only considering pension benefits, and not how the pension premiums paid by the employed are distributed between individuals. The pension reform will permit lower taxes and/or higher public expenditures in the future than if the old system were maintained. How the reduced pension expenditures are spent, is likely to have distributional consequences that are excluded from our analysis since it would mean making speculative assumptions about future policy decisions.

To focus on the horizontal distributional effects from the model for accrual of entitlements, it is also convenient to look apart from indexation and the actuarial adjustments through the flexible pension scheme. The reformed system replaces an almost fixed retirement age of 67 with an individual retirement choice above 62 years. If we include labour supply effects, changes in annual pensions will be a poor approximation for changes in welfare because they will also reflect voluntary shifts in retirement spells.

The overall horizontal distributional effects of the pension reform in 2050 are presented in Figure 7.5. In the figure annual pension benefits with the old and the new system are broken down by pension income percentiles in 2050. A more favourable model for accrual of entitlements before taking lower indexing of benefits than wage growth and adjustments for increasing life expectancy into account means that nobody seems to lose given these assumptions. As adjustments for life expectancy and indexation are the cost cutters of the reform, whereas the system for accumulation of entitlements partially increases expenditures, Figure 7.5 gives a good indication of the distributional consequences. But because of the tightening caused by life expenditure adjustments and indexing the figure is misleading regarding the level of entitlements, and also seen from a fiscal perspective.

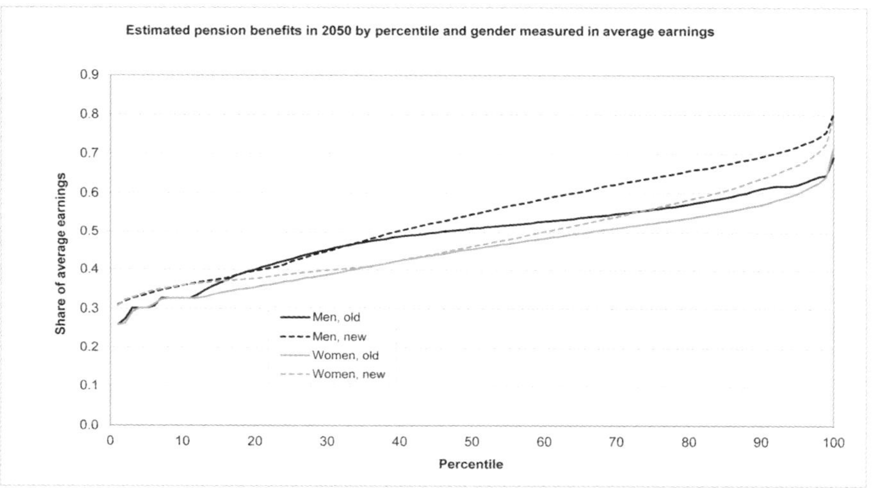

Figure 7.5   Horizontal distributional effects from accrual of entitlements

Because of the closer link between former earnings and accrual of pension entitlements, the distributional effects of the new system are smaller than with the old. The top five pension income deciles seem to gain most from the reform. The gains are largest for the highest income groups, and men gain to a greater extent than women. This result reflects the higher accrual coefficient for pension entitlements and full accrual of entitlements up to 7.1 BPU as shown in Figure 7.1.

For the bottom two deciles, and especially for women, pension levels will also somewhat improve given the assumptions behind the figure. This is mainly caused by the 100 per cent means-testing of the special supplement against supplementary pension with the old system, while the guarantee pension in the new system is means-tested against the income pension with only 80 per cent. The increasing advantage of entitlements for unpaid homecare with the new system is also favourable for women with lower incomes. The pension level for men between the second and the fourth decile, and for women between the third and the fifth is almost unaffected by the reform before lower indexing of benefits than wage growth and life expectancy adjustments are taken into account. Different elements of the modification of the accrual model seem to counteract each other.

Redistribution in Favour of Women over the Life-cycle

The minimum pension benefit and the ceiling on accrual of entitlements cause a strong redistribution in favour of persons with the lowest incomes. And due to lower participation rates and a large degree of part-time work a large part of the women experience low lifetime earnings and thereby low pension benefits. Longer life expectancy also causes the total benefits received as an old-age pensioner to be higher for women than for men for a given level of incomes.

Overall distributional effects over the life cycle from the public old-age pension system also including labour supply effects are shown in Figure 7.6. In this figure we have compared total old-age pension benefits by the corresponding total life time earnings for different income groups and by gender. The comparison is based on the simulated earnings over the life cycle for persons born during the 1990s and is illustrated with the new and the old pension system. For earlier disabled we have calculated their life time earnings as the incomes they could have earned assuming that they had continued to work until the age of 67 with the same relative income as when becoming disabled.

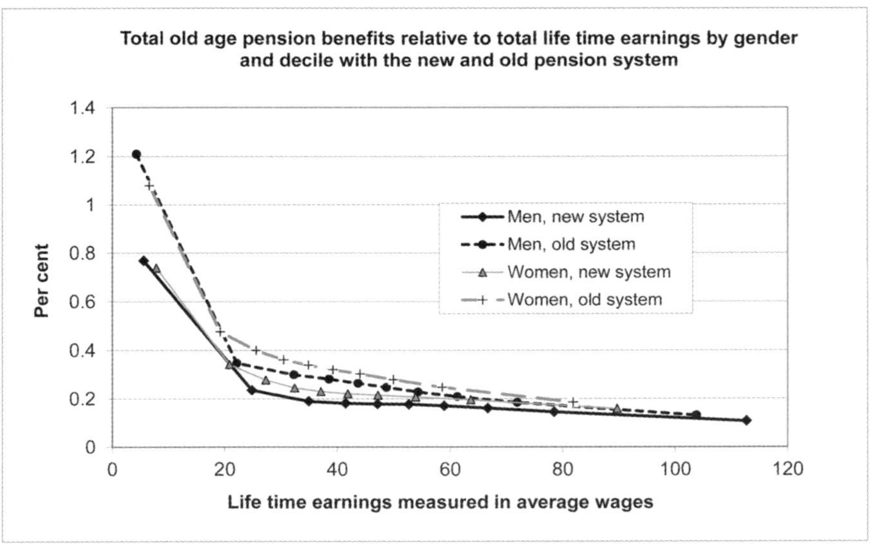

Figure 7.6　**Distributional effects over the life cycle with the new and old system for men and women born during the late 1990s**

Along the X-axis we measure life time labour market earnings in average yearly wages. On each graph the depicted points show the average life time earnings for different deciles and the corresponding old-age benefits received relative to these earnings. As women earn less than men, the female points are to the left of the male points for corresponding deciles (except from the lowest). Women in the first decile on average earn about eight average wages over the life cycle with the new pension system, while the corresponding figure for men is only six. Lower average life time earnings in the first decile for men are caused by a larger share of males among immigrants. Immigrants with at least 10 years of residence in Norway are included in the calculations. Although the level of minimum pension is reduced according to the period of residence, total old-age pension for the lowest decile is about 75 per cent of total life time earnings for both men and women.

On the other hand, the highest male decile for persons born during the late 1990s on average is expected to earn 113 average yearly wages over their working period with the new pension system. For this decile of men total benefits is only expected to correspond to 11 per cent of their life time earnings. For women the decile with the highest income is expected to earn 90 average yearly wages over their working period with the new system, and total benefits constitute 16 per cent of this amount. The strongly downward sloping graphs indicate that the public old-age pension system to a large degree redistributes incomes from persons with high earnings to persons with low earnings. This also means redistribution from men to women as women earn less than men. And even for equal levels of income over the working period women receive higher total old-age pension than men because they live longer and because of entitlements for unpaid homecare.

Figure 7.6 also illustrates overall distributional effects of the pension reform over the life cycle for men and women respectively. The points with the new system are to the right of the corresponding points with the old system as a consequence of assumptions about increased labour supply as a result of the reform, and particularly as a result of postponed retirement.

When labour supply effects are included persons with the highest incomes (and education) are assumed to postpone retirement most, and men more than women. The significant fall in average old-age pensions compared to lifetime earnings in the lower deciles with the new system is caused by the drop in average pensions compared to wages for earlier disabled. Earlier disabled will be transferred to old-age pensions at a fixed age of 67. Although they are exposed for only half of the life expectancy adjustment compared to those who stay in job until they obtain old-age pensions, life expectancy adjustment causes a significant fall in average benefits compared to those who are able to counteract by postponing retirement. Remaining life expectancy at the lower age of retirement (62) is assumed to increase by more than five years from the 1943-cohort, who is the base cohort for the life-expectancy adjustments, to the cohorts born during the late 1990s illustrated in the figure.

From Figure 7.6 we also see that women are slightly more hurt than men as an overall effect of the reform. Men benefitting more than women from the change in the accumulation of entitlements is the main reason. For the lower deciles women on average lose less than men from the pension reform because they are somewhat compensated by a higher accrual of entitlements for unpaid child-care. The guarantee pension, the ceiling in the module for accrual of entitlements and the fact that women live longer than men still result in a considerable redistribution between genders. Due to the life expectancy adjustment former disabled men and women lose if life expectancy continues to grow when disabled are transferred to old-age pensions at the age of 67.

Concluding Remarks

Like pension systems in most other countries the old-age pension system in Norway causes a significant redistribution in favour of persons with lower working incomes, and from men to women. A large part of this redistribution is caused by minimum pension benefits, a ceiling on accrual of entitlements from yearly incomes and pension entitlements from unpaid homecare. Gender neutral financing and benefits in combination with considerably higher life expectancy for women than for men also redistributes incomes from men to women. Survivors' pensions work in the same direction.

Because of the closer link between former earnings and accrual of pension entitlements, the distributional effects of the new pension system are smaller than with the old. This also means a smaller redistribution from men to women as men with higher incomes benefit most / are less hurt by the reform for a given labour supply. Both men and women with higher incomes will probably increase their labour supply as a result of the pension reform mainly by postponing retirement. Over the life cycle the redistribution between men and women caused by the old-age pension system is not much affected. For the lower deciles women on average lose less than men from the pension reform because they are somewhat compensated by a higher accrual of entitlements for unpaid child-care.

References

Blundell, R.W. and MaCurdy, T. 1999. Labour Supply: A Review of Alternative Approaches, in *Handbook of Labor Economics, Vol. 3A*, edited by O.C. Ashenfelter and D. Card. Amsterdam: Elsevier Science, 1559–695.

Christensen, A.M., Fredriksen, D., Lien, O.C. and Stølen, N.M. 2012. Pension Reform in Norway: Combining an NDC Approach and Distributional Goals, in *Nonfinancial Defined Contribution Pension Schemes in a Changing Pension World, Volume 1: Progress, Lessons, and Implementation*, edited by R. Holzmann, E. Palmer and D. Robalino. Washington, DC: The World Bank, 129–55.

Creedy, J. 1990. Lifetime earnings and inequality. *Economic Record*, 67, 46–58.

European Union. 2012. *Pension Adequacy in the European Union 2010–2050*, Report 23 May 2012.

Fajnzylber, E. 2013. Gender Policy and Pensions in Chile, in *Nonfinancial Defined Contribution Pension Schemes in a Changing Pension Pension World, Volume 2: Gender, Politics and Financial Stability*, edited by R. Holzmann, E. Palmer and D. Robalino. Washington, DC: The World Bank, Chapter 13, 113–39.

Fredriksen, D. 1998. *Projections of Population, Education, Labour Supply and Public Pension Benefits – Analyses with the Dynamic Microsimulation Model MOSART.* Social and Economic Studies 101, Statistics Norway.

James, E. 2013. Gender in the (Nonfinancial) Defined Contribution World – Issues and Options, in *Nonfinancial Defined Contribution Pension Schemes in a Changing Pension World, Volume 2: Gender, Politics and Financial Stability*, edited by R. Holzmann, E. Palmer and D. Robalino. Washington, DC: The World Bank, Chapter 10, 3–33.

James, E., Edwards, A.C. and Wong, R. 2003. The Gender Impact of Pension Reform. *Journal of Pension Economics and Finance*, 2(2), 181–219.

James, E., Edwards, A.C. and Wong, R. 2008. *The Gender Impact of Social Security Reform.* Chicago: University of Chicago Press.

Jefferson, T. 2009. Women and Retirement Pensions: A Research Review. *Feminist Economics*, 15(4), 115–45.

Orcutt, G.H., Merz, J. and Quinke, H. 1986. *Micro analytic Simulation Models to Support Social and Financial Policy.* New York: North Holland.

Ståhlberg, A.C., Birman, M.C., Kruse, A. and Sundén, A. 2006. Pension Design and Gender, in *Gender and Social Security Reform: What's Fair for Women?*, edited by N. Gilbert. New Brunswick, NJ: Transaction, 1–44.

Chapter 8

The Redistributive Features of the Italian Pension System: The Importance of Being Neutral

Roberto Leombruni and Michele Mosca

Introduction

The Italian pension system, prior to 1992, was characterized by large and often unjustified disparities of treatment among workers (e.g. public versus private employees; self employed versus employees) and very generous seniority pension schemes. This made up a system that raised big concerns about its fairness and sustainability (Castellino 1995). Starting with the 'Amato' Law in 1992, several reforms have been delivered to harmonize rules across workers and reduce seniority pensions generosity. The 'Dini' Law, in 1995, targeted specifically the issue of inter- and intra-generational redistribution, starting a transition from the PAYG regime to a Notional Defined Contribution one inspired by actuarial fairness, able to ensure at the same time a further step towards long-term sustainability.

Not all disparities of treatment were unjustified ones, though. Actually, the PAYG system was inspired by a strong progressive principle, implemented mainly with a minimum pension benefit; a progressive pension calculation formula; a partial indexation for higher pensions. Since the Dini reform wiped out also this 'good' redistribution, with the exception of the minimum pension, the transition to neutrality may have as a first round effect a tendency towards a higher inequality among the elderly. The latter issue is a topical one – modern pension systems have been a pillar in fighting poverty among the elderly – and a similar concern has been raised in many countries where public pensions have been reduced in size and generosity (van Vliet et al. 2011, Arza 2008, Romig 2008).

The premise of this concern is: was the PAYG regime really progressive? The answer is not obvious, since it depends both on norms and on the career patterns actually realized in the labour market. This means that for all cohorts retiring up to the mid-2020s, for whom the PAYG quota is a substantial part of the pension, the assessment of the redistributive character of the system is by and large an empirical matter.

In principle, to measure redistribution it suffices to compare the (present value of) all contributions paid by a worker with the benefits s/he earned while retired. At the micro level, this gives the actuarial premia/losses each individual receives. If, on average, it is the poor who receive a premium, pensions will be less dispersed than wages, so that at the macro level redistribution is measured comparing inequality in earnings and in pensions.

In practice, data on entire life paths are rarely found in statistical databases, so that a direct measure of redistribution is seldom feasible. About Italy, we may sum up the literature according to three strategies that have been followed to approximate it. The first is the classical one: look at a cross-section and interpret different individuals in different ages as representative of individuals' life paths. This is the approach followed by Mazzaferro and Morciano (2011) and Dekkers et al. (2009), who develop two microsimulations of work and pensions (CAPP_DYN and MIDAS respectively) obtaining, about redistribution, mixed but coherent results. In both studies, in the long run earnings are more dispersed than pensions, which they read as a sign of progressivity. Indeed, in the long run the population has reached a regime phase, so that the assumption that a cross-section is representative of life courses is reasonable. Unfortunately they are not able to derive conclusions about the current situation. While they both find a period at simulation start in which it is inequality in pensions which is higher, they do not interpret the delta as a sign of negative redistribution, but as a composition effect due to the entry into retirement of cohorts of high income workers facing very generous, pre-reforms pension rules.

A second strategy takes again a cross-sectional view, but restricts the analysis around retirement time. Given the distribution of earnings the night before retirement, what is the distribution of pensions? What would it be using a pension calculation formula with no progressivity in it? This is the view taken by Contini and Leombruni (2006) and Ierini et al. (2002), both finding evidence of strong progressivity. The limit of this result is that redistribution revealed around retirement may not be a good approximation of the overall one. Indeed, as early studies about the pension- and tax systems have shown, a very different distributional picture may emerge looking at life course earnings (Harding 1993, Nelissen 1993, 1998, Creedy 1995). This is especially true for the Italian PAYG regime, where individuals with the same wage before retirement, and the same pension after it, do reveal a different actuarial balance when we extend the time horizon. As we will discuss later on, the main sources of the differences are implicit in the pension calculation formula, which implies an actuarial premium to those who retire early (since the pension benefit is linked to seniority, not to age); and to those with highly increasing wage profiles (since the pension benefit is linked to end of career wages, not to lifetime ones).

The last strategy, followed by Borella and Coda Moscarola (2006, 2009), is that of building synthetic careers on which to measure the actuarial balances. They fit models of labour market entry, unemployment and wages, and use the parameter estimates to randomly draw the careers of cohorts of workers from 1945 onwards. Considering retirement at eligibility, they estimate a strong progressivity for the PAYG system, then redistribution diminishes and approaches zero at regime. Switching to a behavioural model with retirement choices the results are confirmed. Here, the limit rests in the use of synthetic careers instead of actual ones. While artificial data may be viable for comparing different policy regimes/cohorts with each other, to convert relative estimates into absolute ones requires a population which closely reproduces the actual careers developing in the labour market.

As we briefly mentioned, this is a demanding task, mostly due to a scant data supply. In a sense, the real challenge when evaluating the actuarial fairness for retirees is to have realistic projections about past careers rather than future ones. Let us consider, as a limit, a situation in which we have a cross section of just-retired individuals. What we need to project their future pension benefits are (typically) simple pension updating rules and good estimates of a few demographic events. But what if we want to compare them with the contributions paid during their life? We have to backward microsimulate their careers back to labour market entry, which is dramatically more demanding. A common situation is a mixed one, in which we have panel data, but only for a career part, so that the issue of having a realistic representation of work trajectories remains a challenging and sensitive one.

The aim of our chapter is tackle this issue, testing several methods to backward simulate work careers to produce as realistic as possible lifetime career patterns in Italy; then to exploit this population and assess, at the individual level, who are the winners and losers under current pension regime and, at the aggregate one, the redistributive character of the system.

A bit surprisingly, with respect to some of the evidence we just reviewed (and a bit worryingly for the cohorts now retiring in Italy), it comes out that the current regime is regressive: it redistributes from poor to rich. The reason is that the career effects completely offset the progressivity of the pension calculation and updating rules. This is not unique in the literature. In two companion studies, Coronado et al. (1999, 2011) arrive at similar conclusions about the US social security system plus some reform proposals of it. They employ the wider notion of income potential, to take into account the value of leisure and home production, and use mortality rates which differ by income, both factors implying a redistribution in favour of the rich. If we buy their qualitative result, our estimates should be considered an upper bound of an even more negative redistribution.

The rest of the chapter is organized as follows. Section 1 details the redistributive mechanisms of current system. Section 2 describes the microsimulation: how we simulate careers back to labour market entry and forward up to retirement. Section 3 presents results and sensitivity analysis. The last section draws our concluding remarks.

The (Changing) Redistribution in the Italian Pension System

The current system is a patchwork of two decades of reforms, which can best be described starting from the redistributive mechanisms of the PAYG regime, since they are, though with a decreasing weight, still active today; and then describing how the reforms modified them.[1]

The Redistribution in the Books

The PAYG regime implemented progressivity mainly with a Minimum Pension Benefit (MBP), in the pension calculation formula and in the pension indexation formula.

The pension calculation applies a typical defined benefit formula. Whatever the contributions paid by a worker during her career, the pension P is equal to:

(1) $P = \alpha\, S\, Y_t$

where α is the accrual rate, S is the seniority (with a maximum of 40) and Y_t is the average of last five years' earnings at final year values (the so called 'pensionable income'):

(2) $Y_t = \sum_{i=0}^{4} Y_{t-i} \prod_{j=1}^{i} \left(1 + \pi_{t-j}\right) / 5$

where π_t is a price index at time t. Progressivity depends on the accrual rate α, which is decreasing in pensionable income. Its base value is 2 per cent, leading to pensions up to 80 per cent of last incomes for long-career workers. For pensionable incomes above the so-called 'pensionable ceiling' (in 2010, €42.364 yearly), the accrual rate decreases as in Table 8.1.

Table 8.1   The decreasing annual accrual rate

Pensionable earnings brackets	After 1998 (Law 66/88)	After 1992 (Law 503/92)
0 to pensionable ceiling (PC)	2	2
PC to 1.33*PC	1.5	1.6
1.33*PC to 1.66*PC	1.25	1.35
1.66*PC to 1.90*PC	1	1.1
1.90*PC and over	1	0.9

After retirement a further redistribution is put in place by the incomplete price-indexation of benefits for the part exceeding two times the MPB. The details have been modified several times: Table 8.2 displays the rules in force in the years we

---

1   Here and in what follows we focus on private sector employees only and limit the review to redistributive features.

will study. As an example, the amount exceeding five times the MPB is currently updated at 75 per cent of the inflation rate.

Table 8.2　　Evolution in the incomplete price-indexation scheme

Pension benefit	1983–1996 (Law 730/83)	1997–1999 (Law 449/97)	2000–2006 (Law 338/00)	2007 on (Law 127/07)
0 to 2*MPB	1	1	1	1
2*MPB to 3*MPB	0.9	0.9	1	1
3*MPB to 5*MPB	0.75	0.75	0.9	1
5*MPB and over	0.75	0	0.75	0.75

The Redistribution in Action

Formulas (1)–(2) actually imply a further redistribution with respect to actuarial fairness. On the one hand, in (1) there is no consideration of age or gender. Concerning gender, the higher life expectancy of women implies that on average they receive benefits for a longer period with respect to men. The overall impact of this is towards progressivity, as we argue in a companion essay, to which we refer the interested reader for a discussion of the gender aspect (Leombruni and Mosca 2012). Concerning age, those who start working earlier may retire, *ceteris paribus*, at a younger age with no penalty in the benefit: they too receive an actuarial premium. The sign of this redistribution cannot be stated *a priori*, since it rests on the empirical relation between age at retirement and lifetime income.

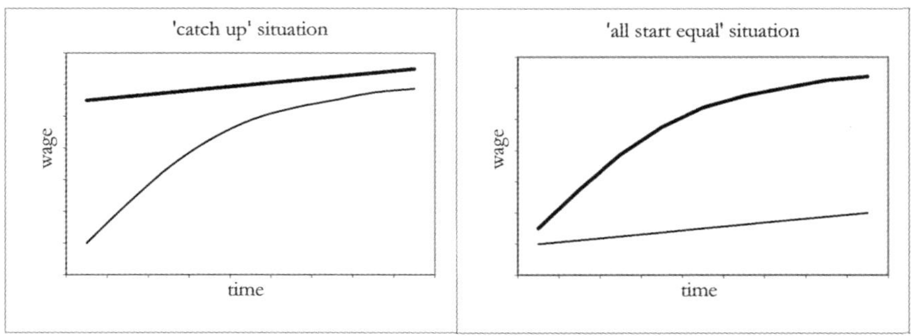

Figure 8.1　　Career profiles at different wage levels

Further, computing pensionable income using end of career wages implies a premium for those with an increasing wage profile. For what concerns redistribution, again, all depends on the empirical relation between wage profiles and life income levels. We may envisage two opposite examples. In Figure 8.1, panel 1, a 'catch up' situation is depicted: it is lower income workers who have steeper wage profiles, but at career end average wages are similar and also pensions will be. Lower income workers are receiving a transfer from higher income ones (positive redistribution). In the opposite 'all start equal' situation (panel 2) higher wage growth workers benefit from a gap in pensionable income which is higher than the gap in lifetime incomes: redistribution is negative. The sign of redistribution then depends on whether careers are closer to a 'catch up' or an 'all start equal' situation.

The Path to Neutrality

The Amato Law did not change the pension calculation formula (1), though it slightly modified the gradient of the accrual rate (see Table 8.1, column 2). Conversely, it addressed the potentially negative redistribution implied by the dynamic career effect, extending to the entire working life the time window over which to compute pensionable incomes. A transition phase was designed, which applies *pro quota* to all workers who are going to retire up to the 2020s, where the time window is progressively extended to 15 (25) years for workers with a seniority higher (lower) than 15 years at the time of the reform.

The Dini Law went further, introducing the principle of actuarial neutrality in the pension calculation formula, which depends only on contributions paid and age at retirement:

$$(3) \qquad P = \delta_{age} \, M$$

where M are accrued contributions, that is the total contributions paid during the working life capitalized at nominal GDP growth rate; while δ_{age} is an age-specific annuity rate which converts M into an actuarially fair benefit. In this way, both the early retirement and dynamic career effects are cancelled. About other sources of redistribution, note that δ_{age} is gender-independent, and that the MPB, although reformed, has not been cancelled.

Again, a long transition was designed: the new regime applies to workers who started working after 1995; it applies *pro quota* to those below 18 years of seniority at 1995; the others are untouched. Summing up, the PAYG regime comprised six redistribution sources:

a. The minimum pension benefit (+);
b. A decreasing accrual rate (+);
c. A partial inflation-indexation for high wages (+);
d. An early retirement effect (+/–, according to prevailing career patterns);
e. A dynamic career effect (+/–, according to prevailing career patterns).

After the reforms, sources a) and c) are still in place, while b), d) and e) have been cancelled, though in a very gradual way. Actually, for all workers who will retire up to 2020 a large part of the pension will reflect all the above effects, so that the redistributive character of the system crucially depends on the sign and size of career effects d) and e).

The Microsimulation Model

The model we built may be defined as a closed population, backward-forward dynamic ageing model without behavioural responses. Our first effort has been that of building a base population made up as much as possible by historical data. We ended up with a database tracking careers from 1975 on, for a representative sample of individuals who retired in 1996–2004. In order to compare contributions paid and benefits received, and in turn to measure redistribution, the missing information we needed to simulate were the past careers of individuals, back to their labour market entry; the future pension rents, updating the pension benefit observed at retirement; a counterfactual neutral rent.

Before getting into details, let us clarify why we do not model behavioural responses. The point is that the actuarially neutral counterfactual we are interested in is an accounting one, not a policy alternative. In other words, we are not asking 'what would happen if individuals faced a neutral system?' In this case, there would plausibly be modifications in the retirement decisions, and the two rents (the factual and the neutral one) would not be comparable with each other, since they would reflect different work career realizations. Our question is an accounting one: 'given actual careers and retirement decisions, what is the actuarial balance of individuals?' This is what we need to assess whether those earning an actuarial premium are on average richer or poorer with respect to those suffering an actuarial loss – that is, what is the sign and size of the redistribution put in place by the system?[2]

In the following, we describe the baseline population we built; then how we backward simulated careers and contributions, and finally how we forward simulated pension careers.[3]

The Baseline Population

We used as a main source the *Work Histories Italian Panel* (WHIP), a longitudinal database developed by the University of Torino with the National Social Security

---

2 An example may help. Assume an individual retired at 60 years old, receiving a benefit of 100, while a neutral rent would have been 80: s/he is receiving an actuarial premium of 20. Assume that, when faced with the neutral rule, s/he would have retired later in order to achieve again a benefit of 100. If we make the computations using the behavioural counterfactual instead of the accounting one, we would mistakenly measure a null actuarial premium.

3 The simulation has been implemented using the Sas® System for the backward simulation of careers, and Statistics Canada's ModGen (Model Generator), to forward simulate pensions under different scenarios.

Administration (INPS), out of a 7 per cent sample of INPS's archives. For each individual, the work career in the private sector is tracked (dependent employment, quasi-dependent work, self-employment activities as artisan and traders), plus retirement and other social security provisions.[4]

From WHIP we selected the employees who retired in 1996–2004, excluding those without a direct transition from work to pension (we allowed a delay of nine months). The exclusion deserves a brief discussion. Actually, bumpy transitions to pension are common in Italy, with periods before retirement spent in various unemployment and partial unemployment benefit schemes (Contini and Leombruni 2006). These measures do redistribute resources, too, we may presume in a progressive way – e.g. temporary layoff contributions are proportional to wage, while the benefits have a ceiling. But also in this case there are countervailing factors – e.g. precarious workers (who on average have lower wages) have a lower probability of being eligible for many schemes, so that they often pay contributions but seldom receive benefits (Leombruni et al. 2012, Banca d'Italia 2011). What the balance is between all factors has not been assessed in the literature yet, so that the inclusion of these workers would confound our results in a difficult-to-interpret way, and shift our focus from the progressivity of the pension system to that of the overall welfare state.

An important limitation of the data is that the reference period, 1985–2004, covers just up to half of careers. As a first, partial solution, we were able to link sampled individuals to the 'Contribution Account' (CA) file, which summarizes all contributions paid from 1973 on, plus information on seniority accrued before 1973. The CA archive is less detailed than WHIP and uses different codes and definitions, but we were able to integrate the two sources, obtaining data on work episodes and wages from 1975 up to retirement (the years 1973 and 1974 being affected by a severe missing data problem on wages).

Table 8.3   Sample description

	1996	1997	1998	1999	2000	2001	2002	2003	2004
N. obs.	901	940	951	877	668	886	955	944	988
% female	21.9	19.6	22.8	22.0	21.1	22.9	22.3	25.6	29.4
Avg age at market entry	19.5	20.3	19.0	18.9	19.8	19.7	19.5	19.7	19.7
Avg age at retirement	56.2	56.9	55.9	56.2	57.0	56.9	57.0	57.5	57.2
Avg pension at retirement	1,449	1,561	1,495	1,522	1,509	1,500	1,415	1,434	1,475
Share of career not observed	41.0	38.2	36.3	34.6	31.7	29.4	28.3	25.5	22.2

Note: The share of work career not observed is computed comparing the average total seniority (in weeks) recorded in the retirement file and the number of worked week observed in the period 1975–2004.

---

4   For further information on the database see http://www.laboratoriorevelli.it/whip.

The baseline population includes nine cohorts of about 900 workers yearly (Table 8.3). They are mostly men, whose career patterns do not change much in the years considered: labour market entry is on average at 19–20 years old, retirement after an average 36 years, at 56–7. Just a slight increase in the age at retirement is recorded, the reforms notwithstanding. A point to be stressed for our aims is that the historical data cover a large part of the careers of those retiring in 2004, so that we will need to simulate only about 20 per cent of them. The oldest cohorts, on the contrary, have up to 40 per cent of the career falling out of our baseline.

In the baseline, we are able to check how the career features relevant for redistribution empirically realize. Figure 8.2, panel a, shows the wage profile for 'rich' ('poor') workers, defined as belonging to the first (fourth) quartile of the wage distribution at career end. It is clear that wages in Italy – at least in those years – follow an 'all start equal' scheme, with wage differentials opening up at prime ages and further widening at career end. This means that we expect the dynamic career effect on redistribution to be negative and relevant.

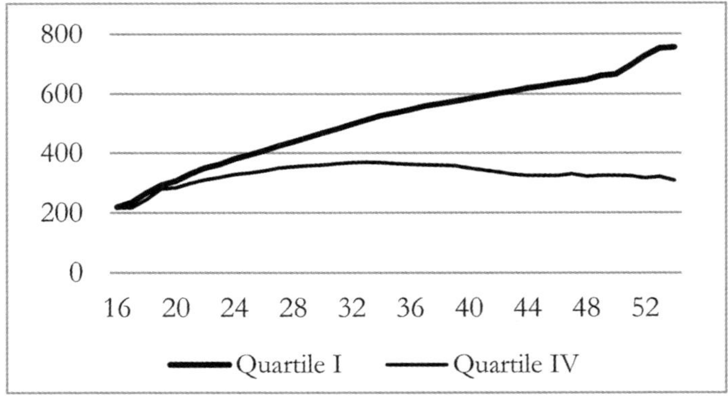

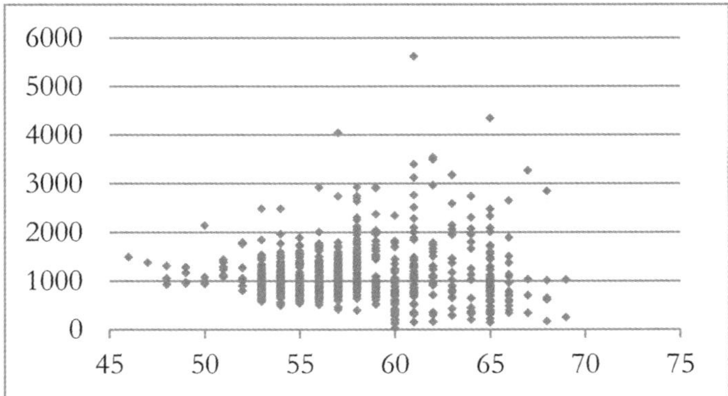

Figure 8.2　　Career features with an impact on empirical redistribution

Regarding the early retirement effect, the relation between lifetime incomes – as measured by the neutral rent (see below) – and age at retirement, is not as clear cut (panel b): the relation is positive and significant, but quite small in size (the correlation index is 0.09). Moreover, at ages 60 and over, we notice a highly dispersed distribution. These are ages when those not eligible for the seniority pensions can apply for the old-age one. It is clear that there are many workers with very low pension rights among them, whose pension is topped up to the MPB. So the disadvantage in retiring later, due to the shorter horizon in which a pension will be received, involves a large group of poorer workers profiting of a high positive redistribution. This means that we cannot assess *a priori* what the balance is between the various factors, and hence whether the early retirement effect is progressive.

Backward Simulation

To simulate individuals' careers from 1975 back to labour market entry we considered separately employment and wage. About the former, the exact number of worked weeks prior to 1975 is actually known, since it can be derived subtracting from total seniority, which is recorded in the retirement file, the sum of all worked weeks observed from 1975 on. Moreover, the summary information on seniority recorded in the AC file is sufficient to locate worked weeks on a yearly basis for most workers. In the cases where the AC revealed undercoverage issues, we did not impute worked weeks, nor wages, but we estimated accrued contributions by inflating the observed ones with a correcting factor proportional to the length of the missing career, estimated on individuals with no missing data.

For the simulation of the weekly wage, on the contrary, we could rely on no individual information, nor on aggregate statistics to align our estimates: the only statistic which can be used as a yardstick to simulate individual wage dynamics is the GDP growth. Our choice has been to take as given the GDP growth (which is known); to model how *average* wages follow the GDP growth; to model how *individual* wages follow a different story with respect to the average. In formulas, we decomposed individual wage growth as in the following:

$$(4) \qquad w_{i,t+1} = w_{i,t} \cdot \left(1 + \overset{\bullet}{w}_{i,t}\right) = w_{i,t} \cdot \left(1 + \overset{\bullet}{GDP}_t + \overline{\Delta}_t + \Delta^2_{i,t}\right)$$

where w_{it} is the weekly wage of individual i at time t; $\overset{\bullet}{GDP}_t$ is the gross domestic product growth rate; $\overline{\Delta}_t$ is the difference between GDP growth and the average wage growth; $\Delta^2_{i,t}$ is the difference between $\overline{\Delta}_t$ and the individual wage growth. Actually, although we model individual differentials around an average wage growth, the flows in-out of employment from one year to the other imply a departure from the average. This suggests for an ex-post alignment to the predicted $\overline{\Delta}_t$.

To model the average wage differentials $\overline{\Delta}_t$ we fitted an AR(2) model in the period 1975–2004 and backward projected it prior to 1975. To model individual wage growth differentials we considered three strategies:

- (baseline) We assumed no heterogeneity in individuals' growth rate ($\Delta_{i,t}^2 = 0$);
- (parametric) We modelled it with a random effect model with an AR(1) error term;
- (non parametric) We imputed it using two variants of propensity score matching.

We tested these strategies in the years 1975–79, masking the known, true information about wages and simulating it back, using the years from 1980 on to estimate the models. To compare the strategies we computed several characteristics of the cross sectional wages in the year farthest from the known data (1975), plus the Gini index on lifetime incomes in the imputed period, since this is our key statistic in the computation of lifetime redistribution. For the sake of comparing the relative performance of models 1–3 only, we used known values of $\overline{\Delta}_t$ instead of predicted ones.

The baseline, interestingly enough, is a good alternative (Table 8.4, column 2). By definition, it keeps the original shape of the distribution – which, as it seems, does not change much in five years. At the opposite site of the ranking, the parametric way was the worst performing (Table 8.4, column 5). The specification considered, that we derived from Borella and Coda Moscarola (2006), ends up in predicting wages whose cross-sectional distribution has a shape dramatically different from the true one. The only statistic on which it reproduces data relatively well is the variability in the individual wage growth rates. Most importantly, the Gini index is 1.2 percentage points higher with respect to the true one. This means that wages are more unequally distributed than in the factual scenario, and the comparison with the Gini index on factual pensions will tend to overestimate redistribution. We tested many other parametric models and specifications, but we were never able to predict a significant share of variance. This is due both to the (known) high importance of idiosyncratic factors in individual wage dynamics, and to the fact that we had to rely on very few covariates. As a consequence, the stochastic term draws tend to overwhelm the dynamics in the predicted values, opening up the distribution and 'normalizing' its shape.

Actually, if the aim is not that of simulating behaviours but just to reproduce a historical dynamic, the need for a parametric and/or structural model is less pressing, and a purely statistical approach may be optimal. The one we tried is propensity score matching used as a donor/receiver imputation technique (Rosenbaum and Rubin 1983, Chen and Shao 2000). Receivers are those entered in the market prior to the first year in which we have data – e.g. prior to 1980 in our test sample. Donors are those entered in the market from 1980 on, for whom we have data about the entire career. The idea is to match donors and receivers

Table 8.4　　A comparison of different simulation techniques of individual wages

		Real data	$\Delta_{i,t}^2 = 0$	PSM – Kernel	PSM – Mahalanobis	Parametric imputation
Weekly wages, year 1975	Mean	376.67	376.67	376.67	376.67	376.67
	Median	345.24	349.13	346.90	355.53	312.90
	Std	170.78	145.07	144.92	131.10	268.25
	Kurtosis	15.31	17.92	16.98	7.67	26.90
	Skewness	2.51	2.63	2.63	1.81	3.34
	Std Individual Δ	0.360	0	0.001	0.146	0.428
Gini index on lifetime incomes 1975–2004		26.7	26.7	26.7	26.4	27.9

with similar wage profiles in the ages in which the career is observed for both. For instance, if the receiver entered in 1976 at the age of 20, wages are observed from when s/he is 24 on. We then look for a donor who started working from 1980 on, with similar characteristics and a similar wage profile for the ages from 24 on. Once a donor is found, its information for the ages 20 to 24 is used to impute wages to the receiver.

We tested two types of PSM imputation: nearest Mahalanobis neighbour within a propensity score caliper; and kernel matching with Epanechnikov weights. The former has a performance almost as bad as with the parametric model (Table 8.4, column 4). The reasons are similar. Although, in a non parametric way, the information used to look for a donor is roughly the same as the parametric model, and we cannot expect to explain a dramatically larger variance share. Moreover, taking a value by a single neighbour is equivalent to imputing both an expected value and a random draw from the error, so that also in this case the shape of the distribution (and the Gini index) tends to rapidly deteriorate. Kernel matching, on the contrary, tends to average out idiosyncratic components, keeping the original shape of the distribution as correctly as when using a unique wage growth rate (Table 8.4, column 3). On most statistics it reaches a better, or very similar performance with respect to the baseline, displaying a good mix of predictive power on the statistics considered.

Forward Simulation

The forward simulation – which is usually the added value in a microsimulation – in our case is almost an arithmetic one, since at time zero we already have completed work careers, the actual retirement choices of individuals, plus information about the (factual) pension received. What we simulate is the following:

- Counterfactual neutral pension. As a neutral benchmark we compute the benefit using the Dini rule without the topping up to MPB. This means that we take the present value of lifetime contributions and convert it into an annuity using the Dini, age-dependent transformation coefficient, which is a good approximation of a neutral system (Belloni and Maccheroni 2006).
- Pension updating. We consider the partial indexation tables reported in Table 8.2, under three inflation scenarios, at 1.7 per cent, 0.7 per cent and 3.2 per cent, which are respectively the last recorded pre-crisis value, and the lowest/highest levels recorded during the crisis.
- Mortality. We consider a fixed horizon, since we want our results net of the redistribution due to random variations in mortality. For the sake of consistency, we used the life expectancies implicit in the Dini rule, which are in the range 83–5 depending on age at retirement (but not on sex). These are a sort-of average of male and female life expectancies and also take into account survivors' rents.

Results

We first present our best estimates, based on the cohort of workers who retired in 2004 – since this is the one granting the most realistic representation of work careers – using the historical partial indexation rules (Table 8.2), the intermediate inflation scenario (at 1.7 per cent), and a discount rate equal to inflation.[5]

Figure 8.3 shows our lower bound estimates of the actuarial premium received by pensioners at retirement – as measured by the difference between factual and neutral rent – and its relation to lifetime income – as measured by the neutral rent. The first, striking evidence is about the generosity of current system, still 12 years after the first reform: almost everybody is receiving a positive actuarial premium. The worker located at the median neutral pension (which is €960 gross monthly) receives a premium of €368, that is, s/he is receiving a factual pension 38 per cent higher with respect to a neutral rent.

The second evidence is the gradient of the premium. At the bottom of the distribution we find individuals whose benefit is topped-up at the MPB (the downward-sloping dots cloud at the left of the figure), for whom the gradient is negative: the lower their neutral rent, the higher the premium they receive. Despite this, the overall gradient shown in the figure with a 2 degree polynomial interpolation is clearly increasing in income. The gradient is particularly steep about the middle of the distribution, while it tends to vanish at high lifetime incomes, where the redistribution operated by the pension calculation formula is stronger.

---

5   We also tested other values for the discount factor, which does not appear to be a key parameter. Results are available upon request.

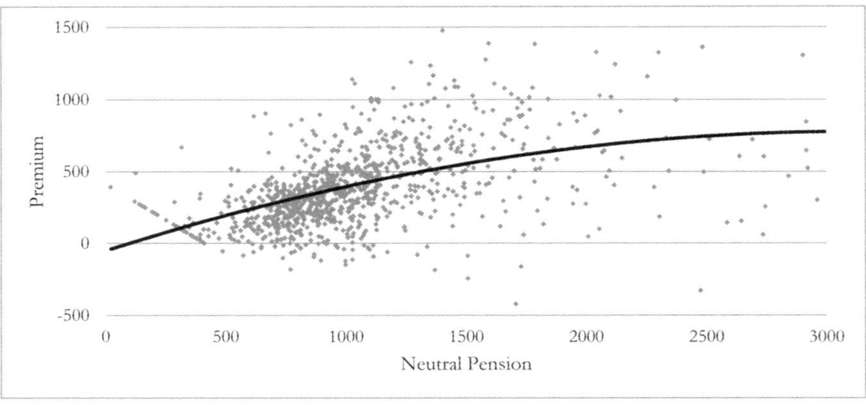

Figure 8.3   Actuarial premia versus lifetime income levels, workers retired in 2004

Table 8.5 delivers similar information, summarized by the Reynolds-Smolensky (RS) index of redistribution (Reynolds and Smolensky 1977). The index is the difference between the Gini coefficient computed on the neutral rent and on the factual one. If the inequality in factual pension distribution is lower than the inequality in the neutral rent one the index will be positive, saying that the pension system is redistributing resources to the poor.

In our case, the RS index measured at retirement is –1.38, that is, redistribution is from the poor to the rich (Table 8.5, first row). The table presents also a decomposition of the index into three parts (Lambert and Aronson 1993): the vertical component measures 'good' redistribution, due to the different treatment (in terms of factual pension) of different workers (in terms of lifetime incomes); the horizontal component measures 'bad' redistribution, due to the different treatment of equals; the third component, also classified as 'bad' redistribution, is the effect of reranking. As it seems, the vertical component – that we associate primarily to the progressivity in the pension calculation formula – is not negligible, but is offset by the 'bad' components.

Looking at the present value of all pension benefits up to mortality two further redistributions take place, due to the early retirement effect and the partial price-indexation of higher pensions. The latter effect is certainly positive but small in size, since the price indexation in rule is mainly the one of Law 127/07, which is the least redistributive. Early retirement, as it seems, ends up in a further negative impact on redistribution, the RS index approaching –2, a decrease mostly due to the strong increase in the re-ranking component.

The results presented may be sensitive to sampling error (we are dealing with cohorts of about 1,000 individuals); to the model adopted to backward simulate careers; and to the choice of inflation and partial indexation scenarios. As a sensitivity analysis, we built what can be considered an upper bound to the RS

Table 8.5   The redistributive character of the pension system, workers retired in 2004

	Rs index	Vertical component	Horizontal component	Reranking
At retirement	−1.38	0.46	−0.17	−1.67
Over the lifetime	−1.97	1.26	−0.24	−2.99

Notes: The RS index over the lifetime uses a fixed horizon at 83–5 years depending on age at retirement, an 1.7% inflation rate and the indexation scheme of L.388/00 until 2007 and of L. 127/07 afterwards. Values are x100.

index of redistribution, obtained measuring the Gini index on the neutral rents computed only on contributions from 1974 on. Recall, from Figure 8.2, that there is a neat tendency to the opening up of the wage distribution with age: it is for ages 25–30 and more that large wage differences start to be noticed. This is confirmed by the Gini index, that, when computed on lifetime incomes excluding workers below 30, raises from 26.7 to 28.4. This means that if we limit the calculation of neutral rents on real data contributions observed from 1974 on, and measure the Gini index on them, we obtain an upper bound for inequality in lifetime contributions and in turn for the RS index.

Figure 8.4, left panel, shows the RS index upper bound, with bootstrapped confidence intervals, computed for the cohorts of retirees in 1996–2004. The first thing to note is that sampling error is sizeable: the same index computed on a very close, independent sample shows noticeable differences, with a confidence interval width of about 2 RS points. The second is that the younger the cohorts, the higher the RS index: this is coherent with the increasing inequality we measure in lifetime contributions as the censoring of initial career gets longer. The third is that the RS index upper bound is either negative or not statistically different from zero, which give robustness to our best estimate of a negative redistribution.

In Figure 8.4, right panel, we turn again to the RS index computed on entire work careers, a (decreasing in time) part of which has been simulated, considering several choices for the backward simulation strategy. To avoid introducing a time bias due to the different partial indexation schemes, we only use Law 127/2007, which is the least redistributive. Also in this case, the first two years – particularly in our best estimate – have a higher RS index. Besides sampling error, and, again, a statistical artifact due to the larger share of simulated career, there are no economic interpretations for this dynamic; on the contrary, the increasing share of the neutral *quota* would imply a tendency towards no redistribution. The main result, however, that of a negative RS index, is largely confirmed.

A final point we want to stress is the big role played by the partial indexation schemes. Table 8.6 reports their impact on redistribution under different inflation scenarios. The inflation gradient is the expected one: the higher the inflation rate, the higher the redistributive impact. Indeed, also, the ranking is confirmed: the most redistributive scheme is to be found in the Law 449/97 (column a), the least

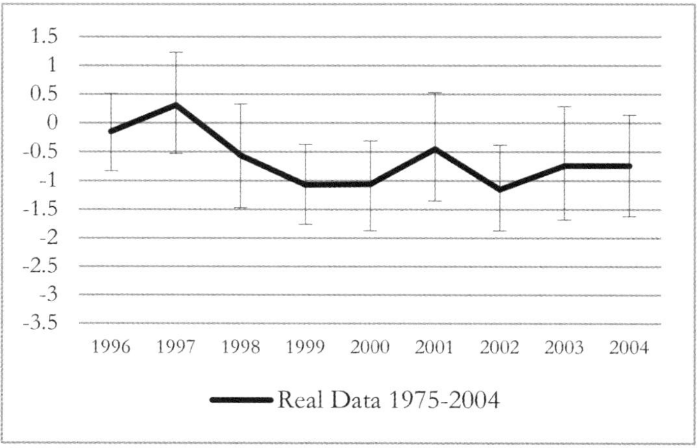

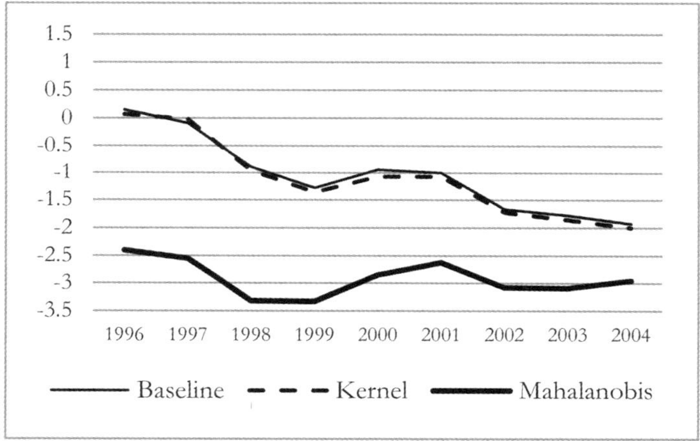

Figure 8.4   The RS index of redistribution. Upper bound with bootstrapped CI, and values computed on partially simulated data, years 1996–2004

one in the Law 127/07 (column c). What is to be stressed is that the delta in the RS index when switching from one scheme to the other is similar or much larger than the distance of the actual system from a neutral one, depending on the inflation scenario. (Remember that we measured an RS index of –1.34 at retirement, see Table 8.5.) In other words, the change in the redistributive character of social security entailed by the Dini reform introducing a contributive formula can be (and has temporarily been) almost undone by a fine-tuning in the price-indexation scheme; a policy action which has rarely been perceived as topical in the public debate.

Table 8.6   **The RS index of redistribution under different inflation and price-indexation scenarios, workers retired in 2004**

	Incomplete Price-Indexation Scheme			
Inflation scenario	1997–1999 (a)	2000–2006 (b)	2007 on (c)	(a–c)
3.2%	−0.26	−1.57	−1.84	1.58
1.7%	−1.05	−1.85	−2.00	0.95
0.7%	−1.69	−2.06	−2.13	0.44

Notes: The RS index calculated over the lifetime considers a fixed horizon mortality at 83–5 years depending on the age at retirement. Note that the values reported in table are centuplicated values.

Concluding Remarks

There is a rising concern in many countries about income inequality and poverty among the elderly, and about a plausible future worsening of the situation due to the transition from old, fully public and generous pension systems, towards new rules where more sustainable and neutral principles are implemented.

Our main policy conclusion, about Italy, is somewhat cross-current: the future is OK; what we should be worried about is the current redistribution put in place by the pension system, which is still moving a great amount of resources between generations, and, within generations, is redistributing from the poor to the rich. Indeed, while the internal validity of our results can rely on a most accurate reconstruction of work careers from labour market entry to retirement, their external validity is limited by the fact that we analysed cohorts of workers who retired up to the mid-2000s. Since we are in the middle of a (very long) transition towards an actuarially neutral system, we may presume that this negative redistribution, when not ceased, is today largely reduced. What should be stressed is that, while the policy maker has been very convinced in ruling a future, well designed system, it has been very undetermined in shaping an effective path to it. Currently, a further reform has been delivered slightly accelerating the transition, the final year of which, however, is still set at the mid-2030s.

A second policy remark has to do with the role of pension updating rules. Although seldom discussed in policy and scientific debate, they provide for a large part of the redistributive features of the system. The impact on the RS index comparing the 1997 and 2007 reforms in the partial indexation are larger in size than the impact on redistribution due to the switch to a neutral system.

We left aside some relevant aspects, relating other welfare measures, gender issues and mortality differentials. About the former, we did not consider workers who at career end had long spells of unemployment, since in the years under consideration they are typically covered by long-term income support measures. While this is a limitation of our results, these are workers who actually benefit (and contribute) to a plurality of social security schemes. Keeping our focus on the functioning of the pension system only, we view our results as a step towards the evaluation of the overall redistributive character of the welfare system. About gender, a general point is that the theme has not been touched by the reforms we examined. Both the PAYG and the Dini formula, as an example, do not consider gender differences in life expectancies. However, mortality differentials are not the only relevant issue on the theme. We take the gender view in a companion essay, where we show that taking into account all features of current pension system functioning, women on average benefit from a positive redistribution, which partly mitigates the career gaps realized in the labour market (Leombruni and Mosca 2012). This means that the first round effect of the transition to neutrality could be that of widening gender differentials in retirement, with a particular concern about the theme of lone mothers.

Finally, we left aside other mortality differences affecting redistribution, the most relevant of which are those by education and socio-economic status, as has been stressed in the quoted studies by Coronado et al. (1999, 2011) and, about Italy, in Mazzaferro et al. (2012), Leombruni et al. (2010) and Belloni and Maccheroni (2006). They are modifiers of redistribution that have an impact also on the Dini regime, which could possibly reveal a regressive character, too. Both issues need the extension of the model to future cohorts of retirees, and, in turn, the modelling of retirement and mortality behaviours, presently not implemented in our model. We leave these aspects to a future extension of our research.

References

Arza, C. 2008. Changing European welfare: the new distributional principles of pension policy, in C. Arza and M. Kohli (eds), *Pension Reform in Europe: Politics, Policies and Outcome*. New York: Routledge, 109–31.

Banca d'Italia. 2011. *Relazione annuale 2010*. Roma.

Belloni, M. and Maccheroni, C. 2006. Actuarial Neutrality when Longevity Increase: An Application to the Italian Pension System. CeRP Working Paper, 47/06.

Borella, M. and Coda Moscarola, F. 2006. Distributive properties of pensions systems: a simulation of the Italian transition from defined benefit to notional defined contribution. *Giornale degli Economisti e Annali di Economia*, 65(1), 95–126.

Borella, M. and Coda Moscarola, F. 2009. Microsimulation of Pension Reforms: Behavioural *vs* Nonbehavioural. *Journal of Pension Economics and Finance*, 9, 583–607.

Castellino, O. 1995. Redistribution Between and Within Generations in the Italian Social Security System. *Ricerche Economiche*, 49, 317–27.

Chen, J. and Shao, J. 2000. Nearest neighbor imputation for survey data. *Journal of Official Statistics*, 16, 113–32.

Contini, B. and Leombruni, R. 2006. From Work to Retirement: a Tale of Bumpy Routes. *Review of Political Economy*, 18(3), 359–78.

Coronado J.L., D. Fullerton and T. Glass. 1999. Distributional Impacts of Proposed Changes to the Social Security System. *Tax Policy and the Economy*, 13, 149–86.

Coronado J.L., D. Fullerton and T. Glass. 2011. The Progressivity of Social Security. The B.E. *Journal of Economic Analysis & Policy*, 11(1), 70.

Creedy, J. 1995. Lifetime Versus Annual Income Distribution. *Working Papers – The University of Melbourne Department of Economics*, 478.

Dekkers, G., H. Buslei, M. Cozzolino, R. Desmet, J. Geyer, D. Hofmann, M. Raitano, V. Steiner, P. Tanda, S. Tedeschi and F. Verschueren. 2009. What are the consequences of the AWG-projections for the adequacy of social security pensions? ENEPRI Research Report, No. 65.

Harding, A. 1993. *Lifetime Income Distribution and Redistribution: Applications of a Dynamic Cohort Microsimulation Model*. Amsterdam: North Holland.

Ierini, V., Marenzi, A., Nobile, L. and Omtzigt P. 2002. Sistema pensionistico e distorsioni redistributive. Working Paper, Università dell'Insubria, Facoltà di Economia, 2002/36.

Lambert, P.J. and Aronson, R.J. 1993. Inequality decomposition analysis and the Gini coefficient revisited. *The Economic Journal*, 103, 1221–7.

Leombruni, R. and Mosca, M. 2012. Le système de retraite italien compense-t-il les inégalités hommes-femmes sur le marché du travail? (The gender gap in Italy. Does the pension system countervail labour market outcomes?) *Retraite et société*, 2012/2, 139–63.

Leombruni, R., Paggiaro, A. and Trivellato, U. 2012. Per un Pugno di Euro. Storie di Ordinaria Disoccupazione (For a fistful of euros. Histories of ordinary unemployment). *Politica Economica*, XXVIII(1), 5–47.

Leombruni, R., Richiardi, M., Demaria, M. and Costa G. 2010. Aspettative di vita, lavori usuranti ed equità del sistema previdenziale. Prime evidenze dal *Work Histories Italian Panel* (Life Expectancy, Wearing Working Conditions and Social Security Fairness. Evidence from the Work Histories Italian Panel), *Epidemiologia e Prevenzione*, 34(4), 150–58.

Mazzaferro, C. and Morciano, M. 2011. Measuring Intra-Generational And Inter-Generational Redistribution In The Italian Old Age Pension System. MEF Working Paper No. 11, Department of the Treasury, Ministry of Economy and Finance, Rome.

Mazzaferro, C., Morciano, M. and Savegnago, M. 2012 Differential mortality and redistribution in the Italian notional defined contribution system. *Journal of Pension Economics and Finance*, 11(4), 500–530.

Nelissen, J.H.M. 1993. The Redistributive Impact of Social Security Schemes on Lifetime Labour Income. Report no. 22, Tilburg University.

Nelissen, J.H.M. 1998. Annual versus lifetime income redistribution by social security. *Journal of Public Economics*, 68(2), 223–49.

Reynolds, M. and Smolensky, E. 1977. Public expenditure, taxes, and the distribution of income: the United States, 1950, 1961, 1970. New York: Academic Press.

Romig, K. 2008. Social Security Reform: Possible Effects on the Elderly Poor and Mitigation Options. CRS Report for Congress 34433, Washington, DC.

Rosenbaum, P. and Rubin, D. 1983. The Central Role of the Propensity Score in Observational Studies for Causal Effects. *Biometrika*, 70, 41–50.

van Vliet, O., Been, J., Koen Caminada, K. and Goudswaard, K. 2011. Pension reform and income inequality among the elderly in 15 European countries. Department of Economics Research Memorandum 2011.03, Universiteit Leiden.

Chapter 9

Simulating Policy Alternatives for Public Pensions in Japan

Seiichi Inagaki

Introduction

The advent of a super-aged society unparalleled in the world is forecast for Japan in the near future due to the rapid progress of a declining fertility rate and an aging population. According to an estimate of the National Institute of Population and Social Security Research (Kaneko et al. 2008), the total fertility rate will stay at the current level of 1.26 or so in 2005, and will not rise in the future. It is far below the replacement level. The life expectancy will extend to 83.37 years from 78.53 years for males and to 90.07 years from 85.49 years for females. As a result, it is expected that the number of elderly people aged 65 years or older will increase from 25,760,000 (20.2 per cent) in 2005 to 36,670,000 people (31.8 per cent) in 2030. It is projected that there will be a great change to the co-resident of families of elderly people such as those living alone (excluding those institutionalized), which is expected to increase from 3,870,000 people to 7,170,000 people (National Institute of Population and Social Security Research 2008).

The public pension scheme in Japan is a two-tier system that consists of a flat-rate benefit called 'the basic pension' and an earnings-related benefit for regular employees (Employees' Pension Insurance). Since the public pension scheme in Japan is based on a social insurance system, and there exist a considerable number of persons who do not pay their premiums, we are concerned about the growing number of the elderly with low pension amounts. Moreover, the number of elderly people living alone, who can expect little private support from their children, will increase significantly.

Under these major changes in the social and economic structure of Japan, we are concerned about the adequacy and sustainability of the public pension scheme in Japan in the future. The 2004 pension reform focused on the sustainability. A ceiling for premiums[1] was set and a new scheme for adjusting benefits was introduced. This is because the conventional approach of raising premiums to maintain the level of benefits has sparked concern among younger generations about how high pension premiums will climb. The adjusting system is called a

---

1   The ceiling is 18.3 per cent of pensionable remuneration for the participants of Employees' Pension Insurance.

'macroeconomic slide system', which reduces the wage indexation and price indexation based on the decrease in the number of insured persons and the increase in life expectancy. The normal pensionable age was maintained at the age of 65. The government made the choice to reduce the pension benefits rather than raise the pensionable age since it is difficult to raise the retirement age. As a result, the financial sustainability was ensured under the basic scenario[2] but the level of benefits will be significantly reduced in real terms.

However, the discussion about the adequacy of the public pension scheme was very poor. The reform plan ensured the replacement rate of 50 per cent at age 65, newly awarded the pension, for a specific single-income couple[3] covered by Employees' Pension Insurance. The replacement rates of the benefit for single persons or double-income couples are generally lower than 50 per cent. Non-regular employed who are not covered by Employees' Pension Insurance will receive the basic pension only, and their benefit level[4] will be very low. The government emphasized the sustainability, and did not provide enough information on the adequacy.

At the same time, there are significant problems such as mismanaged pension records within the public pension scheme resulting in mistrust and causing a national debate on various issues such as introduction of a minimum guaranteed pension financed by tax. The report of the Pension Committee of the Social Security Council (2008) held on 29 September 2008, 'Viewpoints of the investigation of problems remaining after the revision in 2004', shows seven viewpoints, and the first of these raises the issue of the 'revision of pension benefits for the elderly with low pensions and low incomes'. There were differences in opinion on whether or not to introduce a minimum guaranteed pension, but there was no disagreement as to the importance of the first point regardless of each disputant's position on the solution.

What is the current status of elderly people with low pensions and low incomes and will the number of these elderly people increase in the future? Unfortunately, few results of simulations published by the government remain on the several model cases of family finances presently or at a matured stage, and they do not show the results of future estimates such as the distribution of pension amounts. Regarding this point, the interim report of the National Council for Social Security (2008) points out that 'it is difficult to conceive of a great increase in the number of people without pension benefits in the future; rather if the current rate of non-payments for the National Pension continues, a certain proportion (about 2%) of elderly people will be continually without a pension'.

---

2   It assumes intermediate fertility and intermediate economic assumption.

3   The husband is covered by Employees' Pension Insurance (category 2) from age 20 to 59, and the wife has always been dependent on him (category 3). See section 2 for the public pension scheme in Japan.

4   The average take-home pay for regular employees (male) in the year 2009 is 4,296,000 JPY ($48,175; €36,102). The full basic pension is 792,100 JPY ($8,883; €6,657), and its ratio to the take-home pay is only 18.4 per cent.

The purpose of this chapter is to show income distribution among the elderly using a dynamic microsimulation model for Japan, INAHSIM. This chapter then compares the percentage of the poor elderly in the population in order to evaluate income security functions for the elderly among several public pension reform proposals. Finally, it compares additional costs when the proposals are introduced in order to evaluate their financial feasibility.

Brief Overview of the Pension System in Japan

The public pension scheme in Japan was established in the 1960s, and it is a two-tier system that consists of a flat-rate benefit called 'basic pension' and an earnings-related benefit for regular employees. All people in Japan are covered by the basic pension, and are classified by their occupation. Regular employees are classified as category 2 subscribers, and are also covered by Employees' Pension Insurance or mutual-aid associations. Dependent spouses of category 2 subscribers are included in category 3 and others in category 1.

The amount of the basic pension is a flat-rate benefit of 792,100 JPY ($8,883; €6,657)[5] for 40 years of premium paid. A reduced pension is paid according to the number of premiums paid and credited. The normal pensionable age is 65, and an early pension is paid from age 60 to 64. The pension may be deferred until age 70. The reduction rate of the early pension is 0.5 per cent per month, and the increase rate of the deferred pension is 0.7 per cent per month.

Employees' Pension Insurance provides an earning-related benefit, which is 21.924 per cent of an average pensionable remuneration for 40 years of insured period. The normal pensionable age for those born after 1 April 1961 (male) or 1966 (female) is 65. The pensionable age for those born before that day is 60 to 64.

The benefits are automatically adjusted annually according to changes in the cost of living and take-home wages. However, in order to ensure the sustainability, the indexations are reduced by the 'macroeconomic slide system'. The reduction rate is about 1 per cent every year until the sustainability is ensured. According to the 2009 Actuarial Valuation (Ministry of Health, Labour and Welfare, Pension Bureau, Actuarial Division 2010), the reduction is expected to start at the fiscal year 2012[6] and to end at the fiscal year 2038 under the basic scenario.

The premium for category 1 subscribers was a flat rate of 15,100 JPY ($169; €127) per month in 2010. An exemption system of the premium is arranged for low-income earners, but their old-age pension will be reduced according to the exempt period as in formula (1). Since even the full amount of basic pension is not always enough for their old age, the reduced amount would make them very poor.

5　Exchange rates are $1=89.1750 JPY and €1=118.9951 as of 13 January 2013.

6　Since inflation rate was negative in 2012, the 'macroeconomic slide' was not applied.

In addition, a considerable number of people do not pay their premiums, and the growing number of the poor elderly is a matter of concern.

$$Pension = 792,100 \times \frac{[\text{premium paid period}] + [\text{exempted period}] \times 0.5}{480} \tag{1}$$

The premium of the basic pension for category 2 and 3 subscribers is included in the insured person's premium to Employees' Pension Insurance or the mutual-aid associations. The insurers transfer the premium to the basic pension programme. Since employers pay their employees' premium to the insurers, problems such as non-payment of premium do not arise as in the case of category 1 subscribers.

This scheme supposes that most employees are regular workers, and most category 1 subscribers are composed self-employed persons or farmers who do not have a fixed retirement age. It is also supposed that most men and women get married, the single-income family is common, and dependent spouses seldom get divorced. It is not necessary for the level of the basic pension to be high as long as these premises are valid. However, the social and economic structure of Japan has dramatically changed. The number of self-employed persons or farmers has decreased significantly, and many regular employees have been replaced by non-regular employees. As a result, the main component of category 1 subscribers has completely changed from self-employed persons to non-regular employees or the unemployed. In addition, the divorce rate has increased significantly. The premises of the current public pension scheme are no longer valid.

Outline of INAHSIM

Simulation Cycle

INAHSIM[7] is an abbreviation of the Integrated Analytical Model for Household Simulation, and is a dynamic microsimulation model for Japan. It was originally developed in the early 1980s as a household simulation model to accommodate Japan's society. In this model, life events are assumed to occur in annual cycles. The life events incorporated in this model are marriage, birth, death, divorce, international migration, change in health status, change in employment status, estimating earnings, determining pensions, young people leaving home, living with elderly parents, entering an institution, and payment of pension premium.

Key Life Events and Transition Probabilities

Transition probabilities for each life event are given in advance, and it is possible to take into account their future trends. In the assumptions of the baseline scenario, declining trends in first marriage rates and mortality rates are assumed. The future

---

7   Version 3.4 was used for this simulation. See Inagaki (2010a) for details.

trends in the transition probabilities of employment status are also taken in account. The other transition probabilities of the baseline scenario are assumed to continue in the future. Appendices A and B in the online appendix of this book summarize the transition probabilities.[8]

The key life events used in the simulation for the income distribution of the elderly are 'Living with elderly parents', 'Estimating earnings', and 'Determining pensions'.

The first event is living with elderly parents. When elderly people, who do not live with their children, become very old and need care, many children move in to take care of them. This is an important life event to secure the life of the elderly in Japan.

The second event is estimating earnings. Earnings are assumed to conform to a log-normal distribution by sex, age group and employment status. The earnings of each person are calculated by formula (2) using one's z-score. The z-score represents one's ability to earn money, and it is constant throughout one's life. The z-score is assumed to be determined at birth on the basis of one's parents' z-scores. An immigrant's z-score is assigned randomly at his/her entry. The z-scores of the initial population are estimated on the basis of their earnings in the year 2004 by sex, age group and employment status.

$$\text{Earnings} = \exp\left(Mean + SD \times [z - \text{score}]\right) \qquad (2)$$

The third event is determining pensions. The pensionable age for the basic pension is 65 years. The pensionable age for earnings-related benefits is statutorily fixed at 60–65 years and is specified by sex and year of birth. Early and deferred pensions are not considered. The pension amount is estimated on the basis of the pensioner's per cent rank, sex, subscription category and employment status at the age of 35, assuming the distribution of the newly awarded pension amounts. The per cent rank is equivalent to his/her z-score. The pension amount distributions under the current pension system are estimated using the Internet Survey on the Individual Records of Regular Pension Coverage Notice (Inagaki 2012).

It should be noted that individual heterogeneity in earnings is not fully taken into account since the z-score is fixed throughout one's life. Annual fluctuation in z-score is an issue in the future. However, the age-based remuneration system still exists in Japan, and correlation between wages and age is relatively strong.[9]

Regarding economic assumptions, the wage increase and the inflation rate are assumed to be zero. It means that all prices in the simulation results are 2004 prices. In terms of evaluating the income distribution, the effect of the economic assumptions, such as no economic growth, will be limited since people will generally receive

---

8   See http://www.microsimulation.org/resource-centre/new-pathways/.

9   For example, the rank correlation coefficients between ages 20–29 and 30–39 years, ages 30–39 and 40–49 years, and ages 40–49 and 50–59 years are 0.707, 0.796 and 0.843 respectively.

benefits from economic growth equally. However, under no economic growth, the macroeconomic slide system will not work,[10] then, the simulated pension benefits in the future will be overestimated. Therefore, the percentage of the poor elderly in reality will be higher than the simulation results. Evaluating the effect of the macroeconomic slide system is also an issue in the future.

Initial Population

The 2004 Comprehensive Survey of the Living Conditions (CSLC) conducted by the Ministry of Health, Labour, and Welfare is the main source of the initial population.[11] The survey is conducted every three years using large sample sizes. In the 2004 survey, the sample size was 25,091 households and 72,487 household members. The survey covers kinship relationships within household members,[12] marital status, employment status, health status, earnings, pension amounts and other socioeconomic characteristics. The initial population of 49,307 private households and 126,570 household members is prepared by resampling with replacement from the micro-data. The elderly population of 1,212 persons in institutional households is prepared separately and is added to the initial population. In the end, the initial population is 127,782 persons, and reflects Japan's society on a 1/1000 scale.

Prospects of the Elderly in the Future

Percentage of the Elderly by Co-resident Family Type

Figure 9.1 shows the future trends in the percentage of the elderly aged 65 years and older by co-resident family type, divided into the following subtypes: single-person households, couple-only households, those living with married children, those living with unmarried children, other private households and those in an institution. The percentage increases from 19.6 per cent in the year 2004 to 31.8 per cent in 2030, 39.4 per cent in 2050, and 41.0 per cent in 2100.

In the future, the elderly living alone will increase significantly. They will reach 13.2 per cent of the population by the year 2100. The elderly living with unmarried children are also increasing by a large margin, while those living with married children will decrease. These unmarried children are a future case of today's 'parasite singles'.[13] This is a case of parents becoming elderly while

---

10   This system is applied only when the economic growth is achieved.

11   The data used in this study were made available to the author by the Ministry of Health, Labour, and Welfare of Japan, notice number No.0907-7 dated 7 September 2010.

12   Kinship relationships between the persons living in different households are imputed.

13   A Japanese-English term for single adults who live with their parents and do not marry until their late twenties or thirties.

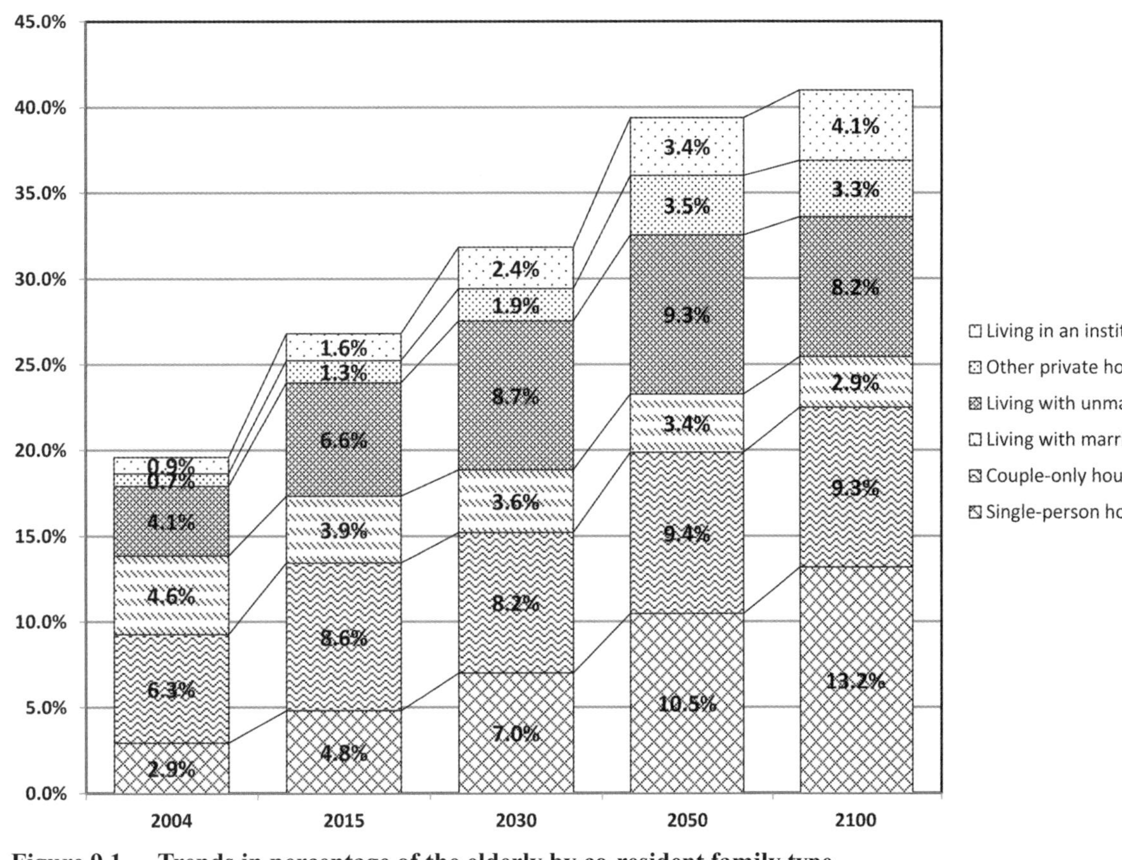

Figure 9.1   Trends in percentage of the elderly by co-resident family type

children are not able to become independent and leave the parental home because they do not have sufficient economic resources due to their unstable employment and, therefore, continue to live with their parents without getting married.

The Distribution of Public Pension Amounts

In 2004, the distribution of public pension amounts to the elderly was wide and there was a small peak of 0.50–0.74 million yen due to the variety of participation periods and pensionable remunerations. However, we will see a peak of 0.75–0.99 million yen after the year 2015, consisting mainly of former category 1 and 3 subscribers. A flat distribution between 1.00 and 2.24 million yen is observed. This is formed by former subscribers of Employees' Pension Insurance (category 2) and beneficiaries of survivors' pensions.

The prospects of the distribution also show that the number of elderly people with very low pensions will not increase even though the elderly will increase in number significantly. This is because of the maturity of the public pension scheme and the establishment of pension rights for dependent wives, which was introduced by an amendment in 1985. Since the participation of dependent wives in the scheme before 1985 was voluntarily, some of them would not be eligible for the public pension. After the amendment, their participation became compulsory as category 3 subscribers, and their basic pension eligibility is guaranteed.

On the other hand, the elderly with very high pensions will significantly decrease in number. This decline is thought to be caused by a reduction in the pension level for men due to the pension fairness adjustment and the transfer of a part of their pensions to their wives' names as basic pension by the 1985 amendment.

The Distribution of Equivalent Income

Figure 9.2 shows the future trends in the distribution of equivalent income. Equivalent income is defined as the total income of the co-resident family divided by the square root of the number of household members. This represents the income level of the elderly adjusted by household size.

In 2004, the distribution is wide due to the variety of living arrangements for the elderly and the broad distribution of their pension amounts. However, the distribution will have a clear peak around 1.75–1.99 million yen after the year 2030, and shows no increase in the number of elderly people with high equivalent income. On the other hand, the number of the elderly with low equivalent income will increase considerably.

Even though the public pension level for the low-pension group will improve, their equivalent income will seemingly not improve. This may be because of the reduction in private support from their co-resident families as a result of the increase in the number of elderly people living alone. In the midst of the decline in the Japanese population, an increase in the numbers of the low-income elderly

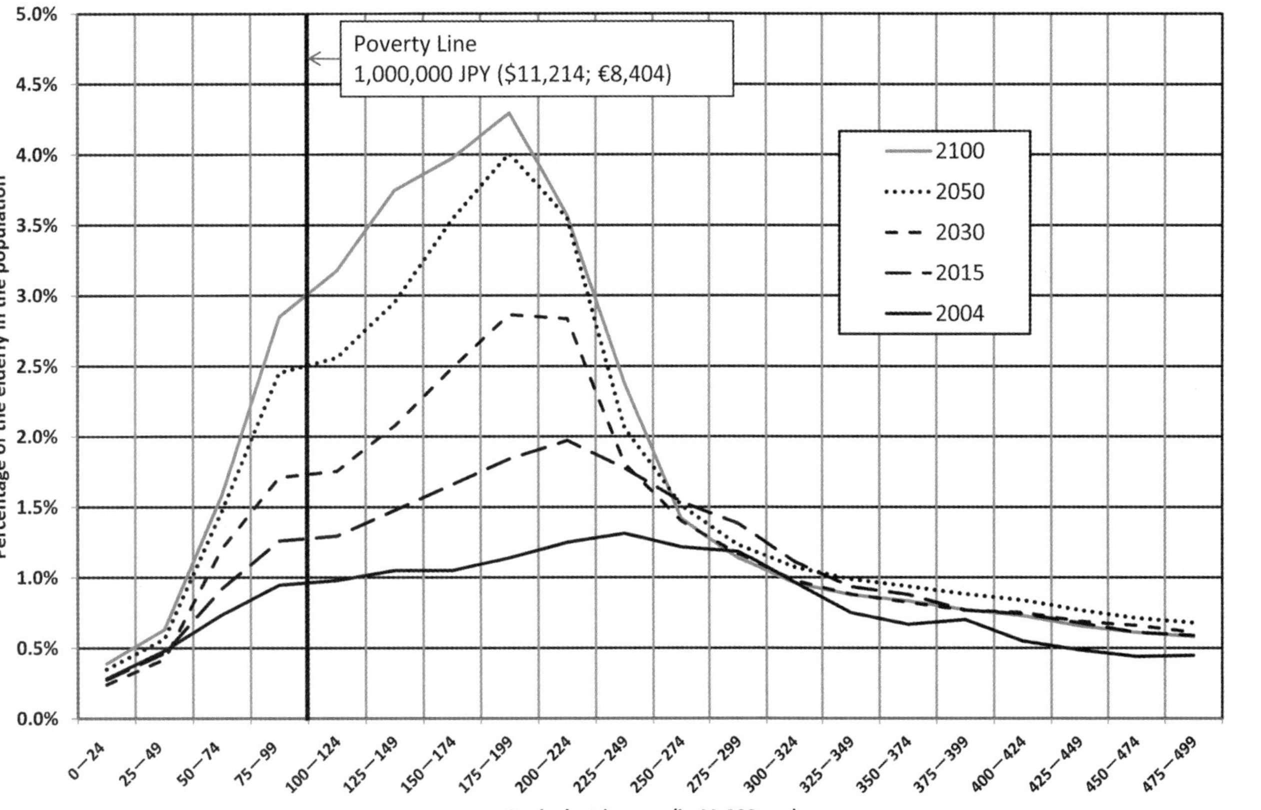

Figure 9.2   Trends in distribution of equivalent income

causes concern. This is because it will lead to expanding income disparity, open the way for social destabilization, and an increase in the amount and costs of public assistance. In such a case, the public assistance system will come to a dead end administratively and financially.

Future Trends in the Poor Elderly in the Population

The definition of poverty is not concrete, but here we consider an equivalent income of 1,000,000 JPY ($11,214; €8,404) as the poverty line. If their equivalent income is less than 1,000,000 JPY in Japan,[14] it is usually very difficult for the elderly to maintain their life without any financial assistance.

Figure 9.3 shows the future trends in the percentage of the poor elderly in the population by their co-resident family type. The percentage will increase from 2.4 per cent in the year 2004 to 3.6 per cent in 2030, 4.8 per cent in 2050 and 5.5 per cent in 2100. Most of the poor elderly represent single-person households. This means that the current pension scheme will not provide sufficient income security for the elderly in the future due to the significant change in their family arrangements.

Proposed Pension Reform Plans and their Evaluation

Proposed Pension Reform Plans

There are many proposals for public pension reform. Here, we consider four reform plans: (A) a uniform earnings-related pension with a minimum guaranteed pension, proposed by the Democratic Party of Japan (DPJ);[15] (B) a fully tax-funded basic pension system, addressed by the National Council for Social Security (2008); (C) a modified version of plan B, based on the proposal of Takayama (2010); and (D) a partially tax-funded basic pension system, proposed by Inagaki (2010b).

The key feature of plan A is the introduction of the minimum guaranteed pension. Its amount was 840,000 JPY ($9,420; €7,059) in the DPJ manifesto. However, the specific values of the level of the earnings-related pension or the threshold amount to provide the minimum pension is not given. In this chapter, we assume the specific values of variables in formulas (3) to (6). The following new formulas are applied to the insured period only after the fiscal year 2015. The pension amount corresponding to the insured period before 2014 is calculated under the current scheme.

---

14   The amount of public assistance for an elderly couple living in Tokyo was 1,443,240 JPY ($16,184; €12,129) in 2012. Its equivalent income is 1,020,525 JPY, and almost same as this poverty line.

15   DPJ is a former ruling party. Currently, the Liberal Democratic Party is the ruling party after the election held on 16 December 2012.

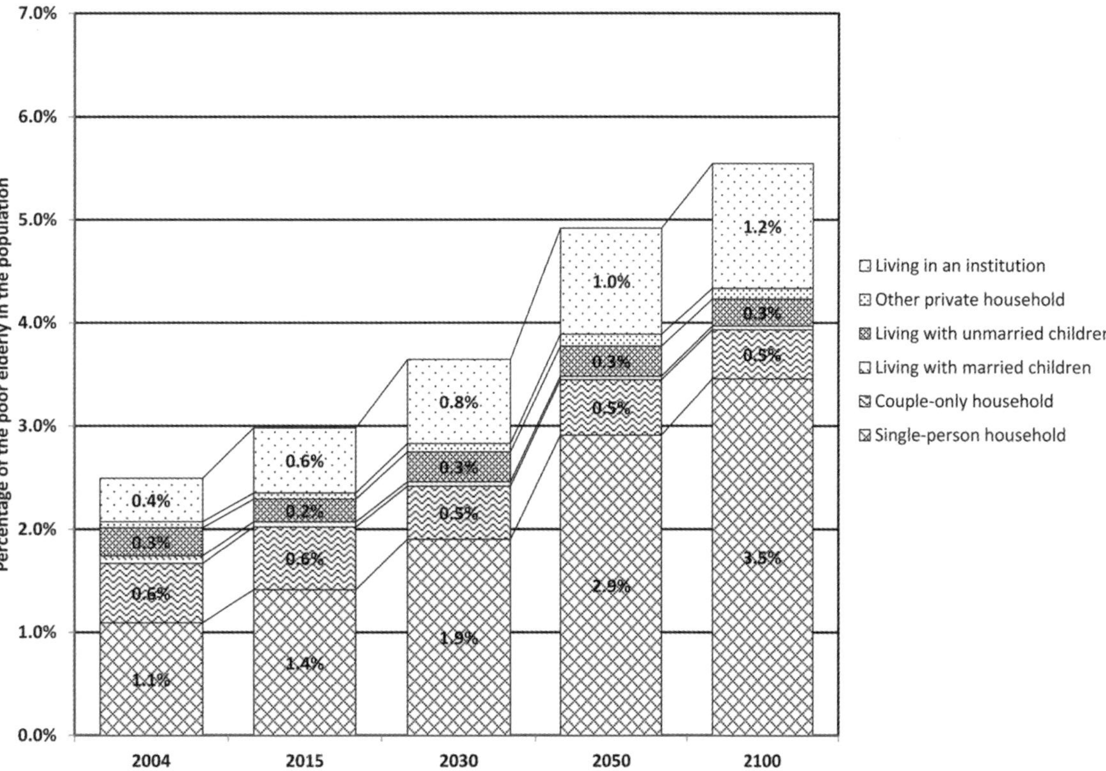

Figure 9.3   Trends in percentage of the poor elderly in the population

$$ERP = [\textit{average earnings}] \times 50\% \qquad (3)$$
$$MGP = 840{,}000 \ \textit{if } ERP < 500{,}000 \qquad (4)$$
$$MGP = 840{,}000 - (ERP - 500{,}000) \times 0.75 \ \textit{if } 500{,}000 \leq ERP < 1{,}620{,}000 \qquad (5)$$
$$MGP = 0 \ \textit{if } ERP \geq 1{,}620{,}000 \qquad (6)$$

Plans B and C are methods to provide a basic pension financed by taxes from the age of 65, and both plans have the same final form. The amount of the basic pension is the same as the full pension under the current scheme of 792,100 JPY. However, there are differences in their transition process. The transition process of plan B is similar to that of plan A. The basic pension amount corresponding to the insured period before 2014 is calculated under the current scheme, while it is calculated as in the fully tax-funded system for the period after 2015. The basic pension amount of plan B is given by formula (7).

$$\textit{Pension} = 792{,}100 \ \times \frac{x + y}{480} \qquad (7)$$

where x is premium paid period before 2014 and y is insured period after 2015.

In plan C, the transition process is accelerated in order that the incidence of the elderly with low pensions is eliminated as quickly as possible. We consider it possible to raise the level of pensions by a certain percentage since all people bear consumption tax after the fiscal year 1989. The basic pension amount of plan C is given by formula (8), where *p* is gradually increased from 35 per cent in 2015 to 100 per cent in 2028.

$$\textit{Pension} = 792{,}100 \times (1 - p) \times \frac{x + y}{480} + 792{,}100 \times p \qquad (8)$$

where x is premium paid period before 2014 and y is insured period after 2015.

The idea of plan D is to immediately introduce a fully tax-funded basic pension system for the late-stage elderly (age 75 and over), and maintain the framework of the current system for the basic pension of the early-stage elderly (age 65 to 74). However, the basic pension for the early-stage elderly is fully financed by insurance premium. The pension formula of this plan is given by formulas (9) and (10).

$$\textit{Pension} = 792{,}100 \ \times \frac{\text{premium paid period}}{480} \quad \text{for early-stage elderly} \qquad (9)$$

$$\textit{Pension} = 792{,}100 \qquad\qquad\qquad\qquad \text{for late-stage elderly} \qquad (10)$$

Plan D may raise concerns of fairness between persons who paid past premiums and those who did not pay. However, it is not a big problem because the actual past payments of insurance premiums are reflected in the basic pension of the early-stage elderly. Actually, the basic pension benefits for 10 years, from age 65 to 74, amount to about 8 million yen, which exceeds the total premium premiums of 40 years at the current premium level of 15,100 yen per month.

Future Trends in Percentage of the Poor Elderly in the Population

The most important purpose of public pension reform is the improvement of income security, especially for the poor elderly. It can be evaluated by simulating the percentage of the poor elderly in the population. Table 9.1 compares its future trends among the current scheme and the proposed reform plans. If the current scheme is maintained, the percentage of the poor elderly will increase from a 2 per cent level of the population in 2004 to a 5 per cent level after 2050, posing a serious problem for Japanese society.

All reform plans have the effect of reducing the proportion of poor elderly people significantly. However, the level and progress of the effect of each plan is very different. In the ultra long-term period, plan A has the most significant effect – for example, a 3.6 point reduction in 2100. On the other hand, in the mid- and long-term period, say, by 2030, plan D is the most effective, and plan C the next. Plans A and B have very little effect.

The difference in progress of the effects is due to the plans' transition process. Plans A and B apply the new pension formula only to the insured period after the fiscal year 2015, and the current formula is applied to the period before 2014. It will take a very long time for the new pension formula to affect the pension amount of the elderly. The existing poor elderly may never reap the benefit of this reform. Therefore, if we opt for plan A or B, it will become necessary to undertake another measure for the poor elderly.

Table 9.1   Trends in percentage of the poor elderly in the population

	Current	Plan A	Plan B	Plan C	Plan D
2004	2.4%	2.4%	2.4%	2.4%	2.4%
2010	2.6%	2.6%	2.6%	2.6%	2.6%
2020	3.2%	3.2%	3.2%	2.8%	2.4%
2030	3.6%	3.4%	3.5%	3.1%	2.8%
2040	4.2%	3.4%	3.9%	3.3%	3.4%
2050	4.8%	3.0%	4.3%	3.6%	3.9%
2060	5.4%	2.6%	4.5%	4.0%	4.3%
2070	5.5%	2.2%	4.4%	4.1%	4.5%
2080	5.6%	2.0%	4.2%	4.1%	4.5%
2090	5.5%	2.0%	4.1%	4.1%	4.4%
2100	5.5%	1.9%	4.0%	4.0%	4.4%

Total Expenditure and Additional Cost of the Public Pension Reform Plans

The Japanese economy is hardly expected to grow in the future since the population will decrease while aging faster. It will be difficult to bear a large expenditure for the public pension in the future. Table 9.2 compares the future trends in total expenditure of the public pension among the current scheme and the proposed reform plans. The total expenditure under the current scheme will reach the maximum level in 2020 and stay at that level by 2050. However, according to the actuarial valuation by the Ministry of Health, Labour and Welfare, Pension Bureau, Actuarial Division (2010), it is financially sustainable under an intermediate or optimistic economic assumption. Though there is a debate about its economic assumption, we assume that the current system is financially sustainable. The additional costs of the proposed reform plans will be essential for evaluating its sustainability.

Table 9.2   Total expenditure and additional cost (in trillion yen)

	Total expenditure of public pension					Additional cost			
	Current	**Plan A**	**Plan B**	**Plan C**	**Plan D**	**Plan A**	**Plan B**	**Plan C**	**Plan D**
2004	40.8	40.8	40.8	40.8	40.8	0.0	0.0	0.0	0.0
2010	45.3	45.3	45.3	45.3	45.3	0.0	0.0	0.0	0.0
2020	50.8	50.8	50.8	52.5	54.1	0.0	0.0	1.7	3.3
2030	50.0	51.2	50.3	52.4	52.9	1.3	0.3	2.4	3.0
2040	51.3	55.7	52.3	54.9	53.9	4.4	1.0	3.6	2.6
2050	49.7	57.8	51.6	54.0	52.6	8.1	1.9	4.3	2.9
2060	46.1	57.3	48.7	50.2	48.9	11.2	2.6	4.2	2.8
2070	41.2	54.1	44.2	44.9	43.6	13.0	3.1	3.7	2.4
2080	35.9	48.8	38.9	39.1	38.0	12.9	3.0	3.2	2.1
2090	30.6	42.1	33.3	33.3	32.4	11.6	2.7	2.7	1.9
2100	26.2	36.2	28.5	28.5	27.7	10.0	2.3	2.3	1.6

The additional costs are also shown in Table 9.2. If the additional cost is large, it is presumably unsustainable. Plan D requires a minimum additional cost, at most 3.3 trillion yen or about 6 per cent of the total expenditure. On the other hand, plan A requires a huge additional cost that exceeds 10 trillion yen or about 38 per cent of the total expenditure in 2100. The additional cost of plan B or C is larger than that of plan D, but it is not huge like plan A. Therefore, plan A seems to be financially unrealistic, but other reform plans seem to be possible.

Conclusion

Japanese society cannot avoid rapid changes such as aging and a shift toward a depopulating society. With the increase in the number of elderly people, the need for social security is also increasing. How should we efficiently distribute the revenue feared to be shrinking to the socially vulnerable?

We illustrated the prospects of the elderly in the future under the current pension scheme by using the Japanese microsimulation model INAHSIM. It shows that the percentage of the elderly with very low pension amounts in the population will not increase. However, the percentage of the poor elderly will increase by a large margin because of the changes in their families, such as the increase in the number of elderly people living alone. The increasing numbers of the poor elderly in the near future will be a serious problem for Japanese society.

Then, simulations were performed for four proposed pension reform plans. Plan A is a uniform earnings-related pension with a minimum guaranteed pension; plan B is a fully tax-funded basic pension system; plan C is a fully tax-funded basic pension system with accelerated transition measure; and plan D is a partially tax-funded basic pension system. The results show that all reform plans will reduce the number of poor elderly people significantly in the future. However, plans A and B are shown to have very little effect on reducing the number of poor elderly people by 2030. Other measures, probably difficult to introduce, would be necessary if we opt for plan A or B.

Regarding additional costs, plan A requires huge costs, whereas the costs of plans B, C, and D are moderate. Plan A is unrealistic. Since plan B has the problem of increasing the number of poor elderly people during the transition period, plans C and D are compelling reform measures.

The author thinks that plan D is the best since it requires minimum additional costs and reduces the number of poor elderly people immediately. In addition, plan D does not change the share of the burden between tax and insurance premium. Under the current scheme, the expenditure on basic pension is financed equally by taxes and insurance premium. Since about half of the elderly are in their early stage and the other half in their late stage, the share will remain unchanged. This advantage can be used to build a consensus among stakeholders. Plan D, of course, meets the seven principles framed by the government panel.

In any case, evidence-based policy making is really important. Macro future estimates such as population projections or the actuarial review of pension schemes are prepared by the government, while micro future estimates such as income distribution are not prepared. Micro future estimates are really important for policy making. Without such micro-based estimates, it is very difficult to evaluate the income security function of the public pension scheme for the elderly. The government should develop and use a microsimulation model like INAHSIM for more enhanced evidence-based policy making.

References

Inagaki S. 2010a. Overview of INAHSIM: A Microsimulation Model for Japan. *PIE/CIS Discussion Paper* [Online], 468. Available at: http://cis.ier.hit-u.ac.jp/Japanese/publication/cis/dp2009/dp468/text2.pdf [accessed: 15 January 2013].

Inagaki, S. 2010b. The Effect of Proposals for Basic Pension Reform on the Income Distribution of the Elderly in Japan. *Review of Socionetwork Strategies*, 4, 1–16.

Inagaki S. 2012. Income Disparities and Behaviour of People Born in 1950s Outline and Analysis of Internet Survey on the Individual Records of Regular Pension Coverage Notice (in Japanese). *Journal of the Japan Statistical Society*, 41(2), 285–317.

Kaneko, R., Ishikawa, A., Ishii, F., Sakai, S., Iwasawa, M., Mita, F. and Moriizumi, R. 2008. Population Projections for Japan: 2006–2055 Outline of Results, Methods, and Assumptions. *The Japanese Journal of Population*, 6(1), 76–114. Available at: http://www.ipss.go.jp/webj-ad/webjournal.files/population/2008_4/05population.pdf [accessed: 15 January 2013].

Ministry of Health, Labour and Welfare, Pension Bureau, Actuarial Division 2010. *Report of the 2009 Actuarial Valuation* (in Japanese). Tokyo: Ministry of Health, Labour and Welfare.

National Council for Social Security 2008. *National Council for Social Security Interim Report* (in Japanese). Tokyo: Office of Prime Minister.

National Institute of Population and Social Security Research 2008. *Household Projections for Japan: 2005–2030* (in Japanese). Tokyo: Health and Welfare Statistics Association.

Pension Committee of Social Security Council 2008. *Viewpoints of the investigation of problems remaining after the revision in 2004* (in Japanese) [Online: 11th meeting, document 3] Available at: http://www.mhlw.go.jp/shingi/2008/09/dl/s0929-9n.pdf [accessed: 15 January 2013].

Takayama, N. 2010. *Public Pension and Child allowance* (in Japanese). Tokyo: Iwanami Press.

Chapter 10

On the Construction of Early Warning Indicators of Old-Age Poverty: The Index-Building versus the Microsimulation Approach

Georg P. Mueller

An Introductory Overview[1,2]

In recent years, social indicators have become more and more important, not only for scientific analyses but also for the public political discourse. In both domains, most of these indicators are used either for describing the current development of society or for criticizing governmental policies (Habich et al. 1994). Apart from a few exceptions (e.g. Rupesinghe and Kuroda 1992, Müller 1999, Müller 2013, Van Walraven 1998) social indicators generally refer to the present or the past, but rarely to the future. This is in sharp contrast to the economic sciences, where there is a considerable interest in constructing and using *early warning indicators*. Typical examples are business indicators for different countries and economic activities (e.g. OECD 2011 or Asian Development Bank 2005). Obviously, early warning indicators are not only useful for business but also for social policy: they allow policymakers to anticipate future social problems and to identify the groups, which are most affected by these problems.

This chapter tries to fill the mentioned gap by proposing and comparing two methodological approaches for constructing early warning indicators of old-age poverty. One of these approaches is conventional *index-building* (McIver and Carmines 1997, Netemeyer et al. 2003) on the basis of statistical aggregates, which describe the size of different population groups. The other is based on *microsimulation* (Harding 1996, Gupta and Kapur 2000, Klevmarken 2008) of individual future poverty risks. Both approaches are based on the same statistical regression analyses of *vulnerability by retirement*, which corresponds to the risk of a person of falling below the poverty line when passing from active work-life

---

1   Parts of this chapter, especially Table 10.1 and Table 10.2 (see Appendix), are based on an earlier German publication of the author, which appeared as Müller (2013).

2   The author is indebted to *Jardena Rotach* (Therwil/Basel) for her help in formatting this chapter.

to retirement. Both approaches also allow calculation of aggregated vulnerabilities of age cohorts, which are considered to be stable over time and thus can be used for making forecasts about the poverty of a cohort, when it reaches the age of retirement.

The ideas outlined in the previous paragraphs are applied to the consequences of retirement in three countries with very different welfare regimes (Esping-Andersen 1990: 74):

i. The *USA* with a *liberal* welfare state that mainly relies on private pension schemes.
ii. *Germany* as a *conservative* welfare state with a life-long protection of group privileges and a strong focus on the responsibility of the family for its weaker members.
iii. *Sweden* as a *social democratic/'socialist'* welfare state, which follows a redistributive egalitarian social policy.

The empirical analyses of these three countries offer not only the opportunity to compare three major welfare regimes but also to compare the different approaches for constructing early warning indicators. It turns out that the microsimulation approach gives additional insights into the future problems of old-age poverty, which are not available when using just the index-building approach.

Social Vulnerability

Theoretical Considerations

Social policy aims at fighting social problems like unemployment, work-accidents or poverty after retirement, which typically mark planned or unplanned transitions in the individual life course. For reaching this goal, most state agencies make use of the following two strategies:

a. The reduction of the *probability of a biographical transition* with negative outcomes (Ranci 2010: 17), e.g. by a labour market policy, which is oriented towards the creation of new jobs. This strategy is of course not usable, if transitions are 'inevitable' such as in the case of the retirement of employees.
b. The reduction of the *probability of harm* due to a biographical transition, which is assumed to have already taken place. The classical instrument of this strategy is the social insurance system for unemployment, work accident, retirement, etc., which covers the cost of a negative biographical transition. Since most of these insurance systems are not perfect, there is a *residual risk of harm,* which defines according to the introductory section the *vulnerability* by a status-transition (Ranci 2010: 17, United Nations 1999: 10).

Since retirement is an 'inevitable' event for all those employees reaching age 60 and more, the current and the future performance of welfare systems with regard to old-age poverty mainly differentiates by their ability to control the vulnerability of different population segments. Current literature (see below) suggests that the remaining vulnerability by retirement of different subpopulations depends on the following three factors:

1. The *type of the welfare state*, which buffers by specific institutional arrangements the risks of retirement to varying degrees (Gelissen 2002: 33). *Social democratic/'socialist'* regimes are assumed be very efficient with regard to the elimination of poverty, also after retirement. For such welfare regimes we expect no group specific vulnerability. As mentioned earlier, *conservative* regimes (Esping-Andersen 1990: 74) rely on the responsibility of the traditional family for their poor relatives. Especially vulnerable under such regimes are categories of persons, which are less well protected by family solidarity like the non-married, the singles, and the divorced. Finally, *liberal* welfare regimes have the weakest welfare state and consequently rely on private pension systems. Thus, social groups with limited resources and no savings are the most vulnerable under such regimes. This especially holds for underclasses, single (female) part-time workers and monoparental families.

2. The *deviance from the normal life course*, on which the pension-system is based on (Meyer and Bridgen 2007b: 238 ff.): the higher the deviance of a group from the normal life course, the higher its vulnerability with regard to poverty by retirement. If we assume that the standard pension-model is made for a couple with at least one breadwinner, then the *non-married, single,* and *divorced* should be especially vulnerable.

3. The *cumulated income* over life-span, which defines in many welfare systems the level of pension benefits after retirement (Meyer and Bridgen 2007a: 7 ff.). Thus, the higher the cumulated income over life-span, the lower the vulnerability by retirement. If this hypothesis is correct, the following groups should be especially vulnerable: *Women,* because of conflicts with family roles and duties, which often entail part-time employment and interrupted professional biographies. *Lower classes* due to their low professional status and salaries. *Immigrants,* because of the delayed entry into the pension system in the country of immigration, where the cumulated income is by the time of retirement not sufficient for a normal old-age pension.

Methodological Considerations

In this chapter, we consider the transition from employment to retirement as a quasi-experiment (Orr 1999: chapter 1), which results either in poverty or non-poverty of the concerned pensioner. Ideally, this experiment should be studied with a pretest/post-test design, which however requires time-series data that are not always available. Thus we propose to use a 1-test design (Orr 1999: 4), which compares for *one* time-point an experimental group of retired persons with a non-retired group approximately at the same age between 55 and 75. The result of this statistical analysis should have the form of an equation, which includes retirement as a binary variable. This allows to make *stress-tests* with *non*-retired persons by turning this binary retirement variable 'on' and 'off' and analysing its effect on poverty. The statistical procedure best suited for this purpose is logistic regression (Aldrich and Nelson 2000: 30 ff.), where the logarithmic odds-ratio

$$\ln[\ p(Poor = 1) / p(Poor = 0)\ ] \tag{1}$$

of the *probabilities p(Poor = 1)* for *poverty* and *p(Poor = 0)* for *non-poverty* is explained by mathematical products

$$Retired * Group\_i\_Membership,\ i = 1, 2, \dots, n \tag{2}$$

of two 0–1-standardized binary variables *Group_i_Membership* and *Retired*. The former binary variable describes whether a person is member of group i or not and the latter whether he or she is retired or not. Thus we propose to estimate in the regression equation

$$\begin{aligned}
\ln[\ p(Poor = 1) / p(Poor = 0)\ ] = a\ & + \\
+\ b_0 * Retired + b_1 * Retired * Group_1_Membership &+ \dots \\
+\ b_n * Retired * Group_n_Membership &
\end{aligned} \tag{3}$$

the parameters a, b_0, b_1, b_2, $\dots$, b_n. By varying in equation (3) the values of the binary variable *Retired* between 0 and 1, it is possible to make stress-tests by calculating the effect of a virtual retirement on the logarithmic odds-ratio (1):

$$\begin{aligned}
V = \ln[\ p(Poor = 1\ \&\ Retired = \mathbf{1}) / p(Poor = 0\ \&\ Retired = \mathbf{1})\ ]\ & - \\
-\ \ln[\ p(Poor = 1\ \&\ Retired = \mathbf{0}) / p(Poor = 0\ \&\ Retired = \mathbf{0})\ ] & = \\
= [a + b_0 * 1\ & + \\
b_1 * Retired * Group_1_Membership + \dots + b_n * Retired * Group_n_Membership]\ & - \\
-\ [a + b_0 * 0\ & + \\
b_1 * 0 * Group_1_Membership + \dots + b_n * 0 * Group_n_Membership] & = \\
= b_0 + b_1 * Group_1_Membership + \dots + b_n * Group_n_Membership &
\end{aligned} \tag{4}$$

Thus, V is just the difference between the odds-ratio (3) for *Retired = 1* and *Retired = 0* and may consequently be considered as an *operationalization* of the vulnerability by retirement. It is highly correlated with the theoretical definition of vulnerability, which we previously defined in the introductory section as the risk of becoming poor by retirement. Due to the 0-1-standardization of the dependent and independent variables, there is a high degree of comparability between the estimates b_i for different groups i: the higher the b_i of group i, the higher its vulnerability V. Moreover, *negative* values b_i may be interpreted as a good protection of the respective group against old-age poverty.

Vulnerability Under Three Typical Welfare Regimes: the USA, Germany and Sweden

In what follows, we will analyse for the USA, Germany and Sweden the vulnerability of selected groups mentioned in the previous theoretical section. This presupposes relatively recent internationally comparable data, which we found in the 2008 dataset of the International Social Survey Programme (ISSP 2008). It offers for a great number of countries, also beyond the frontiers of the EU, the required personal data about different kinds of memberships, like e.g. in the group of the divorced, married or underclass, etc. What is however not directly available, is information about poverty. Consequently, it had to be calculated by dividing the household income by the square-root of the number of persons living in the household. This internationally recognized procedure proposed by Atkinson et al. (1995: chapter 2.3) yields the *standardized* income of a one-person household that can further be used to calculate the median value M of all standardized incomes of a country. Fifty per cent of this median value M defines the national poverty-line, as used in many other publications like e.g. Mitchell (1993: 38 ff.) or OECD (2008: chapter 5). The respective values of Germany, Sweden and the USA are given in Table 10.1 (see Appendix). They allow calculation of the individual poverty/non-poverty of all survey respondents as well as the poverty rates immediately before and after retirement (see Table 10.1 in the Appendix).

With the mentioned individual poverty data and the individual group membership information from the original ISSP-survey, it was possible to perform country specific *binary logistic regressions* based on the formula

$$\ln[\ p(\text{Poor} = 1) / p(\text{Poor} = 0)\ ] = a +$$
$$+ b_0 * \text{Retired} + b_1 * \text{Retired} * \text{Group\_1\_Membership} + \ldots$$
$$+ b_n * \text{Retired} * \text{Group\_n\_Membership} \qquad\qquad (3)$$

which we elaborated in the previous section. In order to exclude effects of ageing not directly associated with retirement, the regression analysis was confined to the age group 55–75. The values of a, b_0, b_1, … , b_n, which we extracted this way from the ISSP data, are given in Table 10.2 (see Appendix), first for an *initial* full model and than for a reduced *final* model. The latter excludes all those variables, which were in the initial model insignificant.

The comparison of the initial with the final models of Table 10.2 reveals some weaknesses of our theoretical reasoning in the previous sections: many explanatory variables like e.g. the gender indicator *female*, are statistically *not* significant and thus do not help us to understand old-age poverty. The best theoretical approach seems to be the *deviance from the normal life course*, which is represented by the demographic variables *Single*, *Divorced* and *Married*. Nevertheless, all really significant parameters b_i have the theoretically expected signs. A more extensive discussion of these signs is given in Müller (2013), where Table 10.2 of the Appendix was first published and analysed in full detail.

Early Warning Indicators

The Methodology of the Index-building Approach

The younger age groups of today are the retired of tomorrow. This trivial wisdom is the essence of the Lexis-diagram in Figure 10.1 (Keyfitz 1985: 45), which describes the ageing of birth cohorts, until they reach retirement (Glenn 2005). The current properties of successive birth cohorts A, B, C, ... (see Figure 10.1) may thus be used for constructing early warning indicators, if these properties are relatively stable and the forecasted time-period is rather short. If the younger cohorts are with regard to their vulnerability by retirement worse off than the older ones, we should be warned about their future old-age poverty. To the contrary, if successively younger cohorts have decreasing index values, we expect under ceteris paribus conditions an improvement of the economic situation of the future retired. Hence, in an earlier article (Müller 2013) we have constructed a measure *V_Index* for describing the vulnerability of successive age cohorts.

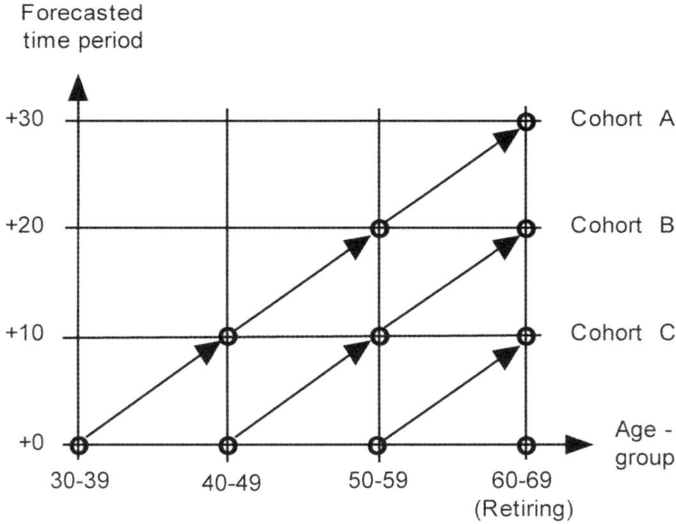

Figure 10.1　A Lexis-diagram of the ageing of cohorts

The aforementioned *V_Index* departs from the previous equation (4), which describes the vulnerability of a person with possible memberships in groups 1, 2, … , n:

$$V = \ln[\, p(Poor = 1 \,\&\, Retired = \mathbf{1}) / p(Poor = 0 \,\&\, Retired = \mathbf{1}) \,] -$$
$$-\quad \ln[\, p(Poor = 1 \,\&\, Retired = \mathbf{0}) / p(Poor = 0 \,\&\, Retired = \mathbf{0}) \,] =$$
$$= b_0 + b_1 * Group\_1\_Membership + \ldots + b_n * Group\_n\_Membership \qquad (4)$$

Due to the 0–1-standardization of the binary variables Group_i_Membership, it is possible to calculate the expected value E(V) of an age-group:

$$E(V) = E[\, b_0 + b_1 * Group\_1\_Membership + \ldots + b_n * Group\_n\_Membership \,] =$$
$$= b_0 + b_1 * E[\, Group\_1\_Membership \,] + \ldots + b_n * E[\, Group\_n\_Membership \,] =$$
$$= b_0 + b_1 * \%\_Group\_1\_Membership *.01 + \ldots + b_n * \%\_Group\_n\_Membership *.01 \quad (5)$$

where *%_Group_i_Membership* is the %-share of the population of a cohort with membership in group i. Since equation (4) is a logarithmic function of an odds-ratio, it makes sense to modify expression (5) by an exponential transformation. Hence we define

$$V\_Index = \exp[\, E(V) \,] = \exp[\, b_0 + b_1 * \%\_Group\_1\_Membership *.01 + \ldots$$
$$\ldots . + b_n * \%\_Group\_n\_Membership *.01 \,] \qquad (6)$$

It can be shown (Müller 2013) that

$$V\_Index = [\, p(Poor = 1 \,\&\, Retired = \mathbf{1}) / p(Poor = 0 \,\&\, Retired = \mathbf{1}) \,] /$$
$$[\, p(Poor = 1 \,\&\, Retired = \mathbf{0}) / p(Poor = 0 \,\&\, Retired = \mathbf{0}) \,] \qquad (7)$$

is just the odds-ratio of poverty after the retirement of a representative cohort member as compared to its odds-ratio before retirement. From equation (6) it is also obvious, that V_Index is a 'classical' index construction (McIver and Carmines 1997, Netemeyer et al. 2003), based on the weighted addition of more elementary variables *%_Group_i_Membership*.

Applications of the Index-building Approach to Germany, the USA and Sweden

In order to assess the future old-age poverty in Sweden, the USA and Germany, we calculated for each of the three countries the V-Index values of the age-groups 40–49, 50–59 and 60–69, which will retire in +20, +10 and +0 years from the base year 2008 of the ISSP survey. The results of these index calculations are presented in Figure 10.2 as well as in the Tables 10.3a–c in the Appendix of this chapter.

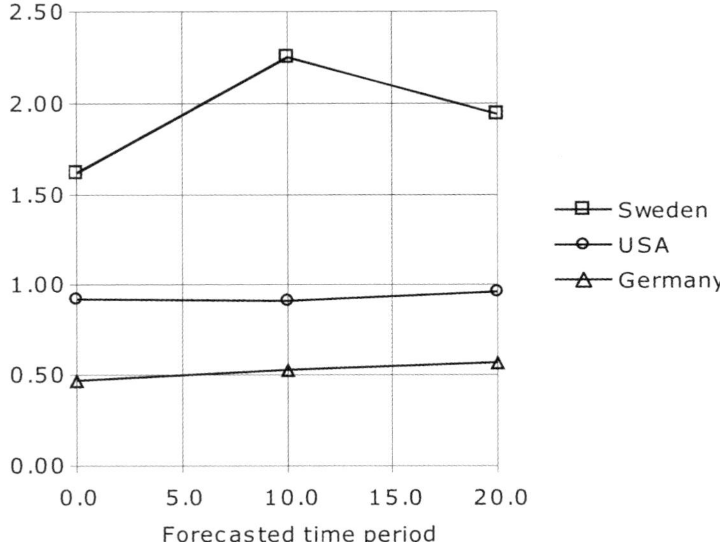

Figure 10.2   The temporal evolution of the V_Index as an early warning of old-age poverty

As Figure 10.2 shows, there is in the long run a general increase of V_Index, which may be considered as an early warning sign of new social problems with poverty after retirement. For Sweden, this increase is rather strong and probably has to do with a relative increase in the population of singles (Müller 2013). For Germany and the USA, however, the increase of the considered early warning indicator is rather moderate. Moreover, in both countries V_Index remains *below* the threshold 1. This means that in Germany and the USA, the 'average' pensioner does not suffer from a welfare system failure: according to equation (7), the odds-ratio of poverty after retirement is lower than the corresponding odds-ratio before retirement. Since the 'average' pensioner is an artificial construct, there is still the politically very relevant question about the share of the citizens, who are really protected by these welfare systems. Similarly, V_Index does not give answers how serious the situation is in Sweden, both in terms of the concerned share of citizens as well as in terms of increased risks of poverty by retirement. Finally V_Index gives no clues about the composition of the future poor old persons. This is in so far a serious shortcoming, as early warning indicators are made for averting the forecasted event by an appropriate policy. Thus they should also inform about the target population of possible counter-measures.

The Methodology of the Microsimulation Approach

Conventional index-building is obviously not enough for a detailed analysis of future old-age poverty. In order to overcome the mentioned problems with over-aggregated information, which are typical for this approach, we propose to *simulate* the *individual* vulnerabilities

$$V = \ln[\ p(\text{Poor} = 1\ \&\ \text{Retired} = \mathbf{1})\ /\ p(\text{Poor} = 0\ \&\ \text{Retired} = \mathbf{1})\ ] -$$
$$-\quad \ln[\ p(\text{Poor} = 1\ \&\ \text{Retired} = \mathbf{0})\ /\ p(\text{Poor} = 0\ \&\ \text{Retired} = \mathbf{0})\ ] =$$
$$= b_0 + b_1 * \text{Group\_1\_Membership} + \ldots + b_n * \text{Group\_n\_Membership} \qquad (4)$$

of cohort members and to aggregate this information only in a second, subsequent step. Thus, as indicated by Figure 10.3, the SPSS software and the ISSP dataset are not only used for the extraction of the regression coefficients b_i of poverty risks, as with the index building method, but also for the microsimulation of individual vulnerabilities of the respondents of the ISSP survey. For those, who are not yet retired, this is some kind of a stress-test, where results can be aggregated by age group and subsequently projected to the future in just the way proposed by the Lexis diagram in Figure 10.1. Thus we are assuming that the composition of cohorts does not change over time. In order to minimize the bias inherent in this kind of projection, the forecasted period is limited to *20 years* and *qualitative* interpretation is more important than quantitative analyses of the outcome of the simulations.

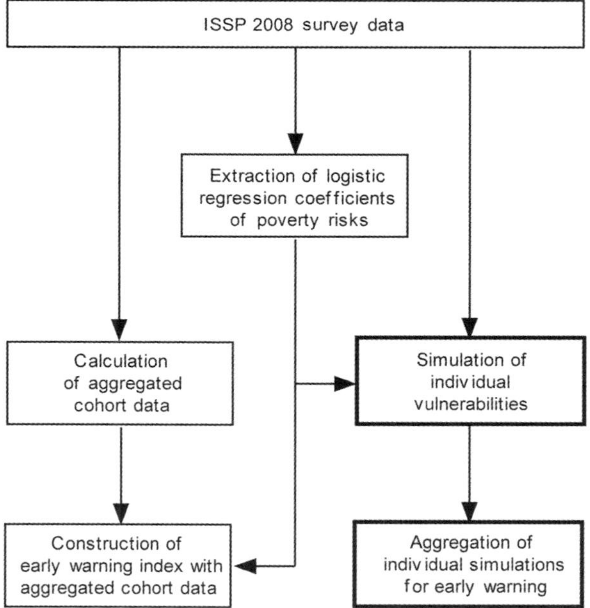

Figure 10.3   The process of early warning by microsimulation (right) as compared with the index building approach (left)[3]

---

3   Boxes with bold frames refer to the specific steps of microsimulation.

The proposed microsimulation approach is not only a supplement but rather a real substitute of the index-building method, presented in the two previous sections: from the equations (5) and (6) follows, that the microsimulation approach also allows the calculation of:

$$V\_Index = \exp[\ E(V)\ ] =$$
$$= \exp[\ E(b_0 + b_1 * Group\_1\_Membership + \ldots + b_n * Group\_n\_Membership)\ ] =$$
$$= \exp[\ mean(b_0 + b_1 * Group\_1\_Membership + \ldots + b_n * Group\_n\_Membership)\ ] \quad (8)$$

as an exponentially transformed mean-value of the *simulated* vulnerabilities. Besides, microsimulation is able to supplement V_Index by the following additional information:

a. V_Share = Cohort related share of vulnerable persons with V > 0. It measures the share of a cohort, for which the welfare system fails.
b. V_Gap = exp[mean(V of persons with V > 0)]. It describes for the vulnerable part of a cohort with V > 0 the gap to the situation, where retirement has no effect on poverty risks. More precisely, V_Gap corresponds to the *factor*, by which the odds-ratio of poverty is increased by retirement (see equation (4)). Thus, ideally V_Gap = ca. 1.
c. V_Group_i: Cohort related share of the group i in the vulnerable persons with V > 0. It is useful for identifying the future vulnerable groups, on which social policy should concentrate, in order to avoid the prophecies of the V_Index.

Applications of the Microsimulation Approach to Germany, the USA and Sweden

In what follows, we will test the microsimulation approach for Germany, the USA and Sweden. For each of these countries, we first show the *simulated* values of V_Index, which are always nearly identical with those *calculated* with the index-building method. Afterwards we interpret the dynamics of V_Index by means of V_Gap and V_Share. Finally we have a closer look at V_Group_i for all those groups i, which have in Table 10.2 (see Appendix) *significant* regression coefficients and thus are of special interest for anti-poverty policies.

Figure 10.4 gives a summary of future old-age poverty for *Germany*, where all three early warning indicators increase. Although the growth of V_Share and V_Gap is much stronger than for V_Index, a German welfare state failure is unlikely for the next 20 years: the vulnerable population V_Share will not exceed 11 per cent and the maximum value of V_Gap = 2.5 (= 10 * 0.25) is still below the corresponding values of Sweden (see Figure 10.6) and the USA (see Figure 10.5). Nevertheless, if measures are taken against old-age poverty, it should focus on the *immigrants*. As the results of our simulations for *V_Immigrated* in Table 10.3a (see Appendix) demonstrate, this group is currently the most important among the

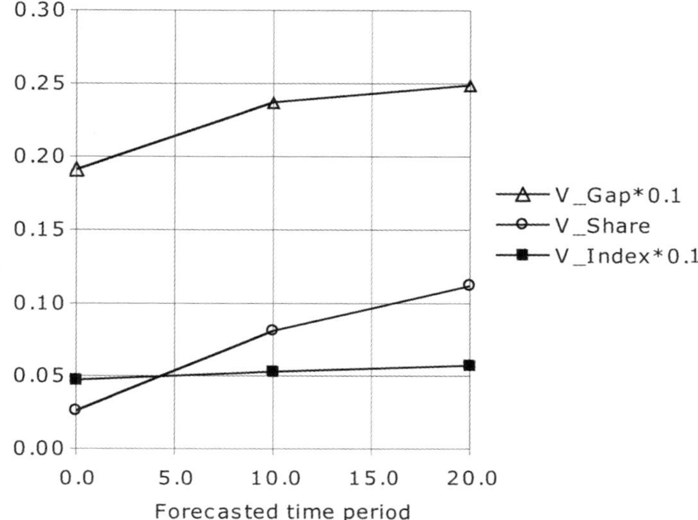

Figure 10.4　Simulated early warning indicators for Germany[4]

vulnerable by retirement and it continues to be in the next 20 years. This finding corroborates a study of Köppe (2010), which also points to the critical situation of the future retired immigrants in Germany.

As we observed earlier, the V_Index values of the *USA* increase only very moderately and stay for the next 20 years below the limit 1 (= 10 * 0.1) (see Figure 10.5). This suggests for the USA a relatively unproblematic future with no real welfare state failure. However, a closer look at Figure 10.5 reveals increasing V_Share values and by the end of the forecasted period, about 30 per cent of the Americans will be exposed to increased risks of poverty by retirement. This process is however alleviated by a decrease of V_Gap. Hence in the future there will be more poor people among the old Americans, their poverty will however be less serious than in the current situation. These contradictory trends probably explain the relative stability of V_Index in Figure 10.5.

If in spite of the stable V_Index values reforms were taken in the USA, they should favour the *divorced* and the *non-married*. According to Table 10.3c in the Appendix (see variables *V_Divorced* and *V_Non-married*), both groups represent a high and even increasing share in the vulnerable population, among others probably due to the individualization of American society. This trend is in sharp contrast to the diminishing shares of the underclass in the future vulnerable population (see Appendix, Table 10.3c, variable *V_Underclass*): in principle its members are still poor but deindustrialization and an increase of general education has made them nearly disappear.

4　Mind the different scales of V_Share, V_Gap (x 0.1!), and V_Index (x 0.1!).

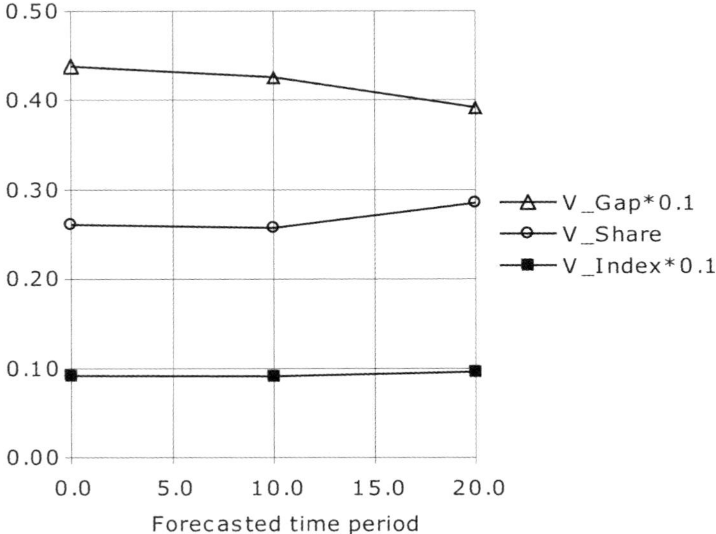

Figure 10.5   Simulated early warning indicators for the USA[5]

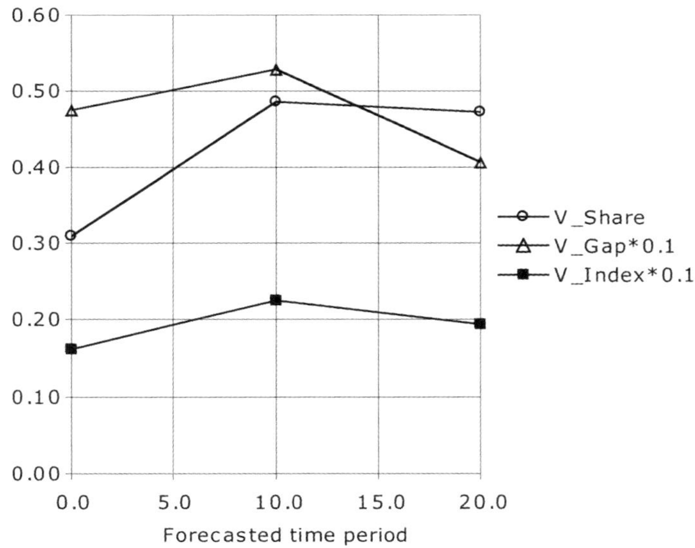

Figure 10.6   Simulated early warning indicators for Sweden[6]

---

5   Mind the different scales of V_Share, V_Gap (x 0.1!), and V_Index (x 0.1!).
6   Mind the different scales of V_Share, V_Gap (x 0.1!), and V_Index (x 0.1!).

Sweden is among the analysed countries the one with the most important increase of V_Index. As V_Share and V_Gap in Figure 10.6 show, an increasing share of the Swedish population is becoming vulnerable, the gap to poverty-neutral retirement is however shrinking. A closer look at the composition of the future vulnerable population in Table 10.3b (see Appendix) reveals in the long run increasing shares of *singles* but decreasing and rather small percentages for the *divorced* (see variables *V_Single* and *V_Divorced*). Hence, the Swedish welfare state seems to have problems with the mega-trend of individualization (Beck 1992: chapter 5): according to the dynamics of *%_Single* in Table 10.3b (see Appendix), the share of the singles in the *total* population will nearly double in the next 20 years, but this increasingly important group is not sufficiently protected against the risk of old-age poverty. Maybe that this is a challenge for the Swedish social democratic welfare culture, which thinks perhaps more in terms of collectivities than in terms of single persons.

Summary and Critique

In this chapter we compared two approaches for making forecasts about the future of old-age poverty in three exemplary countries: one approach relies on conventional methods of index-building, the other on microsimulation. Both are using the same ISSP data and the same parameter estimates, which describe the causes of vulnerability by retirement. The comparison of the two methods shows that the returns form microsimulation are worth the method-specific extra-effort. In addition to early warning by V_Index, the simulation of vulnerabilities at the individual level allows to calculate the share of the vulnerable population (V_Share), its composition (V_Group_i), as well as its gap to risk-free retirement (V_Gap). By means of these simulation based indicators we got in the previous section surprising new insights. To mention a few:

a. On the grounds of the *simulated* V_Share, the welfare system failure of the USA is much more serious than the *calculated* V_Index < 1 made us believe.
b. According to the composition indices V_Group_i, the future old *immigrants* are in Germany the really deprived group that deserves more attention of the welfare state.
c. The future increase of the Swedish early warning indicator V_Index is not a problem of an increasing gap V_Gap to risk-free retirement, but rather of the increasing share of vulnerable population segments V_Share – notably of the singles, as the corresponding index V_Group_i demonstrates.

The aforementioned new insights are based on the assumption that age-groups have *stable* properties, which are propagated to the future and thus enable us to make forecasts about the future retired (see Figure 10.1). For many properties like immigration or the highest acquired level of schooling, this certainly holds true. For demographic variables referring to different marital statuses (*Divorced, Married, Single*), the assumption of the stability of the composition of cohorts is less realistic and thus only acceptable if the forecasted time period does not exceed 20 years and the interpretation of the derived early warning indicators is rather qualitative than quantitative. For more quantitative and more future-oriented predictions, a more dynamic demographic model would be required. Fortunately microsimulation offers the advantage of being flexible enough to also include this kind of additional refinement.

References

Aldrich, J. and Nelson, F. 2000. *Linear Probability, Logit, and Probit Models.* Newbury Park: Sage.

Asian Development Bank 2005. *Early Warning Systems for Financial Crises: Applications to East Asia.* Basingstoke: Palgrave.

Atkinson A., Rainwater L. and Smeeding T. 1995. *Income Distribution in OECD Countries: Evidence from the Luxembourg Income Study (OECD Social Policy Studies 18).* Paris: OECD Publications.

Beck, U. 1992. *Risk Society: Towards a New Modernity.* London: Sage Publications.

Esping-Andersen, G. 1990. *The Three Worlds of Welfare Capitalism.* Cambridge: Polity Press.

Gelissen, J. 2002. *Worlds of Welfare, Worlds of Consent?* Leiden: Brill.

Glenn, N. 2005. *Cohort Analysis.* Thousand Oaks: Sage.

Gupta, A. and Kapur, V. (eds) 2000. *Microsimulation in Government Policy and Forecasting.* Amsterdam: Elsevier.

Habich, R., Noll, H.-H. and Zapf, W. 1994. *Soziale Indikatoren und Sozialberichterstattung (Social Indicators and Social Reporting).* Bern: Bundesamt für Statistik.

Harding, A. (ed.) 1996. *Microsimulation and Public Policy.* Amsterdam: Elsevier.

ISSP 2008. *Module 'Religion III' of the International Social Survey Programme.* [Online] Available at: http://www.gesis.org/issp [accessed: November 4, 2011].

Keyfitz, N. 1985. *Applied Mathematical Demography.* New York: Springer.

Klevmarken, A. 2008. Dynamic Microsimulation for Policy Analysis: Problems and Solutions, in A. Klevmarken and B. Lindgren (eds), *Simulating an Ageing Population: A Microsimulation Approach Applied to Sweden.* Bingley: Emerald Group, Chapter 2.

Köppe, O. 2010. 'Vorboten' der Altersarmut? (Forerunners of Old-Age Poverty?), in H. Dahme and N. Wohlfahrt (eds), *Systemanalyse als politische Reformstrategie.* Wiesbaden: VS Verlag, 241–55.

McIver, J. and Carmines, E. 1997. *Unidimensional Scaling.* Newbury Park: Sage.

Meyer, T. and Bridgen P. 2007a. Private Pensions versus Social Inclusion? Citizens at Risk and the New Pension Orthodoxy, in T. Meyer, P. Bridgen and

B. Riedmüller (eds), *Private Pensions versus Social Inclusion?* Cheltenham: Edward Elgar, Chapter 1.

Meyer, T. and Bridgen P. 2007b. Private Pensions versus Social Inclusion? Three Patterns of Provision and their Impact, in T. Meyer, P. Bridgen and B. Riedmüller (eds), *Private Pensions versus Social Inclusion?* Cheltenham: Edward Elgar, Chapter 8.

Mitchell, D. 1993. *Income Transfers in Ten Welfare States.* Aldershot: Avebury.

Müller, G. 1999. Frühindikatoren zum sozialpolitischen Handlungsbedarf. Das Beispiel der Altersarmut in der Schweiz (Early Warning Indicators and Need for Action by Social Policy: The Example of Old-Age Poverty in Switzerland), in P. Flora and H.-H. Noll (eds), *Sozialberichterstattung und Sozialstaatsbeobachtung.* Frankfurt a.M.: Campus, 169–92.

Müller, G. 2013. Vulnerabilitäts- und Frühwarnindikatoren zur Altersarmut unter verschiedenen Wohlfahrtsregimes (Vulnerability- and Early Warning Indicators of Old-Age Poverty under Different Welfare Regimes), in C. Vogel and A. Motel-Klingebiel (eds), *Altern im sozialen Wandel: Die Rückkehr der Altersarmut?* Wiesbaden: Springer VS, 407–23.

Netemeyer, R., Bearden, W. and Sharma, S. 2003. *Scaling Procedures: Issues and Applications.* Thousand Oaks: Sage.

OECD 2008. *Growing Unequal? Income Distribution and Poverty in OECD Countries.* Paris: OECD-Publications.

OECD 2011. *Economic Outlook.* Paris: OECD-Publications.

Orr, L. 1999. *Social Experiments: Evaluating Public Programs with Experimental Methods.* Thousand Oaks: Sage.

Ranci, C. 2010. Social Vulnerability in Europe, in C. Ranci (ed.), *Social Vulnerability in Europe: The New Configuration of Social Risks.* Basingstoke: Palgrave, 3–24.

Rupesinghe, K. and Kuroda, M. (eds) 1992. *Early Warning and Conflict Resolution.* New York: St. Martin's Press.

United Nations, Department of Economic and Social Affairs 1999. *Vulnerability and Poverty in a Global Economy.* New York: United Nations Publications.

Van Walraven, K. (ed.) 1998. *Early Warning and Conflict Prevention: Limitations and Possibilities.* The Hague: Kluwer Law International.

Appendix[7]

---

7   Go to *http://www.microsimulation.org/resource-centre/new-pathways/* and activate
Chapter 10 Online Appendix GMueller.pdf.

8   Table 10.1 is based on an earlier publication of the author, which appeared as Müller
(2013).

9   Table 10.2 is based on an earlier publication of the author, which appeared as Müller
(2013).

Chapter 11

How Sensitive is Old-Age Poverty to Financial Crisis? A Microsimulation Experiment for Sweden

Elisa Baroni,[1] Thomas Lindh[†] and Gustav Öberg

Introduction

Using the agent based microsimulation model IFSIM at the Institute for Futures Studies, our chapter studies the linkages between the design of the new Swedish pension system and poverty outcomes in old age, and in particular how these outcomes are affected by financial shocks. The model allows for heterogeneity and micro-macro feedbacks that are hard to analyse with conventional theoretical approaches. The issue is topical for Sweden since Swedish pension funds have been experiencing large real losses; –34 per cent on average in 2008 as stated in Orange Rapport (2009). Furthermore, the design of the automatic balancing mechanism (known as the 'brake') in the unfunded part of the public pension is sensitive to macroeconomic, demographic and financial risks. The purpose of our experimental simulations is to explore these risks in a more complex setting than is allowed by analytically tractable models. In this chapter we focus on the financial risks and gendered poverty outcomes in retirement.

The reformed Swedish public pension system first became operational in 1999 for the income pension and then in 2000 the premium pension choice, after a parliamentary decision 1994. In 2003 all changes including the automatic balancing mechanism had been put in operation. Since there is a 20-year transition period with mixed pension rights for the birth cohorts 1934 to 1953, the poverty impact of the pure system cannot be assessed empirically. The new system is a Notional Defined Contribution (NDC) system – 16 per cent of wages – with PAYG financing (the so called *income pension*), and a minor funded system (the *premium pension*) with 2.5 per cent of wages set aside for individual investment in a variety of mutual funds. Saving in the funded premium pension is mandatory.

---

1   We are grateful for comments from participants in the WDA/scala workshop on Pension Challenge and the Financial Crisis, University of St. Gallen, 30 October 2009. Funding from Riksbankens Jubileumsfond, the National Insurance Agency and the Swedish Research Council is gratefully acknowledged. Erik Rosenqvist has provided invaluable research assistance.

There is an additional element of pre-funding in the buffer funds of the PAYG income pension. The funds are invested by five different fund managements on the financial markets. The value of the buffer funds (AP funds) is a crucial element in the balancing of the system. On top of the public pensions, ca. 95 per cent of workers have rights to *occupational pensions*, mainly four different systems collectively agreed by unions and employers. For individuals below the ceiling for the income pension, currently around 80 per cent of the population, it is of limited importance corresponding to around 10 per cent of income, but for the ca. 20 per cent who gets a pension above the income ceiling it is of paramount importance. The occupational pensions also have mixed funding, hence also directly or indirectly depend on the performance of financial markets (directly if DC, indirectly if defined benefit: DB). All in all, the average pensioner is therefore quite exposed to financial risks.

The state offers also a universal minimum benefit (*guaranteed pension*) to all, which is paid out of general taxation and is gradually withdrawn as the individual becomes eligible for a sufficiently high contributory pension (i.e. income pension). Individual income pension rights are accumulated in notional accounts with contributions and grow with an income index reflecting the growth of wages. This index is adjusted downwards by the *automatic balancing mechanism* if it is required to preserve financial stability. The final pension received at retirement is an annuity calculated from the accumulated notional account on the basis of many parameters including life expectancy (unisex life tables are used), the income index growth and any automatic balancing of the buffer fund. In general the income pension represents the largest chunk of an average pension (40–60 per cent). The funded premium pension is subject entirely to market performance and individual investment decisions and represents a smaller share of the final pension (only around 3 per cent today but estimated to represent 15–20 per cent in the fully mature system). The occupational pension, either DB or DC on average represents around 15–20 per cent of the final pension for the average person.

It follows that the exposure of the average Swedish pensioner to the funded part of her pension is therefore ca. 35–40 per cent of the total pension (summing only the state premium pension and the occupational pension). However this exposure is higher if we include downward adjustment of the income pension through the turning on of the automatic balancing mechanism, which would be the case if the value of the state buffer funds shrinks too fast due to a financial shock.

Our aim is to investigate the behaviour of the system with respect to poverty outcomes in old age for different cohorts (e.g. retiring before or after a crisis) also with respect to gender. Even in the absence of a financial crisis, different cohorts do enjoy a different composition in their final pension (e.g. in the share of income pension versus guarantee pension) depending on demographic and macroeconomic conditions prevailing at the time of their retirement. The occurrence of a financial crisis will generate different poverty results depending on when it strikes in relation to these normal variations in pension composition.

Currently, around 35 per cent of women still work part time, a much higher proportion than men (SCB Labour Force Survey, 2011). Also, the average time spent in the labour market is lower for women (ca. 37 years against 40 for men), the average wage is lower (84–92 per cent of that of a man with the same job) and the actual retirement age is earlier (61.6 for women against 62.3 for men if employed at 30 years of age). When it comes specifically to parental leave, we know that for every child 80 per cent of the allowed parental leave is taken out by the woman (Haataja 2009); the woman tends to take out also most of the subsequent leave for caring for sick children up to 12 years old (Ekberg, Eriksson and Fieber 2004).

Women's direct absence from the labour market in connection to childbirth is partially compensated by the Swedish pension system (which contains childcare credits) but due to a multitude of factors, female career prospects are in sum poorer, part time work much more common, and reliance on a higher share of guarantee pension is therefore more frequent than for men.

In order to study the impact of financial crisis on elderly poverty, we have adapted the agent based microsimulation model IFSIM (see Baroni, Žamac and Öberg (2009) for a general model description). It is important to stress that the model is not predictive but a theoretical device to experimentally gauge the net effects of a shock while keeping all other policy parameters constant. Thus, even if we initialize it with Swedish data in this chapter, the outcomes of the basic setup as the model has stabilized would be the same for any country with similar institutions and the model can be recalibrated with a different set of institutions and initial values to simulate any country.

The basic definitions and measurements chosen to describe poverty are relative poverty rates that conform to standard relative poverty indexes as described in e.g. Atkinson (1987). The relative measure of poverty refers to the individual's position within the income distribution rather than her degree of deprivation in terms of absolute human needs. Usually someone is considered 'poor' if their income lies below the poverty line, which is commonly set to 60 per cent of the median income. Household equivalized incomes are used rather than individuals' in order to account for economies of scales related to household size. So our poverty definition refers to someone who lives in a household whose equivalized per capita income lies below the poverty line.

In the next section we describe more closely the relevant basic parts of the IFSIM model. The setup of the specific simulation we report here is described. Then the results are presented, followed by a discussion of these results.

The IFSIM Agent Based Model

The model is initiated with Swedish micro-data from the SESIM microsimulation model (Flood et al. 2006) at the Ministry of Finance as input data and from that simulates an artificial panel of individuals and households for 150 years.[2] The main events simulated are

- Demographic, i.e. whether the individual survives, whether he or she gets married, and if so whether he or she has a child during any specific year while being married.
- Educational, both in terms of the level, i.e. whether the individual is in school or if not what is her highest degree, and the quality of her human capital i.e. how skilled the individual is at any given time. Human capital is accumulated also when in work.
- Labour market status (i.e. if in work, full or part time or retired) is simulated with the restriction that only females may choose their labour supply, and his or her income as a function of accumulated human capital. Retirement is, however, at 65 for everybody.

The last point is a simplified representation of the fact that females in general have more choice regarding their labour supply. Once the income is defined a rudimentary tax and benefit system is implemented to derive disposable income under the restriction that the public budget must be in balance.

The model incorporates four key agents: individuals, households, networks and the State. By agents here we mean JAVA objects belonging to a specific agent class to which certain actions and characteristics are ascribed. Individuals are of course the main agent type being simulated; they are uniquely identified, they can be born, die, mate, procreate, leave home, study, work or retire.

Individuals are grouped into households which are separate agents that have characteristics of their own: a separate household ID, a given size, number of children, household income, a history and special 'links' between household members such as inheritability of certain personal features (e.g. initial skills are inherited as the average of both parents and consumption preferences are shaped by the household consumption).

Networks are less tangible agents but still they exist as separate entities with a specific location and group composition that may affect for example fertility decisions. Networks are lists of individuals grouped by age rather than household (i.e. an individual's network does not directly include his or her household). Networks are programmed to perform certain actions for instance retrieve network characteristics such as mean participation or education rates which are used by the individual agents to make forward looking decisions by learning from their social network. Finally the State is the only single agent in the model i.e. the single class being instantiated only once. The State performs the tax and redistribution functions, including setting a local tax rate to keep the budget in

---

2   Note that in our analysis we disregard the first 80 years since we want to look at a population whose work life falls entirely into the new pension system and who is born within the simulated timespan.

balance, calculating and collecting income tax, paying teachers' salaries, student allowances, parental leave benefits and pensions, and can set some policy targets through which it can affect micro behaviours and macro outcomes.

The main decision making individuals in the model are the individuals but the state also makes a decision about the tax pressure in order to keep a balanced budget.

The individuals use different sets of knowledge to make decisions. Ranging from individual knowledge, that is data that is different for each agent and global knowledge, that is data that is shared between all individuals. For instance, when it comes to the decision to go to college the individual agent looks at its network rather than the wage outcome for the entire population. The female labour decision on the other hand is made on a household level so also the earnings of the men in the model will influence the female labour supply.

The model is a theoretical model in which the micro decisions are made using artificial intelligence, however limited, and the decision making processes are modelled. This in contrast to just assigning empirically estimated probabilities to certain choices. These features make the model fit in more closely with agent based models rather than microsimulation models.

This enables it to be used for combining theories about for instance taxes and fertility choices or taxes and labour supply choices when studying the impact of a financial crisis on the Swedish pension system. This requires that the model is also loaded with a simplified representation of the Swedish pension system, which is described below. It can be used to study what theory has to say about the impact of events on an economic system where the parts of the system are interconnected. This would, according to Speilauer (2009), also give the model features which relate it to a broader class of agent based models.

In an agent based model the agents makes decisions that affects themselves, the environment or the other agents. As stated above the agents in the IFSIM-model make decisions about, for instance, their fertility, labour supply and also their education.

Most of the parameters that are used in the formulas depicting decision processes are attained through calibration against Swedish register data. The known parameters are mostly coming from the Swedish pension system, such as the percent of social contributions going to the funded part of the system and parameters pertaining to the level of guarantee pension.

The main decision making agent in the model is the individual. The fact that the agents are heterogeneous and that the possible combination of variable values would be very large even if the continuous variables in the model where truncated speaks for using a microsimulation, or agent based model, according to Imhoff and Post (1998). In the model the heterogeneity of the agents is important, for instance when it comes to the decision to go to college or not. Since not all agents respond to the shifts in the economy the same way you get, arguably, a more realistic decision outcome where some individuals, even though they are alike in some aspects, may make different choices regarding education even when faced with the same macro conditions.

The modelling of the population in the model is internally consistent, using terminology borrowed from Imhoff and Post (1998). What this means for the modelling of the financial crisis and its impact of the Swedish pension system is that for instance the financial crisis is allowed to affect the levels of the pensions paid out through the balancing mechanism. This affects the amount of guarantee pension paid out through the rules in the pension system relating to the guarantee pension. This in turn affects the tax pressure which through the labour supply is allowed to effect for instance the labour decisions of the women in the model. That decision is also affected by the prognosis the individual agent makes about her future pension levels that is lowered by the brake mechanism of the Swedish pension system. This will give a feedback effect affecting the brake mechanism and so on. Some of the variables influence the level of other variables through rules of thumb and discrete outcomes. This means that the relationship between two variables in the model is not necessarily linear.

The IFSIM Pension System

The pension system is modelled according to the new Swedish system with some simplifications. Thus the description here refers to the IFSIM implementation and does not in all details mimic the actual Swedish pension system. Every retiree is assigned a public pension comprising three elements: a premium pension, an income pension and a guarantee pension.

The premium pension fund collects 2.5 per cent of the individual yearly salary and invests into funds. Since in our model we do not have explicit capital markets, we assume that the returns to such funds are constant. This is to simplify interpretation of other variations in the model. Upon retirement that always takes place at age 65 the value of the fund is indexed by a constant return.[3] These simplifications allow us to focus on automatic balancing by limiting other sources of risk.

The income pension is based on the notional defined contribution accounts where the insured pays 16 per cent of income into a personal account but the contribution is not invested but used to finance current pensioners' expenditure while being earmarked for the future at a given 'interest' determined by the income index. At the time of retirement, the individual will therefore have accumulated a notional pension wealth converted into a yearly pension income. The pension annuity is calculated on the basis of a unisex life expectancy of 20 years at age 65 through an annuitization divisor, which assigns an expected 'interest' of

---

3   In reality the individual has the choice to annuitize the value at retirement to a fixed nominal amount or keep the share in funds and get the value of the annuity recalculated each year. We chose the latter solution to emphasize the financial risk during retirement.

1.6 per cent (corresponding to expected income growth, on the remaining pension wealth after retirement. The actual value of the annuity is adjusted yearly for real growth deviating from 1.6 per cent (i.e. if the growth is lower the pension benefit is reduced and vice versa), as well as occasionally by the brake.

The system's overall balance is assessed by looking at the amount of 'financially sustainable' pension debt in the system. Financial sustainability implies that the expected income pension liability must be set equal to the expected amount of contributions and assets in the system. The amount of expected contributions is obtained by multiplying current social insurance contributions CW by a so called 'turnover duration' factor which roughly measures the average contribution time (i.e. the total payable into each individual account by the current generation of workers, W until retirement). This turnover duration is based on demographics and is kept constant in the model.[4] The amount of projected debt for total income pension benefits S is computed in a similar way, as the sum of the expected pension liability to be paid both to the currently active and to those who have already retired, based on their respective life expectancies.

$$(1) \qquad A_t + \sum_t CW = b \sum_t S$$

A is the value of the buffer funds at time t, the sum of CW represents the estimate of current and future contributions at time t, and the sum of S is the estimate of current and future liabilities for income pensions (both to the active population and to current pensioners). It follows from (1) that $b = (A + \Sigma\, CW) / \Sigma\, S$ is the inter-temporal balancing index required to keep the income pension bill financially sustainable.

Once the income pension is calculated, the individual will be checked to see whether she will be eligible for some guaranteed pension. A guarantee pension will be awarded to all individuals who have an income pension below a level calibrated to the real system.

Beside the public pension, people with an income above 7.5 basic amounts (i.e. average earners and above) contribute into a DB occupational pension which on average pays in retirement around 65 per cent of last earnings (above 7.5 basic amounts, 10 per cent below). The contributions to the occupational pensions vary to keep the system balanced every year, and they increase with age. This is a stylized version of the main four occupational pension systems that is mainly intended to avoid truncating the income distribution of pensioners.

4　In reality the turnover duration is not constant but depends on life expectancy, at which ages people earn money and how many people there are in a certain age group. In our model this variation plays almost no role at all, so we simplified.

The Automatic Balance Mechanism

The decision to index the pension system with average wage growth instead of the growth of the wage sum (the contribution base) made it necessary to have an adjustment mechanism to preserve both financial balance and inter-generational fairness[5] within the PAYG component of the public pension. The automatic balance mechanism was introduced to cut benefits when liabilities were deemed to exceed assets in the system. The brake allows keeping a fixed contribution rate while also preserving the long term financial sustainability of the PAYG system.

Formally the automatic balance mechanism is calculated by the following *Balance Ratio and Balance Index*:

$$(2) \qquad Balance\ Ratio = \frac{ContributionAssets + BufferFund}{PensionLiability}$$

$$(3) \qquad Balance\ Index = BalanceRatio * IncomeIndex \text{ if BR} < 1 \text{ or BI} < \text{Income Index}$$

The balance index – obtained by multiplying the income index by the balance ratio when the brake has hit – remains operational until the balance index equals or is greater than the income index. This means that even after the balance ratio has increased to above unity the balance index will remain in force in order to resume indexation at the income index level and thus restore the level of pension income relative to that of the wage earners. See Figure A1 in the Appendix.

The system's internal rate of return is a function of the growth in the contribution base (e.g. population aging would imply lower growth in the contribution base), of the change in age-related income and of returns to the buffer funds (e.g. a financial crisis).

In practice, the triggering of the balance index means that all notional pension accounts as well as income pensions being paid out will be indexed by the system's internal rate of return rather than the rate of growth in average incomes. As long as the balance index grows slower than the income index, the liabilities will start decreasing relative to contributions.

As Barr and Diamond (2011) note this has some peculiar consequences that so far have not been much debated. Over the period when the automatic balancing index is operative pensioners lose part of their otherwise expected annuities, some of those retiring within the period lose parts of their pension wealth, while those who actively contribute to the system and do not retire until after normal indexing is resumed will ceteris paribus increase their pension wealth!

In order to clarify exactly how this works a formal example can be helpful. Suppose the brake turns down over a period 1 and in period 2 grows to bring the balance index (multiplication factor B_{t+1} / B_t i.e. the gross growth rate in the index in the period) back to the level of the income index W (multiplication factor W_{t+1} / W_t in the period). For an individual with accumulated pension wealth A and

---

5   See O. Settergren, NFT 2/2003.

contributions in each period c, the accumulation of new pension wealth over the same period but without the brake striking would take place according to (ignoring all other differences between scenarios)

$$(4) \qquad A_2 = \frac{W_2 W_1}{W_1 W_0} A_0 + \frac{W_2}{W_1} c_1 + c_2$$

If the brake strikes the accumulation is instead:

$$(5) \qquad A_2^B = \frac{B_2 B_1}{B_1 W_0} A_0 + \frac{B_2}{B_1} c_1 + c_2$$

Simplifying, the difference is:

$$(6) \qquad A_2 - A_2^B = \left(\frac{W_2}{W_0} - \frac{B_2}{W_0} \right) A_0 + \left(\frac{W_2}{W_1} - \frac{B_2}{B_1} \right) c_1$$

By construction the first term is zero since $W_2 = B_2$ (as in period 2 the balance index has reached again the level of the income index). From this also follows that the second term is negative since $W_1 > B_1$. In other words the value of the account at period 2 will be larger than what it would have been if the income indexing would have been on instead. Thus active contributors will, at a given labour supply and income, unambiguously gain compared to a situation when the brake would have been off. As long as pension wealth has not been annuitized (i.e. unless someone retires before the balance is turned off) the effect of the balancing is not only neutralized but total future pension liabilities will actually increase. This simple example can be generalized to more periods to show that any contributions paid during the automatic balancing will have been indexed at a faster rate at the end of the period of automatic balancing than if they had been indexed by the income index. *Ceteris paribus* pension wealth will be higher in the NDC accounts than if indexed by the income index.

Thus the brake has the strange property that those who *can* adjust their labour supply to compensate for the balancing have no direct reason to increase but rather to decrease their labour supply. Those who no longer can adjust their labour supply take the whole hit of the balancing. Those who pay the price in bringing down liabilities will be those who already are retired and those who retire while automatic balancing is in effect and in particular those who annuitize their account when the balance ratio reaches its minimum. In our simulation adjustment of labour supply is exclusively a female prerogative and based on rather myopic expectations formed by observing ten years older peers.

Another issue is that the brake may be triggered by short-term losses as shown in Sundén (2006). This means that even if the system would be sustainable in the long run, short-term market losses could trigger the brake.

Description of Simulation Scenarios

We review our simulation results by comparing a baseline version to one alternative where we simulate an exogenous financial shock. By financial shock we shall mean one year in which the value of funded pension assets drop by an extraordinary rate of 20 per cent and there is no recovery since we want to simulate a burst of a financial bubble.

In principle we can generate data for everything that happens in the model, but we focus on those features of the pension system that are going to be directly affected by a financial shock, namely the value of individuals' premium pension accounts as well as the value of the state's buffer fund, which will affect the system's assets and its internal rate of return. Both premium pension accounts and the state buffer fund are made to drop by 20 per cent.

Since the share of pension income coming from the premium pension is small (roughly 10–20 per cent), the (poverty) impact of the financial crisis is expected to be most felt through its effects on the buffer fund, the automatic balancing mechanism and the income pension. The income pension will grow more slowly for a while and pension accounts of workers will, as shown above, tend to increase in response to an automatic balancing episode, but second order effects working through labour supply for women and incentives for a host of other decisions on education, family formation and so on may cause it to grow slower and perhaps even decrease for a while. The individual impact also depends on where in the lifecycle different individuals are when the crisis hits, e.g. if in late career, in early working years or in retirement.

Our Hypotheses

The timing of a financial crisis releasing automatic balancing matters in relation to an individual's life cycle. Being exposed to a crisis in retirement always implies a loss regardless of indirect effects as discussed above but in other cases indirect effects may moderate responses in other directions. We will investigate whether the following three hypotheses hold as we allow for individual interaction and micro-macro feedbacks:

1. Being exposed to a crisis in working years does not imply a lower amount of pension entitlements. The age and size of contributions is important to determine this outcome in relation to repercussions on labour supply and economic growth. The closer to retirement the more vulnerable an individual should be. **Those who are about to retire when the brake is released are worse off than those who retire during the period it is in effect.**

2. Since liabilities to the working population increases ceteris paribus, the brake may be insufficient to bring back long-term stability and the **financial crisis unleashes repeated brake periods** unless new capital is added to the buffer funds.

In order to test whether these effects go through when we allow for interaction in the population and long-term effects on education and fertility we choose to follow the pension wealth accumulation of three separate cohorts.

Table 11.1   Cohort characteristics

Cohort birth year	Retirement year	Experience of ABM in Baseline	Experience of ABM due to a crisis in 2100
2025	2090	Never	In mid retirement
2040	2105	Never	Just before and at retirement
2065	2130	Never	In early-to-late working years and in retirement

Simulation Results

Our baseline simulation is calibrated to initially reproduce the Swedish demographic parameters, in terms of fertility and mortality rates. This means we are ignoring migration and tend to get no natural population increase. The age-specific fertility rate follows the shape of 2006 Statistics Sweden data, while for mortality we use Statistics Sweden's life expectancy projections by age up until 2055, after which time we fix life expectancy to that level (i.e. a remaining life expectancy of ca. 20 years at 65, assuming that life expectancy will not grow indefinitely). We analyse simulated data between model year 2080 and 2150 for the purpose of our analysis, and over this period we observe a low constant population growth rate. During the initial period we observe an aging population as the old-age dependency ratio (65+/20–64) rises from 0.32 to between 0.42 and 0.43 over the period we study. The total fertility rate also stabilizes around an average of two children per woman (with yearly fluctuations above or below this level).

Over the years 2090–2150 the baseline shows an increasing share of women that choose full time labour supply (from 65 to 68 per cent of all women of working age) and a decrease in voluntary unemployment. Recall that all men work full time.

As the share of workers in the labour force increases due to increased female participation, the growth in GDP per worker decreases over time . Growth rates quickly recover after the crisis. In the model there is no direct connection between production and financial assets so we avoid this feedback to the real economy.

When we let the crisis hit in 2100 the pension system assets suddenly drop by 20 per cent thus reaching the liabilities level. An expected effect of the crisis in 2100 is to set off the automatic balancing mechanism at once. The sudden drop in the buffer fund destabilizes the system by suddenly making assets insufficient to cover liabilities.

Furthermore the crisis leads to automatic balancing striking more often after 2110 and in a more repetitive pattern, see Figure 11.1.

The reason for not starting the experiment at an earlier year is that the pension system in the model should be stable at the onset of the crisis because of the fact that we want to model the impact of a financial crisis on a mature pension system. If we would start the crisis earlier it might be difficult to distinguish the effect of the crisis from phenomena relating to the onset of a partially funded pension system.

Once the brake has been released after the crisis it leads to more frequent striking of the brake. Our standard return of 3.25 per cent to the buffer fund – the same rate used in the baseline projections of the Swedish Pension Authority's Annual Report – is simply not sufficient to restore the buffer to a safe level. Similarly, the drop in pension liability as a percentage of GDP brought on by balancing is not sufficient to compensate for diminishing buffer funds.

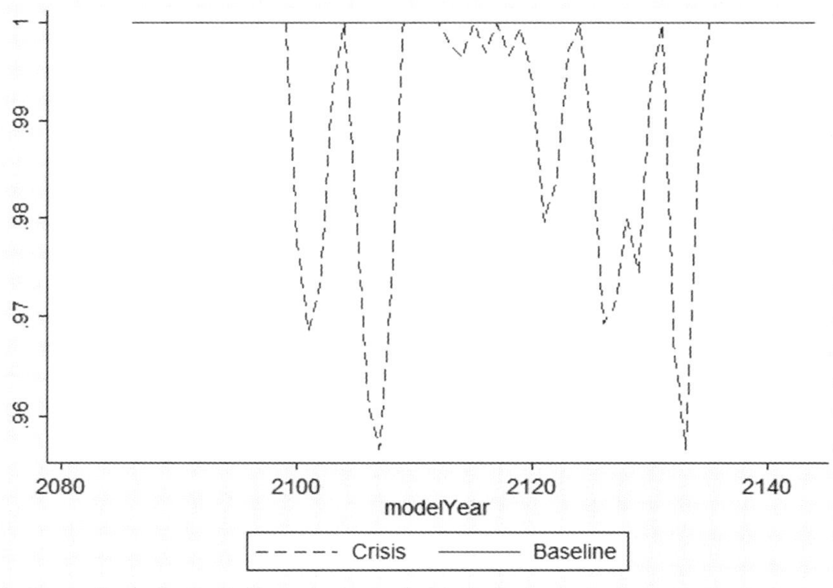

Figure 11.1   Automatic balancing in the crisis scenario and the baseline scenario

Moving on to data on the average gross replacement rate of the elderly, measured as the first public pension relative to the last wage, reaches a maximum around model year 2100, remains high for males (ca. 58 per cent) another 20 years then tends to decrease also for males (ca. 53 per cent by model year 2140). In the crisis scenario the replacement ratio drops heavily at the time of the crisis, especially for men (ca. 51 per cent right after the crisis), reflecting the situation of those retiring during balancing, the recurring balancing episodes leading to lower minima than in the baseline; yet averages are not that different around model year 2140 in the two scenarios, nor is there any obvious change in the gender gaps.

At an aggregate level, the relative poverty rate of women (at 60 per cent of median equivalized household income) of the elderly tends nevertheless to decrease in both scenarios and the difference between genders is vanishing. The latter is an effect due to albeit a small increasing labour market participation of women (who would have been most likely to be poor) in combination with the slowing down of economic growth below 1.6 per cent compressing the income distribution.

Cohort Analysis

We now focus on the three separate cohorts described in Table 11.1 to see how their life cycle incomes and poverty risk evolves. We will later compare these results with the crisis scenario to see whether some of the differences in their retirement outcome can be attributed to experiencing the financial crisis (in particular, the associated balancing mechanism) in different moments of their life-cycle.

Figure 11.2 below shows first of all the value of the three cohorts' respective notional pension accounts up to age 64, as percentage of GDP per worker. Given a situation where no cohort is hit by the brake the accumulation of pension accounts is smooth. Cohort 2025 on average increases its account from about 5.3 of GDP per worker in 2086 to a little more than 5.9 of GDP per worker in 2089. Cohort 2040 has a little more than 5 times GDP per worker 2100 in their average accounts and ends up with almost 5.3 times the GDP per worker in 2104. Cohort 2065 has an account of 5.4 times GDP per worker in 2025 and almost reaches 6.0 in 2029. The fact that cohort 2040 is worse off in terms of average GDP per worker is a consequence of natural variation in GDP over the period we measure (which is different for each cohort) as well as wage and female labour supply variations over the life cycle of each cohort.

From age 65, income pensions are indexed by income growth minus 1.6 per cent (recall that the annuitization factor assumes growth at 1.6 per cent). If we normalize pension incomes to average GDP per worker, they will therefore grow more slowly than incomes over time. In our economy, the average yearly growth rate is 1.8 per cent, but from ca. 2120 the average growth remains mostly below 1.6 per cent . This will therefore also affect the rate at which income pensions will be paid out from that year onwards. Normalized by GDP per worker this means that at faster growth the relative pension income decreases faster.[6] More generally, the fact that income growth decreases over time means that, for a given pension account size, younger cohorts will always get a lower relative annuity compared to older ones. However, as long as the economy has growing GDP per capita younger cohorts accumulate a higher level of pension wealth on average.

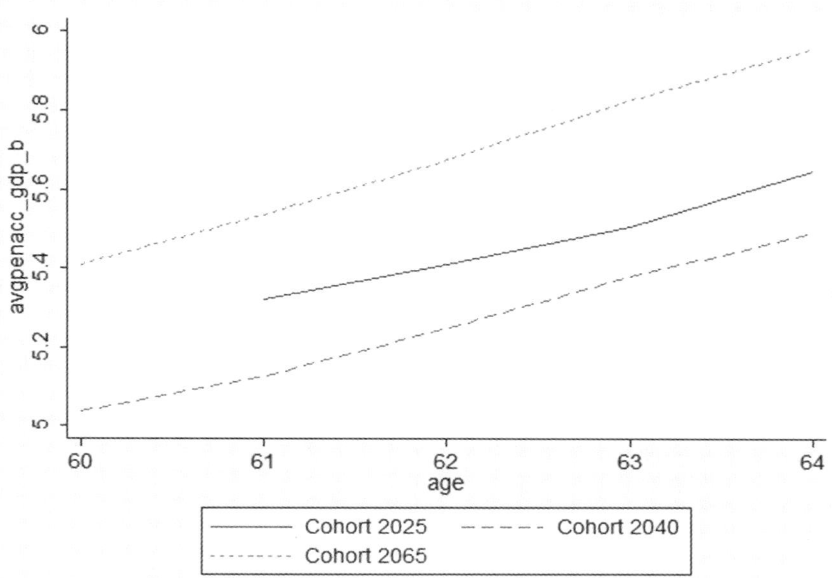

Figure 11.2　Lifetime accumulation of notional pension account by cohort as a proportion of yearly GDP per worker

We thus repeat the same cohort analysis for average income pensions received from age 65 up to 75. Figure 11.3 shows the average income pension for each of our three cohorts from the age of retirement (65) to age 75, expressed again as a percentage of average GDP per worker. Having accumulated similar pension accounts, we see that these cohorts retire with rather similar income pensions in relative terms (and similar rates of decrease over time), between 30 and 33 per cent of average GDP per worker.

When looking at the entire income composition of the average pensioner we also see that the proportion coming from different sources varies only slightly between our cohorts. The average pensioner in cohort 2065 has a slightly lower

---

6　The ratio decreases each year since the denominator increases with the growth rate g and the numerator with g-0.016. Dividing it becomes obvious that the decrease is faster the greater is g.

share of her income from the guarantee pension than cohorts 2025 and 2040. Most noticeably the share of income coming from the funded premium pension and occupational pensions has increased compared to the earlier two cohorts. In general however, we can say that the income composition is pretty stable across cohorts. This average pensioner, of course, represents the collective cohort and has no individual counterpart since most individuals have no guarantee pension and those that have will have very small occupational pensions.

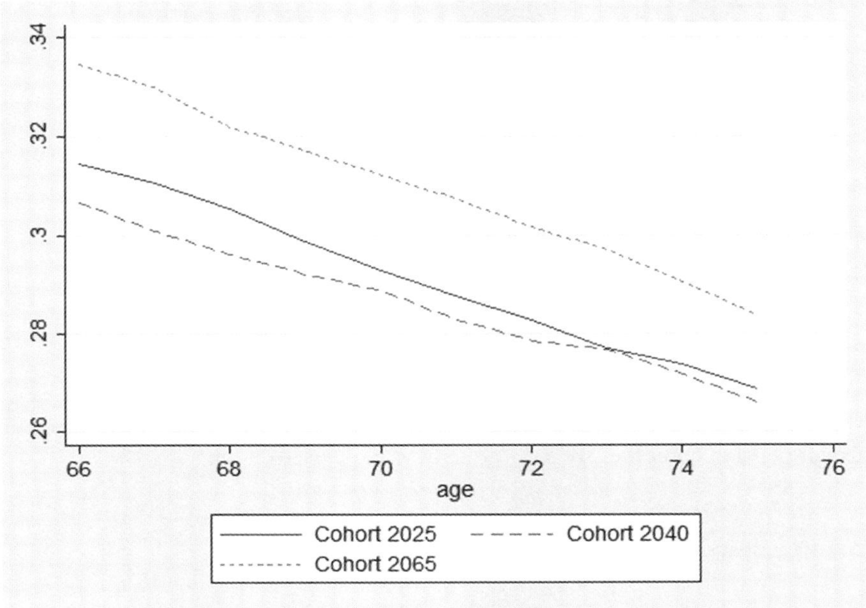

Figure 11.3   Average income pension between 65 and 75 by cohort, as a fraction of average GDP per worker

Turning now to relative poverty statistics, we present below our baseline results for the over 65, defining relative poverty as equivalized household incomes which lie below the poverty line set at 60 per cent of (equivalized) median income (for the whole population). All sources of income contribute to the household disposable income. This means that the poverty statistics is sensitive to household composition changes. We should also note here that the risk of being poor is always associated to having some or all of one's pension coming from the guarantee pension; 95 per cent of those who have some or all of their pension income from the guarantee pension are in fact poor in our model.[7]

---

7   The poverty line in the model varies around 30 per cent of average GDP per worker, and the maximum level of guarantee pension is ca. 33 per cent of the average wage.

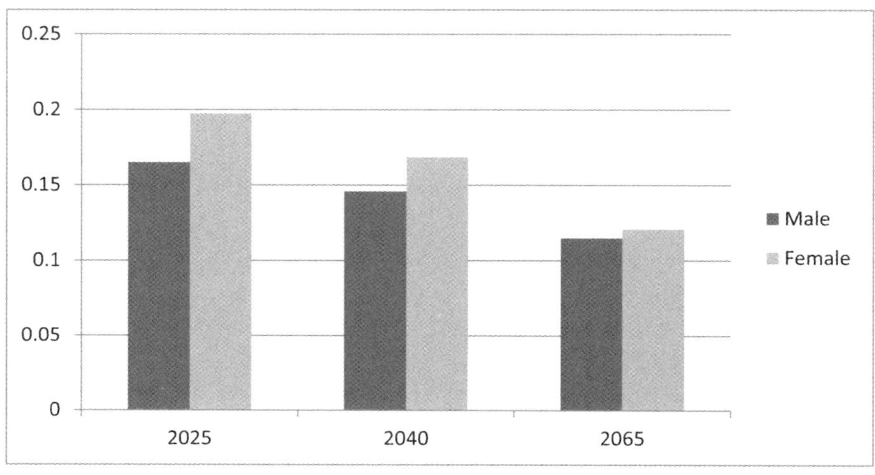

Figure 11.4   Elderly poverty rates (60 per cent) by cohort, age 65–80

Figure 11.4 shows that the highest poverty rates (between 65 and 80 years old) are found in cohort 2025 and 2040. Cohort 2025 experiences thus the highest poverty levels, but we see that cohort 2065 actually have more similar poverty rates for females and males, again reflecting in the cohort dimension the convergence of gender pension outcomes we saw in the baseline cross-section.

Cohort Analysis in the Crisis Simulation

We now move on to see how our three cohorts fare in terms of their pension income under the crisis scenario compared to the baseline. Cohort 2025 will not be affected by the 2100 crisis except for their very last years in retirement. Their age in 2100 is 75 years, but the shift to the balance index has a lag of two years before taking effect. Cohort 2040 will be affected three years before their retirement year (at 62), and beyond retirement, while cohort 2065 will be affected earlier in working years (when they are 37), in later working years as well as in retirement.

We first look at the value of accumulated (notional) income pension accounts by age 64, by cohort in Figure 11.5. The crisis and repeated brake episodes have affected the growth rate of cohort 2065's pension account but at age 62 they have almost entirely recovered. While not making a gain, as would be the case without indirect effects, this cohort has recuperated almost entirely the potential losses but happens to retire during one of the recurring balancing episodes.

Likewise we see that the crisis impacts on cohort 2040 (who are 60 at the time it strikes), reducing the value of the account by age 64 compared to the baseline. We know that for cohort 2040 this is because the balance index has not yet returned to its original level when they are 64. Cohort 2025 of course sees no change.

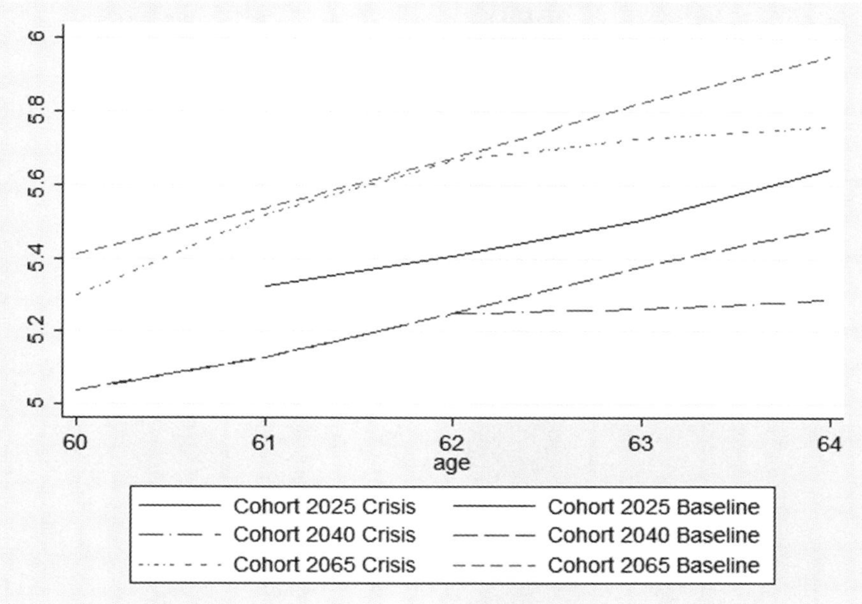

Figure 11.5　Lifetime accumulation of notional pension account by cohort and scenario as a proportion of yearly GDP per worker in the baseline scenario

In Figure 11.6 we use baseline GDP per worker to evaluate the income pensions in the first ten years of retirement in order not to take GDP variations into account in the normalization. Note that this is only part of the public pension. Cohort 2025 has up to 75 years not been affected at all while the other cohorts have slightly worsened their situation, particularly cohort 2040 which was hit by the crisis just before retirement and not given the bonus of gains during the following brake periods. This information is provided in Table 11.2.

Another important effect of the crisis is to suddenly reduce the value of a premium pension account by 20 per cent. In this case, the crisis affects mostly retirees from cohort 2025 and 2040 (who just retires after the crisis) since they see the value of their premium pension suddenly drop by 20 per cent without possibility for this loss to be compensated by their own actions (since those born 2025 are already retired, they do not contribute to the account any longer). In particular, as we clearly see in Table 11.3, cohort 2040 receives a substantially lower premium pension after retirement (in model year 2105). Cohort 2065 instead sees less change in their funded pension due to the fact that its premium account can recuperate most of its pre-crisis value over the years before retirement.

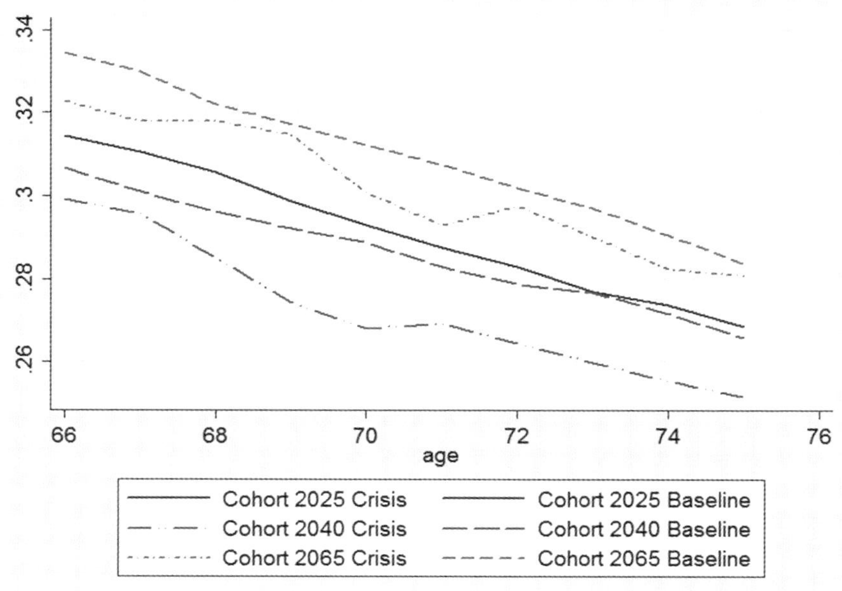

**Figure 11.6   Average income pension by cohort and scenario as a
proportion of baseline GDP per worker**

Table 11.2   Average income pension as a share of GDP per worker

Cohort	Scenario	Age									
		66	67	68	69	70	71	72	73	74	75
2025	Baseline	0.314	0.311	0.306	0.299	0.293	0.287	0.283	0.277	0.274	0.268
	Crisis	0.314	0.311	0.306	0.299	0.293	0.287	0.283	0.277	0.274	0.268
2040	Baseline	0.307	0.301	0.296	0.292	0.289	0.283	0.279	0.277	0.272	0.266
	Crisis	0.299	0.296	0.285	0.274	0.268	0.269	0.264	0.260	0.255	0.251
2065	Baseline	0.335	0.33	0.322	0.317	0.312	0.307	0.302	0.297	0.290	0.284
	Crisis	0.323	0.318	0.318	0.315	0.301	0.293	0.298	0.29	0.282	0.281

We do note a slight increase in labour supply for cohort 2040 (Figure 11.7),
since their expectations of future income pension will be lower due to losses made
in cohorts five years or more older (on whose income they base their projections).
Cohort 2065, however base their expectations on the 10 year older cohort 2055
which is not affected in the same way and hence also increase their labour supply
at age 62.

Table 11.3   Average premium pension by cohort and scenario as a proportion of GDP per worker

Cohort	Scenario	Age									
		66	**67**	**68**	**69**	**70**	**71**	**72**	**73**	**74**	**75**
2025	Baseline	0.089	0.092	0.094	0.097	0.1	0.103	0.106	0.109	0.113	0.116
	Crisis	0.089	0.092	0.094	0.097	0.1	0.103	0.106	0.109	0.113	0.116
2040	Baseline	0.088	0.09	0.093	0.096	0.099	0.102	0.106	0.11	0.114	0.118
	Crisis	0.071	0.073	0.075	0.078	0.08	0.083	0.086	0.089	0.092	0.096
2065	Baseline	0.103	0.107	0.11	0.114	0.119	0.123	0.128	0.133	0.137	0.142
	Crisis	0.095	0.098	0.101	0.105	0.11	0.114	0.118	0.121	0.126	0.131

If we take stock of what we have seen so far, we can therefore say that overall, the cohort which experiences the crisis at the youngest age, while in work (cohort 2065) is only slightly worse off than in the baseline, despite spending a longer amount of time under the ensuing balancing regime with recurring brake episodes.

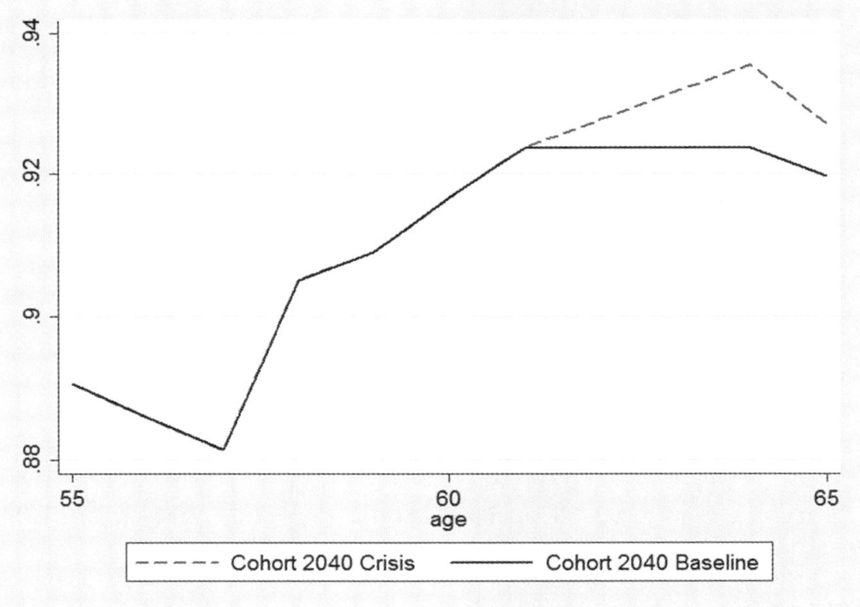

Figure 11.7   Labour supply by scenario for cohort 2040, age 55–65

Looking at the poverty statistics will help summarize which of these effects, i.e. being hit by the brake in retirement or in working year, will prevail in determining the equality in different cohorts.

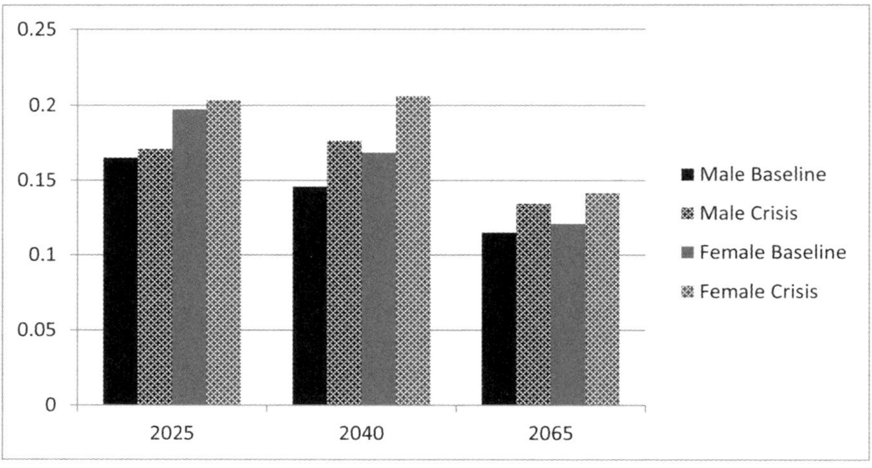

Figure 11.8   Relative poverty among elderly 65–80, by cohort and scenario

The relative poverty statistics aggregated for all cohorts between age 65 and 80 in the crisis scenario show an increase in old-age poverty rates compared to the baseline (Figure 11.8). Cohort 2025 experiences these effects only in late retirement; nevertheless, the increase in poverty rates for both genders is around half a percentage point. Cohort 2040 is the one with the relatively highest increase in elderly poor around three percentage points. Cohort 2065 is much less affected than 2040 with around two percentage points.

Overall they tend to confirm our first hypothesis *that cohorts near retirement are harder hit.* But cohort 2065 is also hit more often after the crisis and just before retirement. In this sense there is not much of a difference with cohort 2040, i.e. both are hit by the brake before retirement so the lower poverty rate characterizing cohort 2065 reflects the general decreasing poverty trend.

Conclusions

Our analysis aims to establish a link between when in the lifecycle one is hit by a financial crisis (and the subsequent on-setting of the automatic balancing mechanism) and poverty outcomes in old age. The analysis is done by looking at three different cohorts.

The main hypotheses that we see confirmed through our simulations are that:

1. The timing of the crisis/automatic balancing in relation to an individual's life cycle matters. In particular, being exposed to a crisis in retirement always amounts to a real income loss although poverty rates do not rise dramatically; being exposed to a crisis in working years has a direct effect

that imply a higher notional pension account but indirect effects on growth rates and repeated releases of the brake may reverse this and for certain it lowers the premium pension account, but this is not enough to make one worse off than someone who is exposed to the crisis in or just before retirement (and who is making a loss in pension benefit while the brake is on). What will be decisive for losses in the working population will be the time left to recuperate and the recapitalization of the buffer funds. Retiring in the middle of a balancing episode will however make you worse off.

2. We do see a clear tendency that once the brake strikes due to a financial crisis it tends to strike more often. The recapitalization by normal returns as the automatic balancing reduces liabilities is insufficient. In part this has to do with the strange property that the automatic balancing tends to increase liabilities to the working population.

What we have shown here is of course only one of many different scenarios. Timing of the recovery from crisis depends on yearly fund return and buffer fund size. We have assumed that the stock market crash is a burst bubble such that there is no recovery in value to be expected except from moderate yearly returns. The general conclusions to draw are that there is a probability that once the brake is released it will tend to be released more often and cohorts near retirement as it is released will tend to take a greater burden. This is due to the design flow that those who can adapt get little reason to do so, while those who cannot adapt bear the burden of rebalancing.

References

Atkinson, A. 1987. On the Measurement of Poverty. *Econometrica*, 55 (4), 749–64.

Baroni, E., Eklöf, M., Hallberg, D., Lindh, T. and Zamac, J. 2009. Fertility Decisions – Simulation in an Agent-Based Model (IFSIM) in A. Zaidi, A. Harding and P. Williamson (eds), *New Frontiers in Microsimulation Modelling*. Vienna / Farnham: European Center Vienna/Ashgate, 265–86.

Baroni, E., Öberg, G. and Zamac, J. 2009. *The IFSIM Handbook*. ArbetsRapport 2009:7. Institutet För Framtidsstudier.

Barr, N. and Diamond, R. 2011. Improving Sweden's automatic balance mechanism. IB#11–2. Center for Retirement Research at Boston College.

Ekberg, J., Eriksson, R. and Friebel, G. 2004. Sharing Responsibility? Short and long term effects of Swedens's 'Daddy Month' Reform. Working Paper Series 3/2004, Swedish Institute for Social Research.

Flood, L. 2008. Sesim: a Microsimulation Approach. *Contributions to Economic Analysis*, 285, 55–83.

Flood, L., Klevmarken, A. and Mitruut, A. 2006. The income of the Swedish Baby Boomers, Working Papers in Economics nr 209. Gothenburg University Business School.

Haataja, A. 2009. Fathers' use of paternity and parental leave in the Nordic countries. Online Working Papers 2/2009. Social Insurance Institution of Finland (Kela).

Imhoff, E. and Post, W. 1998. Microsimulation methods for population projection. *Population: An English Selection*, 10(1), 97–138.

Pensionsmyndigheten. 2009. The Orange Report. Annual Report of the Swedish Pension System SCB. 2011. Labor Force Survey. [Online] 2011. Available at: http://www.scb.se/Pages/Product____23276.aspx [accessed: 20/05/2011].

Spielauer, M. 2009. What is dynamic social science microsimulation? [Online] Available at: http://www.statcan.gc.ca/microsimulation/ [accessed: 29/01/2013].

Sundén, A. 2006. The Swedish Experience with Pension Reform. *Oxford Review of Economic Policy*, 22(1) 22, 133–48.

Sundström, M. and Stafford, F. 1992. Female labour force participation, fertility and public policy in Sweden. *European Journal of Population*, 8, 199–215.

Appendix

Schematic of the working of the automatic balancing index.

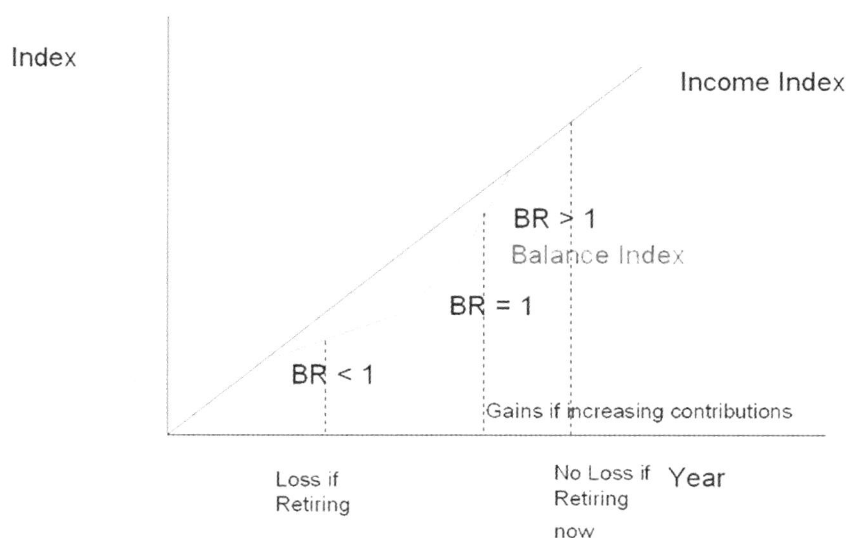

Figure 11.9   Automatic balancing and timing of retirement

Chapter 12

Going Regional: The Effectiveness of Different Tax-benefit Policies in Combating Child Poverty in Spain

Olga Cantó,[1] Marta Adiego, Luis Ayala,
Horacio Levy and Milagros Paniagua

Introduction

According to a large amount of empirical evidence, the consequences of experiencing poverty in childhood are likely to persist for a long time given that employment, educational, health and social outcomes for children growing up in poor families are found more likely to be worse than those for better-off children. The level and evolution of child poverty has become an important concern for social policy in many rich countries in the last decade, particularly since UNICEF (2005) published a report where many developed OECD countries registered an increasingly high rate of child deprivation. In Europe, in particular, there is a large concern that national policies should aim to reduce child poverty risk and promote equality of opportunity in order to facilitate parents' working careers and the achievement of employment objectives within the European Union (EU) 2020 strategy as noted in European Commission (2008). As Corak et al. (2005) and Figari et al. (2009) conclude, there is considerable cross-country variation in the EU in the fraction of the additional household needs arising from having children which is supported from government transfers. In general, they find that, in the European context, countries with the lowest child poverty rates are those in which children benefit a good deal from transfers (not

1   This chapter uses EUROMOD version 5 that was developed with the financial support of the European Commission. EUROMOD is continually being improved and updated and the results presented here represent the best available at the time of writing. Any remaining errors, results produced, interpretations or views presented are the authors' responsibility. This chapter uses data from the Encuesta de Condiciones de Vida for 2007 conducted by the Spanish Instituto Nacional de Estadística (INE). Marta Adiego, Luis Ayala and Milagros Paniagua acknowledge financial support from the Ministerio de Economía y Competitividad (ECO2010-21668-C03-01/ECON). Olga Cantó acknowledges financial support both from the Ministerio de Economía y Competitividad (ECO2010-21668-C03-03/ECON) and from Xunta de Galicia (10SEC300023PR). EQUALITAS is a group of researchers interested in the analysis of inequality and poverty that is financed by a coordinated research project, www.equalitas.es.

necessarily directed to them) such as public support to working mothers and fathers or, also, those countries with a broader tax-transfer system.

Spain is one of the EU countries where the level of child poverty has been highest during the last decade. Child poverty rates in Spain have been consistently over 23 per cent since 1994 while adult poverty rates, even if at high levels too, did not go beyond 19 per cent. The tax-transfer system in Spain is found to be quite narrow. In fact, effective marginal tax rates are found to be one of the lowest of the EU27 together with Greece and Portugal. Regarding public support towards working mothers and fathers Spain also stands out as a country with a relatively low percentage of social expenditure dedicated to the family and children function. However, during the first years of this century and before the start of the Great Recession in 2008 a variety of national and regional policies in Spain extended the level of expenditure on families with children pushing expenditure on cash family benefits as a percentage of total social expenditure from 4.6 per cent in 2001 to 6.6 per cent in 2008. This increase seems to be related both to the creation of a new Spanish central government universal child birth benefit in 2007, but also to the appearance of a large list of new regional governments' tax and benefit policies. So far, little is known about the impact of these new child-related policies on child poverty in Spain. One of the reasons for this is that they have not yet fully been reported in household surveys such as the EU-SILC, but also because, being quite different in terms of design and generosity in each region, there is a general lack of nation-wide institutional information on them. Making use of the tax-benefit model for the European Union – EUROMOD – this chapter simulates the eligibility and receipt of central government policies (both tax deductions and benefits) and assesses their impact on child poverty. Further, we also simulate what would have been the impact of each regional child-related policy if they had been implemented in the whole country. In this sense we aim to point out the main characteristics of the policies that have a higher potential to reduce child poverty in the whole country.

The structure of the chapter is the following. The next section describes the political economy of family policy decentralization in Spain in a general context of social policy design and details the different national and regional cash transfers to families with children that were in place in 2008. Section 2 presents the evolution of child poverty rates in Spain since 1994 and describes the basic structure of all monetary transfers to families with children since the mid-nineties. Section 3 presents some relevant details of our methodology while section 4 discusses the main results of the analysis. The last section concludes.

Family Policies and Decentralization

Decentralization of Social Benefits for Children

Among the different issues related to the optimal design of policies aimed at improving child well-being one outstanding question is the balance between central and local government responsibilities. The question of whether social benefits should depend on local or central governments has attracted great attention from researchers and policymakers. The potential effects of decentralization raise numerous interesting questions and will, without doubt, be a major focus of policy research for years to come. In most OECD countries there has been a continued emphasis on decentralization and greater local responsibilities in the area of social protection and cash benefits. In the European Union, many countries have transferred decision-making power to regional or local governments in the field of targeted cash benefits. In the US one of the changes introduced by the mid-nineties reform of welfare policies was to give more responsibility to the States in the design of these policies. In many low or middle-income countries decentralization of key redistributive programmes has been a corner-stone in the new definition of social protection (Ravallion 1998).

Decentralization, however, has different fundamentals in each case and a variety of ideologies revolve around these processes. Standard economic theory provides reasons related to efficiency and social preferences justifying some kind of decentralization in this field. From a very different side, decentralization of these programmes is also viewed as an opportunity to strengthen democratic development and to mobilize social capital (Klugman 1997, De Mello 2011). Nevertheless, these contributions might not be enough to offset objections that usually come to light. In the case of child benefits, decentralization might produce a mosaic of highly varied schemes, with a striking disparity of regulations and results. Above all, a certain widening of the differences low-income households with children experience regarding rights and access to resources might take place.

The controversy over the relative merits of decentralization of social benefits for achieving higher levels of households' well-being is indeed a frequent topic in the assessment of alternative designs for redistributive policies. Fiscal federalism theories set as their main purpose the analysis of the relationship between central and sub-central government, and its impact on efficiency, equity and macroeconomic stability. In the specific case of redistributive policies, the 'mainline' theory of fiscal federalism stresses that central governments must assume the key role in the provision of redistribution. As stated by Oates (2005), there is clearly some modest scope for decentralized government to play a supporting role in redistributive and macroeconomic policy, but the primary responsibility according to the standard theory rests with central governments. Therefore, central governments must take the lead in macroeconomic stabilization policy, introduce basic measures for income redistribution, and provide efficient levels of output of national public goods.

The main issue lying behind this statement is the possibility of increasing inequalities when income transfers policies are transferred to territorial governments. A redistributive scheme based only on initiatives coming from regional or local governments might produce horizontal inequalities. Due to different budgetary constraints, benefits might differ largely across territories, being higher in those regions where poor households with children are only a small fraction of total population. A second motivation for justifying centralized redistribution schemes is possible inefficiencies arising from geographical mobility. Low-income households with children could move to those jurisdictions where benefits are higher while the richest households could move to those places where the necessary taxes are lower. Regional governments might implement reforms aimed at retaining high-income taxpayers or pushing low-income households out of their jurisdictions through lower benefits for families with children. A well-known process of a 'race to the bottom' could take place. As a result, final benefits could be clearly lower than the necessary standards to provide adequate economic security.

Over the last years, however, general criticisms of decentralization as a sub-optimal design of social policy have been increasingly replaced by more positive assessments of this issue. New lines of analysis have intensively examined the contribution of decentralization to households' wellbeing. This is the case of approaches considering decentralization as a local public good or those emphasizing efficiency and adequacy effects of decentralized schemes of guaranteed income. In practice, as abovementioned, decentralization of child benefits is a common trait in most of the current designs of social protection in OECD countries.

An indirect advantage of a framework with different tax-and-transfer schemes in the same country is the possibility of identifying a set of 'good practices'. Regional experiences may be assessed as a laboratory for the monitoring and evaluation of redistributive policies. In terms of microsimulation analysis a key question might be how poverty or inequality results would change if most regions put into action those developments identified as optimal among the variety of regional experiences.

In this chapter in fact we do not try to evaluate the impact of the decentralization of monetary transfer policies towards families and children in Spain. Instead, our aim is to take advantage of the existence of a variety of regional policies to fight child poverty in order to learn about the potentially most effective policy at the central level, therefore we will put forward descriptive evidence on the capacity of a variety of real child-related policies implemented at the regional level to fight against child poverty in the whole of Spain. This exercise is most interesting given that most other institutional factors are very similar in the different regions of the country.

Child-related Monetary Policies in Spain

Child-related policies in Spain at the central government level in the year we undertake all our simulations include tax credits for children increasing in quantity from first to third child in the family and slightly higher if any of the children are below three years of age. Further there is a specific allowance for children in lone-parent families (see Table A.1 in the online Appendix for a detailed description[2]). Regarding central government benefits, the main monetary transfer is the universal birth benefit of 2,500 euro paid as a lump-sum to parents which in 2008 was received by 480,000 families and summed 1,200 million euro of expenditures to the family-children function in Spain, which is approximately 9 per cent of all expenditures of this kind in the country.[3] Other benefits are a means-tested benefit for low-income households plus a means-tested lump-sum benefit for large households and lone-parents. The first of these is received by a million individuals (children and disabled siblings of a higher age) with a cost of 930 million euro in 2008.

Child-related policies at the regional level include a large list of tax credits that are applicable to households living in the different regions. These tax credits are related to lone-parenthood, new births, child-care or work-life balance. Benefits at the regional level in 2008 are significantly different by regions as we indicate in Tables A.2 and A.4 in the online Appendix. Cataluña, Extremadura, Navarra and País Vasco have universal child benefits for children of different ages, a large group of regions have means-tested benefits while others have universal payments at birth or means-tested benefits at birth. Some regions like Galicia, Navarra and País Vasco have more than one type of child benefit payable to families.

Child Poverty and the Evolution of Child Support in Spain: 1998–2008

Despite the real household per capita disposable income increase between the early seventies and the early nineties and the rise in public expenditure on social protection reflecting the consolidation of the Spanish welfare state, the relative position of children in the income and expenditure distribution did not improve in comparison with that of adults. The evidence presented by Ayala et al. (2006) and Ayala and Cantó (2009) on the evolution of child poverty rates since 1994 show that child poverty estimates base on household microdata suggest that children in Spain have been generally over-represented among the poor.

In Figure 12.1 we depict the evolution of child poverty rates in Spain in comparison with the group of countries within the EU-27 using data from the ECHP and the EU-SILC. Child poverty in Spain has been well over adult poverty since 1994 and it is also well over the EU-27 countries child poverty average since 2005. Further, the strong effects of the economic crisis on Spanish families have implied a rapid divergence in child poverty between Spain and the EU-27 since 2009.

---

2   http://www.microsimulation.org/resource-centre/new-pathways/.

3   Out of total expenditure on the family and children function in Spain in 2008, monetary expenditure is approximately 43 per cent while the rest (57 per cent) is in-kind expenditure. See the Statistics from *Ministerio de Trabajo e Inmigración, Cuentas integradas de protección social en términos SEEPROS, CPS-8, gastos por función y tipo de prestación.*

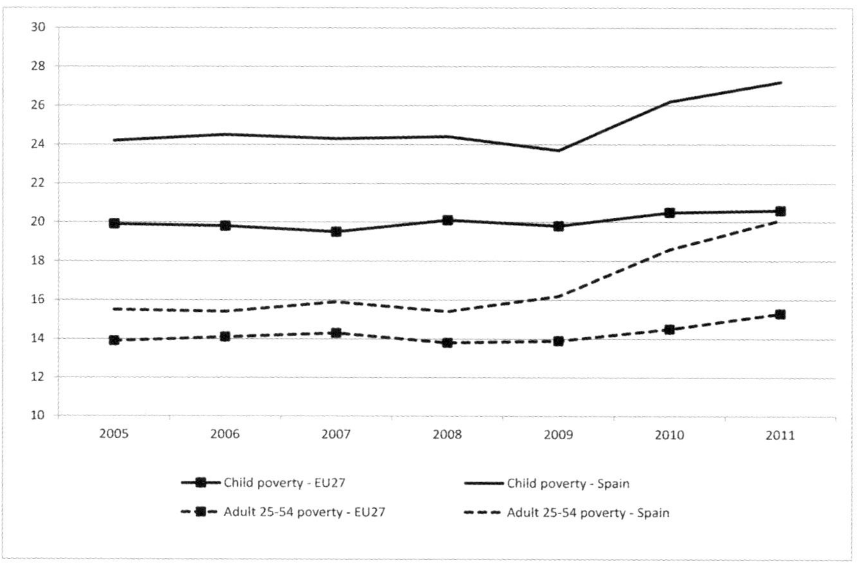

Figure 12.1   Child and adult (25–54) poverty headcounts – Spain and EU27: 2005–11

Source: EUROSTAT. Data from EU-SILC.

In any case, within Spain there are also large differences in the size of child poverty in different Spanish regions as Figure 12.2 shows. Some regions like Andalucía, Canarias, Castilla-La Mancha, Extremadura, La Rioja or Murcia are significantly over the national Spanish child poverty rates while other regions like Navarra or País Vasco are well below it. Using a regional threshold regions such as La Rioja, Madrid and Murcia stand out as those where children are significantly worse-off than adults in the whole Spanish context.

As UNICEF (2005) concludes, there are basically three elements that determine the economic well-being of children: social trends, labour market conditions and public intervention. Regarding social trends, Spain has experienced a large period of changes in social and cultural values since the beginning of democracy. Indeed, during the 1970s, Spain underwent major political and socioeconomic changes which, as pointed out by Cantó and Mercader-Prats (2002), improved children's school enrolment and significantly decreased under-five child mortality rates. These have cohabited with a decreasing fertility rate, an increasing number of non-traditional households, a strongly increasing parents' educational attainment and a slow, but consistent, growth in lone-parenthood. Regarding labour market conditions, Spain registers relatively low female labour market participation rates and a particularly high labour market instability in the European Union context. Interestingly the number of jobless households was not particularly high up until

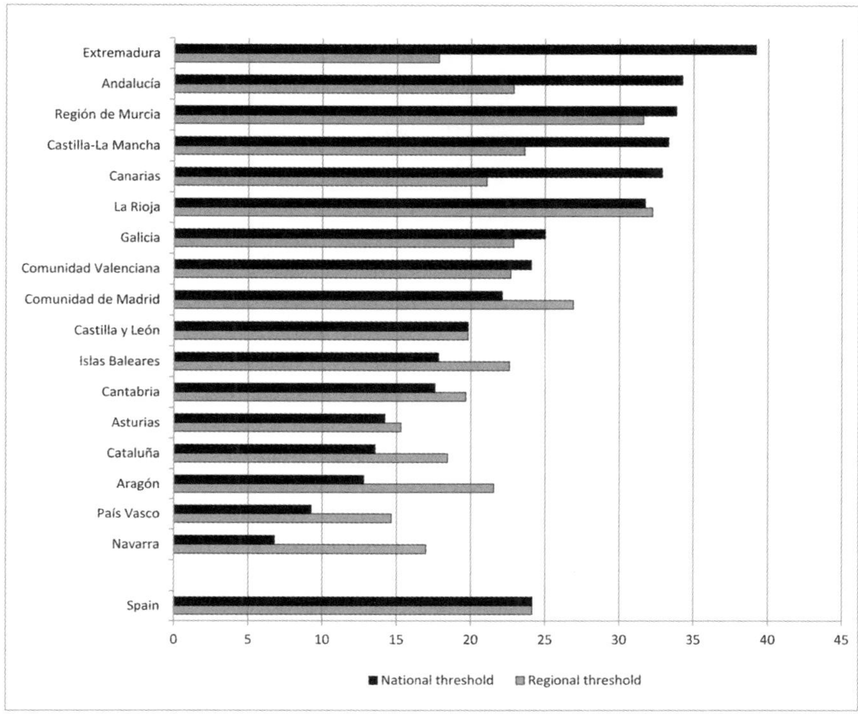

Figure 12.2 Child poverty headcounts for regions 2008 (national, regional thresholds)

Source: Own construction using EU-SILC data for Spain, 2008 (INE).

the arrival of the recession in 2008 even if, in contrast, the percentage of working poor households is one of the highest within the EU-15 countries.

Regarding the development of public intervention towards families with children in Spain at the beginning of the nineties, only a negligible share of social expenditures went to family support even if some cash transfers, such as unemployment assistance, included a family dimension. Family policies in Spain were largely developed during the authoritarian period (1939–75) due to the prominent place assigned by the regime to the role of the family in society. Family allowances and bonuses for families with children were introduced in 1938 and 1945, respectively, and, at the time, implied an important increase in head of household wages.[4] There were several reforms to the system but the main point after the arrival of the new democracy in the seventies was that, even if benefits

---

4   See Valiente (1996) for a good review of family policies in Spain before the end of the first half of the 1990s.

were maintained, payments were never revised so that the high level of inflation during the seventies turned them in an almost negligible transfer for most families.

During the eighties and nineties child support policies in Spain were a central government matter and in 1990 a means-tested child benefit for families with children under 18 (*Prestación por hijo a cargo*) was introduced as income support for families in need compensating them for not benefitting from the family tax credits that had been introduced in the national income tax. In fact, as Levy et al. (2005) underline, the structure of the Spanish system to support families up to the most recent reforms in national and, most importantly, in regional benefits gave a particular emphasis to tax concessions. As we detail in Table A.1 in the online Appendix, in 1998 the main income tax policies towards the family in Spain was a non-refundable tax credit that increased with the number of children.[5]

In terms of benefit policies directly focused on children, in 1998 the only available monetary transfer was a means-tested child benefit available for low-income households with children, received by 16.2 per cent of children in the population in 2000 (see Gaitán 2011). During the beginning of the twenty-first century, some central government policies towards the family have been reformed and some new elements have appeared. Further, as detailed in Table A.2 to Table A.4 in the online Appendix, regional governments have developed an important amount of tax and benefit policies towards children and the family in the first years of this century. This has meant that expenditures in family and children as a proportion of total expenditure on social protection in Spain grew from 2000 to 2008 (see Cantó et al. 2012).

The main change to central government tax policies related to children in Spain was the reform of the child tax allowance (introduced in the 1999), which after the 2007 income tax reform was replaced by a child tax credit.[6] Further, in 2002 a new working mother refundable tax credit was introduced as a tax credit for working women with children below three years of age. Regarding monetary benefits, the means-tested child benefit quantity was revised and increased over the value of inflation a couple of times before 2006 and in 2008 and also a significant increase in the value of the means-test was introduced. Further, in 2007, one of the central government benefits at birth for low-income households with three or more children was made available for lone-parents and disabled mothers. Further, in that same year, the central government introduced a new universal benefit of €2,500 (*Prestación por nacimiento o adopción de hijos*) payable to families at child's birth.

As is clear from Table A.2 in the online Appendix, since the beginning of the twenty-first century, regions have also put forward a large list of policies of a varied monetary weight in order to improve the financial situation of households

---

5   Note that there was also a lone parent joint taxation allowance that made tax schedule brackets larger for these households and provided also larger exemption limits.

6   Note that also the lone-parents' particular tax schedule was substituted by a lone-parent tax allowance in 1999.

with children. These consist in child-related income tax credits (see Table A.3 in the online Appendix) and child-related monetary transfers to families in the form of either universal transfers, universal lump-sum benefits at birth, means-tested benefits and means-tested lump-sum benefits at birth. The differences in policy design and economic relevance of these benefits is large as can be easily understood from the main details of each of them.

Methodology: EU-SILC Data and EUROMOD Model Data, Simulations and Measurement

The Microsimulation Model

This chapter makes use of EUROMOD – a tax-benefit microsimulation model for the European Union.[7] This model has been designed to be flexible enough to take into account the particularities of different national policies but also to provide a common framework for the implementation of policies and the production of comparable results across countries.[8] EUROMOD is unique for a wide range of analysis for international comparative research on the effects of policies and policy reform on income, welfare, poverty, inequality and social inclusion.

Because of its flexible structure, EUROMOD is also a suitable tool for within-country cross-region studies. In the case of Spain, as most benefits and elements of the income tax administered by regional governments are simulated by the model, these policies can be compared and analysed in the same way as EUROMOD is used for cross-country analysis.

Data

The database used by EUROMOD in the case of Spain is drawn from the 2007 national version of the Survey on Statistics on Income and Living Conditions (EU-SILC), known in Spain as *Encuesta de Condiciones de Vida* (ECV), provided by the Spanish Statistics Institute (INE). EU-SILC is a European project of comparative statistics of income distribution and social exclusion. The first aim of EU-SILC is to provide timely and comparable cross-sectional annual data with variables on income, poverty, social exclusion and other living conditions of the households and their members, it also provides longitudinal data with information about individual-level changes over a four year period. The sample size of the ECV survey for Spain is about 13,000 households and 30,000 individuals. Besides, the Instituto Nacional de Estadística de España (INE) has provided EUROMOD with an special breakdown of some particular benefits related to unemployment, old

---

7   See Sutherland (2001).

8   See Lietz and Mantovani (2007) for technical information on the EUROMOD framework.

age, survivor, disability and family benefits, this has turned very useful for the simulations.

The Spanish ECV survey sample is representative at the regional level and regions of residence are identified at NUTS 2 level. The database we use in our analysis is ECV 2007 where household characteristics and incomes reflect those of 2006. In fact, children born in 2007 (96 observations) were excluded from the sample. However, the weights were not scaled up to reflect this exclusion. As a result, the sample used in the model is of 12,315 households (34,490 individuals) projecting a population of 44,200,084 individuals instead of 44,339,161, which would include children born in 2007. In the ECV 2007, income variables are available gross of taxes. Such variables were imputed by the Spanish Statistical Institute based on reported net income. For more information on the net to gross imputation see Paniagua and Méndez (2008). Finally, in order to construct incomes for the years following the baseline we use the Consumer Price Index, the increase in labour costs and a detailed list of nominal increases of benefits in time.

In general, the data from the ECV entering EUROMOD are plausible in terms of labour market and income information for 2006 even if there are some relevant details regarding the macrovalidation of the different income sources and transfers from particular benefits that are not discussed here (see Adiego et al. 2011). Regarding national and regional child benefits, Adiego et al. (2011) report that these benefits are particularly well captured in EUROMOD given that the model provides an excellent estimation of the number of recipients and the quantity of expenditure on them.

Simulation

Different tax credits and benefits to support families with children (henceforth, referred as 'child-related policies') are simulated with EUROMOD. Although the Spanish EUROMOD database is representative at the regional level, its sample size is not sufficient for the analysis of most analysed policies, which are targeted at very specific and rather small population groups. In order to deal with that problem, all regional benefits are simulated as if they applied to the entire Spanish population. Hence, each regional policy is analysed using a sample of 12,329 households instead of an average of some 725 households.

This approach requires a different interpretation of results. Simulations do not measure the real' impact of regional polices but the 'potential' impact they would have if implemented at the national level. One interesting feature of this approach is that it allows one to compare the effect of different policies on a similar population, therefore making the interpretation of results straightforward. On the other hand, given socio-economic and demographic variations across Spanish regions, results produced by these simulations cannot be interpreted as reflecting how these policies effectively work 'in reality'.

The impact of policies was measured using a child-contingent approach.[9] This consists on contrasting simulation results produced using two different databases: one including the full sample and a second using the same sample except for children – which are excluded. Child-targeted policies are measured as the difference in amounts produced by these alternative simulations. Basically, it measures changes in policy amounts due to the presence of children. This approach has some interesting advantages with respect to the standard measurement of the 'face' amount of a policy. First it allows one to measure the impact of policies on a particular population group, irrespective of who the benefit is targeted to (one can measure the impact of child benefits on families with children up to the age of 17 even if these benefits are paid to families up to the age of, say, 20). Second, it produces accurate measures of policies that are not observed directly (child tax credits are, usually, not observed directly but by their impact on final income tax liability). Third, it accounts for policy interactions (for example, changes in child benefits may be compensated with changes in the amount of social assistance).

Finally, it must be noticed that this analysis is based on simulations assuming that all legal rules apply and are fully claimed and complied. Thus, issues such as non-take-up of social benefits and tax evasion are not controlled for. This can result in the over-estimation of taxes and benefits. In addition, the analysis doesn't account for changes in individual behaviour such as labour supply or family formation.

Measurement

Following the United Nations Convention on the Rights of the Child, children are defined as people aged under 18 (i.e. aged 0–17). Generally it is assumed that income is shared within the household such that household disposable income can be used to indicate the economic well-being of each individual within the household ('within household' incidence is not considered).

Household disposable income is defined as original income plus private transfers and social benefits minus taxes and social contributions, aggregated at the household level. Non-cash benefits are not included. Household disposable incomes are equivalized using the modified OECD equivalence scale.[10]

Poverty is measured following the Laeken at-risk-of-poverty approach defined as those living in households with equivalized household disposable income below 60 per cent of the median. The at-risk-of-poverty threshold, based on the EUROMOD ('baseline') simulation for the Spanish 2008 tax-benefit system is

---

9 As Levy et al. (2006) indicate, child contingent income is obtained by using EUROMOD to re-calculate household incomes while disregarding children in the calculation of benefits and taxes received by the household. For more detailed information on these calculations see Corak et al. (2005).

10 This assumes single person = 1; additional people aged 14+ = 0.5; additional people aged under 14 = 0.3.

€7,935 per year per equivalent adult. This threshold is maintained fixed in the assessment of all simulation scenarios.

Results

EUROMOD simulations show that in aggregate terms central government tax credits are the main child-related policies in Spain.

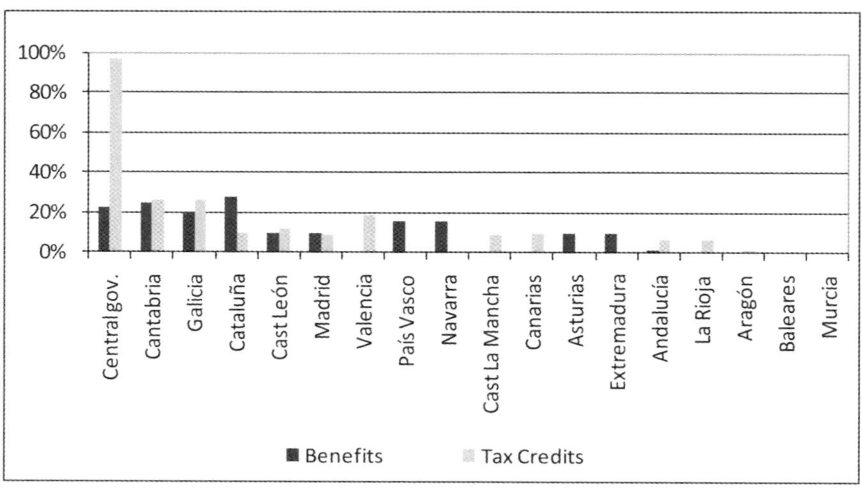

Figure 12.3   Overall coverage of child-related policies in Spain

Note: Percentage of children under 18 in households receiving child-related benefits and/or tax credits.
Source: EUROMOD

These policies cover more than 95 per cent of Spanish children and are by far the largest source of expenditure – amounting, on average, to more than €700 per child under 18 per year. Central government benefits are considerably lower, covering about 20 per cent of children and spending about €200 per child.

There is considerable variation with respect to policies administered by regional governments. However, in general, benefits have a larger role than tax credits. If implemented at the national level, about one in four children would be covered by benefits if choosing those in Cantabria or Catalonia and by tax credits if choosing those in Cantabria or Galicia. As for overall expenditure, Cantabrian and Extremaduran policies amount for more than 200 euro per child (hence more than central government benefits). Policies coming from Navarra, Catalonia or

Galicia also would spend, on average, more than 100 euro per child at the national level.

Table 12.1   Average expenditure per child in euro a year, by type of benefit

	Means-tested		Universal	
	Child	Birth	Child	Birth
Central government	43	2	0	152
Extremadura	0	0	0	223
Cantabria	200	0	0	0
Navarra	169	0	0	11
Cataluña	0	4	124	1
Andalucía	0	5	0	0
País Vasco	0	35	56	0
Castilla León	0	57	0	0
Galicia	49	0	0	0
Asturias	0	0	0	31
Madrid	0	0	0	6
La Rioja	0	0	0	0
Aragón	0	0	0	0
Valencia	0	0	0	0
Baleares	0	0	0	0
Murcia	0	0	0	0
Canarias	0	0	0	0
Castilla La Mancha	0	0	0	0

Note: Total expenditure on means-tested and universal child and birth benefits divided by the number of children under 18 (irrespective of whether the child, her family, receives a benefit). 'Birth benefits' are defined as target at newborn children, remaining benefits are defined as 'child benefits'. Amounts in euro per year.
Source: EUROMOD

Table 12.1 shows the breakdown of benefit spending between means-tested and universal and between children and birth benefits. Means-tested benefits are particularly important in Cantabria, Navarra and, to a lower extent, in Castilla Leon or Galicia. Expenditure on universal benefits is higher in the systems of Extremadura, Catalonia and the Basque Country.

As for the central government, the introduction of the universal lump-sum benefit at birth or adoption, in 2008, represents a change not only in the level of expenditure but also on its composition, shifting the focus from periodic, means-tested benefits to children of all ages to lump-sum, unconditional benefits to newborns.[11]

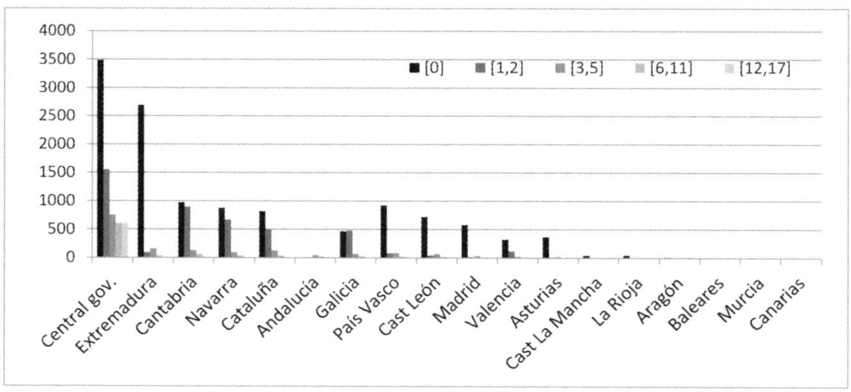

Figure 12.4   Average expenditure per child in euro a year (benefits and tax credits), by age groups

Note: Total expenditure on child-related benefits and tax credits (irrespective of whether the child, her family, receives a benefit). Amounts in euro per year.
Source: EUROMOD

The focus on newborn and young children is also present in most regional policies. Figure 12.4 shows that, on average, spending is considerably larger for children under the age of three. Out of the 17, in nine regions the average expenditure per newborn child exceeds €500 per year (in Cantabria it exceeds €1,000 and in Extremadura €2,500) – see Table 12.1. Children aged one and two also receive on average more than €500 per year in Cantabria, Navarra, Catalonia and Galicia. In no region the average expenditure per child exceeds €100 per year for children aged six or more.

In general, the average spending per child increases with income. Figure 12.5 shows that, for example, while in the bottom quintile the average benefit in Extremadura amounts to less than €50 per child, in the top quintile the amount is more than €400. Due to relatively large income limits ('affluence tests'), also in Cantabria and Navarra, which make use of means-testing, average spending increases with income up to the fourth quintile.

---

11   It should be noted that this benefit was eliminated in 2011 as part of the austerity measures to reduce the public deficit. For an analysis of the distributive impact of austerity measures in Spain, Greece, Estonia and the UK, using EUROMOD, see Leventi et al. (2010).

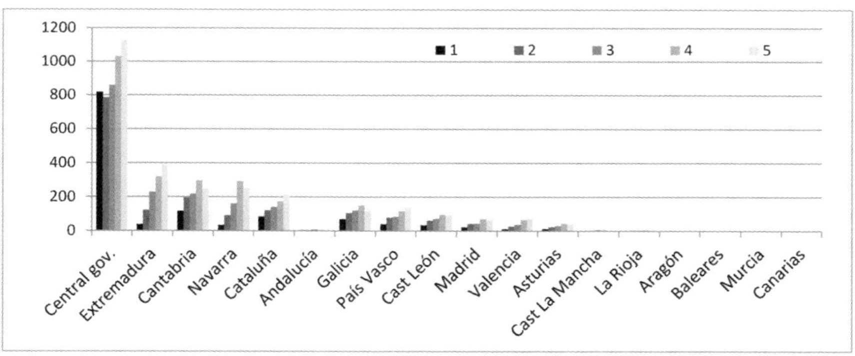

Figure 12.5   Average expenditure per child in euro a year (benefits and tax credits), by income quintiles

Note: Total expenditure on child-related benefits and tax credits divided by the number of children under 18 (irrespective of whether the child, her family, receives a benefit). Amounts in euro per year. Quintiles computed only for children (i.e., each quintile includes one fifth of children) using household equivalized disposable income.
Source: EUROMOD

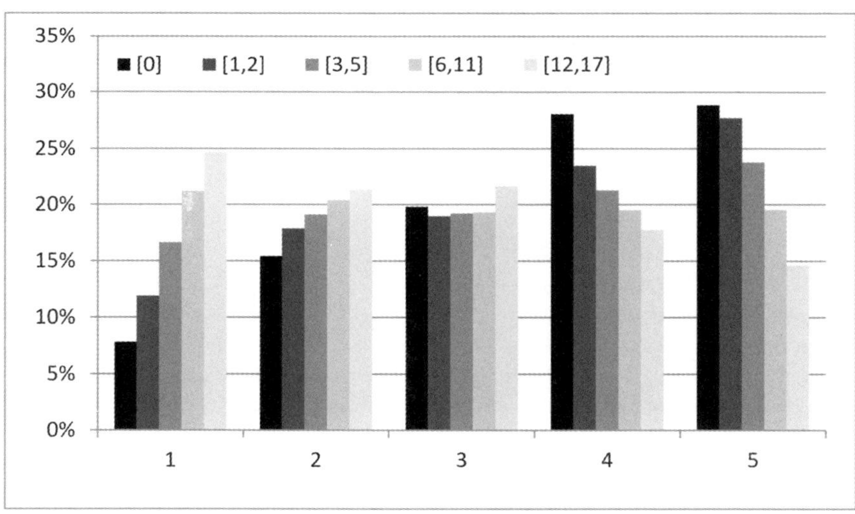

Figure 12.6   Distribution of child age groups by income quintiles

Note: distribution of children from particular age groups by income quintiles. Quintiles computed only for children (i.e., each quintile includes one fifth of children) using household equivalized disposable income.
Source: EUROMOD

This regressive distribution is not due to policies designed specifically to target higher income households with children but because of the distribution of child age groups by income. Figure 12.6 clearly shows how younger children tend to be concentrated in higher income quintiles while older children are concentrated at the bottom part of the income distribution. While only 8 per cent of newborn children are in the first income quintile, 29 per cent are in the top one.[12] Therefore, since young children tend to live in relatively higher income households and child-related policies are focused on young children and lightly or not at all means-tested, on average, spending tends to benefit better-off children.[13]

Regarding child poverty, on the whole, central government policies have a considerably larger role reducing the poverty risk. According to Table 12.2, central government policies reduce child poverty by 4 percentage points (from 26 to 22 per cent), while the best-performing regions achieve around a 1 percentage point reduction. However, the impact of some regional policies is considerably stronger for some particular age groups. Policies from Catalonia, Cantabria, Navarra and, especially, Extremadura reduce the poverty risk of newborn children by more than 2 percentage points. Similarly, policies from Cantabria reduce poverty of children aged one and two by more than 2 percentage points.

The results in Table 12.2 also show that poverty risk increases with children's age while central government policies have a stronger impact in reducing poverty among younger children. Therefore, our simulations suggest that regional benefits and tax-credits reinforce and complement the focus of central government policies on younger children, which, on the other hand, seem to be significantly less vulnerable to poverty than their older counterparts.

---

12   We have checked that the distribution of children by age in our database is similar to that of other sources for Spain for the same year. In particular, using the Household Budget Survey (*Encuesta de Presupuestos Familiares, EPF*) for 2008 we also obtain that newborn children tend to be concentrated in higher income quintiles and older children are more concentrated at the bottom of the income distribution. We should only note that the actual distribution of children of different ages within the distribution of income in the EPF is slightly less polarized regarding newborns than in the ECV: 44 per cent of newborn children in the EPF belong to the two highest equivalent income quintiles while in the ECV this percentage is somewhat higher (57 per cent). The rest of the distribution is most similar between both data sources, for example, approximately 50 per cent of children between 12 and 17 years of age in the EPF are in the two lowest deciles while this percentage is 46 per cent in the ECV).

13   It would be of interest here to differentiate between targeting and level of payment following, for instance, in order to measure the efficiency of each policy in reducing poverty following Beckerman's (1979) approach. This would be a nice extension of the analysis.

Table 12.2   Child poverty risk and reduction, by child's age

	[0]	[1,2]	[3,5]	[6,11]	[12,17]	total
Poverty before all policies	21%	24%	22%	25%	29%	26%
Poverty reduction						
Central gov.	13%	5%	3%	4%	2%	4%
Extremadura	11%	0%	1%	1%	0%	1%
Cantabria	3%	4%	1%	1%	0%	1%
Navarra	2%	1%	0%	0%	0%	0%
Cataluña	3%	1%	0%	0%	0%	1%
Andalucía	0%	0%	0%	0%	0%	0%
Galicia	2%	1%	0%	0%	0%	0%
País Vasco	2%	0%	0%	0%	0%	0%
Cast León	2%	0%	0%	0%	0%	0%
Madrid	2%	0%	0%	0%	0%	0%
Valencia	1%	0%	0%	0%	0%	0%
Asturias	1%	0%	0%	0%	0%	0%
Canarias	1%	0%	0%	0%	0%	0%
Cast La Mancha	1%	0%	0%	0%	0%	0%
La Rioja	1%	0%	0%	0%	0%	0%
Aragón	0%	0%	0%	0%	0%	0%
Murcia	0%	0%	0%	0%	0%	0%
Baleares	0%	0%	0%	0%	0%	0%

Note: Child poverty risk: share of children living in households with equivalized disposable income below 60 percent of the population median (poverty line). Poverty reduction: share of children whose equivalised household disposable income reaches or exceeds the poverty line after child-related policies.
Source: EUROMOD

Conclusions

The level and evolution of child poverty has become an important concern for social policy in many rich countries in recent times given the negative evolution of indicators. Spain is one of the European Union countries where the level of child poverty has been highest during the last decade and where the level of expenditure on family and children function has been around the lowest. Further, the political process in Spain in recent years has resulted in a strong decentralization of many social policies, including those towards families and children. Therefore, in a favourable economic growth context during the period 2003–07, a variety of national and regional child-related policies have been implemented extending the level of expenditure on families with children and pushing expenditure on cash family benefits as a percentage of total social expenditure. This increase appeared to be related both to central and regional government policies but, so far, little was known about the impact of these new child-related policies on child poverty in Spain.

Making use of the tax-benefit model for the European Union – EUROMOD – this chapter simulates the eligibility and receipt of these benefits and assesses their impact on child poverty. Since these benefits are quite different in terms of design and generosity, we simulate what would have been the impact of the child benefits of each region had they been implemented in the whole country.

Our results underline that in aggregate terms central government tax credits are the main child-related policy in Spain. Regarding regional policies, benefits have a larger role than tax credits. The introduction of a universal lump-sum benefit for birth at the central government level in 2007 changed the composition of expenditure towards unconditional benefits to newborns. In fact, newborns and young children are the focus of most national and regional benefits. In general, the average spending per child increases with income even in the case of means-tested benefits, given that the means-test is relatively large. This regressive distribution of benefits is not only due to the policy design but to the distribution of child age groups by household income: younger children tend to be concentrated in higher income quintiles. Regarding child poverty reduction, central government policies have a considerably larger role in reducing poverty risk. However, some regions' policies perform better than others in reducing child poverty at a national level. Policies from Catalonia, Cantabria, Navarra and, most especially, Extremadura reduce the poverty risk of newborn children by more than 1 per cent. In general, our simulations suggest that regional benefits and tax credits reinforce and complement the focus of central government policies on younger children, who, on the other hand, seem to be less vulnerable to poverty than older children in Spain.

References

Adiego, M., Cantó, O., Levy, H. and Paniagua, M. 2011. EUROMOD Country Report, Spain 2006–2009. EUROMODupdate. ISER University of Essex. Available at: https://www.iser.essex.ac.uk/files/euromod/country-reports/CR_ES2006-09_final_5-2-12.pdf [accessed: 12/09/2013].

Ayala, L. and Cantó, O. 2009. Políticas Económicas y Pobreza Infantil, in *Análisis y Propuestas sobre Pobreza infantil en España*. Madrid: UNICEF.

Ayala, L., Martínez, R. and Sastre, M. 2006. *Familia, Infancia y Privación Social: Estudio de las situaciones de pobreza en la infancia*. Madrid: Fundación Foessa, Colección de Estudios.

Beckerman, W. 1979. The impact of income maintenance payments on poverty in Britain. *The Economic Journal*, 89, 261–79.

Cantó, O., Ayala, L., Adiego, M., Levy, H. and Paniagua, M.M. 2013. Going regional: the effectiveness of different tax-benefit policies in combating child poverty in Spain. Euromod Working Paper Series. EM2/12.

Cantó, O. and Mercader-Prats, M. 2002. Child Poverty in Spain from the 70s to the 90s: a static and dynamic approach. *Journal of Applied Social Sciences Studies (Schmollers Jahrbuch)*, 121 Jg., 4–2002, 543–78.

Corak, M., Lietz, C. and Sutherland, H. 2005. The impact of tax and transfer systems on children in the European Union. EUROMOD, Working Paper No. EM4/05.

De Mello, L. 2011. Does fiscal decentralisation strengthen social capital? Cross-country evidence and the experiences of Brazil and Indonesia. *Environment and Planning C: Government and Policy*, 29(2), 281–96.

European Commission. 2008. *Child poverty and well being in the EU: current status and way forward*. Brussels: Directorate General for Employment, Social Affairs and Equal Opportunities.

Figari, F., Paulus, A. and Sutherland, H. 2009. Measuring the size and impact of public cash support for children in cross-national perspective. EUROMOD, Working Paper No. EM6/09.

Gaitán, L. 2001. Contexto y marco conceptual: el Estado de Bienestar, las políticas públicas y los derechos de los niños, in *Las políticas públicas y la infancia en España: evolución, impactos y percepciones*. Madrid: UNICEF.

Klugman, J. 1997. Decentralization: A Survey from a Child Welfare Perspective. Innocenti Occasional Papers, Economic and Social Policy Series, 61. Florence: UNICEF International Child Development Centre.

Leventi, C., Levy, H., Matsaganis, M., Paulus, A. and Sutherland, H. 2010. Modelling the distributional effects of austerity measures: the challenges of a comparative perspective. Research note 8/2010, Social Situation Observatory – Income distribution and living conditions.

Levy, H., Lietz, C. and Sutherland, H. 2005. Alternative Tax-Benefit Strategies to Support Children in the European Union. EUROMOD, Working Paper No. EM10/05.

Levy, H., Lietz, C. and Sutherland, H. 2006. A basic income for Europe's children? EUROMOD, Working Paper No. EM4/06.

Lietz, C. and Mantovani, D. 2007. A Short Introduction to EUROMOD: An Integrated European Tax-Benefit Model, in O. Bargain (ed.), *Micro-simulation in action: Policy analysis in Europe using EUROMOD*. Research in Labor Economics, 25. Amsterdam: Elsevier.

Oates, W.E. 2005. Toward A Second-Generation Theory of Fiscal Federalism. *International Tax and Public Finance*, 12, 349–73.

Paniagua, M. and Méndez, J. 2008. How to achieve the final net income by components in the Spanish ECV. Paper presented at Tax-benefit Microsimulation in the Enlarged Europe: Results from the I-CUE Project and Perspectives for the Future, 3–4 of April, Vienna, Austria. Available at: http://www.euro.centre. org/conferences/icue/files/Paniagua.pdf [accessed: 18 January 2013].

Ravallion, M. 1998. Reaching Poor Areas in a Federal System, World Bank, Policy Research Working Paper, 1901.

Sutherland, H. 2001. EUROMOD: an integrated European Benefit – Tax model – Final Report, EUROMOD Working Paper, EM9/01.

Sutherland, H., Figari, F., Lelkes, O., Levy, H., Lietz, C., Mantovani, D. and Paulus, A. 2008. Improving the capacity and usability of EUROMOD – Final Report, EUROMOD Working Paper, EM4/08.

UNICEF 2005. Child Poverty in Rich Countries 2005, Florence: Innocenti Report card. 6.

Valiente, C. 1996. The rejection of authoritarian policy legacies: family policy in Spain, 1975–1995. *South European Society and Politics*, 1(1), 95–114.

Chapter 13

Combining EUROMOD and LIAM Tools for the Development of Dynamic Cross-sectional Microsimulation Models: A Sneak Preview

Philippe Liégeois[1] and Gijs Dekkers

Introduction

The development of a microsimulation model is typically a slow and – therefore – expensive process. Inversely stated, there is room for efficiency improvements and this chapter suggests one. Often those agencies that enter into dynamic microsimulation already have a static model on a shelf, whether they use it or not. While building a dynamic model, one might want to consider embedding an existing static model in this dynamic framework, to avoid having to create fields in the dynamic model that the static model already possesses. An illustration is the tax-benefit component of the public policy which has to be implemented in all models as far as the distribution of net (or equivalized) disposable income matters.

This chapter makes a first attempt to embed the static microsimulation model EUROMOD (version 31A; Sutherland 2007) for Luxembourg[2] with MIDAS_LU, a dynamic microsimulation forward-looking population model available in Luxembourg as well. The latter is developed by means of LIAM (Life-Cycle Income Analysis Model), a toolbox for the development of dynamic cross-sectional microsimulation models. Originally created by Cathal O'Donoghue

---

1   This research is part of the MiDaL project ('Towards the development of a dynamic Microsimulation toolbox LIAM-II and the complementary implementation of administrative Data needed for dynamic microsimulation of pensions in Luxembourg'), supported by the European Community Programme for Employment and Social Solidarity – PROGRESS (2007–2013), under the Grant VS/2009/0569. The model MIDAS_LU was developed through the REDIS project funded by the Luxembourg National Research Fund under Grant FNR/06/28/19. Any remaining errors, results produced, interpretations or views presented in the chapter are the authors' responsibility. In particular, the chapter does not represent the views of the institutions to which the authors are affiliated.

2   EUROMOD is continually being improved and updated and the results presented here are based on the most recent fully validated version available for Luxembourg at the time of writing.

(O'Donoghue et al. 2009) and subsequently extended through the AIM project (Dekkers et al. 2010), it has been used for model development in several European countries, including Luxembourg.

In embedding the static EUROMOD in the dynamic MIDAS_LU, we make use of the fact that the two show similarities in terms of their contents and internal organization (e.g. discrete time oriented). The reason is clear: both are targeting close final objectives, the analysis of distribution of income and the impact of a change in the tax-benefit system, hence involving similar input data bases and procedures for the computations.

The role of EUROMOD (or a static module like EUROMOD) might be to take care of most tax-benefit computations on a year-by-year basis in an efficient and flexible way. Including it in the dynamic model avoids having to develop these modules specifically for the dynamic model. The dynamic framework would then simply help in making endogenous the life events of the population (e.g. related to demography and employment status) in EUROMOD.

EUROMOD and LIAM Microsimulation Frameworks

The architecture underlying LIAM shows strong similarities with the one governing EUROMOD.[3] The two frameworks therefore share several characteristics that facilitate the linking and combining of those tools. We now describe the main features of the two platforms, underlining relevant technical aspects only.

The EUROMOD Static Microsimulation Model

EUROMOD is an integrated European tax-benefit model for the Member States of the European Union. It allows simulating, among other things, the equivalized disposable income of households through an effective implementation of the structure of the population, the distribution of earnings and the tax-benefit system (Bargain 2007 and Sutherland 2007). It is designed for the simulation and comparison of social policies.

From a technical point of view, EUROMOD output is essentially based on three inputs; the first input is micro-data representative of a population (households and individuals) which can be derived from administrative or survey data (Liégeois et al. 2011). In the EUROMOD version used in the present chapter, micro-data are described in a 'vardesc' file, stored in a Microsoft ACCESS format and read by EUROMOD through an ODBC link. Furthermore, population sub-groups (e.g. several kinds of households) are described in the 'tu' (tax unit) file, and the definition of macro-income variables to be derived from input and simulated data

---

3   This is not a coincidence. Before developing LIAM for his PhD thesis, Cathal O'Donoghue was one of the researchers involved in the first version of EUROMOD.

(e.g. the so-called 'disposable income' of a residence household) is made in the 'il' (income list) file.

The second input is a set of rules on how to calculate taxes and benefits. The rules that describe policies that have to be implemented in EUROMOD are detailed in a 'pol' file and are listed in order of simulation given in a 'spine' file.

The third input is a 'control' file, governing the whole EUROMOD procedure.

It is important to realize that EUROMOD is static in the sense that population is fixed, taken as observed at a given point in time. The policy rules, however, can cover several years, adapting parameters and contents as needed (e.g. describing a structural change in the tax-benefit system and/or monetary drift). The fact that the population under consideration remains unchanged obviously makes a simulation in the longer term less sensible, because an invariant population hypothesis becomes rather questionable. This chapter uses the Luxembourg version of EUROMOD, whose basis is the Luxembourg resident population in 2008. EUROMOD input is derived from survey data, the Luxembourg household panel PSELL3[4]/EU-SILC[5] for 2008 (incomes from 2007).

The LIAM Framework for Dynamic Microsimulation

The Life-Cycle Income Analysis Model (LIAM) is a framework for the development and simulation of dynamic discrete-time cross-sectional-ageing microsimulation models (O'Donoghue 2009). It was created by Cathal O'Donoghue and later completed for the development of the model MIDAS for Belgium, Germany and Italy (Dekkers et al. 2008; idem 2010). Using the routines of MIDAS_Belgium as input, the prospective microsimulation model MIDAS_LU is being developed for Luxembourg. This is an ongoing process, and the version of MIDAS_LU used in this chapter does not include a tax-benefit structure, nor has it been fully validated, which makes economic and social interpretation of the results more questionable. Fortunately, the present chapter aims to show how to link the EUROMOD and LIAM platforms, the socio-economic background serving more as a qualitative illustration. Similarly to EUROMOD, MIDAS_LU adopts the Luxembourg resident population in 2008 as a starting dataset, specifically the Luxembourg household panel PSELL3/EU-SILC for 2008.[6]

Unlike EUROMOD, MIDAS_LU is dynamic. The population is 'aged' and recomposed (e.g. through marriage and divorce) and many relevant states are

---

4　Panel Socio-Economique Liewen zu Lëtzebuerg (http://www.ceps.lu).

5　EU-SILC is an instrument aiming at collecting timely and comparable cross-sectional and longitudinal multidimensional micro-data on income, poverty, social exclusion and living conditions (see http://epp.eurostat.ec.europa.eu/portal/page/portal/microdata/eu_silc, accessed: 23/09/13).

6　Other SILC waves are used to produce 'behavioral' contents for the model (e.g. probabilities of transitions, given personal and households' characteristics, or the estimation of reduced-form behavioural equations).

endogenously determined (e.g. employment-unemployment transitions). These changes are the result of either a deterministic (e.g. 'age + 1') or stochastic process, with the probability of an event depending on personal and household characteristics.

On the other hand, all information needed for the determination of taxes and benefits should be simulated or given as an input to the model through time. If not simulated, hence maintained to its initial value (e.g. rents presently in MIDAS_LU), the content of a variable in the dynamic framework will lose its relevance over time. This is obviously not the case in EUROMOD where the degree of 'detail' we can afford regarding the input dataset and the description of policies is greater (information derived from a rich input dataset, however basically limited to a given year). Furthermore, as said, MIDAS_LU does not presently include a tax-benefit module.

The dynamic microsimulation is governed in LIAM through a number of files whose names often sound similar to those familiar with EUROMOD: general control goes through a 'dycontrol' file, the list of tasks (e.g. policies) in order of simulation for each simulation year is included in 'agespine'. This includes processes as birth, death, labour market transitions, household transitions, factor incomes and social security status transitions. Finally, the identification of variables is done in the 'dyvardesc' file.

LIAM produces a set of ASCII files, containing micro-data regarding household composition, employment status, earnings and incomes, and other endogenous variables.

Table 13.1 compares the two modelling frameworks.

Table 13.1   A first comparison of EUROMOD and LIAM environments

	EUROMOD_based	**LIAM_based**
Procedures / Control		
General control	control.txt	dycontrol.txt dyrunset.txt
List of procedures/ policies	spine.txt	agespine.txt
Description of procedures/policies	tran<...>.txt trap<...>.txt (al_)regr<...>.txt	pol<...>.txt
Data		
Input dataset format	MS-ACCESS & ODBC	<VARNAME>.txt, objtype. txt *(individuals, households)* and linkage.txt *(between individuals, individuals and households)*
List of and main characteristics of variables	vardesc.txt	dyvardesc.txt
Output dataset	TXT or STATA format	TXT format

Combining EUROMOD and LIAM

The main message from the previous section is that the two models, EUROMOD and MIDAS_LU, are complementary. Building on output from MIDAS_LU, encompassing household composition and individual characteristics (including gross labour income), we show now how EUROMOD can be used for the tax-benefit computations. Thus, the objective of the present chapter is to show *how* linking EUROMOD and LIAM can be done (rather than *why*).

We start from the description of a population given for an initial year under consideration (2008, incomes from 2007) and derive the distribution of disposable income for the 'same' population[7] in the future, where the latter situation is based on simulation results of MIDAS_LU. The present exercise covers the years 2008–18, but this may easily be extended. The main lines governing the interchange between EUROMOD and MIDAS_LU are as follows. For each year passing (one only if static framework), households are examined in turn, life events are simulated (dynamic framework only) and taxes and benefits computed (static framework). Finally, net income is derived and descriptive variables and indicators, such as the distribution of equivalent income, can be derived and examined.

Table 13.2 summarizes the steps needed for the exercise, if EUROMOD is used after MIDAS_LU for the tax-benefit side of the computations.

Table 13.2   Towards a link between EUROMOD and LIAM platforms

Steps	Task	Remark
1	Preparing input dataset for MIDAS_LU (LIAM)	Mainly based on PSELL3/EU-SILC 2008 (incomes from 2007)
2	Running MIDAS_LU	STATA Outputs (households and individual characteristics, incomes) for years 2008, 2009, etc. (up to 2018 in the present exercise)
3	Preparing input datasets for EUROMOD	A few variables have to be redesigned (when definitions inconsistent in static and dynamic frameworks) One MS-ACCESS dataset for each year, together with its ODBC link
4	Preparing parameter sheets for future public policies in EUROMOD	Mainly 'pol' files concerned, but also 'control' file and possibly 'tu' and 'il' files (see Table 13.1)
5	Running EUROMOD	TXT outputs
6	Analysis of results	Based on years 2008–2018

---

7   Nevertheless progressively 'aged' and recomposed (through marriage, etc.).

After the first step, the dynamic model MIDAS_LU changes the population structure (individual characteristics and household composition) and gross labour incomes in the simulation years. In the present exercise, we consider a consumer price indexation of 2.5 per cent per year together with an exogenous real growth rate for the hourly-wage which is 1.8 per cent per year (on average) between 2008 and 2018.

In the third step, the output from the dynamic model is used to generate several input files for EUROMOD. In EUROMOD, the micro-data are stored in a Microsoft ACCESS format and then read by EUROMOD through an ODBC link. This implies that, when several input databases have to be considered, each corresponding to one simulation year, with information from MIDAS_LU, one ODBC link and an ACCESS file must be created for each year. Finally, some variables must be recomposed in order to conform to the EUROMOD framework.

Of course, we need a 'control' file for each modified input dataset from MIDAS_LU. Furthermore, public policies must be anticipated and parameterized in EUROMOD for the various years, which is done through the 'pol' files. In the present exercise, we are considering a simple evolution. New policy 'systems' are created for the years 2008–18. Regarding income taxation, tax brackets are assumed to follow consumer price indexation, and hence to increase by 2.5 per cent per year. Family allowances are imposed a one-shot increase by 13.1 per cent (2.5 per cent to the power 5) in 2013. The 'Minimum Social Wage' is indexed taking into account both consumer price index and the real growth rate of hourly-wage.[8] This reference is playing an important role in the determination of many tax-benefit amounts (e.g. for the computation of social contributions whose tax-basis is top-limited to five times the Minimum Social Wage). Social assistance is also indexed on prices.

The various runs of EUROMOD for the successive years are based on 'control' and 'pol' files. We keep the scenarios relatively simple by assuming no changes in the 'spine', 'tu' and 'il' files.

In the last step, EUROMOD is then simulated on the basis of the micro-datasets pertaining to the simulation years between 2008 and 2018. Some key results of this exercise will be presented in the next section.

MIDAS_LU and EUROMOD have a small overlapping area, since an 'uprating' procedure of monetary variables is conceivable in EUROMOD so as to take monetary evolution of income elements into consideration. However, gross income depends on behaviour (labour supply) as well and such changes are not taken into account in EUROMOD. We have therefore chosen to model the development of earnings within MIDAS_LU through an earnings equation, rather than uprating (nominal and real components) over time in EUROMOD.

This chapter describes a first attempt to interlink the two models EUROMOD and MIDAS_LU, and their 'dialogue' is clearly yet not complete. The dynamic model MIDAS_LU, developed in the LIAM framework, is based on the same

---

8   Minimum Social Wage = €1,570.28 per month as of 1 January 2007.

dataset as EUROMOD, and development was done keeping the EUROMOD input set of variables in mind, thereby making the two as consistent as possible. Yet full consistency was not always possible; sometimes, the definition of variables had to be changed, for example when categories defined in EUROMOD were inconsistent with those used in MIDAS_LU; and some variables necessary in EUROMOD but not simulated in MIDAL_LU had to be directly derived from the initial EUROMOD dataset.

For example, the 'Highest Education Achieved' variable is categorized ['COEDUACH': (0) Not completed primary level, (1) Primary, (2) Lower secondary, (3) Upper secondary, (4) Tertiary] in EUROMOD, to be compared to [(0) Do not know, (1) Up to lower secondary, (2) Lower than tertiary, (3) Tertiary] in MIDAS_LU. Thus, after simulation through MIDAL_LU, nobody was given level 1 ('Primary') in EUROMOD. As another example, the compound EUROMOD-variable 'Employment Status' is not directly available from the MIDAS_LU output, and therefore was derived from dichotomous MIDAS_LU ('inwork', 'employee', 'unemployed', etc.). Finally, some variables including 'Maintenance payments – COMAINTY' or the 'Housing tenure – COTENURE' are not simulated in MIDAS_LU, and the values in the EUROMOD starting dataset were therefore assumed constant.

However, these are minor adjustments since the final 'static' and 'dynamic' datasets are close enough to make the output of MIDAS_LU a possible input for EUROMOD.

Analysis of Results

This section presents some key results from combined MIDAS_LU / EUROMOD simulations described earlier, with the objective of emphasizing the impact of complementing one model with another. The first subsection makes more explicit the simulation scene and its limitations. Then, the next subsection gives details about the population changes over the period 2008–18 and their impact, together with that of policy reforms, on the distribution of equivalized disposable income and inequalities.

The Global Simulation Scene and Limitations

Combining EUROMOD and MIDAS_LU allows us to evolve both population (including gross income) and policies ('systems', in EUROMOD), in unison or separately. Population characteristics and the development of gross labour income are dealt with by the dynamic model while public policy is simulated through the static model.

Starting with the Luxembourg household panel PSELL3/EU-SILC, an input dataset for MIDAS_LU is created, describing the population in 2008 and incomes in 2007. MIDAS_LU then generates outputs for the years 2008 to 2018, specifically on individual and household characteristics and gross earnings. Other sources of revenue, like social unemployment benefits or pensions,[9] are not yet included in MIDAS_LU. Given that some of those resources are not simulated in EUROMOD either but rather copied from the input dataset, they are simply considered evolving through time, in the present exercise, in conformity with the uprating rules applied in EUROMOD for monetary variables.

Another limitation is due to the transition between an input which is observed data (year 2007) and the first output year involving simulated results, including the population characteristics (year 2008). This is the reason why we choose the year 2008 and the first MIDAS_LU output wave as the reference point both for the analysis of results and for the EUROMOD starting input. Successive waves will be compared to that basis.

Moreover, it was not possible to take weights of households (and individuals) into account in the dynamic model (see Dekkers and Cumpston 2011), and consequently neither in the static model. Finally, MIDAS_LU modelling of household size and composition is based on a set of sometimes crude and simple rules. One example is the so-called 'Get A Life' rule in MIDAS_LU, which makes a single adult leave his or her parents' household after a certain age. As a result of this rule, multigenerational households and other complex residence households cannot exist. This leads to a population configuration in terms of nuclear households (parents with dependent children) rather than residence households which are the standard reference basis, in the assessment of adequacy measures based on observed data (Liégeois et al. 2011).

Those limitations, together with the lack of validation discussed in the section 'The LIAM Framework for Dynamic Microsimulation', show that these simulations are as yet incomplete. The chapter, however, aims only to highlight issues pertaining to combining the static EUROMOD with a dynamic model.

Population Changes and Evolution of Inequalities

Table 13.3 shows that individual and household characteristics are subject to change as a result of the demographic ageing process.

Not surprisingly, the proportion of elderly in the population is progressively increasing,[10] while the proportion of young decreases. Household size is consistently

---

9   Pensions, like other kinds of resources, raise a few additional difficulties. Like many other countries, those benefits depend on past history of the recipient (and maybe that of his/her relatives), including incomes and working periods of time. Such cumulative individual variables are not generated in the MIDAS_LU model yet (this will change soon for 'new' individuals) and then not made available for EUROMOD simulation here. Moreover, the question whether a feedback from EUROMOD to MIDAS_LU might be needed is still to be explored.

10   However, the rapid evolution observed might be questionable. The validation of the model will help us to understand more about that and might induce adaptations (see section 'The LIAM Framework for Dynamic Microsimulation').

Table 13.3   Evolution of population characteristics

Characteristics	Categories	2008	2013	2018
Age (in proportion of individuals)	Age < 18	27%	26%	23%
	18 = < Age < 59	59%	56%	55%
	Age > = 60	14%	18%	22%
Type of household (in proportion of nuclear households)	Single (< 65)	20%	28%	34%
	Single (65+)	6%	7%	8%
	Single with dependent(s)	9%	11%	14%
	Couple 0 dep	23%	20%	20%
	Couple 1–2 dep	33%	25%	17%
	Couple 3+ dep	10%	9%	7%
Number of dependents (*) (in proportion of nuclear households)	0 dependent	49%	55%	62%
	1 dependent	22%	20%	18%
	2 dependents	19%	15%	11%
	3+ dependents	11%	11%	11%

Source: MIDAS_LU and own computations.

(*) A dependent is a member of a nuclear household but not a parent (e.g. young child).

decreasing, with increasing single-individual (nuclear) households and a lower average number of dependent children per household.

Further to those demographic changes, income is evolving (through real and nominal growth of the hourly wage and due to individual choices and life events) and the public policy is progressively adapted (see section 'Combining EUROMOD and LIAM').

This chapter now briefly presents a few indicators based on the distribution of equivalized disposable income.[11] The focus is mainly on understanding the impact of modelling decisions.

A first key conclusion from the 'POL-POP' line in Table 13.4 is that inequality is gradually increasing over time, with a change in Gini coefficient from 0.2531 to 0.2815 between 2008 and 2018. A comparable evolution is shown by the at-risk-of-poverty rates, Atkinson indices and inter-decile ratio. Such an evolution results from demographic changes, behavioural reactions, economic variations and social policy adaptations. The lines 'POP_2008' in Table 13.4 shows the results of the simulation with fixed population and changing policy, with policy systems implemented as described for 2013 and 2018. Finally, lines 'POL_2008' in

---

11   The equivalized disposable income is the ratio of total disposable income (= earnings – social contributions – taxes + social benefits, summed up for the members of the household), corrected for differences in household size and composition through the 'OECD-modified scale' (1, 0.5, 0.3). Each member of the household is then attributed this equivalized disposable income.

Table 13.4 represents the simulation results keeping public policy unchanged at 2008 while changing population and gross labour income only.

Table 13.4　Inequality indicators, impact of modelling and evolution

Inequality indicators	Configuration (II)	Year (I)		
		2008	**2013**	**2018**
Gini	POP_2008	0.2531	0.2452	0.2389
	POL_2008	0.2531	0.2752	0.2983
	POL_POP	0.2531	0.2667	0.2815
Poverty rate	POP_2008	14.6%	9.0%	4.0%
(60% of median equivalent	POL_2008	14.6%	18.1%	18.9%
income)	POL_POP	14.6%	15.8%	18.7%
Atkinson index	POP_2008	0.050	0.047	0.045
(inequality aversion = 0.5)	POL_2008	0.050	0.061	0.072
	POL_POP	0.050	0.057	0.063
Atkinson index	POP_2008	0.175	0.163	0.153
(inequality aversion = 2)	POL_2008	0.175	0.207	0.241
	POL_POP	0.175	0.193	0.210
P75 / P25	POP_2008	1.99	1.98	1.98
	POL_2008	1.99	1.90	1.92
	POL_POP	1.99	1.89	1.92
P90 / P10	POP_2008	3.09	2.90	2.73
	POL_2008	3.09	3.54	4.13
	POL_POP	3.09	3.28	3.54

Source: MIDAS_LU, EUROMOD and own computations
(I) INCOME year
(II) POP_◇ and POL_◇ are the scenarios with fixed population (and gross earnings) and policy, respectively. POL_POP is compound scenario including population and policy changes.

The demographic changes and policy changes appear to have an opposite impact on the indicators shown in Table 13.4. Keeping demographics constant and including only policy changes (which is equivalent to simulating EUROMOD in stand-alone and no uprate of monetary variables) results in the Gini going down from 0.2531 to 0.2389 and has also an impact on the left-side of the income distribution (see the Poverty rate or Atkinson indices). In contrast, taking only demographic changes into account while keeping public policy constant (or, simulating MIDAS_LU in stand-alone) results in inequalities going up. Figure 13.1 illustrates the observation another way. The distribution of income in terms of deciles is represented, and its evolution through time under the two regimes (policy *versus* population constant) emphasized.

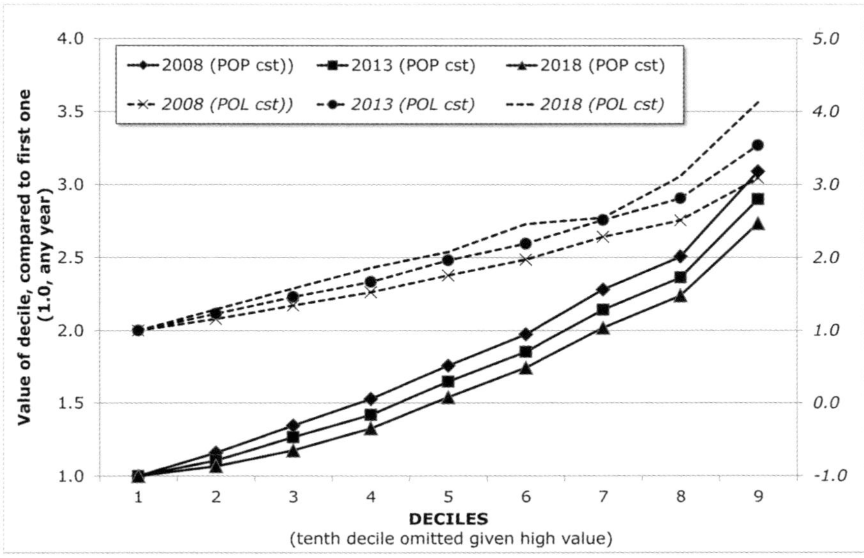

Figure 13.1　Evolution of income distribution through time

Full lines refer to the 'population constant' and left axis. Dotted lines refer to the 'policy constant' and right axis.
Source: MIDAS_LU, EUROMOD and own computations.

This opposite contribution can be highlighted in still another way. In Table 13.5, the transition from 2008 to 2013 (respectively 2018) is done in two sequential steps. In a first step, the policy system is changed, while the population characteristics are maintained at their 2008-level. The second step complements the first one in that it adds the demographic changes to the simulation results of the first step. Thus, the combination of the simulation results of the two models brings the 2008 starting dataset to the 'final dataset' in 2013 (resp. 2018). Not surprisingly, the first step (policy change only) again causes a reduction in inequality, while the second step (population change) is doing the opposite. Both steps imply some vertical redistribution (reducing inequalities), but the second step also results in an important increase in horizontal inequity, which more than compensates for the vertical effect. Thus, the combination of the two steps leads to an increase in inequality as measured by the Gini coefficient.

Table 13.5   Inequality indicators, evolution and impact of modelling

Inequality indicator	FIRST step (changing POLICY)		SECOND step (changing POPULATION)	
	FROM : POP_2008 ... and POL_2008 (I)		**FROM** : POP_2008 and POL_2013	*... or POL_2018*
	TO : POP_2008 and POL_2013	*... or POL_2018*	**TO** : POP_2013 and POL_2013...	*... or POP_2018 and POL_2018*
Gini : Initial (1)	**0.2531**	0.2531	0.2452	0.2389
Gini : Final (2)	0.2452	0.2389	**0.2678**	0.2814
Gini : Initial – Final (3) = (1) - (2) = (4) - (5)	0.0079	0.0142	–0.0226	–0.0425
Reynolds-Smolensky index of vertical equity (4)	0.0081	0.0148	0.0515	0.0805
Re-ranking index of horizontal inequality (5)	0.0002	0.0006	0.0741	0.1229

Source: MIDAS_LU, EUROMOD and own computations.
(I) See note (II), Table 13.4.

Conclusions

This chapter discusses a first attempt to combine the static model EUROMOD with the dynamic MIDAS_LU model.

The static model EUROMOD, on the one hand, is well-suited to deal with the immediate impact of changes in the tax-benefit system. It can also incorporate some changes in the monetary variables through the uprating procedure. On the other hand, MIDAS_LU includes demographic developments, policy hypothesis and evolutions, and behavioural reactions.

A first conclusion is that the combination of the two models is indeed possible, and that the two models are complementary enough for this combination to be meaningful. However, the combination at this stage suffers from some shortcomings that confine the possibilities. At present, the dynamic model MIDAS_LU does not provide all the variables that EUROMOD needs (e.g. capital income, replacement revenues like pensions, etc.) and this becomes increasingly problematic when simulations go further in the future. In the EUROMOD environment, such information, if not simulated, can sometimes be partially derived from raw input data (PSELL3/EU-SILC) and maintained constant for a few years projection when needed. But – again – this option of invariance is less valid in the longer term.

Part of this limitation is purely contextual and will disappear in the future, when MIDAS_LU will have been progressively completed.

Moreover, the dynamic model can generate nuclear households only and does not deal with 'weights' of households and individuals, which makes a strong limitation regarding social indicators that should be set on the basis of residence households and in a 'weighted' configuration.

We also show that demographic changes (including the development of gross incomes) and developments in the tax-benefit system can play a role in an opposite way, regarding the distribution of equivalized disposable income and inequalities. In the present exercise, inequalities are shown to decrease between 2008 and 2018 due to policy changes. But demographic changes play a significant role and result in increase of inequalities, which outweigh the policy effect, leaving a situation where the society is more unequal in 2018 than in 2008. This might highlight the value of a combination of dynamic and static modelling over static modelling on its own.

Finally, future research will involve combining further the latest versions of the two models. On the one side, EUROMOD is being updated at the moment (in the scope of the EUROMODupdate project) and the new model will soon be made available for Luxembourg. This new version also involves a new interface for the programmers. The dynamic model MIDAS_LU, on the other hand, was developed using the LIAM toolbox, using routines developed for MIDAS_Belgium. Today, a new fully redesigned toolbox, 'LIAM 2', was recently developed in the context of the MiDaL project (Dekkers et al. 2011). This improved package will allow for the development of a next-generation version of MIDAS_LU, which will then be combined again with the new version of EUROMOD.

References

Bargain, O. (ed.) (2007) *Micro-simulation in action: policy analysis in Europe using EUROMOD*. Amsterdam: Elsevier.

Dekkers, G., Buslei, H., Cozzolino, M., Desmet, R., Geyer, J., Hofmann, D., Raitano, M., Steiner, V., Tanda, P., Tedeschi, S. and Verschueren, F. 2008. What are the consequences of the AWG projections for the adequacy of social security pensions? An application of the dynamic micro simulation model, MIDAS, for Belgium, Italy and Germany. Final report of the AIM project [FP6-2003-SSP-3] OJ C243 of 10.10.2003.http://www.plan.be/publications/publication_det.php?lang=en&TM=30&IS=63&KeyPub=781 [accessed: 24/09/13].

Dekkers, G., Buslei, H., Cozzolino, M., Desmet, R., Geyer, J., Hofmann, D., Raitano, M., Steiner, V., Tanda, P., Tedeschi, S. and Verschueren, F. 2010. The flip side of the coin: the consequences of the European budgetary projections on the adequacy of social security pensions. *European Journal of Social Security*, 12(2), 94–120.

Dekkers, G. and Cumpston, R. 2011. *On weights in dynamic-ageing microsimulation models*. Paper presented at the 3rd General Conference of the International Microsimulation Association, Stockholm, Sweden, June 8th to 10th.

Dekkers, G., de Menten, G. and Liégeois, P. 2011. LIAM 2 – *A tool for the development of dynamic microsimulation models: a sneak preview*, presented at the 3rd General Conference of the International Microsimulation Association, Stockholm, Sweden, June 8th to 10th.

Immervoll, H. and O'Donoghue, C. 2001. Towards a Multi-purpose Framework for Tax-Benefit Microsimulation: A Discussion by Reference to MMEANS, a software system used for constructing EUROMOD, a European Tax-Benefit Model, EUROMOD Working Paper, EM2/01, Department of Applied Economics, University of Cambridge. Available at: https://www.iser.essex.ac.uk/publications/working-papers/euromod/em2–01.pdf [accessed: 26/09/13].

Liégeois, P., Berger, F., Islam, N. and Wagener, R. 2011. Cross-validating administrative and survey datasets through microsimulation and the assessment of a tax reform. *International Journal of Microsimulation*, 4(1), 1–18.

O'Donoghue, C., Hynes, S. and Lennon, J. 2009. The Life-Cycle Income Analysis Model (LIAM): A Study of a Flexible Dynamic Microsimulation Modelling Computing Framework. *International Journal of Microsimulation*, 2(1), 16–31.

Sutherland, H. 2007. EUROMOD: the tax-benefit microsimulation model for the European Union, in Gupta, A. and A. Harding (eds), *Modelling Our Future: population ageing, health and aged care*. International Symposium in Economic Theory and Econometrics. Elsevier, 16, 483–8.

Chapter 14
An Overview of Binary Alignment Methods in Microsimulation

Jinjing Li[1] and Cathal O'Donoghue

Introduction

Microsimulation models typically simulate behavioural processes such as demographic (e.g. marriage), labour market (e.g. unemployment) and income characteristics (e.g. wage). The method uses statistical estimates of these systems of equations and then applies Monte Carlo simulation techniques to generate the new populations, typically over time, both into the future and when creating histories with partial data, into the past.

As statistical models are typically estimated on historical datasets with specific characteristics and period effects, projections of the future may therefore contain errors or may not correspond to exogenous expectations of future events. In addition, the complexity of micro behaviour may mean that simulation models may over or under predict the occurrence of a certain event, even in a well-specified model (Duncan and Weeks 1998). Because of these issues, methods of calibration known as alignment have been developed within the microsimulation literature to correct for issues related to the adequacy of micro projections.

Scott (2001) defines alignment as 'a process of constraining model output to conform more closely to externally derived macro-data ("targets")'. There are both arguments for and against alignment procedures (Baekgaard 2002). Concerns directed towards alignment mainly focus on the consistency issue within the estimates and the level of disaggregation at which this should occur. It is suggested that equations should be reformulated rather than constrained *ex post*. Clearly, in an ideal world, one would try to estimate a system of equations that could replicate reality and have effective future projections without the need for alignment. However, as Winder (2000) stated, 'microsimulation models usually fail to simulate known time-series data. By aligning the model, goodness of fit to an observed time series can be guaranteed'. Some modellers suggest that alignment is an effective pragmatic solution for highly complex models (O'Donoghue 2010).

---

1   The authors are grateful to Rick Morrison, Howard Redway and Steven Caldwell for helpful discussions over time in relation to alignment in microsimulation models. We are grateful to the Luxembourg AFR grant scheme for supporting this research.

Over the past decade, aligning the output of a microsimulation model to exogenous assumptions has become standard despite this controversy. In order to meet the need for alignment, various methods, e.g. multiplicative scaling, sidewalk, sorting based algorithm etc., have been experimented along with the development of microsimulation (see Morrison 2006). Microsimulation models using historical datasets, e.g. CORSIM, align the output to historical data to create a more credible profile (SOA 1997). Models that work prospectively, e.g. APPSIM, also utilize the technique to align their simulation with external projections (Kelly and Percival 2009).

Nonetheless, the understanding of the simulation properties of alignment in microsimulation models is very limited. Literature on this topic is scarce, with a few exceptions such as Anderson (1990), Caldwell et al. (1998), Neufeld (2000), Chénard (2000a, 2000b), Johnson (2001), Baekgaard (2002), Morrison (2006), Kelly and Percival (2009) and O'Donoghue (2010). Although some new alignment methods were developed in an attempt to address some theoretical and empirical deficiencies of earlier methods, discussions on empirical simulation properties of different alignment algorithms are almost non-existent.

This chapter aims to fill this gap by documenting the known alignment implementations and evaluating the simulation properties of these algorithms in microsimulation. It compares the alignment processes, probability transformations, and the statistical properties of alignment outputs. Alignment performances are tested using various evaluation criteria, including the ones outlined in Morrison (2006).

Alignment in Microsimulation

This section discusses the purpose of alignment in a microsimulation model and the common practise of their statistical implementation. Baekgaard (2000) suggests two broad categories for alignment:

- Parameter alignment, whereby the distribution function is changed by adjustment of its parameters;
- *ex post* alignment, whereby alignment is performed on the basis of unadjusted predictions or interim output from a simulation.

This chapter focuses on the *ex post* alignment methods, as they are the most common form of alignments in microsimulation. In most cases, a microsimulation model applies this prediction process to all observations individually without constraint at aggregate level. However, this may lead to a potential side effect: the output of the predication, although it may look reasonable at each individual level, may not meet the modeller's expectation at the aggregate level. For instance, simulated average earnings might be higher or lower than that assumed, or the employment rate is out of range of expectations. Therefore, alignment is introduced as the step after the initial prediction in order to impose an *ex post* constraint.

Models of binary discrete events such as in-work, employment status, disability status etc. typically produce probabilities of the event occurring as output. These models can be expressed in the following generic form:

$$y_i^* = X_i \beta$$

Where X is the independent variable and β is the coefficient, is a latent variable that is not observed directly. In the case of the logit model, y_i^* is translated to y_i using logistic distribution, therefore y_i is predicted to have a value of 1 with the probability

$$\frac{\exp(X_i\beta)}{(1 + \exp(X_i\beta))}.$$

Although there is some theoretical debate surrounding alignment usage, alignment is *de facto* widely adopted in the models built or updated within last decade, e.g. DYANACAN (Neufeld 2000), CORSIM (SOA 1997), APPSIM (Bacon 2009). Many papers, e.g. Baekgaard (2002), Bacon (2009) and O'Donoghue (2010), have discussed the main reasons for alignment, and summarize them as follows:

Alignment may be used to address the unfortunate consequences of insufficient estimation data or poor predictive performance by incorporating additional information in the simulations. Since no country has an ideal dataset for estimating all the parameters needed for microsimulation, modellers often make compromises, which adversely affects the output quality. Alignment is sometimes used to mitigate the impact of some of these errors.

Alignment provides an opportunity for producing scenarios based on different assumptions. Examples include the simulation of alternative recession scenarios on employment with different impacts on different social groups (e.g. sex, education or occupation).

Alignment is instrumental in establishing links between microsimulation models of the household sector and the macro models. It is a crucial step to reach a consistent Micro-Macro simulation model (see Davies 2004).

Alignment can be used to reduce Monte Carlo variability though its deterministic calculation (Neufeld 2000). This is useful for small samples to confine the variability of aggregate statistics.

Alignment Methods

In order to calibrate a simulation of a binary variable, we need a method that can adjust the outcome of an estimated model to produce outcomes that are consistent with the external total. At the time of writing, there is no standardized method for implementing alignment in microsimulation. Given that different modellers may have different views or needs, it is not surprising that various binary alignment methods have appeared.

Papers by Neufeld (2000), Morrison (2006) and O'Donoghue (2010) provide descriptions on some popular options for alignment used in the literature. Existing documented alignment methods include

- Multiplicative Scaling;
- Sidewalk Shuffle, Sidewalk Hybrid and their derivatives;
- Central Limit Theorem Approach;
- Sort by predicted probability (SBP);
- Sort by the difference between predicted probability and random number (SBD); and
- Sort by the difference between logistic adjusted predicted probability and random number (SBDL).

Multiplicative Scaling

Multiplicative scaling, which was described in Neufeld (2000), involves undertaking an unaligned simulation using Monte Carlo techniques and then comparing the proportion of transitions with the external control total. The average ratio between the desired transition rate and the actual transition is used as a scaling factor for the simulated probabilities. The method ensures that the average scaled simulated probability is the same as the desired transition rate. The method, however, is criticized by Morrison (2006) as probabilities are not guaranteed to stay in the range 0–1 after scaling, though the problem is rare in practice as the multiplicative ratio tends to be small.

Algorithm 1: Multiplicative Scaling Alignment Method

Input: p_i (predicted probability obtained from the model), t (target probability), N (total number of observations)

Output: q_i (updated predicted probability)

Pseudo Code:

$$r = t / \left(\frac{1}{N} \sum_{i=1}^{N} p_i \right)$$

$$q_i = r p_i$$

Sidewalk Method

The sidewalk method was first introduced in Neufeld (2000) as a variance reduction technique, which was also used as an alternative to pure Monte Carlo simulation. It keeps a record of the accumulated probability from the first observation to the last one. As long as there is a change of the integer part of the accumulated probability, the observation is assigned with an outcome value of 1.

Neufeld (2000) developed an alignment method that is a hybrid of Monte Carlo and the sidewalk method. DYNACAN adopted this approach with non-linear adjustment to the equation-generated probabilities, combined with a minor tweaking of the resulting probabilities depending on whether the simulated rate is ahead of or behind the target rate for the pool during the progress and some randomizations (Morrison 2006). The method calibrates the probabilities through nonlinear transformation instead of using predicted probabilities directly (SOA 1998). Sidewalk Hybrid method requires two arbitrary parameters, which decides how similar the output is to standard Monte Carlo or standard sidewalk method.

Algorithm 2: Sidewalk with Nonlinear Transformation

Input: p_i (predicted probability obtained from the model), t (target probability), N (total number of observations), η (maximum difference before probability adjustment, 0.5 in the original paper), λ (adjustment factor, 0.03 in the original paper)

Output: y_i (simulation output)

Pseudo Code:

Find a so that $t = \dfrac{1}{N}\sum_{i=1}^{N}\dfrac{ap_i}{1+(a-1)p_i}$

$q_i = \dfrac{ap_i}{1+(a-1)p_i}$

Randomize order of observation

T=0 (counter)

For i=1 to N:

$$c = \min\left(\frac{q_i}{2}, \frac{1-q_i}{2}, \lambda\right)$$

$$\text{if } \left(\sum_{j=1}^{i}q_j - T\right) > \eta: \quad c = -c$$

$r \leftarrow$ random number $(0,1)$

$$y_i = \left((r+c) < q_i\right)$$

$$T = T + y_i$$

restore observation order

The Central Limit Theorem Approach

The Central Limit Theorem approach is described in Morrison (2006). It utilizes the assumption that the mean simulated probability is close to the expected mean when N is large. It manipulates the probabilities of each individual observation on the fly so that the simulated mean matches the expectation. A more detailed description of the method can be found in Morrison (2006). As all the methods we have discussed so far, this method does not need any sorting routine.

Algorithm 3: Central Limit Theorem Approach

Input: p_i (predicted probability obtained from the model), t (target probability), N (total number of observations)
Output: y_i (simulation output)
Pseudo Code:

    T=0 (counter)

$$P_i \leftarrow \sum_{k=i}^{N} p_k$$

    For i=1 to N:

        $r \leftarrow$ random number (0,1)

        $q_i = p_i (tN - T) / (P_N - P_{i-1})$

        if $(p_i > r)$

            $y_i = 1$

            $T = T + y_i$

        Else

            $y_i = 0$

Sort by Predicted Probability (SBP)

O'Donoghue (2001) and Johnson (2001) first documented sorting based alignment algorithms. This type of algorithm involves sorting of the predicted probability adjusted with a stochastic component, and selects the desired number of events according to the sorting order. It is seen as a more 'transparent' method (O'Donoghue 2010) although it can be computationally more intensive due to the sorting procedure. Many variations of these methods have been used in the past years. In this section, we discuss the commonly used variations: sort by predicted probability (SBP), sort by the difference between predicted probability and random number (SBD), and sort by the difference between logistic adjusted predicted probability and random number (SBDL).

    Sorting by probability method essential picks up the observations with highest p_i^* in each alignment pool. One consequence, however, is that those with the highest risk are always being selected for transition. In the example of in-work, the higher educated, all other things being equal would be selected to have a job. In reality, those with the highest risk will on average be selected more than those with lower risk, but not always be selected. As a result some variability needs to be introduced. Kelly and Percival (2009) propose a variant of this method, where a proportion (typically 10 per cent of the desired number) are selected when the sorting order is inverted, so as to allow low risk units to make a transition.

Algorithm 4: Sort by Probability

Input: p_i (predicted probability obtained from the model), t (target probability), N (total number of observations)
Output: y_i (simulation output)
Pseudo Code:
       sort by p_i from largest to smallest (assume the new index is j)
       $y_i = (j \leq Nt)$
       restore observation order

Sort by the Difference between Predicted Probability and Random Number (SBD)

Given the shortcoming of the simple probability sorting, Baekgaard (2002) uses another method, which sorts by differences between predicted probability and a random number. Instead of sorting the probability p_i^* directly, it sorts q_i, which equals to the difference between p_i^* and a random number r_i, a number that is uniformly distributed between 0 and 1. Mathematically, this sorting variable can be defined as follows:

$$q_i = \text{logit}^{-1}(\alpha + \beta X_i) + r_i$$

A concern about this method is that the range of possible sorting values is not the same for each point. In other words, because the random number $r_i \in [0,1]$ is subtracted from the deterministically predicted p_i^*, and the sorting value takes the range $q_i \in [-1,1]$. For each individual, q_i will only take a possible range $[r_i - 1, r_i]$. As a result, when p_i^* is small say 0.1, the range of possible sorting values is $[-0.9, 0.1]$. At the other extreme if p_i^* is large say $= 0.9$, then the range of possible sorting values is $[-0.1, 0.9]$. Thus because there is only a small overlap for these extreme points, an individual with a small p_i^* will have a very low chance of being selected even if a low value random number is paired with the observation.

Algorithm 5: Sort by the difference between predicted probability and random number (SBD)

Input: p_i (predicted probability obtained from the model), t (target probability), N (total number of observations)
Output: y_i (simulation output)
Pseudo Code:

    $r_i \leftarrow$ random number $(0,1)$
    $q_i = p_i - r_i$
    sort by q_i from largest to smallest (assume the new index is j)
    $y_j = (j \leq Nt)$
    restore observation order

Sort by the Difference between Logistic Adjusted Predicted Probability and Random Number (SBDL)

An alternative method described in Flood et al. (2005), Morrison (2006) and O'Donoghue et al. (2008) mitigates the range problem of SBD by using logistic transformation. This method takes a predicted logistic variable from a logit model, $\text{logit}(p_i) = \alpha + \beta X_i$ combined with a random number r_i that is drawn from a logistic distribution to produce a randomized variable. The sorting variable can therefore be described as follows:

$$q_i = \text{logit}^{-1} (\alpha + \beta X_i + r_i)$$

r_i is a logistically distributed random number with mean value 0 and a standard error of $\pi / \sqrt{3}$. Since the random number is not uniformly distributed as r_i in the previous method, it produces a different sorting order.

Algorithm 6: Sort by the difference between logistic adjusted predicted probability and random number (SBDL)

Input: p_i (predicted probability obtained from the model), t (target probability), N (total number of observations)
Output: y_i (simulation output)
Pseudo Code:

    $r_i \leftarrow$ random number $(0,1)$
    $l_i \leftarrow \ln (1 / r_i - 1)$
    $q_i = l_i + \ln\left(p_i / (1 - p_i) \right)$
    sort by q_i from largest to smallest (assume the new index is j)
    $y_j = (j \leq Nt)$
    restore observation order

Methods of Evaluating Alignment Algorithm

In order to evaluate the simulation properties of all alignment algorithms, it is important to define what we need to compare, and what the criteria are. Although different alignment methods have been briefly documented in a few papers, there is little discussion on the differences among these methods' statistical properties. This chapter tries to evaluate different algorithms and compares how they perform under different scenarios.

Objectives of Alignment

The objectives of alignment, discussed in Morrison (2006) and O'Donoghue (2010) serve as the basis of our evaluation criteria. From a practical point of view, a 'good' alignment algorithm should be able to replicate the aggregate statistics as in the alignment target (Neufeld 2000, Morrison 2006) and preserve the relationship between deterministic and explanatory variables (O'Donoghue 2010). Ideally, it should also retain the shape of distributions in different subgroup and inter-relations unless there is a reason not to do it.

Indicators of Alignment Performance

In order to assess the alignment algorithms with very different designs, the chapter uses a set of quantitative indicators that can measure the simulation properties according to the criteria discussed earlier. The indicators include a target deviation index (TDI), which measures the difference between the external control and the simulation outcome, and a distribution deviation index (DDI), which measures the distortion of the relationship between different variables and inter-relations.

Target Deviation Index (TDI)

Assuming among N observations, the ideal alignment ratio is t and the final binary output after alignment for observation i is y_i. Target deviation index (TDI) is defined as

$$TDI = t - \frac{1}{N}\sum_{i=1}^{N} y_i$$

It is a percentage number ranged 0 to 1, and shows how the alignment replicates the external control. Higher values imply the outcome is further away from the external control.

Distribution Deviation Index (DDI)

In order to evaluate the second and the third criteria, it is necessary to find an indicator that can reflect how well the relationships are preserved and how different the new distribution is from the old one. This section uses a self-defined distribution deviation index (DDI) to evaluate the second and third criteria in choosing an alignment method. Assuming we are going to evaluate the distribution distortion in a single alignment pool via a grouping variable X. X could be anything like age, gender, or age gender interaction etc. N observations can therefore be divided into $n(X)$ groups with N_j observations in group j. If we define t as the external target ratio for alignment, $y_{j,i}$ as the binary output for observation i in group j after alignment and $p_{j,i}$ as the original probability for observation i in group j before alignment. A distribution deviation index (DDI), therefore, can be defined as

$$DDI = \sum_{j=1}^{n(X)} \frac{N_j}{N}\left(\frac{1}{N_j}\sum_{i=1}^{N_j} y_{j,i} - \frac{a}{N_j}\sum_{i=1}^{N_j} p_{j,i} \right)^2$$

$$\text{Where } a = tN \bigg/ \sum_{j=1}^{n(X)}\sum_{i=1}^{N_j} p_{j,i}$$

a is the ratio between exogenous total target and total accumulated probability in the dataset before alignment. The DDI indicator describes how well the micro-simulated data retain the relationships between dependent variable and variable X. Essentially, DDI calculates the sum of squares of differences weighted by the number of observations. It measures the differences between distributions before and after alignment in multiple dimensions, depending on the vector X. When X is an independent variable, it measures the distortion introduced between the independent variable and the dependent by alignment. The indicator is positively correlated with the alignment deviation, it increases when the aligned distribution departs from the original and decreases when the distributions are getting alike. DDI has a range of 0 to 1. When the dataset preserves the shape of distribution perfectly, the index has a value of zero. It increases when the difference of two redistributions grows, with a maximum value of one.

Datasets and Scenarios in Alignment Algorithm Evaluation

This chapter constructs several scenarios to test the performance of each alignment method. Each scenario represents a potential statistical error that alignment methods try to address or compensate in a microsimulation model.

Baseline Scenario

Assuming there is a binary model expressed as following

$$y_i = \text{logit}^{-1}(\alpha + \beta x_i + \varepsilon)$$

α, β are the parameters in the equation, and ε is an error term which follows a logistic distribution with zero mean and a variance of $\pi / \sqrt{3}$. To simplify the calculation in the evaluation, we assign $\alpha = 0$, $\beta = 1$. x is randomly drawn from a standard normal distribution $N(0,1)$. The number of observation in the synthetic dataset is 100,000.

Second Scenario: Biased Alpha (Intercept)

The second synthetic scenario aims to replicate a monotonic shift of the probabilities. This is commonly used in scenario analysis, where a certain ratio, e.g. unemployment rate, is required to be increased or decreased to meet the scenario assumptions.

By manipulating the intercept of the equations, it is possible to shift the probabilities across all observations. In this scenario, α is changed to -1 while everything else is constant. The result is a monotonic, but non-uniform change in the probabilities. A non-uniform transformation is required to make sure the probabilities are still bounded within the range of $[0,1]$. The transformation in this scenario is monotonic but non-uniform. Contrary to the previous scenario, the error structure and the number of observations stay the same in this setup. Table 14.1 highlights the statistical differences between this scenario and the other ones.

Third Scenario: Biased Beta

The third synthetic test scenario introduces a biased slope β in the equation. This represents a change in the behaviour pattern which could not be captured at the time of estimation (e.g. the evolution of fertility pattern). In this scenario, one may assume that the behaviour pattern shifts over time. This particular setup tests on how alignment works as a correction mechanism for behaviour pattern correction.

The simulated dataset in this scenario is generated with $\beta = 0.5$, half of its value in the baseline, and therefore creates a different distribution of probability. Since x has a mean value of 0, the change does not affect the total sample mean of y at the aggregate level. The transformation would yield a different distribution but with an unchanged sample mean.

Unlike the first and second scenarios, the transformation in this scenario causes a non-monotonic change in probabilities. Observations with low probability ($p < 0.5$) in the baseline scenario have increased probability since their x have negative values, while the observations with high probability ($p > 0.5$) have a lower probabilities compared with the baseline scenario.

As an overview, Table 14.1 summarizes the changes of alpha and beta in different scenarios and compares the key statistics. As seen, all scenarios have the same number of observations except the first one. The mean value of outcome variable ranges from 0.277 to 0.5, and the target for alignment (external value) is 0.5 across all scenarios.

Table 14.1   Overview of the synthetic data scenarios

| | Scenario | | |
Synthetic Scenario	**Baseline**	**1**	**2**
Number of observations in estimation	100,000	75,000	100,000
Number of observation in simulation	100,000	100,000	100,000
Mean value of outcome variable	0.500	0.330	0.303
α	0.000	−0.695 (0.008)	−1.000
β	1.000	0.998 (0.010)	1.000
Target ratio for alignment		0.50	0.50

N.B.: Coefficients in the first scenario are estimated using logit model. Standard errors are included in the brackets.

Evaluation Results

Table 14.2 lists four key indicators obtained when evaluating using synthetic datasets, which contains the Target deviation index (TDI) and Distribution deviation index (DDI). DDI calculation uses the percentile of dependent variable as the grouping variable.

Table 14.2   Properties of different alignment methods in synthetic dataset test

Method	TDI	DDI
Scenario 1: Biased alpha (intercept)		
Multiplicative scaling	−1.41%	0.61%
Sidewalk hybrid with nonlinear adjustment	0.00%	0.03%
Central limit theorem approach	0.00%	0.65%
Sort by predicted probability (SBP)	0.00%	11.50%
Sort by the difference between predicted probability and random number (SBD)	0.00%	0.30%
Sort by the difference between logistic adjusted predicted probability and random number (SBDL)	0.00%	0.03%
Scenario 2: Biased beta coefficients		
Multiplicative scaling	−0.18%	0.90%
Sidewalk hybrid with nonlinear adjustment	−0.01%	0.84%
Central limit theorem approach	0.00%	0.91%
Sort by predicted probability (SBP)	0.00%	11.50%
Sort by the difference between predicted probability and random number (SBD)	0.00%	0.87%
Sort by the difference between logistic adjusted predicted probability and random number (SBDL)	0.00%	0.88%

As seen in Table 14.2, all alignment methods except multiplicative scaling, in all scenarios, have less than 0.01 per cent deviation from the target number of event occurrence while multiplicative scaling shows a deviation up to 1.41 per cent from the target during the evaluation. The result is largely driven by the design of the algorithm, as multiplicative scaling cannot guarantee a perfect alignment ratio although the expected deviation is zero. The sidewalk hybrid method sometimes has a slight deviation (less than 0.01 per cent), as the non-linear transformation may not be always perfect under existing implementation.[2] Central limit theorem methods have built-in counters that prevent the events from manifesting when the target is met. Sorting based algorithms only pick the exact number of observations required, which is why their target deviation index (TDI) is always zero.

In terms of the distribution distortion, DDI reflects how well the relative relations between variables are preserved after alignment. In the first scenario, sidewalk hybrid and SBDL method gives the best result while in the second scenario, where the synthetic dataset modifies the slope of x_p, all methods have similar DDI values except SBP. The results show that SBP method heavily distorts the original distribution of the probabilities across all scenarios using percentile grouping. DDI effectively measures a weighted size of the gap between the correct and the aligned distribution. It seems that there is no method consistently outperforming across all scenarios. Overall, alignment algorithms work much better when beta remains stable, e.g. scenario 1. This may be due to the nature of these algorithms as the 'differencing' and 'logit transformation' operations assume monotonic changes in the probabilities.

Conclusion

This chapter reviewed and discussed six common binary model alignment techniques, including multiplicative scaling, hybrid sidewalk method, central limit theorem approach and sorting based algorithms (including its variations). The evaluations report a mixed result of alignment performances. It shows that the selecting the 'best' alignment method is not only about the algorithm design, but also the requirements and reasoning in a particular scenario.

Overall, multiplicative scaling is the easiest to implement, and fastest to compute method for alignment. Nonetheless, it cannot perfectly align to external control as the events are calculated purely based on the calculated probabilities. Moreover, due to lack of restrictions in the algorithm design, the outcome produced by the multiplicative scaling method is subject to higher fluctuations

---

2 The process usually requires several iterations and it is computationally expensive (Neufeld 2000). Our test model used in this chapter stops its calibration when the iteration only improves the average probability by no more than 10^{-8}. This increases the calculation speed but sometimes results in imperfectly aligned probabilities. Details of the calibration steps can be found in the book published by Society of Actuaries (SOA 1998).

than by other methods. The central limit theorem approach tends to have similar statistical patterns with the multiplicative scaling method except it can match the alignment target more precisely. The method is slow when implemented in Stata and the performance is similar to multiplicative scaling except target control.

Sidewalk hybrid with nonlinear adjustment is a more complicated method due to its nonlinear adjustment. It exhibits a similar pattern with one sorting based method, *sort by the difference between logistic adjusted predicted probability and random number* (SBDL). Because of the logistic transformation applied in both algorithms, both methods are good at handling the error of intercept in logit model.

As to the sorting based algorithms, the *sort by probabilities (SBP)* distorts the internal distributions heavily in both tested scenarios. The method, by design, over-predicts the observations with higher probabilities and under-predicts the observations with lower probabilities. However, the method is easy to implement and does not involve random number sorting. Its simulation properties suggest that *SBP* can be potentially used for imputation, but is not ideal for forward or backward simulation. *Sort by the difference between predicted probability and random number (SBD)* and *Sort by the difference between logistic adjusted predicted probability and random number (SBDL)* are similar in terms of computation steps, but they produce very different distributions of probability. *SBDL* works better with logit model, especially when the intercept is used for alignment calibration.

As the results show, each alignment method has its own advantages and disadvantages. For a microsimulation project that is speed oriented, *multiplicative scaling* seems to be a good choice. In a project where speed is not the major concern, the choice might depend on the reason for alignment. For instance, if alignment is used to create a shift in intercept, *SBDL* or *sidewalk hybrid with nonlinear transformation* may be the best choice. In addition, for microsimulation analysis with the focus on distributional analysis, *SBP* may not be the ideal because of its distortion of distributions.

Understanding the simulation properties is not an easy job as there are many implicit and explicit assumptions in every simulation project. The evaluation method used in this chapter also has its own limits. While the evaluations covered the most common scenarios, the sources of errors in a real simulation are more complex. Further work is required to understand the simulation properties of different methods under different assumptions and more complicated error structures. In addition, algorithms should also be evaluated on some real-life datasets in order to understand the impact of alignments in real-life projects.

References

Anderson, J.M. 1990. Micro-Macro Linkages in Economic Models, in Lewis, G.H. and Michel, R.C. (eds), *Microsimulation Techniques for Tax and Transfer Analysis*. Washington, DC: Urban Institute.

Bacon, P.B. 2009. Microsimulation, Macrosimulation: model validation, linkage and alignment, NATSEM Working Paper.

Baekgaard, H. 2002. Micro-macro linkage and the alignment of transition processes: some issues, techniques and examples, National Centre for Social and Economic Modelling Technical Paper.

Caldwell, S., Favreault, M., Gantman, A., Gokhale, J., Johnson, T. and Kotlikoff, L.J. 1998. Social Security's Treatment of Postwar Americans, NBER Working Paper No. W6603.

Caldwell, S. and Morrison, R. 2000. Validation of longitudinal microsimulation models: experience with CORSIM and DYNACAN, in Mitton, L., Sutherland, H. and Weeks, M. (eds), *Microsimulation Modelling for Policy Analysis: Challenges and Innovations*. Cambridge: Cambridge University Press.

Chénard, D. 2000a. *Earnings in DYNACAN: distribution alignment methodology*, Paper Presented to the 6th Nordic Workshop on Microsimulation, Copenhagen, June.

Chénard, D. 2000b. Individual alignment and group processing: an application to migration processes in DYNACAN D, in Mitton, L., Sutherland, H. and Weeks, M. (eds), *Microsimulation Modelling for Policy Analysis: Challenges and Innovations*. Cambridge: Cambridge University Press.

Davies, J.B. 2004. Microsimulation, CGE and Macro Modelling for Transition and Developing Economies. UNU/WIDER research paper.

Duncan, A. and Weeks, M. 1998. Simulating transitions using discrete choice models. *Proceedings of the American Statistical Association*, 106, 151–6.

Flood, L., Jansson, F., Pettersson, T., Sundberg, O. and Westerberg, W. 2005. SESIM III – A Swedish dynamic micro simulation model, Handbook of SESIM.

Johnson, T. 2001. Nonlinear Alignment by Sorting, CORSIM Working Paper.

Kelly, S. and Percival, R. 2009. *Longitudinal benchmarking and alignment of a dynamic microsimulation model*, IMA Conference Paper.

Morrison, R. 2006. Make it so: event alignment in dynamic microsimulation. DYNACAN paper.

Neufeld, C. 2000. Alignment and Variance Reduction in DYNACAN, in Gupta, A. and Kapur, V. (eds), *Microsimulation in Government Policy and Forecasting*. Amsterdam: North-Holland.

O'Donoghue, C. 2001. Redistribution in the Irish Tax-Benefit System, PhD Thesis, London School of Economics, UK.

O'Donoghue, C. 2010. Alignment and calibration in LIAM, LIAM working paper.

O'Donoghue, C., Hynes, S. and Lennon, J. 2008. The Life-Cycle Income Analysis Model (LIAM): A Study of a Flexible Dynamic Microsimulation Modelling Computing Framework, *International Journal of Microsimulation*, 2(1), 16–31.

Scott, A. 2001. Computing strategy for SAGE: 1. Model options and constraints. Technical Note 2. London, ESRC-Sage Research Group.

SOA 1997. Chapter 5 on CORSIM, Society of Actuaries, [http://www.soa.org/files/pdf/Chapter_5.pdf, accessed: 10/06/10].

SOA 1998. Chapter 6 on DYNACAN, Society of Actuaries, [http://www.soa.org/files/pdf/Chapter_6.pdf, accessed: 10/06/10].

Winder, N. 2000. Modelling within a thermodynamic framework: a footnote to Sanders. Cybergeo: *European Journal of Geography* Systèmes, Modélisation, Géostatistiques, 138(5).

Chapter 15

Simulating the Expenditures of Scottish Households: A Two-step Microsimulation Approach to the Cairngorms National Park

Eveline van Leeuwen

Introduction

Although globalization is increasingly affecting our world and modern telecommunication and transport modes make the world appear smaller, the interest for what is happening locally is increasing as well. This is partly due to the growing availability of detailed data sources and the enduring interest of researchers and policy makers in understanding what drives what at different spatial levels. For example, the question of how local residents appreciate their environments and how they use facilities that are available is still very relevant. People become more mobile: commuting longer distances is not abnormal anymore; going abroad for holidays a few times a year seems standard. Furthermore, by using the Internet, services and products can be obtained from all over the world. However, using the Internet and finding jobs within half an hour's drive is not an always possible, not even in Western Europe.

Several policies, at the EU, national and local level, focus on less accessible, often rural areas. There is a concern for the future of these areas where often young people move out and the elderly stay behind. The question is how vital those areas are and how sustainable in terms of the provision of important services to their inhabitants. Nowadays, new economic activities are developing in rural areas, such as recreation and tourism. The decrease in agricultural and industrial activity has led to a decline of service provision in the countryside. The increase in other activities can, however, compensate for this lack of provision. The countryside, with its characteristic peace, space and local identity becomes increasingly important to urban centres and urban dwellers.

An interesting example is the Cairngorms National Park. For Scottish standards, this park is quite well accessible (by train from Edinburgh and by car from Aberdeen). It is an area with several smaller towns and many tourists who enjoy the hiking possibilities in summer and skiing opportunities in wintertime. The status of National Park attracts many visitors, but also comes with sometimes-strict rules that can restrict economic development (CNP 2010a). Therefore, local policy makers are very concerned with how the current residents use local facilities. Within the context of the FP7 project SMILE, which aimed to analyse the trade-offs and synergies that exist between the different objectives related to sustainable development, they requested more detailed insights into this topic. However, there is a lack of consistent detailed information for this area.

Therefore, it was decided to collect as much local information as possible in order to perform a microsimulation (MSM) of the local population. MSM is a technique that aims at modelling the likely behaviour of individual persons, households, or individual firms, combining communicative qualities together with more analytical qualities. In simulation modelling, the analyst is interested in information relating to the joint distribution of attributes over a population (Clarke and Holm 1987). In these models, agents represent members of a population for the purpose of studying how individual (i.e. micro-) behaviour generates aggregate (i.e. macro-) regularities from a bottom-up approach (e.g. Epstein 1999).

The aim of this research is to create a detailed picture of all residents of the CNP with characteristics related to shopping and employment. One of the strong advantages of MSM is its ability to link different datasets at the micro level (van Leeuwen et al. 2010). Another advantage is that the result, the database of simulated persons, can be used for several purposes and analyses. One of our purposes described in this chapter is insight in the spatial shopping behaviour of the CNP residents. In future research, this will be an important input for the creation of a multi-level input-output table that describes the linkages between the CNP and the wider Scottish economy. An important input for the MSM is data from a questionnaire sent to local households early 2010 asking them about where they buy different types of products and services. Furthermore, we use a detailed marketing database that also includes a lot of information about shopping behaviour. We use a combination of matching and MSM techniques to get the most extensive picture.

In this chapter, we will first elaborate on the determinants of spatial shopping behaviour. Then we will focus on the CNP population using secondary data and questionnaires. Following that, the methodological framework will be presented and the simulations will be described. The final section shows the results, followed by the conclusions.

Determinants of Spatial Shopping Behaviour

When analysing the consumer behaviour of households, three important groups of factors should be considered. These are: 1) the consumer with all its characteristics, 2) the characteristics of the shop or retail centre including its location, and 3) the reason for shopping, or kind of product purchased (van Leeuwen and Rietveld 2010).

Socio-economic characteristics of consumers are fundamental in that they affect, for example, the degree of consumer spatial mobility (Hubbard 1978). When looking at consumer related factors, a higher level of income seems to be related to a higher share of purchases outside town (Herman and Beik 1968, Thompson 1971, Papadopoulos 1980). Apparently, households with a higher income are better able to bear the costs of shopping around (Huff 1959). In addition, they might be interested in products or services that are not locally available.

Another important consumer-related factor is age. It is often stated that older persons are less mobile and therefore are more likely to shop close to their place of residence (see Pinkerton et al. 1995, Powe and Shaw 2004, Papadopoulus 1980). They are also supposed to be more attached to the local area. However, attachment can also be measured by length of residence (Brown 1993) or satisfaction with the community. New inhabitants might still have links with their former place of living, while people that have always lived in one place might also have stronger social links to the local businesspeople.

A next relevant consumer related factor is the family situation, such as whether a family has young children. Herman and Beik (1968) and Miller and Kean (1997) found that households with young children do more shopping locally.

A final important variable is the place of work of the consumer. As Papadopoulos (1980: 57) described, sometimes consumers would not consider travelling a longer distance for their shopping; but once a consumer reaches a larger trade centre, for whatever other reason (such as work), shopping appears to become a significant secondary activity.

Besides these consumer-related factors, supply factors, related to the shop or retail-centre, affect the shopping behaviour of households. However, since we are only focusing on the Cairngorms National Park, we assume that the supply factors are similar to the whole CNP population. However, we do distinguish different types of purchases (third group of factors).

Methodological Framework

As mentioned earlier, the main aim of this research is to get a detailed picture of the population of the CNP, specifically related to their spatial shopping behaviour. Our two main data sources are results from a questionnaire, which was held early 2010 and a dataset we obtained from ADMAR, a company that collects marketing lists and enhance datasets. Those two datasets both provide very detailed micro-level information. Within the questionnaire, the focus was on where people buy different types of products and services. The ADMAR dataset contains more information about internet use, gas and electricity use, the kind of house people are living in, etc. Table 15.1 shows the data that both datasets include. Besides the already mentioned information, the two datasets also have similarities through which they can be linked, those are: household size, household age, length of residence, tenure and household income. Since the level of detail of the information differs, 'XX' indicates a good level of detail, and 'X' a poorer level of detail. An example is employment status, for which the questionnaire includes the status of up to two adults in the household, as well as the number of hours. The ADMAR dataset only includes information about the head of household and the CNP data tells us the total number of persons with a job.

Table 15.1   Available information in two datasets and totals for the CNP

	SMILE questionnaire	**ADMAR**	**CNP data**
Household size	XX	XX	
Age per person	XX	XX	
Length of residence	XX	XX	
Why living here	X		
Expenditures amount	XX	X	
Expenditures location	X		
Buy through internet	X	XX	
Tenure	X	X	
Housing characteristics		XX	
Household income	X	X	X
Employment status	XX	X	X
Type of job	XX		X
Location of job	XX		X
Owning a car	X	XX	

Figure 15.1 shows the framework of our research approach. Based on insights from the literature and insights from the SMILE questionnaire constraint variables for the matching and MSM procedures were selected. Furthermore, statistics on the current situation of the CNP were collected from various sources, such as reports from the local authorities. The matching procedures will result in a new and more heterogeneous dataset, the SMILE/ADMAR micropopulation as described below. This will be used for the final microsimulation procedures.

Households in the CNP

Cairngorms National Park

The Cairngorms National Park is one of the most sparsely populated parts of the United Kingdom and is currently home to some 17,200 individuals.

The Park's population is on average older than elsewhere in Scotland, and continued ageing creates both challenges and opportunities for providers of public and private services (CNP 2010b). Like all of rural Scotland, the area is experiencing large-scale out-migration of older teenagers in pursuit of education and of a wider range of opportunities. However the overall population of the Park

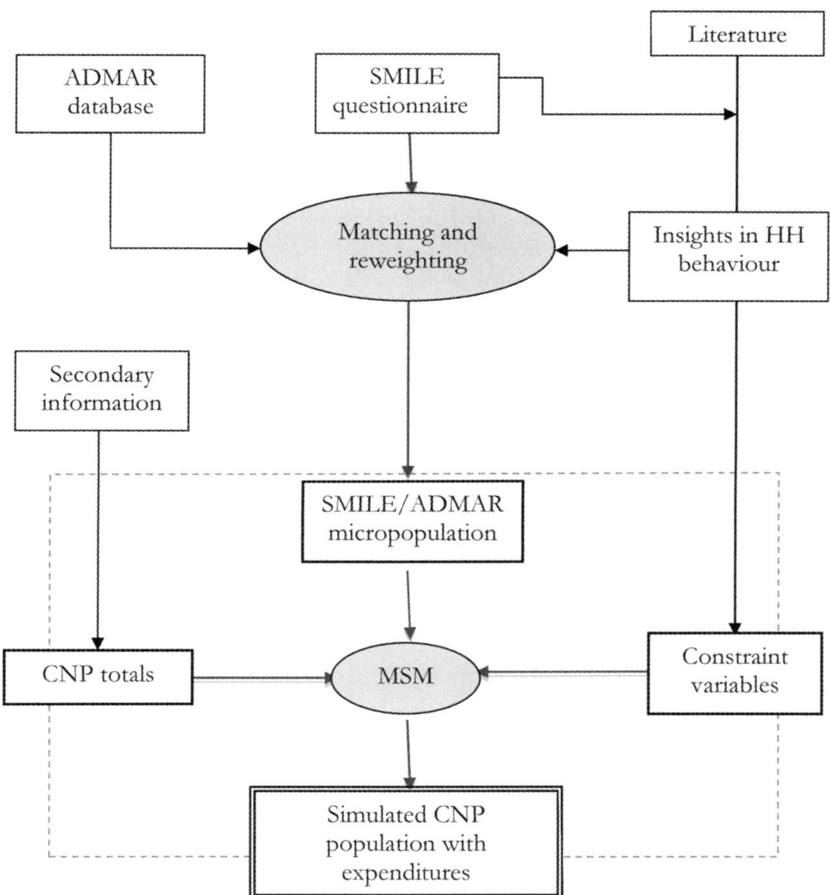

Figure 15.1   Methodological framework

has increased almost 5 per cent since designation, and projections suggest it will reach 20,000 by 2040. Currently more than 250 more people come to the Park than leave each year, with most of these new residents being of working age (ranging from their twenties to their fifties). Few other rural areas can demonstrate an attraction to youngsters.

There are a total of 11,500 people economically active in the Park. Of these, 9,000 are employed, around 2,000 are self-employed (a very large proportion by national standards), 200 are unemployed and the balance is full-time students. The last five years, the unemployment rates of around 2 per cent in the Park were significantly lower than in the rest of Scotland (4 per cent). Two thirds of all jobs are in private sector services, including retailing and tourism. One in six are employed in the public sector (a smaller share than national averages), whilst goods-producing industries, such as manufacturing, agriculture and construction, also account for one job in six. Over the past ten years most of the expansion in jobs has taken place in tourism related industries, with some in financial and business services (CNP 2010b).

The beautiful landscape, and in particular the mountains, draw tourists. Tourism, including accommodation, catering and visitor attractions, accounts for almost 30 per cent of all value added created in the Park (£115 million). This is a higher proportion than any other part of Scotland (CNP 2010b).

The sparsely populated nature of the permanent population, along with the physical challenges of the landscape means that connectivity and access to services can be challenging. Several of the Park's villages belong among the most geographically remote communities in Scotland, as measured by the Scottish Index of Multiple Deprivation. Telecommunications meet basic standards, but wireless coverage and the penetration and bandwidth of wired communications are on the agenda for improvement. Overall, the household income of people in the Park is relatively low, around 84 per cent of the average Scottish income. However, in general the Park's residents enjoy a high standard of economic wellbeing with only isolated pockets of deprivation evident. The health of residents is generally good, significantly better than average, and crime is broadly low (CNP 2010b).

Questionnaire: Expenditures

An important reason to conduct this survey was to get a better insight in the expenditures of households living in the CNP, and in particular where those expenditures take place. Therefore, we asked the households to indicate the amount of expenditures for several product and service groups over the previous four weeks (January), as well as the location of those expenditures (Park, adjoining municipalities, Rest of Scotland, Rest of UK, Rest of the World and Internet). In addition, we asked what they like about the Park and what their main motive is for moving here. Invitations were sent out by post and the questionnaires could be filled in on paper with a free return service and on the internet. Unfortunately, the response rate was rather low; from the 1,000 invitations which included a paper version of the questionnaire and a free response envelope, and the 1,000 with only an invitation to fill in the questionnaire online, in total 100 responses were received. No significant differences between the paper and online responses are found. The main reasons for the low response rate are assumed to be the low number of people with internet access, the bad weather in that period with a lot of snow which made is less easy to post the response, and the high number of questionnaires that already took place in the CNP.

However, the 100 filled-in questionnaires provide us with very detailed and important information. Figure 15.2 shows how on average the household budget is spread over different product and service categories. It shows only the most important categories. Not surprisingly, most money is spent on food and groceries.

Secondly, gas and petrol, both for car and heating purposes, form an important part of the expenditures. Most money spent on services goes to the repair of vehicles, and to gifts and contributions.

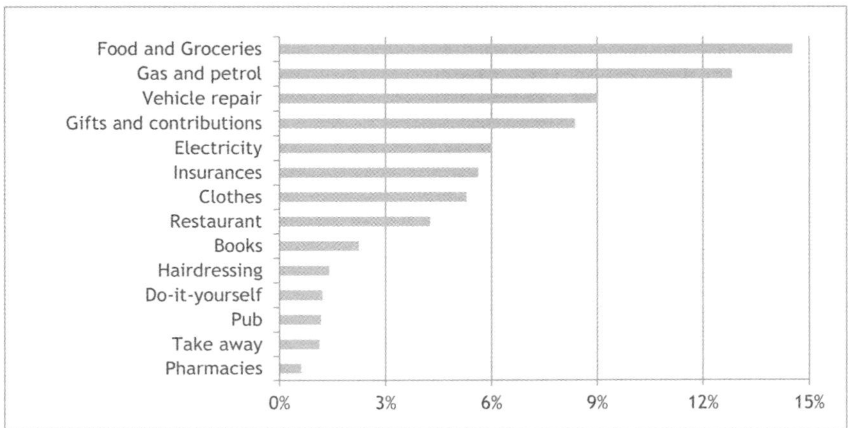

Figure 15.2   Share of total household expenditures on a selection of products and services

Both for expenditures on products and on services, For the Park is the most important location: 42 per cent of the products and 50 per cent of the services is bought here. The adjoining areas are relatively more important for products than for services. Interestingly enough, in the rest of the UK (RUK) as much as 14 per cent of all services are bought. These services are mainly insurance and to a smaller extent gifts and contributions.

Since our main interest lies in the Park, Figure 15.3a shows the share of different product categories bought in the Park, together with the average amount of expenditures spent by those who did actually buy something. Again, the importance of the spending on food and groceries becomes clear, but it also appears that only half of it is bought in the Park. The other half is bought in the adjoining areas. The second largest purchase is gas and petrol. Around 40 per cent of this is bought in the Park, a little more in the adjoining areas where the supply might be better.

Products that are often bought in the Park are wood for fuel, as well as pharmaceuticals and books. However, the amount spent on these articles is relatively low.

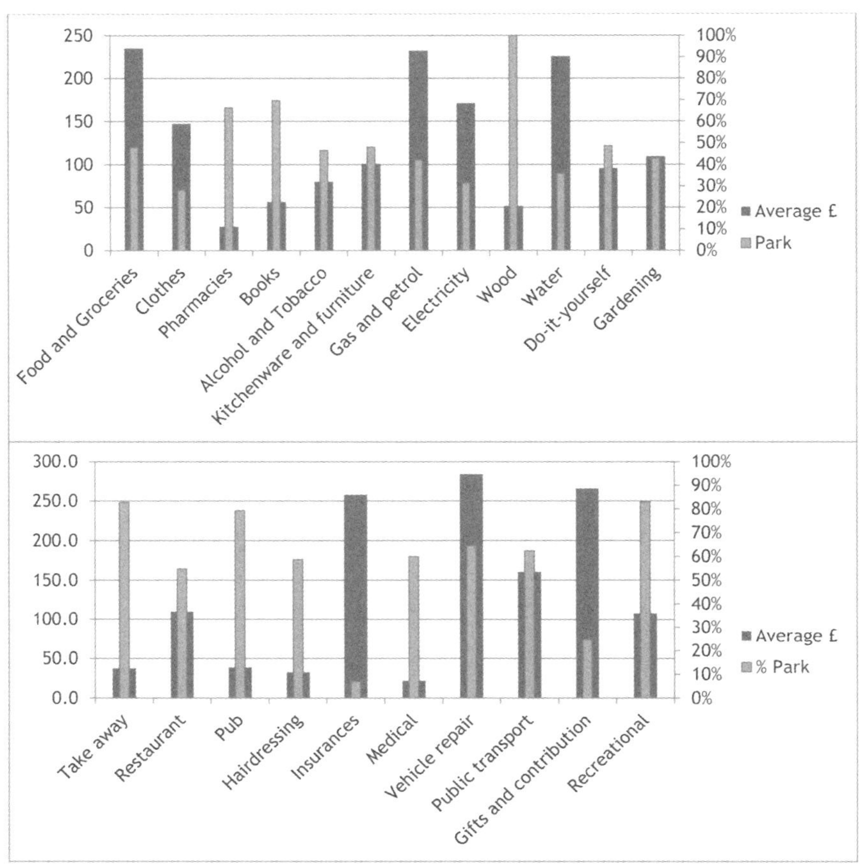

Figure 15.3   Amount of money spent on different product groups and services and the share spent in the Park

When looking at services (Figure 15.3b), it appears that quite some money is spent on insurance, gifts and contributions and vehicle repair as we saw earlier. However, only most of the budget on vehicle repair is spent in the Park. As mentioned earlier, most insurance is bought outside Scotland, a lot of the gifts and contributions are also spent outside the Park. Services for the Park that are important are take-away food, drinks in the pub and recreational services.

Questionnaire: Types of Households

In order to get a better insight in the differences between different types of households we run simple bivariate Pearson's correlations. It appears that the size of expenditures is mainly related to household size and household income.

Table 15.2   Result of the hierarchical cluster analysis based on share of products bought in the Park and in the adjacent areas

Characteristics	Cluster 1	Cluster 2	Cluster 3	All
# households	37	21	21	79
HH size	2.1	2.2	2.7	2.3
HH age	57	59	46	55
Children under 8	.08	.10	.29	.14
Years living in CNP	27	40	13	27
HH income	7.1	5.1	7.1	6.6
The biggest advantage:				
Job in Park	.13	.32	.24	.21
Job outside the Park	.03	.00	.05	.03
Nice house	.28	.00	.19	.18
Family always lived here	.28	.47	.14	.29
Recreation possibilities	.25	.32	.33	.29
Landscape	.56	.42	.43	.49
Job in Park	.43	.52	.52	.48
Job adjacent	.35	.05	.48	.30
Job far	.08	.05	.10	.08
Expenditures Park	29%	86%	14%	40%
Expenditures ROS	37%	12%	80%	42%
Expenditures RUK	15%	2%	3%	8%
Expenditures ROW	19%	0%	3%	10%

Furthermore, Park shoppers are often smaller and older households with a relative low income that have lived in the area for a long time. They like that their families have been living in the same area for a long time as well. The ones that don't shop in the Park but in adjacent towns often are larger households, younger and with children. In addition, they often have a job in the adjacent areas, and that is also why they prefer to live in the CNP.

Secondly, we performed a hierarchical cluster analysis. This procedure attempts to identify relatively homogeneous groups of cases (or variables) based on selected characteristics. The hierarchical cluster analysis confirms the finding of the correlations. When we perform the cluster analysis on the share of products bought in the Park and the share of products bought in the adjacent areas, we find three meaningful clusters: the first one of 37 households, the second one of 21 households and the third one of 21 households as well. The characteristics of the households in the clusters allow us interpreting them.

The first and biggest cluster can be indicated as the 'average' households. When comparing their characteristics with those of the total group, the biggest differences appear in how they appreciate the Park, with a relative low value for the availability of a job in the Park and a slightly higher appreciation of the houses.

Furthermore, they buy in general a little more than a quarter of their products in the Park and the same share in the rest of Scotland. In addition, they buy quite a lot through the internet and in the rest of the UK.

The next two clusters show more differences. Cluster 2 can be described as households that do most of their expenditures in the Park (86 per cent). They often have been living in the Park for a long time, on average 40 years, and they generally have a lower income. They appreciate the Park for the jobs and because their family always lived there. Furthermore, they generally do not have a job in the adjacent areas.

The third cluster consists of slightly larger households, more often with small children. They have been living in the Park for a relatively shorter period, on average 13 years. Furthermore, they often have a job in the adjacent areas, which might also be (part of) the reason why do a relatively large part of their shopping in that area, as much as 80 per cent in the rest of Scotland.

Based on the literature review and this analysis of the SMILE dataset, we select as relevant constraint variables for the matching and MSM procedures household size, household age, household income, length of residence and job location.

Two-step Microsimulation Procedure

In order to simulate the population of the Cairngorms in the best possible way, we take a two-step approach. Firstly, we link the SMILE questionnaire population consisting of around 100 households, to the 2,000 households in the ADMAR database; secondly we will fit the matched households to the total CNP population.

When comparing the two datasets, it appears that the ADMAR dataset has a very high share of younger households, and both datasets too low shares of older households (see the online Appendix 15.1[1] for the structure of the two datasets compared with the actual structure of the population of the Cairngorms). Furthermore, both datsets include a lower share of one-person and of low-income households. In particular, the share of households with high income that responded to the SMILE questionnaire is very high compared to the actual population structure.

The MSM techniques we used were developed by Robin Lovelace and Dimitris Balllas from Sheffield University (Lovelace and Ballas 2012). An often recognized disadvantge of iterative proportional fitting (IPF) techniques are the non-integer weights. An alternative to this is 'integerization' of IPF weights: the translation of a continuous variable into a discrete number of unique or 'cloned' individuals. Lovelace and Ballas developed an iterative proportional fitting technique that recognizes that IPF weights consist of both 'replication weights' and 'conventional weights', the effects of which need to be separated. The procedure consists of three steps: 1) separate replication and conventional

---

1   http://www.microsimulation.org/resource-centre/new-pathways/.

weights by truncation; 2) replication of individuals with positive integer weights; and 3) probabilistic sampling. Their results show that this 'truncate, replicate, sample' (TRS) is fast and accurate compared with deterministic approaches to integerization. The algorithms are coded using the R-language.

Matching SMILE Data and ADMAR Database

Matching is a technique that is often used in combination with MSM. However, usually this is used in the combination with dynamic models, where actors change over the years. For example, males and females may have to be matched to form partnerships, individuals matched to form groups, and households matched to dwellings (Cumpston 2010). Here, we use it for a static MSM approach, in which a population is simulated at just one point in time. Since we have two rich datasets available, with at least four similar variables, matching allows us to join the information. In this procedure, based on household size, income level, age group and years of residence, similar households are matched and the additional information from both datasets is joined, furthermore a more heterogeneous database in terms of household characteristics is created.

Basically, this matching procedure is a combination of reweighting and matching, since the number of households is not the same. The algorithm, developed by Sekhon (2010), matches the two datasets based on size, income, age and years of residence. This was not done by a unique match, but in such a way that cases from the smaller SMILE questionnaire were returned to the dataset and could be drawn multiple times. The result of this grouped multivariate matching procedure is a vector of the positions of matches of the first argument (ADMAR database) in the second (SMILE database).

The application separates the matching problem into subgroups defined by a factor. At the beginning of the matching procedure the cases are grouped in five groups based on household size. In addition, the variables income (9 classes), age group (3 classes) and years of residence (8 classes) were used. Thus, all households with size one from the SMILE questionnaire were matched to one-person households from the ADMAR dataset using the other three variables.

In addition, the application allows setting different levels of sensitivity, or tolerance, for the matching. Because income level and years of residence are more detailed than age and household size, we allowed different 'tolerances' for a match. For age the caliper was set to half and for income to one standard deviation, for years of residence it was set to two standard deviations. Since only observations within the caliper are considered for a match, this results in an optimal matching procedure given the nature of the data.

As a result 1,530 households were matched. As Figure 15.4 shows, household size matched exactly, with no deviations because it was used to make the sub-groups. The age-group variable matched 1,350 times, 118 times there was a deviation of +1. This clearly shows the effect of the different calipers. Since the caliper for income and years of residence was larger, more deviations can be found. For years of residence this even resulted in deviations of +/–3. However in these cases, the other variables were exactly matched.

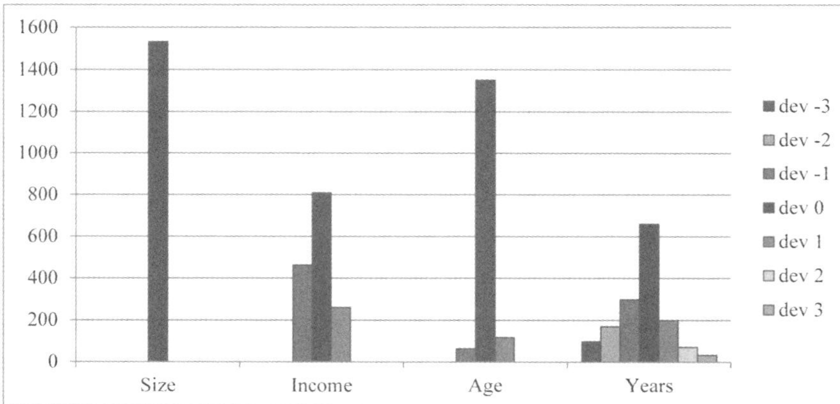

Figure 15.4   Deviations resulting from the matching procedure

The two databases are not only matched but also checked since certain variables are either similar or complementary. An example is the retired part of the population. From the 1,530 linked households, 328 households are retired according to the ADMAR database and 339 according to the questionnaire dataset. The difference between the two is mainly due to households that are old enough to retire but who are currently still working.

As a result of this first step we have a database of 1,530 existing households with information about their energy expenditures, Internet use etc., from the ADMAR database, and linked to that more detailed spatial shopping behaviour from the SMILE questionnaire.

CNP Microsimulation

For the CNP the data availability is very limited. The census dates back from 2001 and for the rest local information (at the low geographical scale) is scarce. Data sources we use are from the general register office of Scotland and from a strategic report commissioned by the CNP. From that information we can simulate a total of 7,500 households and 15,750 persons for the year 2007 (General Register Office for Scotland 2010).

For this simulation we combine a multivariate with a univariate approach because not all variables are present in a multivariate way. The constraint variables we will use are: income level, age, household size and commuting, which are included in a multivariate way. In addition, we use income level (low, medium, high) and commuting out of the Park (job in Park, job outside Park, no job) as univariate constraints.

The Cairngorms economic baseline report tells us that in- and out-commuting is not very significant in the Park. First of all, its location is too far from major centres of employment. Secondly, the Park does not have enough jobs to attract in-commuters, apart from people living in small villages just outside the CNP borders. According to the report, in 2008 there were 9,000 jobs in the CNP, 2,000 self-employed and around 1,800 persons were commuting out of the Park, 1,500 into the Park. In this study, we will simulate a working population with 16 per cent out-commuters, based on the mentioned figures. The working population consists of 65 per cent of the total population; the retired population consist of 25 per cent of the total. We use a figure of 2 per cent of the working population that is unemployed.

For the income levels, we use the Household Income Percentiles by Local Authority (based on CACI Paycheck 2010 data). Based on the data for Moray and Angus (two large local authorities in the Park) the classes used in the questionnaire can be translated to the situation in 2007. For better results, we aggregated this to three main groups: low, medium and high income.

Appendix 15.2 shows for the four constraint variables the difference between the actual situation in the CNP and the simulated households. As can be seen, the differences are very small. Concerning age, the middle group (between 35 and 59) is a little underrepresented. However, this difference is only 3 per cent. Concerning the size of the households we see a small overestimation of the households with children. In addition, the lower incomes are a little underrepresented and the higher incomes overrepresented but the differences are relatively small.

Evaluation and Results

In this chapter, we showed an approach of how a database of around 100 cases can be linked to one of 2,000 cases, which is finally simulated to fit a total population of 8,000 households. The advantage is that a more heterogeneous population can be simulated. A disadvantage is that at the end a small number of households could be cloned much more often than others. This is indeed what Figure 15.5 shows: when we only use SMILE, the weights range from 23 to 521 with a standard deviation of 90. When using the matched dataset, that already includes a first step of reweighting, the weights of the SMILE variables range from 1 to 573, with a standard deviation of 118. However, by using an optimal matching instead of an exact matching procedure, the population became 30 per cent more heterogeneous (i.e. 30 per cent more different households only based on age, size, income and commuting). In addition, the matching procedure allowed adding new variables to the analysis.

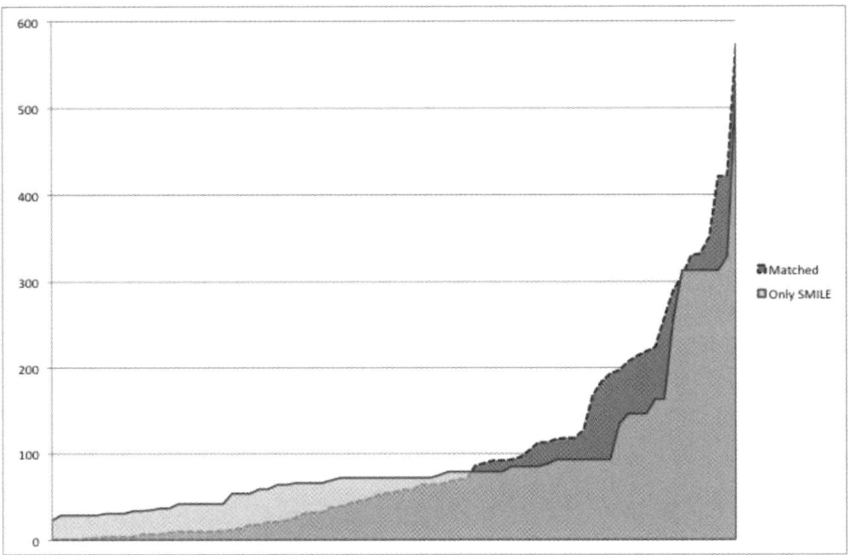

Figure 15.5   Weights of the SMILE variables when using the matched population or only the SMILE population

The weights of the ADMAR variables are more balanced. They range from 1 to 107 with a standard deviation of 9.

The final results of our approach are a detailed picture of the Cairngorms population about internet accessibility, energy use, spending on several services and products and the location of these expenditures. It appears that almost half of the CNP households has internet access. Furthermore, they spend per month on average £87 on electricity, around £650 on products and £350 on services in total. More than 38 per cent of those expenditures are done in the Park. This is quite a high level and very useful information for our future research on the economic situation of the CNP.

Conclusions

In this chapter, we showed how the advantages of MSM, in particular the possibilities to link different datasets, can be used by simulating the CNP population. When detailed information is poor, for example because of a disappointing response from a survey, microsimulation can be very useful to borrow strength from other reliable data (using matching and benchmarking techniques) and make the survey more reliable.

The focus was on household characteristics that affect the share and location of expenditures on products and services. A very detailed questionnaire that was returned by 100 households was combined with a larger and extensive database of ADMAR. This was done by a grouped multivariate matching procedure. This matched dataset was then used as an input for the MSM. A static deterministic approach resulted in a good picture of the Cairngorm residents with information about Internet use, electricity use, spending on goods and services and the location of this spending.

Although this approach has some disadvantages, mainly that some of the results are still based on a relatively small sample (100 of the 8,000 households) and that through the two-step procedure, one household got a weight of almost 600, there are strong advantages. First of all, the optimal matching procedure (instead of exact matching) resulted in a more heterogeneous population in terms of age, income, size and commuting. Secondly, it allowed the inclusion of additional variables. These new variables from the ADMAR dataset have also much more balanced weights.

Acknowledgements

The collection of the data was funded by the European through the SMILE project (Project no. 217213, Socioeconomic Sciences and Humanities (SSH) Collaborative Project FP7-SSH-2007-1). The author wishes to thank the partners of the SMILE consortium; in particular, Keith Matthews, from the Macaulay Institute, and Masood Gheasi, from the VU University Amsterdam, should be thanked for their important contributions.

References

Brown, R.B. 1993. Rural community satisfaction and attachment in mass consumer society. *Rural Sociology*, 58, 387–403.

Clarke, M. and Holm, E. 1987. Microsimulation Methods in Spatial Analysis and Planning. *Geografiska Annaler*, 69 (B2), 145–64.

CNP 2010a. *Cairngorms National Park Local Plan*. Cairngorms National Park Authority.

CNP 2010b. *The Economic and Social Health of the Cairngorms National Park 2010*. Cairngorms National Park Authority.

Cumpston, J.R. 2010. Alingment and matching in Multi-purpose household Microsimulation. *International Journal of Microsimulation*, 3(2), 34–45.

Epstein, J.M. 1999. Agent-based Computational Models and Generative Social Science. *Complexity*, 4(5), 41–60.

Hermann, R.O. and Beik L.L. 1968. Shoppers' movements outside their local retail area. *Journal of Marketing*, 32, 45–51.

Hubbard R. 1978. A review of selected factors conditioning consumer travel behaviour. *Journal of Consumer Research*, 5, 1–21.

Huff, D.L. 1959. Geographical aspects of consumer behaviour. *University of Washington Business Review*, 5, 27–37.

Leeuwen, E.S. van, Clarke, G.P. and Rietveld, P. 2009. Microsimulation as a tool in spatial decision making: simulation of retail developments in a Dutch town. In A. Zaidi, A. Harding and P. Williamson (eds), *New Frontiers in Microsimulation Modeling*. Farnham: Ashgate, 97–123.

Leeuwen, E.S. van and Rietveld, P. 2011. Spatial consumer behaviour in small and medium-sized towns. *Regional Studies*, 45(8), 1107–19.

Lovelace, R. and Ballas, D. 2013. 'Truncate, replicate, sample': a method for creating integer weights for spatial microsimulation. *Computers, Environment and Urban Systems*, 41(September), 1–11.

Miller, N.J. and Kean R.C. 1997. Factors contributing to inshopping behavior in rural trade areas: implications for local retailers. *Journal of Small Business Management*, 35(2), 80–94.

Papadopoulus, N.G. 1980. Consumer outshopping research: review and extension. *Journal of Retailing*, 56(4), 41–58.

Pinkerton, J.R., Hassinger E.W. and O'Brien, D.J. 1995. Inshopping by residents of small communities. *Rural Sociology*, 60, 467–80.

Powe, N.A. and Shaw, T. 2004. Exploring the current and future role of market towns in servicing their hinterlands: a case study of Alnwick in the North East of England. *Journal of Rural Studies*, 20, 405–18.

Sekhon, J.S. 2011. Multivariate and Propensity Score Matching Software with Automated Balance Optimization: The Matching package for R. *Journal of Statistical Software*, 42(7), 1–52.

Thompson, J.R. 1971. Characteristics and behavior of out-shopping consumers. *Journal of Retailing*, 47, 70–80.

Chapter 16

Using Excel as a Front End to a Microsimulation Model on Energy and Water Concession Pricing

Robert Tanton, Marcia Keegan and Quoc Ngu Vu

Introduction

Microsimulation is a natural choice when modelling rules applied to people or households. It is commonly used for modelling Tax/Transfer systems, which consist of a series of rules that determine how much a person pays in tax or receives in benefits (Immervoll and O'Donoghue 2001; Percival, Abello and Vu 2007). Other uses for microsimulation models are modelling eligibility to certain programmes, for instance, legal aid (Virtual Worlds Research 2011) and electricity concessions.

The electricity market in Australia has a highly complex pricing system, with charges calculated according to how much electricity a household uses; different tariffs for using electricity out of peak periods; different tariffs for different providers; and a number of concessions for households on low incomes. This means that calculating the effect of a price change for a particular tariff is difficult, as the change may not affect all consumers. Further, some of the consumers will be receiving a concession, so the price change will not affect all consumers equally.

Because of this complexity, a microsimulation model is an ideal tool to calculate how a change in pricing will affect revenue and the concessions being paid. The microsimulation model developed by NATSEM for the Independent Pricing and Review Tribunal (IPART) in New South Wales, Australia, uses survey data from IPART, and applies complex rules to these data to model electricity pricing. This means the user can implement a number of different scenarios, and look at the effect on revenue for the electricity companies and the amount of concessions that the consumers are entitled to.

IPART required projections of any scenarios to 2015–16. The data required to do this was developed from projections on the future costs of concessions, based on a price inflation factor; and the projected number of customers. This information comes from IPART and ABS population projections, and the projections can be changed in the user interface. The start year for the model (Year 0) is currently 2010–11, and the final projected year is 2015–16. The base dataset from IPART is then reweighted to these projections from IPART. This is described further in the Data section.

One of the significant advances with this model was the use of Excel for an interface. This was done due to the complexity and number of parameters being fed into the model, and because IPART required an easy to use model operating from their desktop. Using Excel allows the user to copy/paste data from other workbooks; calculate values for parameters which are dependent on other cells in the workbook, or even in a different workbook; and make changes to a large number of parameters at one time by linking parameters through formulae.

Excel was only used as an interface to the model because the programming language for Excel (VBA) was not powerful enough to model the complex rules. Therefore, the programming language SAS was used as a back-end to the model with Excel as the front end passing the parameters to SAS.

This chapter shows how a complex microsimulation model designed to model elaborate rules like electricity tariffs can be implemented in a powerful programming language, but then presented to the end-user in a form they are familiar with (an Excel spreadsheet). This chapter does not present results from this model or validation of the model as these are commercial in confidence. The chapter describes the structure of the model, and specifically shows how Excel can be used as an interface for a complex microsimulation model written in a more powerful language.

The next section covers the data; the following section covers the model; the following section covers the Excel interface; and the final section concludes.

Data

Datasets

The IPART Concessions model was based on two surveys collected on behalf of IPART. The surveyed households were in the target regions of Sydney, Illawarra, Blue Mountains, the Hunter Valley, Gosford and Wyong. The survey, aimed at the person responsible for paying household bills, recorded the social and demographic characteristics of the household, the type of dwelling, types of appliances and gas, electricity and water consumption for the household. In addition, the surveys are linked to the household's recent utility bills, so accurate information on utility use, expenditure and utility supply company can be used. One of the two surveys was conducted in the Hunter, Gosford and Wyong area in 2008, the other in the Sydney, Illawarra and Blue Mountains area in 2010.

These two surveys were taken in different years and in some cases had different classifications for certain variables. In particular, the question on income provided different income brackets, and needed to be updated for wage growth. Income brackets used in the Hunter, Gosford and Wyong survey (2008) were uprated to 2010 figures based on growth rates estimated from the 2007–08 Survey of Income and Housing Costs. Respondents' incomes in Hunter, Gosford and Wyong were then matched to the income brackets in the Sydney, Blue Mountains and Illawarra survey. If a respondent to the former survey was in an income bracket that clearly overlapped a bracket in the latter survey, they were allocated this new income bracket. If there was any ambiguity about which income bracket the household should be in, a Monte Carlo process was used to allocate the respondent's income bracket.

In addition to this, the client also provided data on the pricing structures of utility providers in the survey areas. This data was complex as many utility providers have different pricing mechanisms. The pricing plans of eight electricity providers and four gas providers are simulated, along with four region-specific water providers (Sydney, Hunter, Gosford and Wyong).

Finally, benchmarking data was necessary to ensure that the surveyed population from the two surveys could be weighted to represent the New South Wales population in the target areas. This benchmarking data was primarily drawn from the 2006 Census (ABS 2007), which was the most recent version of the Census available at the time. The benchmarking focused on dwelling types and family types by postcode, and was updated using regional population growth rates and projections out to 2015 from the Australian Bureau of Statistics (ABS 2010).

Data were also needed for the number of households in each region who hold some sort of concession card – either Health Care Card (for low income earners) a Seniors Card (for people aged over 65 in receipt of the Age Pension) and a Department of Veterans' Affairs card (for war veterans and their families). Data from NATSEM's in-house static microsimulation model, STINMOD, was used to estimate recent rates by region of concession card ownership, and this was projected to 2015.

Reweighting

As discussed earlier, households in the IPART model are based on participants' survey responses and their electricity, gas and water bills. As well as utility use, expenditure and concession card usage, it asks questions about the household, its occupants and their income. To ensure that the distribution of utility consumption lines up with that for New South Wales, the survey respondents had to be weighted so that any results from the model were relevant to the total New South Wales population totals. This was done for the base year, and projections available from the ABS were used for the projected years. To be specific, survey responses were weighted by household type, dwelling type, region and household use of a concession card. Data sources for benchmarking are discussed in the previous section.

The first step of the process was to match Census categories to survey categories, and to match up data classifications between the two surveys. This involved reclassifying dwelling types and family types. The final three dwelling types used for weighting were: detached home; semi-attached home (e.g. villa, townhouse, duplex); or flat/apartment. The family types used were couple only, couple with mostly young children (aged 15 and under), couple with mostly older children (aged over 15), single, single parent with mostly young children, single parent with mostly older children, and other (mixed families and group households). Where possible, ABS projections of these estimates were also used to benchmark the projected years.

The reweighting process was undertaken using GREGWT, a SAS macro developed by the Australian Bureau of Statistics (Bell 2000), which allows users to generate weights for a dataset based on external benchmarks (see Singh and Mohl 1996 for a general description of the method). Several benchmark datasets were generated, classified by benchmark (concession card, dwelling type and family type) and by year of simulation (six years in total); for a total of 18 benchmark datasets, classified by region. For each year in the model, GREGWT allocated a weight to each household such that total weights added up to regional targets. In addition to this, GREGWT was used to create another weight representing each household's importance in New South Wales – that is, households were also weighted by concession card, dwelling type and family type, but not by region.

The Model

The System Being Modelled

The system being modelled is the NSW Electricity Concessions system, which is managed by IPART. The concessions system provides electricity concessions for customers, provided by the NSW State Government. IPART is the NSW Government regulator that determines maximum prices that can be charged for energy, water and transport services in NSW, as well as the concessions that can be applied. These concessions include pensioner, student and unemployed concessions. These concessions are given to consumers by the energy, water and transport companies; and then reimbursed by the State Government. The aim of the IPART Concessions model is to identify how much these concessions cost the NSW Government, and provide IPART with the ability to model 'what if' scenarios based on different levels of concessions and different numbers of concession card holders.

The tariff structures are also complicated, and based on amount of usage (so there is a stepped system of charges); time of day the energy is being used; and the type of residence.

Structure

The IPART Concessions Model is written in the SAS programming language. The SAS language was used because other models at NATSEM, including STINMOD, a static Tax/Transfer microsimulation model, use SAS. This allows code sharing between models, but it also means there is considerable experience in SAS at NATSEM, making it an obvious choice for a new model.

The IPART Concessions model starts with the reweighted surveys of households in the area as described in the Data Section. For each of these households, a number of modules are run to calculate electricity, gas and water bills, and also rebates. These modules are run sequentially against each of the surveys for the base year and for five projected years of data. These modules, in the order that they are run, are:

- SURHHMAIN – The main module. This module reads the Excel interface data into SAS, and then calls the other modules in the order described below. Once all the modules have run, this module writes the output datasets to Excel workbooks and returns control to Excel.
- ALLPARMS – This module defines a number of arrays, which assign the tariff structures and parameters for Electricity, Gas, Water and Energy rebates.
- ELEC – This module calculates the electricity bill for a household, based on a number of different tariffs and rates. The calculation of the electricity bill is a complex procedure, taking into account fixed charges and consumption charges according to different levels of consumption (so the consumption charge is stepped according to use).
- GAS – This module calculates the Gas charges. While not as complex as the Electricity charges, Gas users can be on a contract tariff or a regulated tariff. On both tariffs, households are charged according to blocks of use, but there are different charges for each block in each tariff.
- WATER – This module calculates the water charge. The water charge is based on consumption, and is a stepped charge, so as a household uses more water, the per kilolitre charge increases. The sewerage charge and stormwater and drainage charge is also calculated in this module. The sewerage charge is calculated as a per cent of the water used, and the stormwater charge is a fixed cost.
- EN_REBATE – This module calculates the energy rebate for a household. An energy rebate is provided to concession card holders and households with an Energy Accounts Payment Assistance (EAPA) voucher. These vouchers are used to assist financially disadvantaged people experiencing difficulty paying their electricity or gas bill because of a crisis or emergency situation. The concession card holder rebate can be set as either a fixed amount or a proportion of the bill, while the EAPA is a fixed amount available for one bill (the holder sends the voucher in with the bill to get a A$30 discount). The rebate is first applied to the electricity bill, and any remaining rebate is applied to the gas bill.
- WA_REBATE – This module calculates the water rebate. A water rebate is provided to concession card holders and households suffering financial hardship through a Payment Assistance Scheme (PAS).
- TIDY – This module aggregates some of the variables for the output, and defines some categories for the final output.

A base run is conducted for each year, with no change to the parameters, and this base run is then used to compare the new scenarios. The user interface described in the next section then allows the client to adjust a number of parameters for the current year and each year projected, which are then used to re-run the modules against the same households and to compare the results to the base run. This will show the effect of changing the parameters on the outputs.

Interface

While the model has been written in SAS, the SAS programming language does not have a very user-friendly interface. There is a system called SAS/AF, which can operate as a user interface, and this is used in NATSEM's STINMOD model, but support and programming skills for SAS/AF are limited. For this model, we therefore used an Excel interface and ran SAS in the background.

The advantage of this technique is that it allows the user to enter parameters into an Excel workbook, to copy and paste parameters into the workbook, or do other manipulations to a set of parameters in Excel before running the model. Visual Basic for Applications is then used to create menus for the user to run the model, and screens to change global parameters before finally running the model.

The first screen that a user sees when running the model is a screen allowing the user to create a new scenario; create some output for a previously run scenario; look at some output from a scenario; manage scenarios; and an Administration page that allows the user to change where output is saved, adjust take up rates, and allow debugging. There is no Save Scenario page, as scenarios are automatically saved when a new scenario is created. Figure 16.1 shows the start menu.

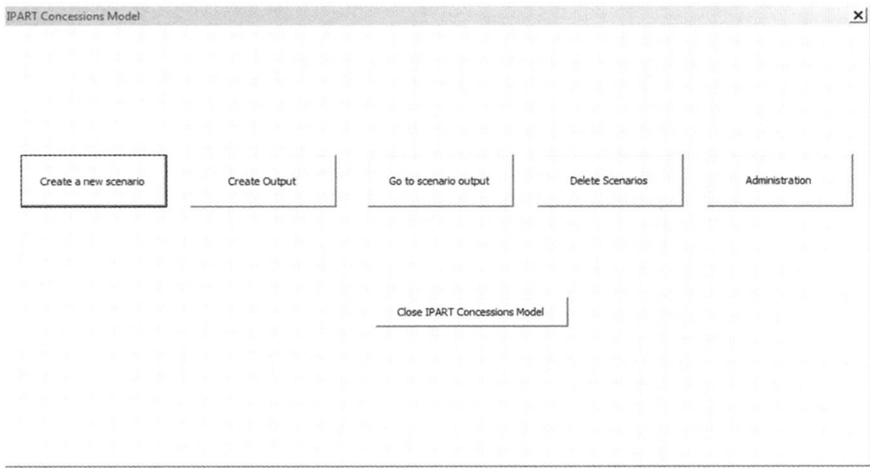

Figure 16.1   Opening view of IPART model

If a user creates a new scenario, then an Excel workbook (the interface workbook) with a number of sheets for different parameters is opened for the user to enter new rates and rebates for electricity, gas or water. The parameters entered on these sheets are complex and include rates for different suppliers, different charge rates (fixed and variable), and projections to 2015–16. There are separate worksheets for electricity, gas and water prices, rebates and inflators to inflate the prices to future values. Overall, there are about 5,500 parameters which can be changed, including 3,000 for the electricity pricing sheet alone.

Once the user has entered the required changes, a drop-down menu in Excel is used to run the model. On running the model, the user is presented with another screen to enter some global parameters. These global parameters include whether to use fixed amounts for rebates or proportions, whether all households should be put on a regulated gas tariff or use the tariff from the survey, etc. These global parameters are then written to named ranges in the interface workbook so that they can later be read into SAS.

Once these parameters have been set, the model is run. To do this, assuming SAS is installed on the host machine, SAS is run as an object using the ExcelVBA commands:

```
Dim SAS As Object
Set SAS = CreateObject("SAS.Application")
```

This will open an occurrence of SAS which code can then be submitted to from Excel. For debugging purposes, SAS is left open so the log can be seen; but SAS can also be run so it is not visible to the user using the ExcelVBA statement:

```
SAS.Visible = False
```

SAS statements can then be submitted to SAS using the SAS.Submit statement in ExcelVBA:

```
SAS.Submit ("%Let scen=" & chNewScenName & ";")
```

This will assign a macro variable in SAS called scen to the value of the ExcelVBA variable named chNewScenName. This ExcelVBA variable was entered into a form when the user was asked for the name of the new scenario.

Once some initial parameters are passed to SAS from ExcelVBA, the interface workbook is closed so it can be read in SAS, and the first SAS module is run:

```
SAS.Submit ("%Include SURHHMAIN;")
```

Other parameters are passed to SAS using named ranges in the Excel interface workbook, which was why it had to be closed before starting the first module. From within SAS, Excel workbooks can be read using the command:

libname interfce excel path="&install.User Interface\Data\Scenarios\&scen\ Interface.xls"

where &install is a macro variable containing the path where the model is installed. This &install macro variable was created in SAS from ExcelVBA using a SAS.Submit statement in the same way the scenario name was created in SAS using ExcelVBA. Named ranges from the Excel workbook can then be read into SAS using the code:

data e_price_all ; set interfce.e_price; run ;

This will read the named range called e_price in the workbook interface (which is the interface workbook that the user entered their detailed parameters into) into a SAS dataset called e_price_all. A number of these datasets are read in (electricity price, gas price, water price, rebates). These datasets, which contain the new parameters, along with the global parameters set in the Excel VBA screen, are then used in each of the modules.

Once all the modules are run, the results need to be written to Excel workbooks. The model writes to two Excel workbooks, one which contains detailed information for every household on the survey; and one that contains Excel pivot-tables that summarize the information. The SAS datasets are written to Excel using the SAS code:

Libname res_sum excel "&install.User Interface\Data\Scenarios\&scen\ Results\Summary Results_sur.xls" ;
data res_sum.raw_results ;
set out3sury1 out3sury2 out3sury3 out3sury4 out3sury5 out3sury6 ;
run ;

where out3sury1 are the results for Year 1, out3sury2 are the results for Year 2, and so on to Year 6. These SAS statements will write the results to a new worksheet in the Summary Results_sur workbook called raw_results, and pivot tables can be based on this worksheet. This needs to be a new worksheet in the Excel workbook, but we also need to create the pivot tables and maintain the links to the data worksheet. The way we do this is to design the pivot tables on one worksheet using a sheet of raw results from the model, then delete the worksheet with the raw results and keep the worksheet with the pivot table. The SAS code then writes the new sheet of results, using the same worksheet name as the original worksheet of data, and the pivot table is refreshed using the new data.

Once SAS has finished, Excel needs to know so it can take control again. This is done by SAS writing a short file to the host computer; and Excel pausing until this file appears. In SAS, the command is simply:

data 'C:\IPartFinished.sas7bdat'; run;

and in ExcelVBA, the code is:

```
Do While Not fso.FileExists("C:\IPartFinished.sas7bdat")
       Application.Wait (Now() + TimeValue("00:00:05"))
Loop
```

The new results are now in a workbook called Summary Results_sur.xls. These pivot-tables then need to be updated, as they are currently still based on the old sheet that was used to design the pivot tables. The simplest way of doing this is to add some ExcelVBA code to the Summary Results_sur.xls workbook when it is first created:

```
Private Sub Workbook_Open()
                ThisWorkbook.RefreshAll
End Sub
```

This code will update all the pivot-tables with the new data when the workbook is opened.

Conclusions

This chapter has outlined a new microsimulation model developed at NATSEM that uses an innovative Excel interface to allow a large number of parameters to be changed. These parameters can also use formulae in Excel, and can link into other workbooks, providing a much more powerful interface than a simple interface developed through a programming language like C#, Java or Visual Basic. Global parameters are then entered through simpler screens designed using ExcelVBA Forms.

The user (IPART) has found the Excel interface a powerful tool to run the model. The Excel interface allows them to conduct calculations in other workbooks or worksheets and copy/paste them into the main interface sheet. It also allows formulae to be used, so it is easy to use Excel formulae to increase a concession amount by 5 per cent and re-run the model.

This type of interface has also been used at NATSEM for spatial microsimulation models, where if one considers allowing 10 parameters to change for 1,400 areas, this gives 14,000 potential parameters to change. Using an Excel workbook allows us to categorize and simplify the process of changing these parameters, including allowing easy copy/pasting between areas, or inflating between years using a formula.

References

ABS 2007. Australian Census 2006 Basic Community Profile, cat. no. 2001.0. Canberra: Australian Bureau of Statistics

ABS 2010. Regional Population Growth, Australia, 2008–2009, cat. no. 3218.0. Canberra: Australian Bureau of Statistics

Bell, P. 2000. GREGWT and TABLE macros – Users guide. Canberra: Australian Bureau of Statistics

Immervoll, H. and O'Donoghue, C. 2001. Towards a multi-purpose framework for tax-benefit microsimulation. EUROMOD Working Paper Series EM2/01.

Percival, R. Abello, A. and Vu, Q.N. 2007. STINMOD (Static Income Model), in A. Harding and A. Gupta (eds), *Modelling Our Future: Population Ageing, Health and Aged Care*. Amsterdam: Elsevier B. V.

Singh, A.C. and Mohl, C.A. 1996. Understanding calibration estimators in survey sampling. *Survey Methodology*, 22, 107–15.

Virtual Worlds Research. 2011. Scottish Legal Aid Simulation. [Online] Available at: http://www.virtual-worlds.biz/demonstrations/slas/ [accessed: April 13 2011].

Chapter 17

Modelling Sequences of Events with Chain Graph Models

Marcus Wurzer[1] and Reinhold Hatzinger[†]

Introduction

Graphical Modelling can be seen as a type of multivariate analysis that is of particular usefulness in very complex multivariate systems with complicated structures of dependency. Graphical Models are, as well as Structural Equation Models, an extension of the Path Models introduced by Wright (1921), but in contrast to SEMs, they can also be used to model categorical variables (Wermuth 2003). Additionally, Graphical Models get input from other analysis techniques, including Log-linear Models and Covariance Models, as Whittaker (1990) points out. Furthermore, the principles of independence and conditional independence are important contributors. Darroch, Lauritzen, and Speed (1980) were the first ones to bring together these techniques and principles and showed that Graphical Models are a subset of Log-linear Models that allow – under certain assumptions – a simple interpretation of the underlying dependence structure. Since many modelling tasks in microsimulation involve a high number of potentially influential predictors and/or chains of dependencies between (blocks of) variables, Graphical Models are useful in the sense that they alleviate the task of structuring these multivariate systems.

In the next section, the authors will provide a short introduction to some of the most important concepts and definitions of Graphical Modelling. The following shows the link to microsimulation modelling and gives an outline of a selection strategy that can be used to fit such models. Finally, two examples will illustrate the usefulness of this approach in microsimulation modelling practice.

Graphical Models – Basic Ideas and Concepts

This section will clarify the underlying assumptions for the usage of Graphical Models, as well as showing how graphs are set up and how they can be used for model selection. It is mainly based on the short introduction into Graphical

1   The authors would like to thank the Austrian Federal Ministry of Labor, Social Affairs and Consumer Protection for funding this project.

Modelling given by Christensen (1997). Of course, a complete description of all aspects of Graphical Modelling is not possible in the context of this chapter, and so we refer the interested reader to the works of Edwards (2000) and Lauritzen (1996), in addition to the above-mentioned book by Whittaker (1990).

Composition of a Graph

Our starting point is a multivariate system where the variables can be categorical or continuous. These variables may be associated and we are interested in a graphical representation of the dependence/independence relationships present between them that allows us to read the corresponding model directly from the graph. To draw such a graph, we follow the guidelines that can be found in, e.g., Cox and Wermuth (1996), but do not use all of the elements defined there. The elements we need are the following:

- A node (vertex, point) represents a variable in the multivariate system.
- Edges (lines) connect pairs of nodes. They correspond to two-way interactions between the variables.
- Arrows (directed edges) are used to connect independent and dependent variables.
- A box can include multiple variables. Variables (i.e., vertices, points) in one box are treated on an equal footing. This means that they can only be connected with undirected edges which correspond to a symmetric analysis of the joint distribution of these variables. Asymmetric dependencies, allowing for the distinction between variables regarded as responses and variables regarded as explanatory, are only possible between different boxes.

It is important to have a one-to-one correspondence between model and graph, i.e., each graph generates exactly one model and each model has exactly one graphical representation. This is only guaranteed if certain assumptions are made, the most important one being that Graphical Models are determined by their two-way interactions, which means that whenever a model contains all two-factor terms generated by a higher-order interaction, it must also include this higher-order interaction to be graphical. Consider the following graph:

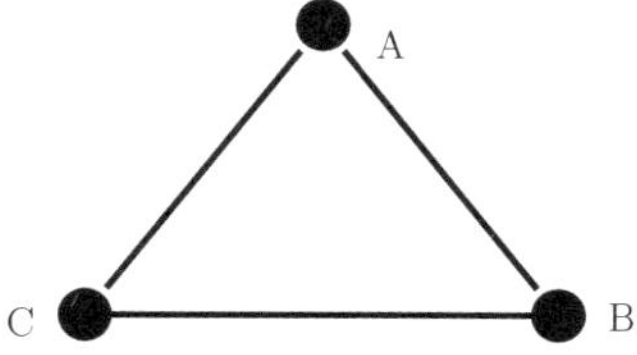

Figure 17.1   A simple undirected graph

The undirected graph (no arrows are present) contains two-way interactions between A and B, A and C, and B and C. Following Christensen's notation, the model could be written as [AB][AC][BC]. This wouldn't be a Graphical Model because it contains all two-way interactions, but not the three-way interaction. Therefore, the Graphical Model that corresponds to the graph can only be [ABC]. In terms of the interpretation of Graphical Models, each absent edge represents some sort of conditional or marginal independence between two nodes, whereas the presence of an edge denotes some important conditional or marginal association.

Recursive Causal Models

As it was briefly mentioned above, Graphical Models cannot only be used to analyse symmetric dependencies between variables, causal relationships may also be part of the model to be analysed. It is important to say that causation can only be established using substantive knowledge and cannot be inferred from the data. That the Causal Models are recursive means that no factor may be used to explain itself, neither directly nor indirectly. Recursive Causal Models can include three types of factors:

- Purely explanatory variables
- Intermediate variables which serve as response to some factors and as explanatory variables to others
- Purely dependent variables

Recursive Causal Models can be subdivided into Directed Acyclic Graphs (DAGs) and Block Recursive Models (Chain Graph Models). In DAGs, vertices are only connected by directed edges and all vertices are in a certain order, so they can be numbered. The joint density f_V of the numbered vertices $v_1, v_2, \ldots, v_n$ factorizes into a product of densities:

$$f_V = f(v_1)f(v_2|v_1) \ldots f(v_n|v_{n-1}, \ldots, v_1)$$

Since the conditional densities can be specified freely, for each response we can use an arbitrary univariate response model if all prior variables are included as covariates. The factorization can directly be read off the graph. If an arrow is missing between two vertices, this means that they are independent *given all prior variables*. This is the main difference between DAGs and undirected graphs where a missing connection corresponds to independence between the two variables *given all remaining variables*.

Since it is quite uncommon in social science practice to have systems that only include causal relationships, it is beneficial to introduce Chain Graph Models where all variables are assigned to blocks (boxes). These assignments are based on partial orderings of the variables: the ordering is only present between blocks; within blocks, the variables are not ordered. Accordingly, variables within a block can only be connected by undirected edges. Edges between blocks are always directed. Therefore, Chain Graph Models incorporate properties of undirected graphs and DAGs: If a line or an arrow is missing between two variables, they are independent given all prior (directed) and concurrent (undirected) variables. The choice of a model for each block is independent of the choices for all other blocks, just like the model choice for each step in a DAG. The following graph gives an example of a Block Recursive Model:

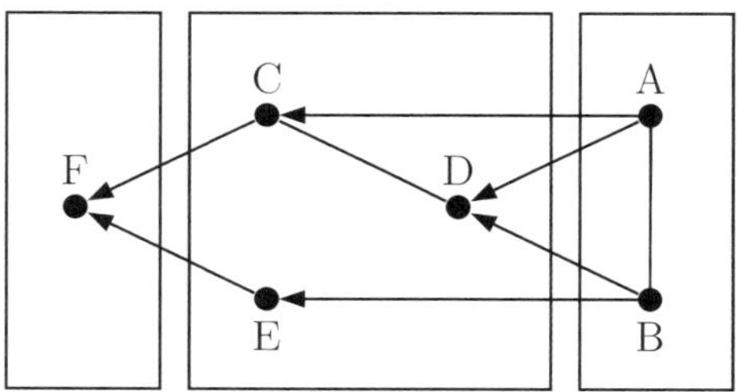

Figure 17.2   A Block Recursive Model

The purely explanatory variables A and B are located on the right-hand side. The box in the middle contains the intermediate variables C, D, and E. In the box on the left we find the purely dependent variable F. An example for the independence relations in this graph would be that D and E are independent given A, B (prior) and C (concurrent).

Practical Use of Graphical Models in the Microsimulation Context

The Connection between Sequences of Events in Microsimulation and Chain Graph Models

Although there are some exceptions like LifePaths (Statistics Canada 2002) that use continuous time, the majority of the dynamic microsimulation models (e.g., APPSIM (Cassells, Harding and Kelly 2006), SESIM (Flood 2008), SAGE (Zaidi and Rake 2001)) are discrete time models. This means that the sequence of the events that are simulated in the model has to be chosen by the researcher on the base of substantive knowledge in advance, a task that is not always trivial. If the sequence of events becomes very complex, for example when involving a large number of potentially influential variables or showing a complicated dependence structure, the joint probability distribution of the involved random variables can only be unsatisfactorily modelled with classical statistical models.

It becomes clear that this approach of putting events into a certain order is quite similar to the one outlined for the Chain Graph Models above. Therefore, these Models are of particular usefulness in the microsimulation context as they can be used to model complete sequences of events instead of concentrating on single regression equations for each event in the chain in turn. As an example, the whole educational career of a person can be formulated as a Chain Graph Model instead of having distinct models for the events involved, firstly modelling the choice of primary school, then the choice of secondary school, the drop-out from secondary school, choice of tertiary education, etc.

The Cox-Wermuth Selection Strategy

Several selection strategies to fit Graphical Models are available, for instance the Edward-Havránek procedure (Edwards and Havránek 1985, 1987). As Blauth (2002) states, if the number of variables in the model is not small, most of these procedures are very time-consuming. An even greater disadvantage is that in the case of mixed variables the maximum-likelihood estimation often does not converge. Cox and Wermuth (1996) propose a selection strategy that bypasses the multivariate problem by fitting the Chain Graph approximately with a series of univariate conditional regressions, based on the factorization of the joint density as described above. This heuristic approach allows the maximization of the joint likelihood by reducing the problem to maximizing the likelihood for each factorized submodel. The strategy can roughly be divided into two steps that are carried out repeatedly:

- In the first step, a check for non-linearities and possible second-order interactions is performed. More complicated terms, e.g., higher-order interactions, are ignored for reasons of parsimony (Cox and Wermuth 1994).
- In step 2, a series of forward and backward selections is carried out to find the appropriate model for the current sub-problem.

In detail, the starting point is the explanation of the purely dependent variable in block 1. This response is regressed on all of the intermediate and all of the purely explanatory variables, following the two steps outlined above. Next, this approach is replicated for the intermediate variable in block 2, then follows block 3 etc. If two or more variables fall into a block that has to be explained, all of them are taken as being dependent in turn, the remaining ones (of the same block) constituting additional explanatory variables at any one time.

It goes without saying that the validity and explanatory power of the results generated by this procedure are dependent on the quality of the data entered, just like in classical statistical modelling. This means that the automatic selection doesn't release the researcher from the obligation of checking the data for outliers, dealing with missing values etc. beforehand.

When the model has finally been fitted, the corresponding model graph is drawn. Its appearance is a little bit different from the graphs already defined above. The boxes are not drawn since the block structure can be directly read off the graph and if there are undirected edges present, this corresponds to a correlational relationship between two variables, and not to an interaction effect (these are not depicted in the graph). In the next section, we will provide an example that makes use of this selection strategy.

Two Microsimulation Applications

Our R (R Development Core Team 2012) implementation of the Cox-Wermuth selection strategy allows the fitting of a Chain Graph Model for metric and categorical random variables from exponential families and thus incorporates the class of Generalized Linear Models in the chain. The methods used are Gaussian, Binary and Multinomial Logistic, and Poisson Regression. We present two applications in the microsimulation context, where the first one deals with aspects of health, and the second, more complex one, is related to housing.

Modelling Activities of Daily Living (ADL)

We are modelling two aspects of health, namely possible limitations in activities people usually do (adl) being the response variable of primary interest, and the presence of chronic diseases (chron), constituting the response variable of secondary interest and being explanatory variable for (adl) at the same time. We suppose that these variables could (to a certain extent) be explained by the amount of work (full time/part-time) (ftpt) and the level of education (edu) of a person. As background variables that are purely explanatory, we consider age and gender (sex) as possibly important. The data is taken from the EU-SILC (EU Statistics on Income and Living Conditions) Survey 2008. Our first task is to define the types of the input variables and the structure of the model (see Figure 17.3).

	row.names	type	block	var4	var5	var6	var7
1	year	NA	NA				
2	pid	NA	NA				
3	chron	bin	2				
4	adl	categ	1				
5	age	cont	4				
6	sex	bin	4				
7	edu	categ	3				
8	ftpt	bin	3				
9							

Figure 17.3   R Data Editor used to define the structure of the model

- In the first column, the names of the variables are given.
- In the second column, we insert the type of the variable. In our example, we have the binary (*bin*) variables *sex*, *chron* and *ftpt*, the polytomous (*categ*) variables *adl* and *edu* and the continuous (*cont*) variable *age*.
- In the third column, we assign each variable to a block. We start with the purely dependent variable (*adl*) in block 1. We suppose that this variable could be influenced by the presence of some chronic disease, so the intermediate variable *chron* is located in block 2. The next block of intermediate variables contains *edu* and *ftpt*, *sex* and *age* are assigned to block 4. Variables that we do not want to be part of the analysis get an NA in this column (here: Survey year (*year*) and Person ID (*pid*)).

As soon as the structure of the model has been defined, we are able to start the Cox-Wermuth procedure on the given data set. We use the first step of the iterative process to show how the procedure works for our example:

1. The current dependent and independent variables are defined. According to the type of the dependent variable that has been specified, the appropriate model family and test are chosen (Binary Logistic Regression for *bin* type variables, Poisson Regression for *count* type variables etc.). The algorithm starts with variable *adl* in Block 1, so a Multinomial Logistic Regression is performed where *adl* is regressed on all variables belonging to the same or a preceding block.
2. The algorithm checks for second-order interactions and non-linear relationships.
3. If any relevant terms were found in step 2, a forward selection procedure is used, trying to add each of these terms in turn, based on the tests defined in step 1 of the Cox-Wermuth Selection Strategy (see above).
4. A backward selection based on the AIC-criterion (Akaike 1974) is performed.
5. For the remaining variables, the second-order interaction terms are added to the model, followed by another AIC backward selection.
6. Like step 5, but for non-linear relationships.

Upon completion of the last step, the final model for the target variable adl has been found, and the procedure is repeated for the remaining variables, the next one being chron since it is the only variable in block 2. A summary for each target variable is available after the model fitting process. Looking at these summaries in Table 17.1, we see that for each binary or continuous dependent variable one regression equation is present. If the dependent variable is categorical with more than two categories, the number of equations equals the number of categories minus one, according to the number of pairwise comparisons with the baseline category that are possible.

Table 17.1   Univariate regression equations related to the activities of daily living (purely dependent variable)

Response	Explanatory variables			
adl1	*chron*	*age*	*chron:age*	*const.*
est. reg. coeff.	5.09	0.05	−0.03	−7.37
st. error	1.04	0.02	0.02	0.94
z value	4.89	2.42	−1.22	−7.80
adl2				
est. reg. coeff.	5.00	0.05	−0.04	−4.97
st. error	0.41	0.01	0.01	0.31
z value	12.28	6.56	−4.81	−15.82
Chron	*age*	*const.*		
est. reg. coeff.	0.04	−3.16		
st. error	< 0.01	0.14		
z value	14.30	−22.87		
edu1	*age*	*poly(age, 2)*	*sex*	*const.*
est. reg. coeff.	−0.02	30.43	0.32	3.34
st. error	0.02	2.43	0.38	0.87
z value	−1.13	12.51	0.84	3.85
edu2				
est. reg. coeff.	0.00	−7.56	−0.42	4.97
st. error	0.02	2.00	0.37	0.86
z value	−0.13	−3.78	−1.12	5.87
…				
edu10				
est. reg. coeff.	0.04	−10.21	−0.51	0.13
st. error	0.02	0.11	0.43	1.01
z value	2.18	−89.98	−1.20	0.13
Ftpt	*age*	*poly(age, 2)*	*sex*	*const.*
est. reg. coeff.	0.02	−19.19	2.56	−3.72
st. error	< 0.01	3.20	0.09	0.17
z value	5.37	−5.99	28.35	−22.09
Age	*const.*			
est. reg. coeff.	39.70			
st. error	0.15			
z value	269.60			
Sex	*const.*			
est. reg. coeff.	−0.21			
st. error	0.03			
z value	−8.35			

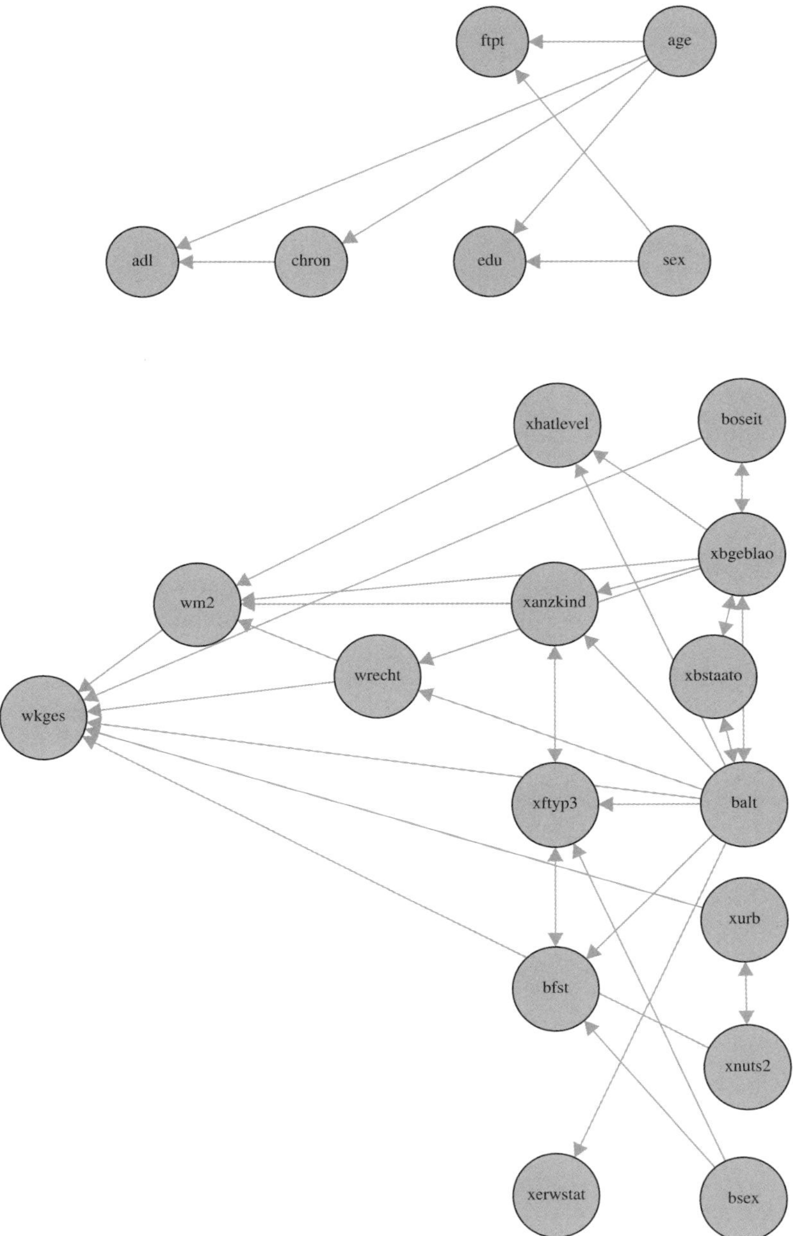

Figure 17.4 **Dependency structures of the fitted models for activities of daily living (upper part) and monthly housing costs (lower part)**

adl has three categories, therefore two equations are given (*adl1*, *adl2*). The baseline category here is *no, not limited*, *adl1* corresponds to the comparison with *yes, limited*, *adl2* with *yes, strongly limited*. adl depends on the presence of chronic diseases and the age of a person, the latter entering the equation as a linear term. The interaction effect between the predictors complicates the interpretation – an effect plot helps to overcome this problem (not depicted here). We conclude that for persons not suffering from a chronic disease (*chron*: 0), the odds of being limited or strongly limited in the activities of daily living (*adl*: 1 or 2) increase with age, whereas not being limited becomes more unlikely (*adl*: 0). For people with a chronic disease, age makes little difference. Bearing in mind that not all responses have the same levels of measurement, the estimates of all the other regression equation can be interpreted in a similar fashion (*edu* has 11 different categories, not all of the 10 equations are included in Table 17.1).

It is possible to derive an adjacency matrix from these models. A one in this matrix complies with a pairwise connection (the row variable being the predictor), a zero stands for conditional independence of two variables. For example, since age is a significant predictor in all of the univariate regressions, four ones are present in the corresponding matrix row, associated with the (dependent) column variables *chron*, *adl*, *edu*, and *ftpt*.

In addition, by plotting a graph of the fitted model (the upper part of Figure 17.4), we are also able to find sequences (chains, paths) that we can interpret (see also Wermuth 2003). For the fitted model, only one sequence is present: Age has a positive effect on developing a chronic disease. Those having a chronic disease are more likely to be limited in their usual activities.

Note that each arrow present in the graph directly relates to a variable in one of the regression equations, e.g., *chron* pointing to *adl* corresponds to the first term of the first regression equation given in Table 17.1. The input for this graph is the adjacency matrix presented above where the ones generate the arrows. Therefore, four arrows originate from the *age* node, pointing to the variables *chron*, *adl*, *edu*, and *ftpt*.

Modelling Monthly Housing Costs

The second example uses Austrian microcensus data (Statistik Austria 2006) and includes three housing variables of interest, namely the total monthly housing costs (*wkges*), living space (*wm2*) and dwelling type (*wrecht*). Additionally, level of education (ISCED) (*xhatlevel*), marital status (*bfst*), family type (*xftyp3*), number of children in the family (*xanzkind*), labour status (*xerwstat*), gender (*bsex*), age (*balt*), degree of urbanization (*xurb*), federal state (*xnuts2*), citizenship (*xbstaato*), country of birth (*xbgeblao*) and the number of years the person has lived in Austria (*boseit*) are incorporated in the analysis. We use the same procedural method as above, but set aside the presentation of the multitude of regression equations. Looking at the model graph (lower part of Figure 17.4), we see numerous dependencies and several chains of events, a discussion of which is beyond the scope of this article.

Conclusion

Graphical Models can be a valuable tool for model selection when the dependencies between variables have a complicated form or when the number of variables gets very large. Beyond that, the representation of the fitted model in form of a graph makes the interpretation much more practicable. The authors have presented an implementation in the statistical programming language R that allows fitting such models on the basis of a heuristic approach proposed by Cox and Wermuth. Currently under development, it is planned to release an R package in due time. Since the principle of factorization holds, more complex methods, for example Random Effect Models, could be used at certain stages of the modelling process, but in this case it would not be possible to automatically select models anymore.

References

Akaike, H. 1974. A new look at the statistical model identification. *IEEE Transactions on Automatic Control*, 19(6), 716–23.

Blauth, A. 2002. *Model selection in graphical models with special focus on genetic algorithms*. Berlin: Logos.

Cassells, R., Harding, A. and Kelly, S. 2006. *Problems and Prospects for Dynamic Microsimulation: A Review and Lessons for APPSIM* [Online: National Centre for Social and Economic Modelling, University of Canberra]. Available at: http://www.canberra.edu.au/centres/natsem [accessed: 12 January 2013].

Christensen, R. 1997. *Log-linear models and logistic regression*. Second edition. New York: Springer.

Cox, D.R. and Wermuth, N. 1994. Tests of linearity, multivariate normality and the adequacy of linear scores. *Applied Statistics*, 43(2), 347–55.

Cox, D.R. and Wermuth, N. 1996. *Multivariate dependencies*. Boca Raton, FL: Chapman & Hall/CRC Press.

Darroch, J.N., Lauritzen, S.L. and Speed, T.P. 1980. Markov fields and log linear interaction models for contingency tables. *Annals of Statistics*, 8(3), 522–39.

Edwards, D. 2000. *Introduction to graphical modeling*. Second edition. New York: Springer.

Edwards, D. and Havránek, T. 1985. A fast procedure for model search in multidimensional contingency tables. *Biometrika*, 72(2), 339–51.

Edwards, D. and Havránek, T. 1987. A fast model selection procedure for large families of models. *Journal of the American Statistical Association*, 82(397), 205–13.

Flood, L. 2008. SESIM: A Swedish Micro-Simulation Model, in A. Klevmarken and B. Lindgren (eds), *Simulating an Ageing Population – A microsimulation approach applied to Sweden*. Bingley, United Kingdom: Emerald Group Publishing Ltd., 55–84.

Lauritzen, S.L. 1996. *Graphical models*. Oxford: Clarendon Press.

R Development Core Team 2012. *R: A language and environment for statistical computing* [Computer software manual]. Vienna, Austria. Available at: http://www.R-project.org (ISBN 3-900051-07-0) [accessed: 12 January 2013].

Statistics Canada 2002. *The LifePaths Microsimulation Model – An Overview* [Online: Statistics Canada]. Available at: http://www.statcan.gc.ca/microsimulation/pdf/lifepaths-overview-vuedensemble-eng.pdf [accessed: 12 January 2013].

Statistik Austria 2006. *Mikrozensusdaten ab 2004 – Interviewerhandbuch inkl. Merkmalsbeschreibung der AKE-Variablen* [Computer software manual].

Wermuth, N. 2003. Analysing social science data with graphical markov models, in S.R.P. Green and N. Hjort (eds), *Highly structured stochastic systems*. Oxford: Oxford University Press, 33–9.

Whittaker, J. 1990. *Graphical models in applied multivariate statistics*. Chichester: Wiley.

Wright, S. 1921. Correlation and causation. *Journal of Agricultural Research*, 20, 162–77.

Zaidi, A. and Rake, K. 2001. *Dynamic Microsimulation Models: A Review and Some Lessons for SAGE* [Online: London School Of Economics]. Available at: http://www.lse.ac.uk/collections/sage [accessed: 12 January 2007].

Chapter 18

Education in the Norwegian Microsimulation Model MOSART

Hege Marie Gjefsen

Introduction

Educational characteristics are highly correlated with labour market outcomes. This is reflected in the Norwegian microsimulation model MOSART[1] where education is an important factor in explaining the behaviour of the individuals in the labour market and other outcomes through life. Educational background affects several events over the lifecycle in this model. It is a factor in deciding the individual risk of unemployment and disability, as well as life expectancy. The model does not distinguish the self selection mechanism from the causal effect of education on later demographic and labour market outcomes. Only the correlations between educational choices and later outcomes are included in the model, and this can be interpreted as a combination of the self selection-mechanism and a causal relationship.

By using the MOSART model it is possible to produce projections of the number of students distributed over fields and levels. The model also produces projections for level of education, of both the population as a whole and the labour force. Information about the educational background of the population and labour force is important for example for estimating future public expenditure and uncovering possible labour market imbalances.

First, the Norwegian school system is described, followed by the main features of the MOSART model. Then the econometric modelling and the estimates resulting from it for each of the transitions in the model are discussed; finally, projections of labour supply and population by educational background are presented. The tables and figures are based on the data used to estimate the transition probabilities, unless stated otherwise.

---

1   MOSART is a Norwegian acronym for 'Model for micro simulation of education, labour supply and social security'.

The Norwegian School System

Overview of the Norwegian School System

The Norwegian educational system consists of 10 years of compulsory education, followed by three or four years of high school. Most students complete compulsory education at 16.

Upper secondary education is not compulsory, but approximately 95 per cent of each cohort continue their education by starting in high school directly after completing their compulsory schooling. In Norway, high school education is divided into two areas: vocational education programmes and programmes in general studies. Students in general programmes attend upper secondary education for three years. The main model for vocational education is based on two years of schooling and two years of vocational training as an apprentice in an enterprise.

While most of the youths start upper secondary schooling the semester after completing compulsory schooling, all of them do not complete their education. In recent years, about two-thirds of each cohort have completed high school five years after leaving compulsory schooling (Statistics Norway 2012a). General studies are the largest field of education at this level. Almost 50 per cent of high school students complete their education in general studies. Most of the students who do not complete upper secondary education follow vocational programmes. While the completion rate varies across vocational fields, it is lower than for general programmes. The field of education is an important factor in deciding the risk of leaving school without formal qualifications.

Certain educational programmes do not belong to the tertiary education group, even though most of the students attending them have a high school certificate. The schools at this level are not accredited to offer degrees on a tertiary level. These programmes are referred to as post-secondary, non-tertiary education, and consist of vocational courses with varying duration. Some provide pre-degree foundations, while others are extensions of vocational programmes in high school. Post secondary, non-tertiary education is equivalent to level 4 at the ISCED 1997-scale[2] (UNESCO 2006).

Completed high school is necessary to enter most kinds of tertiary education. However, there are rules giving persons with informal qualifications the possibility of entering tertiary education if they are 25 years or older.

Most of the study programmes at lower tertiary level are of three years duration, while teacher education takes four years. Students obtain bachelor's degrees after completing three years of study. Upper level tertiary education comprises of education at Master's level. Master's degrees are obtained by studying in a Master's programme for two years subsequent to a bachelor's degree. Included in this level of education are also some professionally oriented degrees and integrated Master's degrees. These are completed after five or six years of studies, depending

---

2   International Standard Classification of Education.

on the programme. Most people who complete professional studies and university studies have found relevant work within six months of graduation (Arnesen 2010).

Education in the MOSART Model

People make educational choices every semester, and students can change the field of their studies without difficulties. Paths to the same kind of proficiency differ, which makes it more difficult to fit educational choices into a model. To carry out an econometric analysis of their educational choices, we need a modelling framework where the population can make educational choices in a way that corresponds to reality. This framework is created by looking at four educational choices prospective students make. The first is to start an educational activity. Conditional on entering, the students choose which level of education to attend. Conditional on the level, the field of study is chosen. The next choice is whether or not to complete their studies in that particular year. If a student does not complete the education, he or she can choose to continue the ongoing education, or quit before completion.

Choices are made once a year in the sequence given by the flow chart in Figure 18.1. When the choices described in italic are made, no further choices are made until next year.

Figure 18.1 shows how transitions are made in the educational module of the MOSART model. The modelling of a person's educational activities and attainment starts when graduating from compulsory education. For immigrants, the simulation starts when arriving in Norway. Each year, a person makes a decision about whether to start an educational activity or not. Otherwise, they return to being outside education. No further educational choices are made until the next year.

Persons starting a new educational activity will choose which educational category to attend. Because there are as many as 28 educational categories to choose from in the MOSART model, the choice of educational category is separated into two separate choices. The student first chooses the level of education to attend, i.e. degree level. The possible levels of education are upper secondary school in general studies, upper secondary school in vocational studies, folk high school[3] lower tertiary education or higher tertiary education.

If choosing vocational upper secondary education, or short or long tertiary education, a choice of field of study is made. The combination of choice of level and field of education gives 28 educational categories. All individuals starting an educational activity are registered within an educational category.

The registered students then choose whether or not to complete the education. If completing the ongoing educational category, they go back to being outside education, and can make new educational choices the next year. If not completing, they choose whether or not to continue in the same educational programme.

---

3   Folk high school and military officer training.

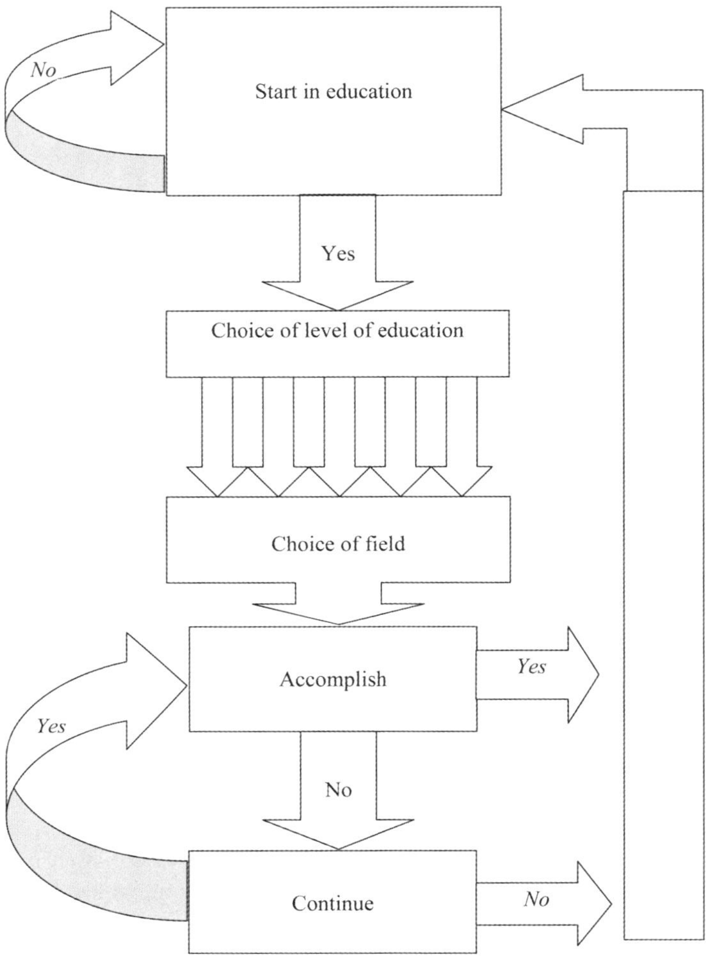

Figure 18.1 Educational transitions

Continuing in education is defined as being registered within the same educational category the following year. To continue in education is in most cases necessary to complete the education, as the propensity to complete an education is low when having spent a short time in it, and increases with the time spent in that particular education. For students choosing to continue in their ongoing educational activity, a new choice about completing the education is made the following year. Personal characteristics, such as age and time spent in education will then have changed, and so will the educational propensities. If choosing not to continue, the person goes back to being outside education, and can make a new decision about starting education the following year.

In addition to these choices, the model allocates updated educational attainment for those who were not registered as students the previous year. Persons outside any educational activities can each year have their educational attainment updated. The cycle repeats itself until the person passes away. The population can go in and out of education throughout life, but the probability of starting an educational activity is drastically reduced after the age of 30.

Education Profile

The level of education has been rising over the last decades, but now seems to be settling. An expansion of tertiary education has been observed, and an increased propensity to take education has been the result.

Seven fields of education are specified at upper secondary level in the model. There is one general programme, and the remaining six programmes are vocational. Men and women make different educational choices at higher secondary level. The number of men and women who enter upper secondary education is similar, but women choose general studies programmes to a higher extent than men. More women with general studies high school proficiency means that more women will enter tertiary education, as general studies high school proficiency is a prerequisite for starting a tertiary education.

Short tertiary education is divided into nine fields. This level of education corresponds to level 5 on the ISCED scale. More women than men start in lower tertiary education. This could partially be explained by the fact that more men than women have vocational high school proficiency, and are thus ready to enter the labour market after completion. There are several fields of study which are heavily dominated by women at this level, the most important being the teacher education, nursing and healthcare, and other health studies.

Long tertiary education consists of two-year Master's degrees following a bachelor's degree, and integrated Master's degrees or professionally oriented degrees. The fields represented in the model are humanities and arts, education, social sciences, law, economics and administration, engineering, other fields of sciences, medicine, dental studies, other studies in health and social services, and other tertiary education of higher degree. There are differences in the fields of education chosen by men and women similar to what is seen in lower tertiary education.

Some people have their educational attainment updated without being registered as students. In Table 18.1, the share having their educational attainment updated without being students is presented. For some fields, it is much more likely to obtain proficiency without being a student than for others.

Table 18.1   Proportion of the graduates gaining educational attainment without being registered as students

Upper secondary education	
Economics and administration	17.9
Electronics, mechanics and machinery	20.9
Building and construction	33.8
Other fields of science and trade	20.2
Health subjects	44.0
Other	23.3
General studies	8.1
Short tertiary education	
Humanities	10.6
Education	8.9
Social sciences	9.9
Economics and administration	18.8
Engineering	7.0
Other fields of sciences	11.6
Nursing and care giving	8.0
Other fields of health	5.8
Other	17.4
Long tertiary education	
Humanities	6.5
Education	7.2
Social sciences	8.7
Law	4.4
Economics and administration	21.3
Engineering	4.9
Other fields of sciences	21.7
Medicine	28.2
Dental studies	23.8
Other health studies	10.9
Other	44.4

In vocational studies, it is possible to obtain proficiency by working and taking a qualifying exam. Persons following such a track will not be registered as students. Medicine, dental studies and economics and administration are the most important courses for students taking the whole degree outside Norway. This could explain the high share of graduates obtaining their qualifications without being registered as students in these subjects. Immigrants will in some cases have their education registered and approved in Norway, and such a registration will also lead to updated educational attainment without any registered educational activities the year before.

In several educational programmes, there are requirements for proficiency and results in earlier education to be accepted into a study programme. In the MOSART model, there are no such restrictions.

The MOSART Model

Overview of the MOSART Model

The MOSART model is a microsimulation model used to analyse the pension system, public expenditure and the labour supply. Educational background has been an important characteristic in the MOSART model from the start. The probability of starting an education after the age of 30 is low. Educational background can therefore be regarded a fixed characteristic. Educational attainment is highly correlated with later labour market attachment and demographical events.

In the MOSART model, every person in the population has a transition probability for each possible choice at every point in time (Frekriksen 1998). The transition probability is calculated by using the estimates of how the characteristics influence the probability of making a transition, together with each person's characteristics. When running the model the individual transition probabilities are matched by drawing a random number between 0 and 1. The event takes place if the transition probability assigned to a particular person is higher than this random number. Having a high transition possibility means that the probability of the random number being below the transition probability is high, but it is still possible that persons having a high risk of making a certain choice will choose differently. The drawing of the random numbers is discussed in Fredriksen (1998).

Events are simulated in a given sequence, and earlier simulated events can influence the transition probability of the next event. The transition probabilities are conditional on earlier events. The MOSART model is a dynamic micro simulation model. A dynamic micro simulation model enables analysis of the life course of individuals. The whole population is included in the simulation.

Information about educational background is important to projections about the future labour supply. The MOSART model is used to produce projections of the labour supply by both educational level and field. The projections can be matched to corresponding projections for demand, and imbalances in the future labour market can be detected. These analyses have been made since 1993 (Bjørnstad et al. 2010).

Data and Definitions

Administrative register data from Statistics Norway are used when updating the information on educational background. Movements into education are registered for all students aged 16 and older in Norway. There are also data on the highest completed education. In Statistics Norway, movements in and out of education have been registered since 1974. There is also information about educational background from the population censuses. Register data on the highest completed education are updated every year in November.

The ISCED standardization changed the registration of completed education in tertiary education from 1998. With the new standard, education is only registered as completed if the education has lasted for at least two years.

All immigrants coming to Norway are assigned to the category unknown education (Fredriksen 1998). Immigrants can have their education approved and registered by applying for it, and some do also enrol in the Norwegian education. The number of immigrants is expected to rise in the future, and so will the number of persons having unknown education. A survey was carried out in 2012 with the purpose of improving the information about the educational background of immigrants.

Econometric Modelling

A number of conditions influence educational choices. Personal taste and interests may be the most important factors, but they are both difficult to measure. Earlier educational decisions are an indication of personal taste and interests, and are included in the model as explanatory variables.

In some cases, the explanatory variables could affect the transition probability differently for different subgroups, i.e., there could be interactions between the explanatory variables. In the MOSART case, the age effect and effect of time spent in education differs for educational subgroups. To solve any problems concerning interaction of the explanatory variables, the estimation has been done separately for subgroups of the population. Estimating the transition probabilities separately allows the effect of the explanatory variables to be different for the subgroups. To allow for further interactions between the explanatory variables, interaction dummies are included. Logistic regressions are used to estimate transition probabilities, and multinomial logit models are used when modelling choice of level and fields of education.

Transition rates in the educational module in the MOSART model are decided by the effects found in the econometric modelling together with observed characteristics. Observed characteristics could change with the simulation. The observed characteristics and how they affect the transition probabilities will decide the development of student numbers and the level of education in the population and labour force, together with the demographical development.

Starting in Education

The propensity to start an educational activity is estimated separately for a series of subgroups. The subgroups are specified using a combination of educational attainment and the educational activities the year before.

Age dummies are included as explanatory variables, together with dummies for highest completed education within each subgroup. Dummies for time spent both in and outside education are also included. Time spent in and outside education is an indication of interest and ability in education. The cost of starting in education could be higher if having spent long time outside the educational system. Year fixed effects are included to account for any variation in the propensity to start in education due to business cycles, variation in capacity and cohort effects. There may be business cycle effects on the opportunity costs of education, and further on the number of students wanting to go into education (Card 1995). Business cycles are not included in the projections made by the MOSART model, but it is necessary to take the fluctuations from the estimation period into account. A dummy for being under the newest school reform 'Kunnskapsløftet' (The Knowledge Promotion Reform) is added, together with dummies for combinations of age and highest completed education for those with a high school degree in vocational studies. The propensity to start in education differs highly between the programmes attended, and there age effects for those between 19 and 21 interacted with the field of education for the programmes in vocational high school education are included.

For the decision of entering education, the decision is conditional on being outside education, i.e. not continuing the education from the previous spring. Equations 1 and 2 expresses the probability that person i chooses to enter education at time t, given her individual characteristics and the fact that she is outside education, as a function of her own educational characteristics and age at time t, as well as the year the decision is made. All educational characteristics are collected in a vector *edu*.

$$1 \quad P(y_{it} = start \mid x_{it}) = \frac{e^{x_{it}{}'\beta_{start}}}{1 + e^{x_{it}{}'\beta_{start}}}$$

$$2 \quad x_{it}{}'\beta_{start} = \beta_{0\_start} + \beta_{age\_start} age_{it} + \beta_{edu\_start} edu_{it} + \beta_{year\_start} year_{it}$$

Choice of Level and Field

When deciding the educational category of the students starting in education, there are two separate decisions to make, both level and field. In both decisions, a multinomial logit model is used. The estimation of the probability to choose a level is conditional on starting in education. The alternative levels to choose from are folk high school, a high school education in general studies, a high school education in vocational studies, a short tertiary education and a long tertiary education. The choice of which level to attend is estimated separately according to the highest completed education and gender.

Age and highest completed education within the subgroup are included as explanatory variables for the choice of level of education. Year fixed effects, dummies for having completed the highest completed education the previous spring, and a dummy variable for being under the latest school reform are included.

The regression equation for the probability that a person i chooses educational level j conditional on having chosen to start in education is given in equations 3 and 4. The possible levels are county college or its equivalent, high school education in general studies, high school education in vocational studies, and short tertiary education or long tertiary education.

$$3 \quad P(y_{it} = levelj \mid x_{it}) = \frac{e^{\bar{x}_{it}'\bar{\beta}_{levelj}}}{1 + \sum_{j=1}^{4} e^{x_{it}'\beta_{levelj}}},$$

where j is the alternative levels of education different from the reference outcome.

$$4 \quad x_{it}'\beta_{levelj} = \beta_{0\_levelj} + \beta_{age\_levelj} age_{it} + \beta_{edu\_levelj} edu_{it} + \beta_{year\_levelj} year_{it}$$

After choosing a level, the students choose which field to attend. The choice of field is estimated separately according to the highest completed education. Earlier educational attainment reflects both interests and abilities, and could restrict later choices.

Choosing a field of education is conditional on the student having chosen the relevant level. A multinomial logit model for each level is specified. For each level, there are n fields of education.

$$5 \quad P(y_{it} = fieldj \mid x_{it}) = \frac{e^{\bar{x}_{it}'\bar{\beta}_{fieldj}}}{1 + \sum_{j=1}^{n} e^{x_{it}'\beta_{fieldj}}}$$

$$6 \quad x_{it}'\beta_{fieldj} = \beta_{0\_fieldj} + \beta_{age\_fieldj} age_{it} + \beta_{edu\_fieldj} edu_{it} + \beta_{year\_fieldj} year_{it}$$

The number of fields of study depends on the level. The probability to choose field j within the n available fields is described by equations 5 and 6.

Completing and Continuing Educational Activities

When deciding the propensity to complete an education a person is in, the effect of the explanatory variables varies according to the kind of education taken. The subgroups are estimated according to ongoing education and gender. Explanatory variables included are age, highest completed education, the education attended, and how much time spent in it. Time in education is defined as total number of years spent in education at the relevant level. In the case of attending a vocational track in high school, interaction terms between time spent in education and the programme attended are included as the duration of the study programmes varies.

The probability of completion is given by equations 7 and 8. In the following regressions, the variable called edu_{it} is a vector including information about former completed education and ongoing education for each person i at time t.

$$7 \quad P(y_{it} = completion \mid x_{it}) = \frac{e^{x_{it}'\beta_{completion}}}{1 + e^{x_{it}'\beta_{completion}}}$$

$$8 \quad x_{it}'\beta_{completion} = \beta_{0\_comp} + \beta_{age\_comp}age_{it} + \beta_{edu\_comp}edu_{it} + \beta_{year\_comp}year_{it}$$

The students who do not complete their education can either continue in the same educational track, or leave education without completion. To continue in an educational activity is defined as being in the same educational field the following year. The same explanatory variables as for the decision to complete education are used when modelling to continue. The probability to continue is given by equations 9 and 10.

$$9 \quad P(y_{it} = continue \mid x_{it}) = \frac{e^{x_{it}'\beta_{continue}}}{1 + e^{x_{it}'\beta_{continue}}}$$

$$10 \quad x_{it}'\beta_{continue} = \beta_{0\_cont} + \beta_{age\_cont}age_{it} + \beta_{edu\_cont}edu_{it} + \beta_{year\_cont}year_{it}$$

Educational Attainment Without Being a Student

Individuals outside education can have their educational attainment updated without starting in education. The propensity to have a new educational attainment without being a student is estimated separately for a series of subgroups. The subgroups are specified from information about educational attainment and time spent in the Norwegian educational system, and any educational activities not completed.

There are controls for age, year fixed effects and educational characteristics to decide whether their proficiency is updated without being a student. Educational characteristics are in this case highest completed education, the last educational activity that was not completed, time spent in that activity, and time spent outside education. The estimations are conditional on not being in education the year before. The probability to have the educational attainment updated without being a student is expressed in equations 11 and 12.

$$11 \quad P(y_{it} = obtain\_proficiency \mid x_{it}) = \frac{e^{x_{it}'\beta_{prof}}}{1 + e^{x_{it}'\beta_{prof}}}$$

$$12 \quad x_{it}'\beta_{prof} = \beta_{0\_prof} + \beta_{age\_prof}age_{it} + \beta_{edu\_prof}edu_{it} + \beta_{year\_prof}year_{it}$$

Projections of Labour Force by Education

In this section we will make projections of labour supply within different educational groups. Projections are here based on transitions probabilities being the same in the future as the average between 2007 and 2011. The projections are based on the Norwegian population projections from 2012. For a more detailed description of the modelling of population projections, see Brunborg et al. (2012).

The propensity to start in education increased up to about 2000, due to both increased capacity and behaviour. Since then, educational propensities have remained fairly constant, and the further increase in the educational level of the population is caused by the fact that older generations with a generally low education are replaced by new generations, who have a higher propensity to enrol in education, and therefore have a higher educational level in general.

Educational background is highly correlated with labour force participation. By combining information about inflows and outflows in education with information about the demographic development and labour force participation for the subgroups, it is possible to use the MOSART-model to project the labour force by education. The analysis could be extended by projecting the labour supply under different assumptions regarding education, labour force participation, demography etc. The results presented in the following are based on assumptions of constant educational propensities and constant participation rates. A significantly higher number of persons with higher education among the young generations compared to the elderly are one of the main driving forces in this model (Bjørnstad et al. 2010). Educational propensities have remained fairly constant in Norway since the start of this decade.

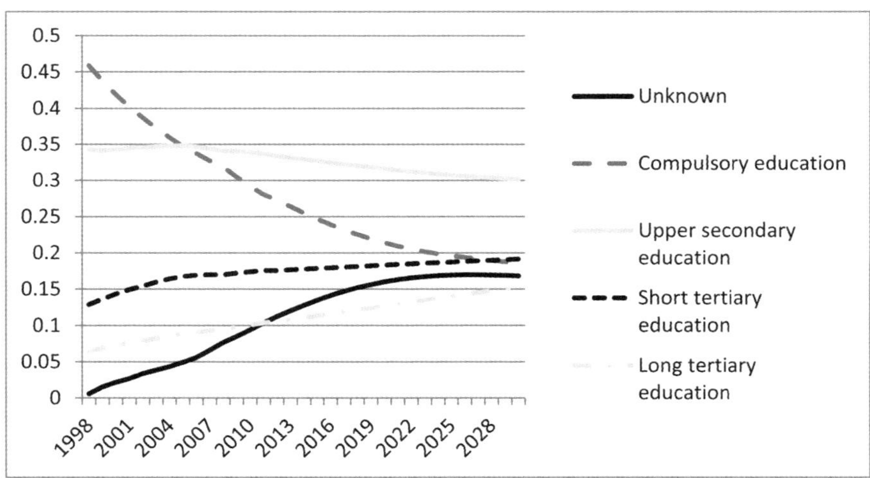

Figure 18.2   Labour force by level of education. Share of labour force

The share of the labour force with no more than compulsory education is therefore expected to decline towards 2030 as presented in Figure 18.2. Having compulsory education as the highest completed is considerably more common in the older cohorts. When the old cohorts are replaced by younger, the share of the labour force with only compulsory education decreases. The share with upper secondary education as the highest is expected to remain constant towards 2030. It is expected to be a significant increase in the number of persons with tertiary education, both at the absolute and relative level. The number of persons with unknown educational background in the labour force is also expected to increase because of the high immigration.

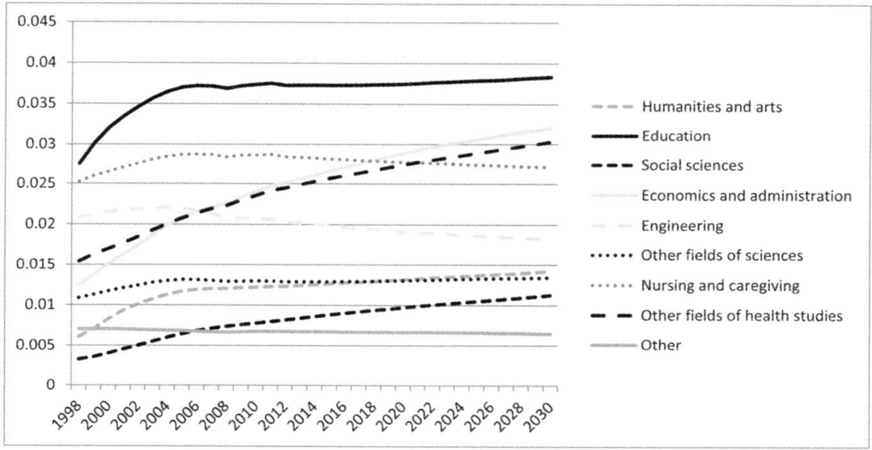

Figure 18.3   Projections of the labour force with short tertiary education as the highest. Share of labour force

The share with education in social sciences is expected to increase. This is also the case for economics and administration. The share with education in economics and administration is one of the fields with the highest growth. The share of the labour force with an engineering degree at the bachelor level is declining, and the same is the case for the share with other kinds of education in natural sciences. The share with education in other kinds of health studies is increasing. Further studies of the personnel in the educational sector can be found in Roksvaag (2012b). The definition of teachers is however not the same as in the MOSART model.

Most kinds of education at Master's level are projected to experience an increasing share of the labour force in this general approach. The exceptions in these projections are medicine and dental studies, but these are very small groups compared to the others, and are therefore difficult to project with this kind of approach. A more in-depth analysis of the personnel in the health sector can be found in Roksvaag (2012a). The number of persons with education in economics

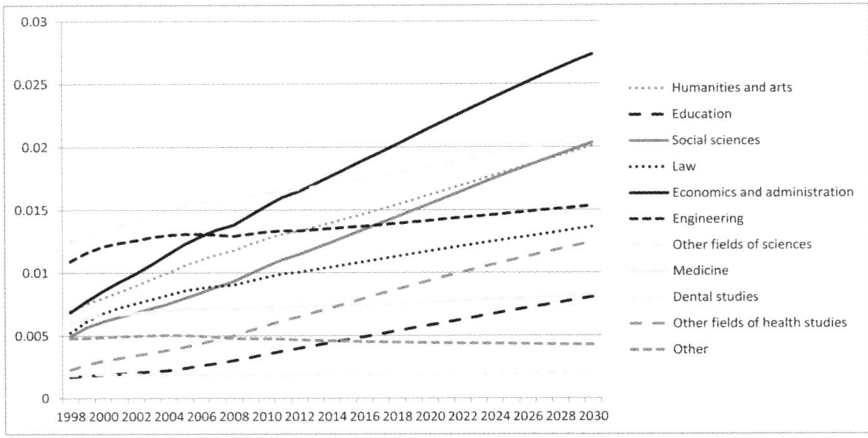

Figure 18.4   Projections of the labour force with long tertiary education as the highest. Share of labour force

and administration grows at the highest rate. Social sciences and other fields of health studies than medicine and dental studies also grow with a high rate.

Concluding Remarks

All parts of the Norwegian educational system have been reformed over the last 10 years, and an update of the MOSART model was necessary. Transitions in and out of the educational system have been estimated using a series of logistic models and Norwegian register data.

Projections show that the level of education in both population and labour force is expected to rise. The share of the population with compulsory education is replaced by younger cohorts with higher educational level. Due to immigration, the share of the population with unknown education is also expected to rise. Some educational groups are expected to grow with a higher rate than the others. There is an increase in the share of the labour force and population with education in economics and administration, social sciences and humanities at Master's level. The projections also show an increase in the share with education in health studies.

An updated educational module in the MOSART model is important when projecting public expenditures, because labour market participation is strongly dependant on education. It is also essential when projecting labour supply. An educational model gives a broad range of possibilities for analysing effects of demographical changes and changes in the educational behaviour.

References

Arnesen, C.Å. 2010. *Kandidatundersøkelsen 2009*. Rapport 18/2010. Oslo: NIFU STEP.

Bjørnstad, R, Gjelsvik, M.L. et al. 2010. *Demand and supply of labour by education towards 2030*. Rapport 39/2010. Oslo: Statistics Norway.

Brunborg, H., Texmon, I. and Tønnesen, M. 2012. *Befolkningsframskrivninger 2012–2100: Modeller og forutsetninger.* ØA 4/2012. Oslo: Statistics Norway.

Card, D. 1995. The Wage Curve: A Review. *Journal of Economic Literature*, 33, 785–99.

Drage, N., Havnes, T. and Sandsør, A. 2012. *Kindergarten for all: Lung run effects of a universal intervention*. Discussion Paper 695. Oslo: Statistics Norway.

Fredriksen, D. 1998. *Projections of Population, Education, Lobour supply and Public Pension Benefits – Analyses with the Dynamic Microsimulation Model MOSART*. Social and Economic Studies 101. Oslo: Statistics Norway.

Greene, W.H. 2008. *Econometric Analysis*. 6th edition. New Jersey: Pearson Prentice Hall.

Ministry of Education and Research. 14.11.1996. *Dette er grunnskolereformen*. Available at: http://www.regjeringen.no/nb/dokumentarkiv/regjeringen-brundt land-iii/kuf/veiledninger/1996/reform-97-dette-er-grunnskolereformen.html ?id=87403 [accessed 30/01/2013].

Norwegian State Educational Loan Fund. 2011. *Fag og nivå 2010–2011-gradsstudenter.* Available at: http://www.lanekassen.no/nb-NO/Toppmeny/ Om_Lanekassen/Statistikk/utlandsstatistikk/Elever-og-studenter-i-utlandet/ Studenter-fag-og-niva/Fag-og-niva-gradsstudenter-2010-2011[accessed 30/01/2013].

Roksvaag, K. and Texmon, I. 2012a. *Arbeidsmarkedet for helse og sosialpersonell fram mot år 2035*. Report 2012/14. Oslo: Statistics Norway.

Roksvaag, K. and Texmon, I. 2012b. *Arbeidsmarkedet for lærere og førskolelærere fram mot år 2035*. Report 2012/18. Oslo: Statistics Norway.

Samordna Opptak. 2012. *Realkompetanse*. Available at: http://www.samord naopptak.no/info/opptak/andre-veier-til-opptak/realkompetanse/ [accessed 30/01/2013].

Statistics Norway. 2012a. *Fakta om utdanning 2012 – nøkkeltall fra 2010*. Kongsvinger: Statistics Norway.

Statistics Norway. 2012b. *Utdanningsnivå – om statistikken*. Available at: http:// www.ssb.no/vis/emner/04/01/utniv/om.html [accessed 30/01/2013].

UNESCO. 2006. *ISCED 1997*. Available at: http://www.uis.unesco.org/Library/ Documents/isced97-en.pdf [accessed 30/01/2013].

Chapter 19

What are the Driving Forces behind Trends in Inequality among Pensioners? Validating MIDAS Belgium Using a Stylized Model

Gijs Dekkers[1]

Introduction

Possible future trends in the development of pension adequacy are usually simulated using dynamic microsimulation models. These models are very complex and include many different processes. This, and the many individual interactions, make it difficult to see which procedures and relations underlie the observed simulation results. Hence, the discussion of simulation results, and especially trends, tends to be based on 'common sense reasoning' using only a few fundamental parameters. As an example, the discussion of the simulation results of the Belgian version of the MIDAS model (Dekkers et al. 2010) hinges on fundamental relations between demographic ageing, the indexation of pensions to the development of wages, and inequality of pensions and the poverty risk among pensioners.

If this strategy to explain the simulation results from a dynamic MSM is valid, then a simple stylized model describing these fundamental relations should be able to capture the long-term trends reflected by the dynamic microsimulation model. Making this case is a first goal of this chapter.

A second goal of this chapter is to propose this approach as another strategy to reduce the black box problem of dynamic microsimulation models and therefore to validate these models. Morrison (2007: 5) defines the validation of any model as 'the comparison of the model's results to counterpart values that are known or believed to be correct, or that are consistent with one's assumptions, [or] other trustworthy models' results'. The results of the stylized model could then be comparable to those of a dynamic microsimulation model (henceforth MSM), and the results from the former could be used to validate the latter.

---

1 The author wishes to thank Jinjing Li, Frank Vandenbroucke, Asghar Zaidi and the participants of the 'European Workshop on Dynamic Microsimulation', Brussels, 4 March 2010, the Séminaire Scientifique 2010, Caisse des depots, Bordeaux, France, 29 March 2010, and the 3rd General Conference of the International Microsimulation Association, Stockholm, June 2011, for comments on an earlier version of this chapter. The stata code of the model presented in this paper is available upon request.

Of course, a meaningful comparison requires that the stylized model reflects the same fundamental parameters that the MSM does. This chapter uses such a simple model to show some general relations between indexation, retirement age, demographic ageing and the inequality of pensions. The results of this stylized model are then compared to simulation results of MIDAS Belgium.

The Base Model

Suppose a basic model which starts in period t = 0 and simulates up to period 100. In the starting year, there are 100 individuals of each age. Individuals are born at the age 0 and die at the age of 100. So each period, one individual is born and one dies. For all others, their ages increase by one each period. In this simple setting, in each period t ≥ 0, there are 100 individuals, each of a different age. So, age_t = [0, … , 100], t = [0, … , 100].

Next, assume that everybody retires at 60 and dies at 100, and assume furthermore that the pension benefit at 60 equals €100. Finally, the model is expressed relative to the development of wages, and we suppose that pensions lag behind the development of wages with a constant fraction Ψ per year. Equivalently, in any year, pensions decrease with a rate Ψ with increasing age. So in the starting year 0, pension benefits of an individual of age ≥ 60, denoted $p_{0,age}$, equals €100 times $(1-\Psi)^{age-60}$, and pensions at time t > 0 then amount to

$$P_{t,age} = \begin{cases} p_0(1-\psi)^t, & if \quad age_0 > 60 \\ 100(1-\psi)^{t-(60-age_0)}, & if \quad age_0 < 60 \ \& \ age \geq 60 \end{cases} \quad (1)$$

With age_t or age equals age_0 + t. The condition $age_t \leq 100 \ \forall \ t$ applies to all equations, and is therefore left out. The first line of (1) describes those that are retired in the starting year 0, and the second line describes the pension benefit of those that retire between 2000 and t.

The top pane of Figure 19.1 plots the pension benefits $P_{t,age}$ for a situation where Ψ equals 1.25 per cent. The pension benefit of an individual pensioner obviously decreases over time (or – equivalently – with age) but as the age distribution itself remains constant over time, so does the distribution of pensions. Hence, the base setup of this simple model results in inequality being constant over time, and being higher with a higher value of the parameter Ψ. Inversely stated, the higher this parameter, i.e. the more benefits of those in retirement lag behind the development of wages over time, the more the benefit of older pensioners decreases; not in amounts but relative to the development of wages, and the higher income inequality will be. Indeed, a value of Ψ = 5% results in the Gini being equal to 33 per cent; a more realistic value of Ψ equal to 1.25 per cent still causes the Gini to be equal to 8.55 per cent.

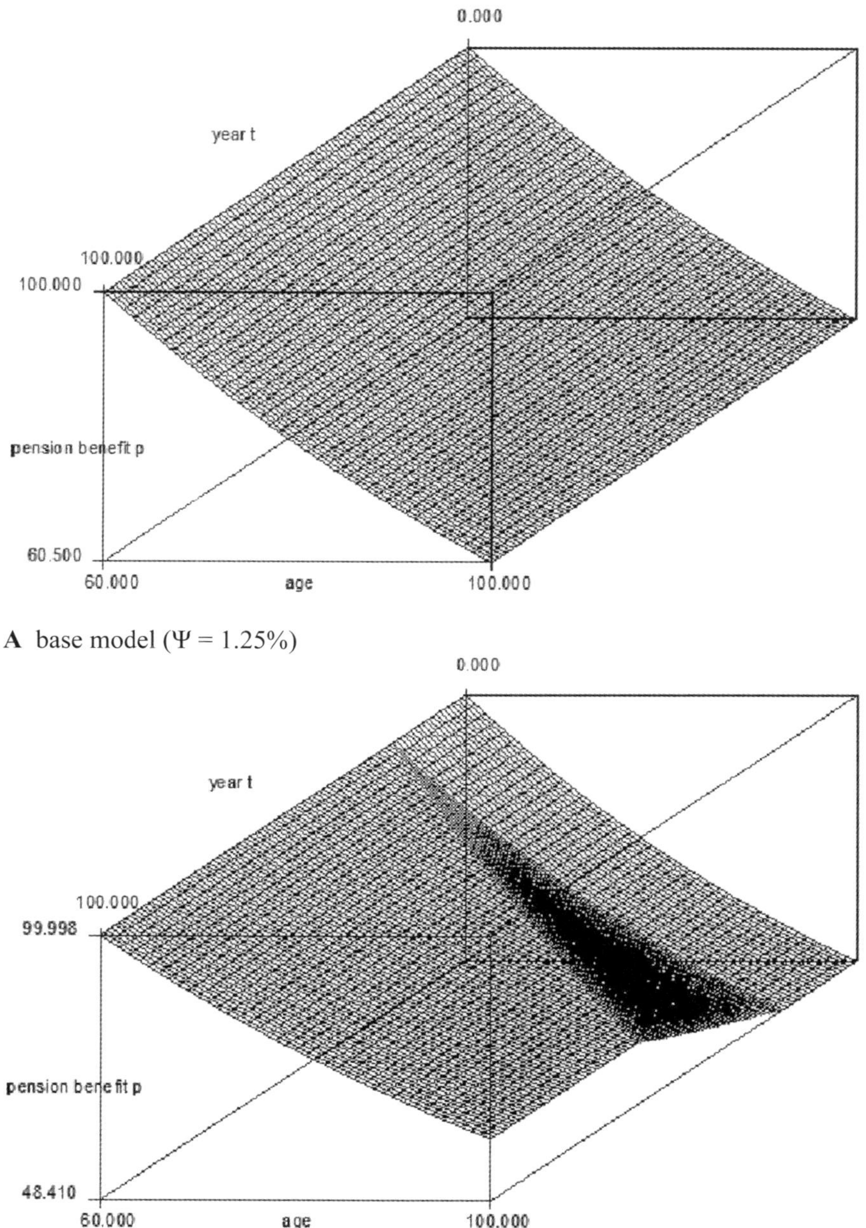

A base model (Ψ = 1.25%)

B Ψ decreases from 1.8 to 1.25 in t = 20

Figure 19.1   **Base model (Ψ = 1.25%) and a change of the indexation parameter**

The next sections will introduce various extensions of this base model. We set off by considering the impact of an inter-temporal change of the indexation parameter Ψ, in combination with changes of the retirement age. Next, the impact of the two driving forces behind demographic ageing – changes in fertility and mortality – will be considered separately as well as jointly.

Changes of the Indexation of Pensions, and the Impact of the Retirement Age

A first extension of the model is to allow for intertemporal one-shot changes of the lag-parameter Ψ. The Belgian case shows that this is a relevant extension. The Ageing Working Group (EC 2007: Table 3.1, 53) assumes in its projections on the financial sustainability of pensions in Belgium that pension benefits lag 1.25 per cent behind the development of wages. Fasquelle et al. (2008: 2) however show that this lag was on average 1.8 per cent between 1956 and 2002. This difference implies a reinforcement of the future link between wages and pension benefits. What will be the impact of this reinforcement on inequality? Suppose that the lag parameter changes from Ψ_1 to Ψ_2 in the period *cht*, with $0 < cht < 100$. The pension benefit of an individual of age in year t equals

$$
P_{t,age} = \begin{cases}
p_0(1-\psi_1)^t, & if & (age_0 > 60)\,\&\,(t < cht) \\
p_0(1-\psi_1)^{cht}(1-\psi_2)^{(t-cht)}, & if & (age_0 > 60)\,\&\,(t \geq cht) \\
100(1-\psi_1)^{t-(60-age_0)}, & if & (age_0 < 60)\,\&\,(age \geq 60)\,\&\,((60-age_0) < cht)\,\&\,(t < cht) \\
\dfrac{100(1-\psi_1)^{cht}(1-\psi_2)^{(t-cht)}}{(1-\psi_1)^{(60-age_0)}}, & if & age_0 < 60\,\&\,age \geq 60)\,\&\,((60-age_0) < cht)\,\&\,(t \geq cht) \\
100(1-\psi_2)^{t-(60-age_0)}, & if & (age_0 < 60)\,\&\,(age \geq 60)\,\&\,((60-age_0) \geq cht)\,\&\,(t \geq cht)
\end{cases} \tag{2}
$$

The first and third lines of equation (2) are simple replications of (1) and pertain to the years before the change of Ψ in *cht*. The second line describes the situation where the lag variable changes for those that were retired in the starting year. The fourth line describes the pension benefit at time t of someone who retires after the starting year, but before the year cht in which Ψ changes. Finally, the fifth line reflects the situation of someone who retires after *cht*. Of course, the condition $\Psi_1 = \Psi_2$ causes (2) to collapse again to (1).

What happens when Ψ decreases from 1.8 to 1.25 in $cht = 20$? This is shown in the right pane of Figure 19.1. The pension benefit at death (shown at the east surface of the box) starts to gradually increase, shown at $t = 20$, which depicts a situation where the lag between wages and pensions (i.e. the relative decrease of the latter over time) becomes smaller. The surface at that time starts to increase up the x-axis, meaning that the average pension at each age increases. Furthermore, the downward slope of the surface becomes smaller (compare the slope at the south side of the box with the north side). The relative decrease of the benefit to older retirees indeed is slowed down as a result of strengthening the link between pensions and wages, not only relative to workers but also to younger retirees (who retired later). As a result, the inequality of pension benefits will gradually decrease. After a while, the oldest individuals who have had their pension up rated under the weak linkage regime, will decease, and the population of pensioners will increasingly consist of those that only have had their pensions indexed under the more generous regime.

Hence, inequality will settle down at a lower level. This development is shown in Figure 19.2. For the time being, consider only the development of the Gini with retirement age 60 and the lag-parameter Ψ decreasing from 1.8 to 1.25 in t = 20. This is the full line in Figure 19.3 that must be set against the left vertical axis. These results hence are equivalent to the results shown in Figure 19.2. The Gini starts off a bit higher than 0.12 and remains on that level until t = 20. Then a gradual decrease sets in, and inequality stabilizes again around t = 60 at a level around .085. The transition phase is therefore 40 years and this obviously is equal to the number of years that an individual is in retirement. This confirms that the new 'steady state' is reached when all individuals who have had their pension uprated under the weak linkage will have deceased.

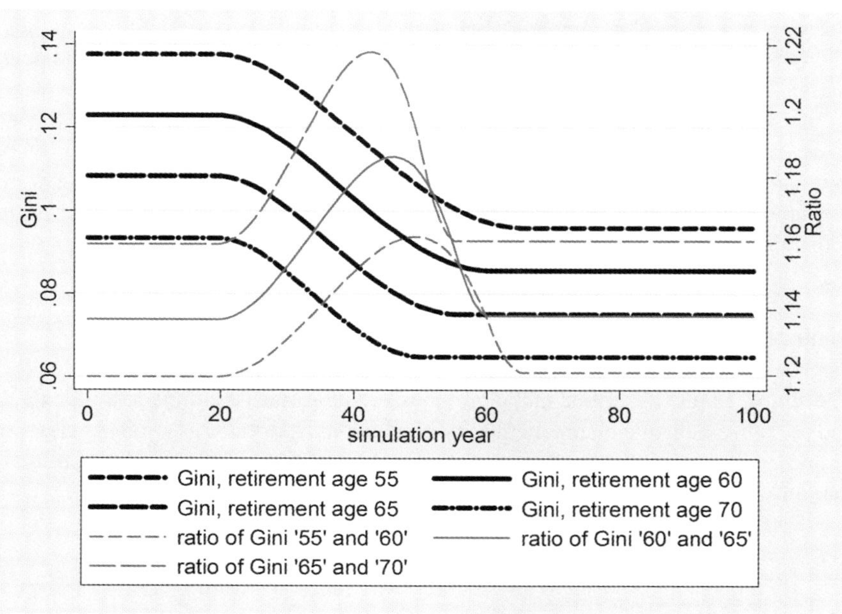

Figure 19.2   The impact of a decrease of Ψ from 1.8 to 1.25 in t = 20 on the inequality of pension benefits

The number of years that a typical individual is in retirement therefore sets the transition phase following a change of the indexation parameter. Or, the higher the retirement age, the shorter the transition phase. But let us look at this interaction of the retirement age and changes of the indexation parameter Ψ in more detail. First of all, the various dotted lines Figure 19.2 above show the impact of the indexation parameter when the typical individual does not retire at 60, but at 55, 65 or 70 years old. Given the value of the indexation parameter Ψ, the lower (higher) the retirement age, the higher (lower) inequality, because one receives the pension benefit for more (less) years and the total lag ($\Psi^{(100\text{-age of retirement})}$) therefore increases (decreases).

The retirement age hence does not only affect the level of inequality, it also affects how fast the system reacts to changes of the indexation parameter Ψ. This is shown by the grey lines in Figure 19.2 that must be compared to the right vertical axis. The long-dotted line shows the ratio of inequality with retirement age 65 and 70; the full line shows the ratio of inequality with retirement age 60 and 65. Finally, the short-dotted line shows the ratio of inequality with retirement ages 55 and 60. The fact that the highest retirement ages results in the highest curve reflects an increasing marginal impact of an increasing retirement age. Put differently, if the retirement age is low, then a change of the retirement age by one year has a smaller impact on inequality as when the retirement age is high. The reason for this is that the numbers of years that one receives a pension benefit decreases with an increasing retirement age. An increase of the retirement age by one year hence has a proportionally stronger impact if one is closer to the age of death. Furthermore, the higher the retirement age, the faster inequality reacts to a change in the indexation parameter Ψ, and the sooner the impact wears off. A society with a low retirement age digests a change of the indexation parameter considerably more slowly, not only relative but also marginally.

Demographic Ageing, Indexation and Inequality

The simple model described in the previous section shows the impact of indexation and the retirement age on the inequality of pensions. It does so assuming a situation of no demographic ageing. So inequality is a direct function of the distribution of the individual pension values P:

$$Gini_t = F\left\{P_{t,60}, \quad \cdots \quad, P_{t,age>60}, \quad \cdots \quad, P_{t,100}\right\} \tag{3}$$

where F denotes the steps to derive the Gini out of the vector of pensions. The values of $P_{t,age}$ are again derived using equations (1) or (2). In this section, the retirement age is again equal to 60.

Now demographic ageing can be the result of past changes in the fertility rates, or by decreases in mortality rates, i.e. a continuous increase of life expectancy. If there has been an important but temporary increase of the fertility rate in a certain period, then this will result in a 'baby boom generation', that is, a cohort that is larger than the surrounding cohorts. A second process that can result in demographic ageing is a continuous increase of life expectancy. This model can mimic both processes and therefore simulate their impact on pension inequality.

Demographic Ageing Resulting from a 'Baby Boom Generation'

The first reason for demographic ageing is the existence of a 'baby boom generation', caused by past changes of the fertility rate. In the stylized context of our model, this can be reflected by a non-uniform distribution of age in the initial period t=0. Denote Π_t the vector of pensions P at time t. Then equation (3) can be written as

$$F\{\Pi_t\} \text{ with } \Pi_t = \left| P_{t,60} \quad \cdots \quad P_{t,age>60} \quad \cdots \quad P_{t,100} \right| \text{ or}$$

$$\Pi_t = \left| P_{t,60} \quad \cdots \quad P_{t,age>60} \quad \cdots \quad P_{t,100} \right| \begin{vmatrix} 1 & . & 0 & . & 0 \\ . & . & . & . & . \\ 0 & . & 1 & . & 0 \\ . & . & . & . & . \\ 0 & . & 0 & . & 1 \end{vmatrix} \tag{3'}$$

A simple extension of this model then is to include the impact of ageing by introducing weights w, as $Gini_t^W = F\{\Pi_t^W\}$ and

$$\Pi_t^W = \left| P_{t,60} \quad \cdots \quad P_{t,age>60} \quad \cdots \quad P_{t,100} \right| \begin{vmatrix} w_{t,60} & . & 0 & . & 0 \\ . & . & . & . & . \\ 0 & . & w_{t,age>60} & . & 0 \\ . & . & . & . & . \\ 0 & . & 0 & . & w_{t,100} \end{vmatrix} \tag{4}$$

with $w_{0,age0}$ = N(43, 23) and $w_{t,age}$ = $w_{0,(age-t)}$. The variable $w_{t,age}$ is essentially a frequency weight used to change the proportional size of age-groups in order to reflect the impact of ageing. In the basic model, in real terms, there are 100 individuals in time t ≥ 0, each of a different age (so, age_t = [0, ... , 100], $\forall$ t = [0, ... , 100]. Now we weigh this dataset by $w_{0,age0}$ in the starting year t = 0 in such a way that the distribution of age_0 has mean 43 and standard deviation 23. These figures are derived from the Belgian PSBH dataset of 2002, used as the starting dataset of the MIDAS-model. So the weights only adapt the distribution of age in the starting year t = 0 instead of having just one individual for each age in the starting dataset, this (weighted) number is now normally distributed around the age of 43. This is shown in pane A of Figure 19.3. The ageing process itself remains as it was before. In the later years, the weight obviously remains the same as the individual ages. Thus, for example, the weight that the 45-year-old has at $t = 5$ is equal to the weight of the 40-year-old in $t = 0$. This is analogous to a larger or smaller cohort moving upwards in an age-pyramid graph. Finally, the weight of any newborn cohorts is again equal to 1, as in the base-variant. This reflects that the change in fertility is not permanent and that the base situation will in the very long run be restored. The resulting distribution of $w_{t,age}$ is for various years shown in the panes A to C of Figure 19.3. Remember that demographic ageing is here represented as the result of past changes in the fertility rates. The short run impact of weighing the dataset at $t = 0$ to reflect demographic ageing is shown in pane A of Figure 19.3.[2] The median of the age distribution shifts to the right as the modal cohort becomes older. Furthermore, the distribution gradually becomes skewed to the left as the base situation (where all cohorts are of equal size) is restored. This is especially the case in the long run, as shown in pane B of Figure 19.3. Here, we see that the baby boom cohort shifts to the right even further. Once the right tail of the 'bump' reaches the age of decease (100), its size decreases and the distribution becomes more platykurtic. This reflects the situation that the baseline, where every cohort is the same size, is starting to be restored. In $t = 90$, all members of the baby boom cohorts have deceased, all cohorts are again of the same size and the distribution function is uniform.

The pane C of Figure 19.3 shows the densities of age > 60 for the same years as in pane B of the same figure.

In the starting year, the modus of the age distribution is 43 and thus well below the retirement age of 60. As a result, age is almost equally distributed in pane C of Figure 19.3, and there is only a small impact in the youngest ages. But as t increases, the oldest members of the baby boom cohorts enter into retirement. As a result, the frequency of younger ages increases at the expense of older ages (see the line of $t = 30$ in pane C of Figure 19.3). Around $t = 17$, the majority of the members of the 'baby boom' cohorts will have reached the retirement age. At this point, the frequency of older age groups increases at the expense of those of younger age groups (see the line of $t = 60$). After that, as shown in the previous Figures, the members of the baby boom cohorts decease, and the age distribution returns back to its normal, horizontal, shape (see the line of $t = 90$), which is very close to the shape in the starting year.

---

2   Note that the KDE of $w0,age$ does not fit a normal distribution. This is because in generating the weight, the corresponding ages were not bounded (i.e. they could be negative or more than 100), whereas the KDEs shown in Figure 19.1 reflect the truncated distribution of age.

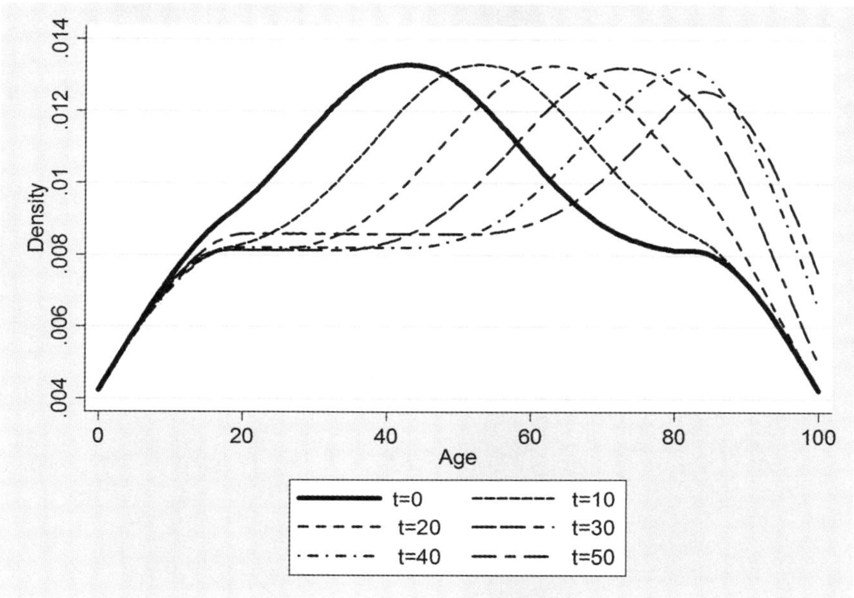

A t ≤ 50

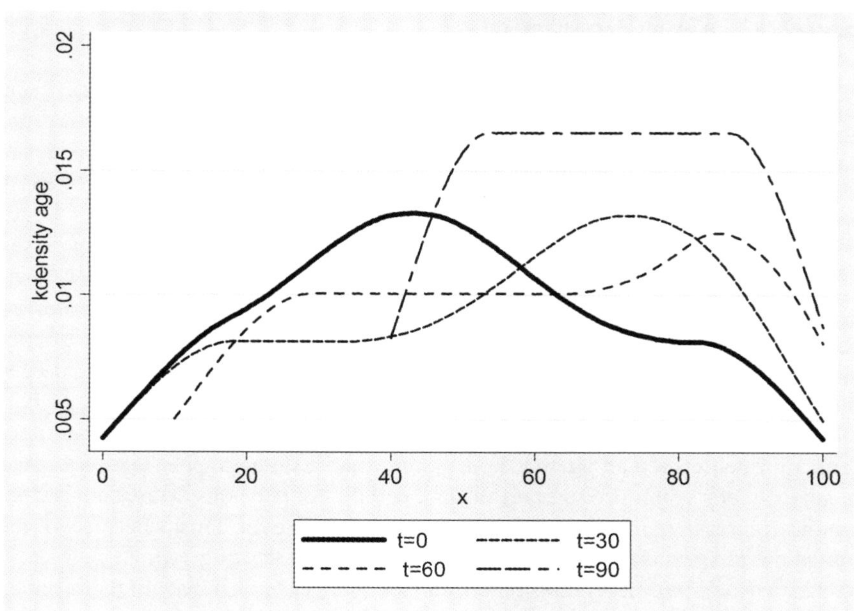

B t ≤ 90

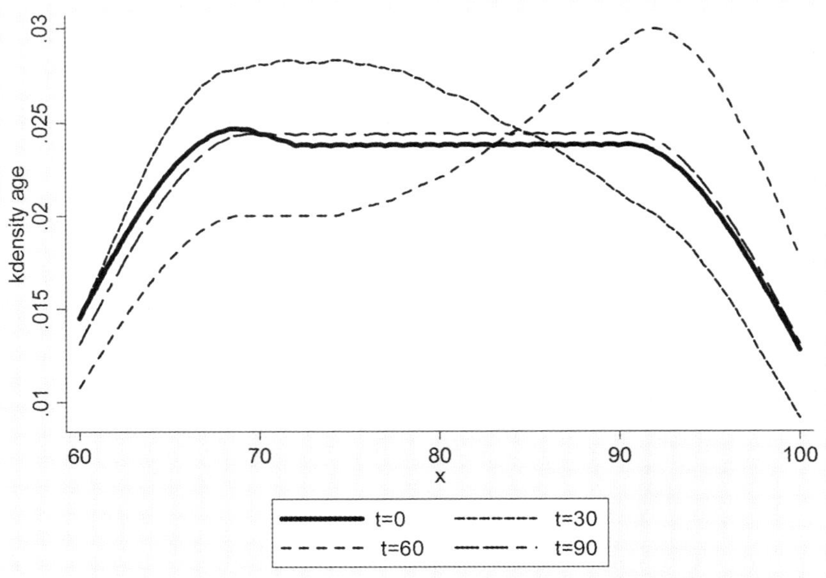

C age ≥ 60 at t ≤ 90

Figure 19.3   Kernel density of age

Now what is the impact of introducing demographic ageing in our model? The pane A of Figure 19.4 shows the impact using various values of Ψ, ranging from 5 per cent to 0.5 per cent. This figure confirms that inequality increases with the value of the lag. Secondly and not surprisingly, the impact of ageing increases with the size of the lag. Indeed, when pensions increase by the same rate as wages (Ψ = 0), then changes in the age distribution of pensioners have no impact on the distribution of pensions. The impact of ageing on inequality of pensions increases with the size of Ψ. The third conclusion is more surprising and is that the impact of this first type of demographic ageing appears limited. It is only when we apply an unrealistically high value for the lag (Ψ = 2.5% or more) that a pattern emerges in the development of the Gini of pensions. This confirms Harding's (1993) conclusion that uprating to social policy hypotheses has a considerably stronger impact on pensions than ageing. Fourth and finally, demographic ageing caused by adjacent baby boom cohorts results in inequality of pensions decreasing at first, and then increasing, after which it returns to its stable level. This is because of the typical pattern pertaining to this type of ageing. In the starting year as well as t = 90, age is nearly uniformly distributed, and inequality of pensions will therefore be on or close to its 'base situation value'. But as time goes by, the oldest members of the baby boom cohorts enter retirement. As a result, the average age of pensioners will decrease, and this cet. par. will cause the inequality of pensions to decrease.

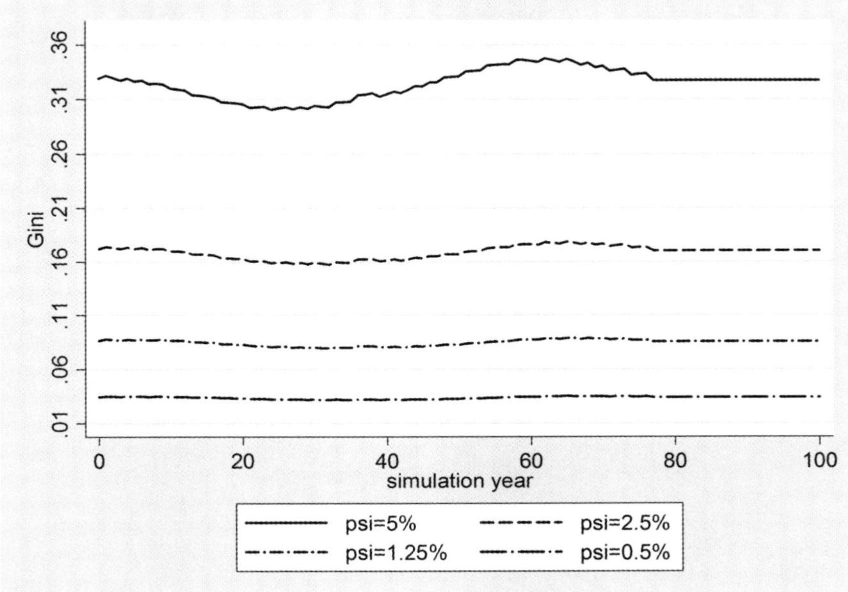

A changes of fertility rates

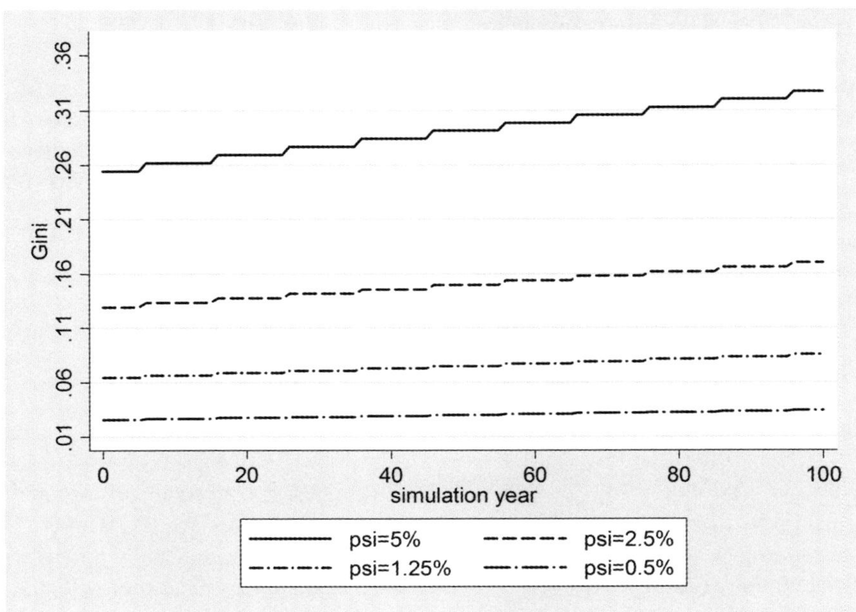

B a continuous increase of life expectancy

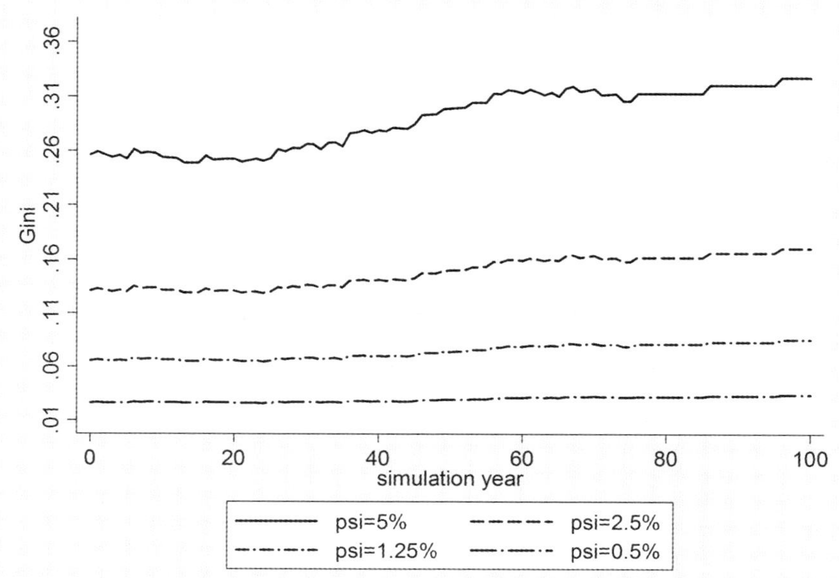

C compound effect

Figure 19.4   The impact of ageing on pension inequality

Around t = 17, the majority of the 'baby boom' will have reached the retirement age. At this point, the average age of the pension recipients will slowly start to increase – and so will inequality of pensions. This increase will continue until the last pensioners of the baby boom cohorts have deceased, and from that year on, inequality will settle down to its base value.

Demographic Ageing Resulting from a Continuous Increase in Life Expectancy

This is a very simple extension of equation (3), where the ending age of 100 is replaced by a variable that depends on time

$$Gini_t = F\left\{P_{t,60}, \quad \dots \quad , P_{t,age>60}, \quad \dots \quad , P_{t,x}\right\} \tag{5}$$

with x = g(t) $\forall$ t = [0, ... , 100]. According to the most recent demographic projections, life expectancy at birth in Belgium will increase by 10.19 and 9.52 years over a period of 60 years (between 2000 and 2060) for men and women (see FPS Economy (2009)). This section shows the consequences of assuming that the age of death x increases by 10 years, from 90 in period 0 to 100 in period 100. Hence, x in equation 5 equals [90+((100-90)/100) × t].

Starting in period 0, the age of death increases. As pensions decrease with Ψ for every year that one is in retirement, the level of the pension at death decreases as well. Given the indexation parameter Ψ, the pension benefit at death decreases, and we can therefore expect the inequality of pensions to increase. This is shown in pane B of Figure 19.4 showing the positive impact of an increasing life-expectancy on income inequality.[3] This figure again confirms that a higher value of the indexation parameter Ψ obviously makes the inequality of pension benefits more vulnerable to changes in life-expectancy. In the extreme, when all pensions follow wages, the level of pensions will be independent of the age of the pensioner, and the inequality of pensions will be unaffected by whatever demographic change.

Hence, demographic ageing consists of two separate effects. First of all, there is ageing caused by past ruptures in the fertility rate. This causes some cohorts to be larger than others. Ageing occurs as such a large birth cohort becomes older. Secondly, ageing can occur through an increase of life-expectancy. The impact of the first underlying factor of demographic ageing on pension-inequality is ambiguous in that it depends on the median (or modal age group) of the distribution. In contrast, increasing life expectancy cet. par. has an unambiguously increasing impact of the inequality of pensions. Finally, pane C of Figure 19.4 shows the combination of the two demographic phenomena.

As in the previous figures, the baseline level of inequality increases with the indexation parameter Ψ. Equally obvious, the developments in pane C of Figure 19.4 are a combination of the results depicted in pane A and B; the positive trend in inequality is caused by the development of life-expectancy, whereas the development of the baby boom generation through the various phases of retirement, causes the actual level of inequality to 'wobble' around this trend. At any moment in time, the actual level of inequality of pensions is therefore a function of the indexation parameter Ψ and demographic ageing. In this, the impact of the former is considerably more important in explaining the level of pension-inequality than the latter.

Comparison with Results of the Belgian MIDAS Model

To what extent do the simulation results of the stylized model reflect possible future trends in inequality among pensioners? Or, inversely stated, to what extent do the results from the stylized model validate those of the MSM?

---

3   Note that the simulation results of pane B of Figure 19.4 describe a situation where life expectancy gradually increases to 100, the level used in the previous simulations. Hence, the level of inequality in the last simulation year, $t = 100$, equals that in the starting year in the pane A of the same Figure, given the level of Ψ.

This section compares the results of the stylized model presented in the previous sections to validate the simulation results from the Belgian version of the dynamic MSM MIDAS (henceforth MIDAS_BE).[4]

In its original setup, MIDAS was developed in the context of a European-funded FP7 project called AIM, and was designed to simulate future developments of the adequacy of pensions in Italy, Germany and Belgium, following wherever possible the projections and assumptions of the AWG. MIDAS_BE starts from the PSBH cross-sectional survey dataset representing a population of all ages in 2002 (8,488 individuals). MIDAS consists of different modules, the demographic module, the labour market module and the pension module. The pension module of MIDAS_BE simulates first-pillar old-age pension benefits for private sector employees, civil servants and self employed. Furthermore, it simulates the Conventional Early Retirements (CELS) benefit, the disability pension benefit for private sector employees, and – finally – the widow(er)s' pension benefit, again for private sector employees, civil servants as well as self employed. The results of the fertility and mortality routines in the demographic module of MIDAS are aligned to the demographic projections of the AWG.

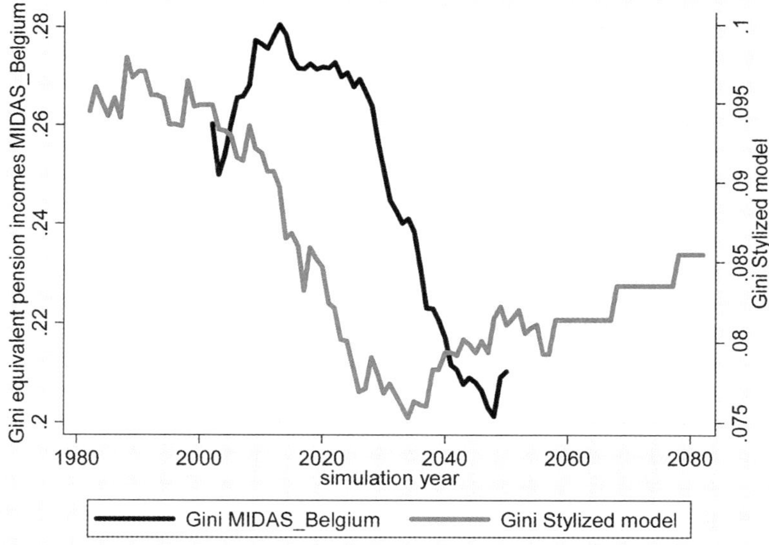

Figure 19.5   Comparison of the results with those of MIDAS_Belgium

---

4   For a thorough discussion of MIDAS and its simulation results, please consult Dekkers et al. 2010. Note that the version of the model used in this chapter is today replaced by a new version that runs on an administrative dataset of about 2.2 million individuals, or one-fifth of the Belgian population. See High Council of Finances 2012, page 83 and further, and Dekkers et al. 2013.

The variants applied in the stylized model and discussed in previous sections of this chapter were chosen deliberately to fit the assumptions of MIDAS wherever possible. The age distribution of our stylized model had been based on the PSBH in 2002; the development of life expectancy is based on projections of the FPS economy (2009). Furthermore, the AWG assumes a lag of ongoing pensions of 1.25 per cent per year from 2002 onwards, whereas Fasquelle et al. (2008: 2) show that this lag was on average 1.8 per cent between 1956 and 2002. As the stylized model simulates the same decrease in period $cht = 20$, the starting year in the above Figure 19.5 is set to 1982 so that $cht = 20$ coincides with 2002.

The Gini of equivalent total pension benefit generated by MIDAS_Be (from now on referred to as 'the MIDAS series') is the black line in Figure 19.5 and should be compared to the left scale. It is equal to the inequality of pensions depicted in Figure 2 of Dekkers et al. 2010. The Gini of pensions generated by the simple, stylized model (henceforth 'the stylized model series'), is simulated taking into account both types of ageing (weighting of the age-groups and an increase of life expectancy of 10 years over 100 simulation years), a decrease of Ψ from 1.8 to 1.25 per cent and, finally, a retirement age of 60. The Gini resulting from this 'full' version of the stylized model is the grey line in Figure 19.5 and should be compared to the right scale.

Next the results shown in Figure 19.5 are discussed. First of all, the comparison between the stylized model series in Figure 19.5 and pane C of 19.4 reveals that the impact of the indexation variable Ψ on inequality is considerably stronger than the impact of ageing. This can also be seen by comparing pane C of Figure 19.4 with the series in Figure 19.2. Secondly, the scales on the right and left vertical axes of Figure 19.5 are different. Inequality in the MIDAS-series is considerably higher than that of the stylized model, among other things because the latter assumes away all earnings inequality. But even though the level differs, the development of both series is remarkably comparable, and the same goes for the proportional size of the drop of inequality over time. It appears that the stylized model series precedes the MIDAS-series with roughly 20 years. The decrease of the MIDAS-series itself is reflected by the stylized model series, so remains to explain why the former follows the latter with such delay.[5]

There are at least three possible explanations for this delay in the MIDAS-series. First of all, the stylized model assumes fully equal earnings, causing all pensions to be equal to 100 euro in the year of retirement. This assumption of fully equal earnings is of course a gross simplification relative to the MIDAS model. Even though toned down by the redistributive elements in the pension system, increasing earnings inequality from about 2005 on causes the inequality of pensions to increase over time as well. This effect is reinforced by an increase of the annual productivity growth rate from 1.5 to 1.8 in 2010 (see Dekkers et al.

---

5   In fact, should the simulation results of the two models have been 'too much' alike, then one could have questioned the value added of expensive and time-consuming dynamic microsimulation models over the easy and straightforward stylized model.

2009, section 4.3.1., page 101). Relative to the stylized model series, the impact of earnings inequality on pension inequality thus increases in later decades. Inversely stated is the impact of the changing indexation parameter on the MIDAS-series in the first decade countered by the impact of increasing earnings inequality.

A second reason for the delay is that the stylized model is affected by a few parameters, among which the indexation parameter Ψ is the most important. In contrast, the Belgian version of MIDAS includes many other parameters (op. cit., section 4.3.1., page 101), linking the development of ceilings, floors and minimum pensions to the development of wages. Also, inequality of pensions in the latter model is based on equivalent household income, meaning that changes in the size and composition of the households in the sample affect the simulation results.

Third, the pension module of MIDAS_BE not only includes employees' pension benefits, but also civil servants' pension benefits, early retirement benefits and minimum pension benefits. The indexation regime linking the development of these benefits to that of wages differs from the employees' pensions' indexation regime.

In short, the simulation results in MIDAS_BE are a composite of many different pension types, indexation regimes and various other effects and changes, most of them unrelated to the change of the indexation parameter of employees' pensions. It therefore is not surprising that the simulation results of MIDAS_BE react more sluggishly to the change of this indexation parameter than the stylized model does.

Finally, in line with the goals of this chapter, this resemblance between the simulation results of the two models makes it possible to use the stylized model to shed light into the black box that the MSM is. The simulation results of the stylized model confirm that the strengthening of the link between wages and benefits is clearly the most important determinant of the development of inequality; only in the long run does demographic ageing, and especially the continuous increase of life expectancy, have a positive impact on inequality.

Conclusions

This chapter presents a simple model that relates the indexation of pensions in conjunction with demographic ageing and the retirement age, to the development of inequality of pensions. This results in several conclusions. First, the more pensions lag with the development of wages, the higher inequality of pensions at any point in time. Furthermore, the higher the retirement age, the lower the inequality of pensions. Third, the higher the retirement age, the faster inequality of pensions reacts to changes of the lag of pensions to the development of wages. Fourth, the two underlying causes of demographic ageing each have a different impact on the inequality of pensions. The impact of a baby boom generation on inequality is ambiguous and depends on the average age of this generation. If its members are young pensioners, inequality of pension benefits is reduced. As the members of the baby boom generation become older pensioners, inequality increases even slightly above its base level. The second cause for demographic ageing, an increasing life expectancy, has an unambiguous increasing impact on the inequality of pensions.

Finally, the stylized model suggests that the impact of the indexation regime is the most important determinant of the development of inequality; only in the long run does demographic ageing, and especially the continuous increase of life expectancy, cause inequality to increase.

These findings obviously are not new. However, they are generated by a very rudimentary model; anyone can therefore see how the simulation results are generated and how the conclusions come about. This stylized model, developed in Stata, will be available upon request from the author, and can easily be adapted to the circumstances of other countries.

The simulation results from the stylized model are then compared to the simulated prospective development of pensions' inequality in the MIDAS_Be model. The base level of inequality is obviously considerably different, and the simulation results of the latter react more sluggishly to the change of the indexation parameter than the former.

One possible reason for this delay is the impact of earnings inequality on pension inequality; extending the stylized model with earnings inequality is a subject for future research. But besides that, the simulation results of the stylized model seem to validate the results of MIDAS_BE.

References

Dekkers, G., Buslei, H., Cozzolino, M., Desmet, R., Geyer, J., Hofmann, D., Raitano, M., Steiner, V, Tanda, P., Tedeschi, S. and Verschueren, F. 2009. What are the consequences of the European AWG-projections on the adequacy of pensions? An application of the dynamic micro simulation model MIDAS for Belgium, Germany and Italy, ENEPRI Research Report No 65, AIM WP4. http://shop.ceps.eu/BookDetail.php?item_id=1780 [accessed: 23/09/2013].

Dekkers, G., Buslei, H., Cozzolino, M., Desmet, R., Geyer, J., Hofmann, D., Raitano, M., Steiner, V, Tanda, P., Tedeschi, S. and Verschueren, F. 2010. The flip side of the coin: the consequences of the European budgetary projections on the adequacy of social security pensions. *European Journal of Social Security*, 12(2), 94–120.

Dekkers , G., Desmet, R., Fasquelle, N. and Weemaes, S. 2013. The social and budgetary impacts of recent social security reform in Belgium. Paper presented at the IMPALLA-ESPANET International Conference 'Building blocks for an inclusive society: empirical evidence from social policy research', Luxembourg, 18 and 19 April, 2013.

European Commission EC. 2007. Pension Schemes and Pension Models in the EU25 Member States, European Economy Occasional Papers, n. 35/2007.

Fasquelle, N., Festjens, M.J. and Scholtus, B. 2008. Wel-vaartsbinding van de sociale zekerheidsuitkeringen: een overzicht van de recente ontwikkelingen, Working paper 8–08, Federal Planning Bureau, Brussels.

FPS Economy, S.M.E'.s, Self-Employed and Energy. 2009. Demografische indicatoren – Bevolkingsvooruitzichten 2007–2060. http://economie.fgov.be/nl/binaries/CoefBelg_nl%5B1%5D_tcm325-34234.xls [accessed: 23/09/2013].

Harding, A. 1993. *Lifetime Income Distribution and Redistribution: applications of a micro simulation model*, Contributions to Economic Analysis, vol. 221. Amsterdam: North Holland.

High Council of Finances / Conseil Supérieur des Finances. 2012. *Rapport Annuel du Comité d'Etude sur le Vieillissement.*

Morrison, R. 2007. DYNACAN Validation, Unpublished Working Paper, the DYNACAN team.

Chapter 20

An Investigation of the Sensitivity of a Dynamic Microsimulation Model of Urban Neighbourhood Dynamics

Mark Birkin and Nicolas Malleson

Background

In this chapter we discuss a dynamic spatial microsimulation model of a city region. The overall approach is to characterize the population as a series of individuals with specific demographic attributes, in which the core attributes are age, gender, occupation, marital status, health and ethnicity. The individuals are combined into households, and acquire further properties (tenure, housing type) in addition to membership qualities (household size, age and occupation etc. of the head). Populations are characterized using synthetic estimation procedures, so that for any small area the individuals are realistic, but not in any meaningful sense real or identifiable. More detail on the estimation of initial or baseline populations is provided by Harland et al. (2012), while the dynamics are discussed by Wu et al. (2010). The population of quite large cities, or even countries, can be represented quite comfortably in this way using the computational resources now available. For a discussion of potential world models with billions of individual 'agents' then see Epstein (2009). Some of the computational issues and infrastructures to support complex processing of such large datasets (specifically, spatially dynamic models) are reviewed by Birkin et al. (2010).

The development of dynamic microsimulation models is technically challenging and an intellectually valuable activity in its own right (e.g. Willekens (2009), Morrison (2009), for other examples with a high pedigree). The broader purpose of the models is often to provide indicative forecasts, or at least projections, of the future state of a city. Such projections may have considerable value in the planning of infrastructure, resource allocation and policy formulation (Ballas et al. 2005). One of the major problems is then how to validate such models in order to build both confidence and credibility. In the second part of the chapter, we suggest a variety of methods by which validation can be approached. It will be proposed that 'backwards simulation' (BackSim) is a technique worthy of investigation in this regard. In simple terms, the idea is to run the model in reverse and to test the results of this process against historical information. A straightforward approach to this problem is outlined. Following this description, the method is applied to the city of Leeds, in which the dynamic model runs backwards for a decade and the demographics of the city is compared across a ten-year interval. Finally, a wider discussion of the contribution and potential value of the backcasting technique will be provided.

Approaches to Model Validation

The first point to make about validation is that it is a crucial step, the value of which is – in the opinion of these authors – insufficiently recognized by the academic community in general. One of the most common excuses for failing to validate models is that if one looks to the future, then comparison of scenarios is never unbiased or straightforward because there are always so many confounding factors (although what this implies about the robustness of the models is an interesting matter for conjecture). Another typical hedge which is regularly offered by the agent-based modelling community is that models are not actually well-suited for policy testing or real world scenarios but rather more intellectually refined thought experiments about systems of interest. Under these circumstances the possibility of useful, interesting and above all robust relationships between the parameters of the models and comparable processes in the real world is open to question (cf. O'Sullivan 2008). In the context of this chapter, then, one relevant trend to note is an increasing coming together – in the UK at least – of the regional science and regional studies communities (Batey 2010). While the former are highly oriented towards models and theory, the latter have a much stronger policy emphasis. Taking the models from theoretical constructs towards policy applications demands fuller consideration of the validation question.

The next issue is whether calibration and validation are not in fact closely related, or at least different sides of the same coin. While there may be some truth in this, at least one confounding factor here is the question of equifinality which has been widely recognized in complex systems modelling. This principle essentially states that a large number of different models can usually be calibrated to a unique data set. Since these models can be expected to exhibit variations in their future behaviour (hence their effectiveness as projection tools) then some further means of distinguishing between approaches is needed.

A method which is popular in the microsimulation community is alignment. Here what typically happens is that detailed outputs from some sophisticated, highly specified and probably data intensive process are simply adjusted to make sure that they match to some established projection. For example, in recent experimental work this method was used to constrain small area projections from the dynamic models which are under discussion here. The obvious problem here is the extent to which the 'established' techniques are themselves reliable. On the one hand, official government projections have a degree of self-fulfilment about them, given their tendency to provide a basis for planning and policy decisions regarding economic development, housing and infrastructure. On the other hand, the methods adopted by the National Statistics agency (ONS) have been called into question at the highest level. For example, in evidence from the British Society of Population Studies to the House of Lords Committee on Public Service and Demographic Change, members of the National Population Projections Expert Panel concluded that 'ONS needs to invest further … if they are to answer the reasonable questions made of them'. The function of microsimulation is not simply to disaggregate macro-level models, but to provide a mechanism for the enhanced representation of demographic processes. In short, therefore, within demographic microsimulation specifically some more sophisticated means of 'micro-macro' integration is required than the alignment of micro projections to aggregate forecasts, although the further point could be made that a comparison between models could perhaps form one part of a bundle of techniques for establishing confidence.

Another interesting idea is to build a repository of forecasts (Hirschfield 2010) in which academics and planners engaged in the problem of future-watching are encouraged, even obliged, to make deposits for posterity of their ex-ante assessments of the impact of policy scenarios and interventions. Such a repository could rather quickly begin to provide a useful evidence base for the evaluation of model performance, and fits well with deeper shifts towards freedom of information and open science (Birkin 2012). Whether such an effort can actually get off the ground, and who might support it, remains unclear, and time lag between the provision of a forecast, the effect of a policy, and its evaluation, will always be an issue. One suspects that the *ceteris paribus* argument advanced earlier also applies here.

A third option which we advocate here is the prospect of operating the models in reverse. The idea of backcasting has some currency in the earth science disciplines, in which for example models of tectonic activity are used to predict historical events such as earthquakes and volcanic eruptions. However we are unaware of any such applications in either microsimulation or regional science more generally, and therefore feel emboldened to characterize this slightly differently as backwards simulation, or *backsim* for short. We suggest that taking a dynamic model, running it backwards in time and comparing the resulting outputs to historic data could potentially be quite a valuable technique in assessing the viability of such a model. In the next section two different ways in which a backsim might be implemented will be considered.

Models, Methods and Data

Before considering the methodology for backcasting, it is useful to review briefly the way in which the dynamic model itself is constructed.

The microsimulation model considers a number of key socio-demographic attributes for both individuals and households:

Individual characteristics:

- The *age* of each individual is simulated as the age last birthday.
- *Gender* is distinguished as male or female.
- *Marital status* is allocated to one of three categories (married, single, or widowed/divorced).
- *Headship* is assigned to a 'representative person' in each household.
- *Occupation* is allocated according to different categories of those in work (i.e. skilled manual, professional etc.) as well as students, retired, unemployed and the economically inactive.
- *Ethnicity* is grouped into four broad classes.
- *Health status* is based on a three point self-recorded scale.

Household characteristics:

- *Locations* are assigned to a small geographic neighbourhood, the output area (OA) comprising approximately 100 households.
- *Tenure* is assessed in one of four ownership categories.
- *Household size* is a count of the number of individual residents.
- *Housing type* distinguishes the nature and characteristics of the property (e.g. detached or terraced house; apartment).

The population of Leeds is represented simply as a list of households and their individual members represented as vectors of attributes. For example, Table 20.1 shows the first six households in the file. The four numbers on the first line represent the characteristics of a household. This entity is located in area 1 (Aireborough), with three residents and is a terraced house (type = 2) which is owner-occupied (tenure = 1). The next three lines of the table or database represent the characteristics of each household member. The first individual is aged 40, male and married, who is considered the head of household (or HRP). He is a white (ethnicity = 1) manual worker (occupation = 3) in good health (health status = 1). He has a wife aged 35 and a daughter who is four years old. The second household contains a single person, the third has two members, and so on. The microsimulation file for Leeds includes 301,505 households and 724,426 individuals in this form – thus it is a synthetic representation of every individual and household in the city.

The means for the generation of this baseline population (2001) is discussed in more detail in Harland et al. (2012). The method is based on a raking procedure which these authors refer to as Iterative Proportional Sampling. For each OA the total count for each attribute and characteristic (i.e. white ethnic group, manual worker and so on) are derived from the 2001 Census Neighbourhood Statistics. Although some small numbers may be adjusted slightly for the protection of anonymity, this provides an essentially accurate representation of the univariate distribution for each small area. The neighbourhood totals are combined with

Table 20.1   A selection of simulated households

Household 1	1	3	2	1			
Individual 1	40	1	1	1	1	3	1
Individual 2	35	2	1	2	1	5	1
Individual 3	4	2	1	2	1	5	1
Household 2	1	1	4	1			
Individual 1	37	1	1	1	1	5	1
Household 3	1	2	2	1			
Individual 1	26	1	1	1	1	2	1
Individual 2	26	2	1	2	2	5	1
Household 4	1	1	2	1			
Individual 1	80	2	2	1	1	5	1
Household 5	1	1	4	1			
Individual 1	30	2	1	1	2	2	1
Household 6	1	2	2	1			
Individual 1	59	2	2	1	2	3	1
Individual 2	66	1	2	2	3	5	1

conditional probabilities from the Sample of Anonymised Records (SAR), also from the 2001 Census. This provides reliable intelligence about the interaction between cells (for example, that a white resident is in a manual occupation) but only for a 2 per cent sample of the population which can be tagged spatially to a regional scale (in which a typical region is an aggregate of 10,000 or more OAs).

The dynamic model runs in single year steps. One complete iteration of the model comprises nine separate modular operations. The model can be executed for any city or region in Great Britain. More details on the individual model components are provided by Wu et al. (2010). A brief summary follows.

- Module 1 (M1). Births. This module consists of the application of fertility probabilities to all of the adult females considered to be 'at risk' of maternity (in the age range 15–49). Separate probabilities are applied by age, marital status and small area of residence. The data are combined from vital statistics including age and marital status of mothers for each census ward (in which the ward is an aggregation typically in the order of 20 OAs, but nonetheless still quite a small local area).
- M2. Ageing and survival are applied to individuals as a Monte Carlo process again using Office for National Statistics (ONS) Vital Statistics.
- M3. Inward migration uses spatial data from both the national census 2001 and International Passenger Statistics (IPS) to compute individual and household movers into each local area.
- M4. Outward migration also uses census and IPS data to represent individual and household moves to other regions and countries.

- M5. Household formation is a module which is used to simulate the fragmentation and unification of households and their members using longitudinal from the British Household Panel Survey (BHPS). For example, a new couple setting up home would usually result from the fragmentation of two households from which a 'child' departs, and the unification of two newly formed single households as a cohabiting pair.
- M6. Change in health status is another simulation process using longitudinal data (from BHPS) to trace transitions from one health category to another according to the age and gender of each household member.
- M7. House-building uses a rate of production for new housing stock in each area, which is approximated from strategic documents which are in the public domain for individual local planning authorities.
- M8. Local migration (generation of movers) exploits longitudinal data which suggests movement propensities for different socio-demographic groups.
- M9. Local migration (selection of destinations) uses inter-area movement patterns for 2001 census Special Migration Statistics to infer local spatial preferences for the migrants generated in the previous module (M8).

Therefore a single iteration of the model consists of the following sequence of operations – {M1-M2-M3-M4-M5-M6-M7-M8-M9). In order to reverse the model, one might simply apply the inverse of each of these processes in succession i.e. {M9'-M8'-M7'-M6'-M5'-M4'-M3'-M2'-M1'}. For example, in M2 an individual aged 44 at the start of the period will be 45 at the end of the period (assuming survivorship). In module M2', the individual would be aged 43 at the end of the **backcasting** period.

However in some other cases the transitions are more difficult to represent, and may even be quite hard to conceptualize. For example M2' also necessitates the resurrection of individuals who are no longer alive, while M1' requires that infant children be returned to the maternal womb! Reverse engineering the operation of the dynamic simulation modules to this level would be quite demanding of both time and effort. The current algorithm therefore evaluates a slightly more straightforward but workable procedure. This can be seen as an exploratory precursor to more detailed work if the overall BackSim framework starts to look like an interesting and useful idea. The current (reduced) implementation comprises the following steps:

- Step 1: Run the model as normal {modules M1 to M9 inclusive}.
- Step 2: Assign each household to one of N types.
- Step 3: For each household type N and each area I calculate a rate of change through the dynamic simulation period.
- Step 4: In order to reverse the dynamics, apply the reciprocal of the rate of change to each household according to its type. A random number is drawn, and if the rate of change is greater than 1 (and its reciprocal is less than 1)

then if the random number is in the appropriate range then this household is eliminated when the model is reversed. If the reciprocal rate of change is greater than 1 then the household is a candidate to be 'cloned' in backsim, in which case a duplicate will be created in order to represent an increase in households of this type.

In order to make this procedure operational, an important question is clearly how to represent household types. In the demonstration which follows, we simply define 28 household types as the exhaustive combination of household composition (four groups) and age of head (seven groups). The groups for household composition are single male, single female, 'couple' (two people), and 'family' (any group of three or more people in a household). The age groups are under 24, 25–34, 35–44, 45–54, 55–64, 65–74, and 75+. In another experiment a much more detailed assignment of 80 types with eight age groups, five household types and two ethnicities was evaluated but this option yielded too many small groups and rendered the reversing procedure unstable. Clearly there is scope here for further investigation and greater sophistication and some of these possibilities are reviewed further in the discussion (see the section 'Discussion and Next Steps').

Model Results

The model was initialized for base year 2001. A synthetic population was created using known aggregate distributions from the UK census. Transition rates for the dynamic model are estimated from a variety of sources including the Registrar General's Vital Statistics (births and deaths by small area), International Passenger Survey (international migration flows), census 'special migration statistics' (sub-national and local migration flows), and the British Household Panel Survey (marriage, household formation, and changing health status). The BackSim procedure was executed through ten complete iterations in order to create an approximation to the population of Leeds in 1991. Each of these iterations comprises the steps outlined in Section 3 above, thus the nine dynamic simulation modules, then the reversing procedure which eliminates or clones households according to their type. We compared the populations for 1991 from the simulation model against the census data for the same year (www.mimas.ac.uk).

Demographic change by age group is considered in Figure 20.1, which shows a comparison of the 1991 and 2001 populations by five-year cohorts. The pattern of actual change (Figure 20.1a) shows four peaks of demographic expansion: i) a growth in the high school population reflects high birth rates in the mid-1980s (a period of increasing prosperity in the UK economy); ii) inflation of the student population associated with expansion of Higher Education throughout the 1990s; iii) a growth in the cohort aged in their late 30s and early 40s reflects the passing through of the 'baby boom' generation of the 1960s; iv) demographic expansion amongst the most elderly age groups. Each of these peaks is separated by a rather pronounced trough.

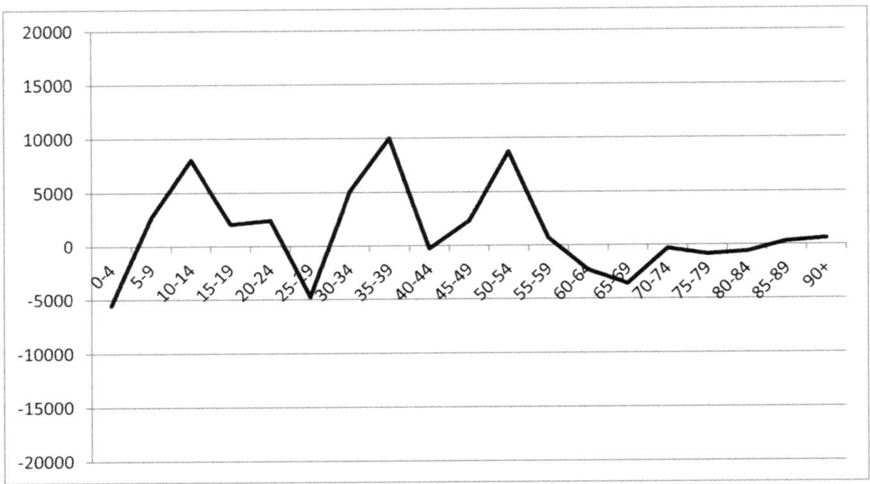

Figure 20.1a   Demographic change by cohort (actual)

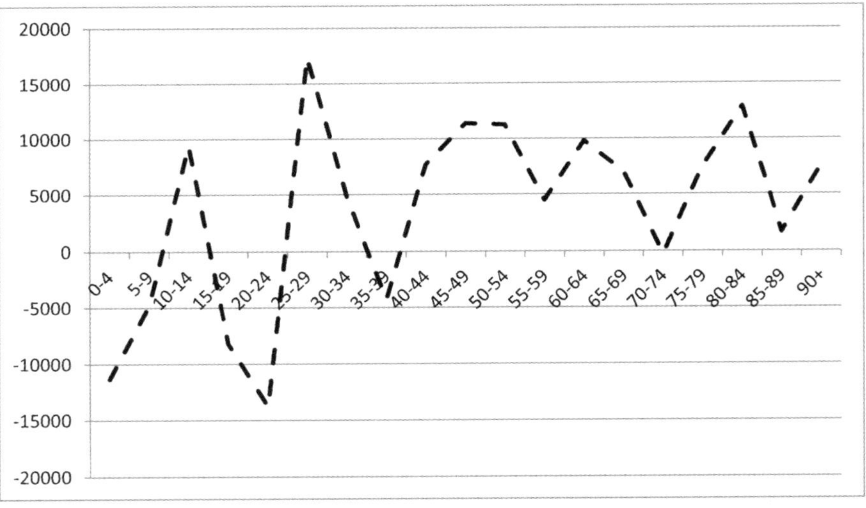

Figure 20.1b   Demographic change by cohort (modelled)

In comparing the model results (Figure 20.1b) then in general one can suggest that the pattern is reassuringly similar. In particular, equivalent troughs can be seen for schoolchildren, students, baby boomers and the elderly, with equally well-defined troughs in between. The most notable differences between the two profiles are that the students appear to be a little bit younger in the model than they are in the real data, and there is an unexplained 'double peak' in the model in the baby boom years. The model 'expects' much larger increases in the very elderly than are seen in the real data, and in this case it is the model which perhaps better represents our a priori expectations. Here there may well be some issues of compatibility between the two censuses relating to the treatment of residential and institutional populations (which is most significant for the very elderly as so many find themselves in homes or hospitals).

Preliminary spatial analysis of the data is undertaken in Figure 20.2. Here we are looking at differential population growth across 33 census wards of Leeds during the same period. The pattern of change (Figure 20.2a) shows consistent population expansion across most of the outlying, suburban areas of the city such as Aireborough, Garforth and Morley. The most concentrated growth is in the student area (Headingley), but there are also areas of population contraction in some of the more deprived inner city areas. Once again there is a degree of similarity between the modelled and real pattern. Nevertheless there are also some interesting and potentially significant points of difference. In the real data Headingley appears as the major hotspot, as noted previously, but in the simulation growth is stronger in the neighbouring areas, and also in the city centre.

A number of processes could be accounting for these differences. The most significant point to note is that the simulation uses transition data from the base year 2001. Because student expansion in Leeds was quite pronounced through the 1990s, by the end of the decade these neighbourhoods were beginning to reach further out – hence the model is tending to extrapolate this pattern by predicting higher levels of growth in some of the more outlying areas. In a similar way, the regeneration of some of the more central areas, particularly the Leeds waterfront, is a process that probably accelerated most at the end of the 1990s and into the new millennium, so again the model is perhaps representing a trend which was not fully established in the early part of the simulation period. Finally, a cluster of areas to the south and east of the city centre are losers of the population in the model, but this effect is not represented in the actual data. Some kind of distortion in the local housing market seems to be the most likely cause of this mismatch.

In a final piece of analysis, we assess the social and ethnic mix of the city from the BackSim procedure. Figure 20.3 shows the changing population of each ethnic sub-group as the model is reversed back to 1991. The structure shows a close match between the modelled and observed distributions. In spite of recent trends such as the influx of migrants from the EU 'new accession' countries then at this level of aggregation at least the long-term patterns appear to be robust and reliable.

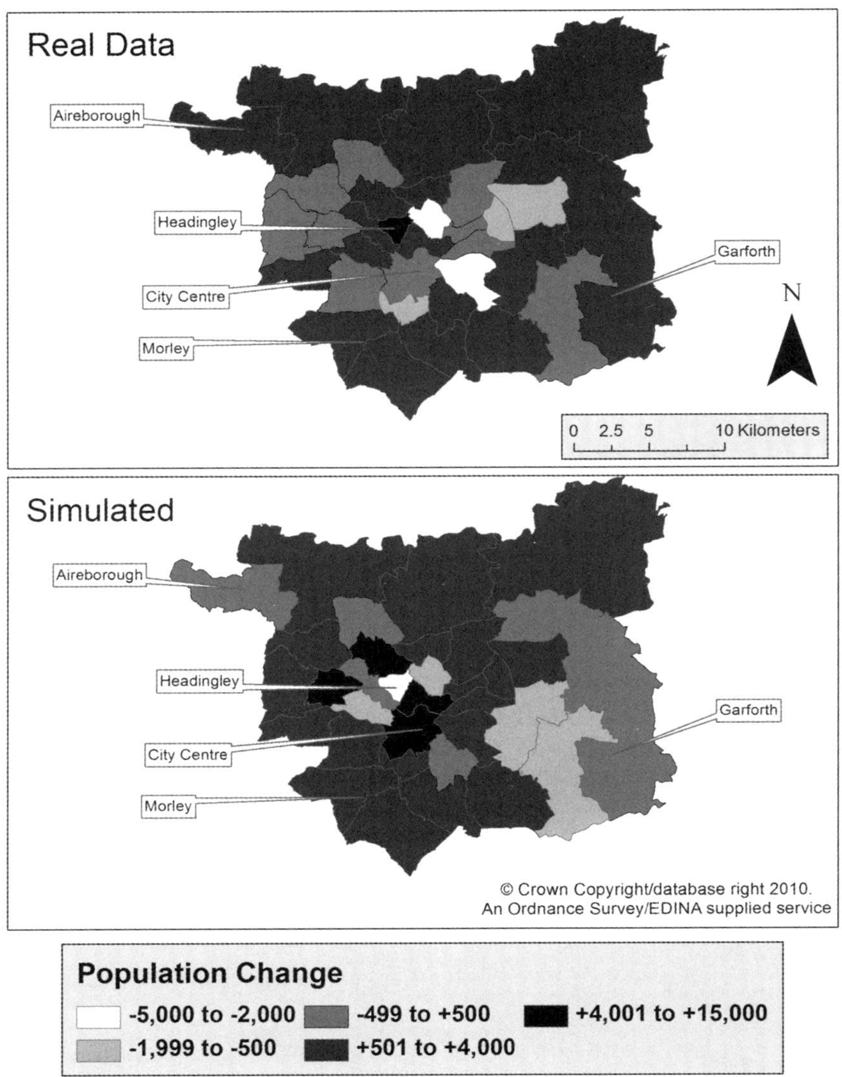

Figure 20.2   Comparison of population change by area, 1991–2001

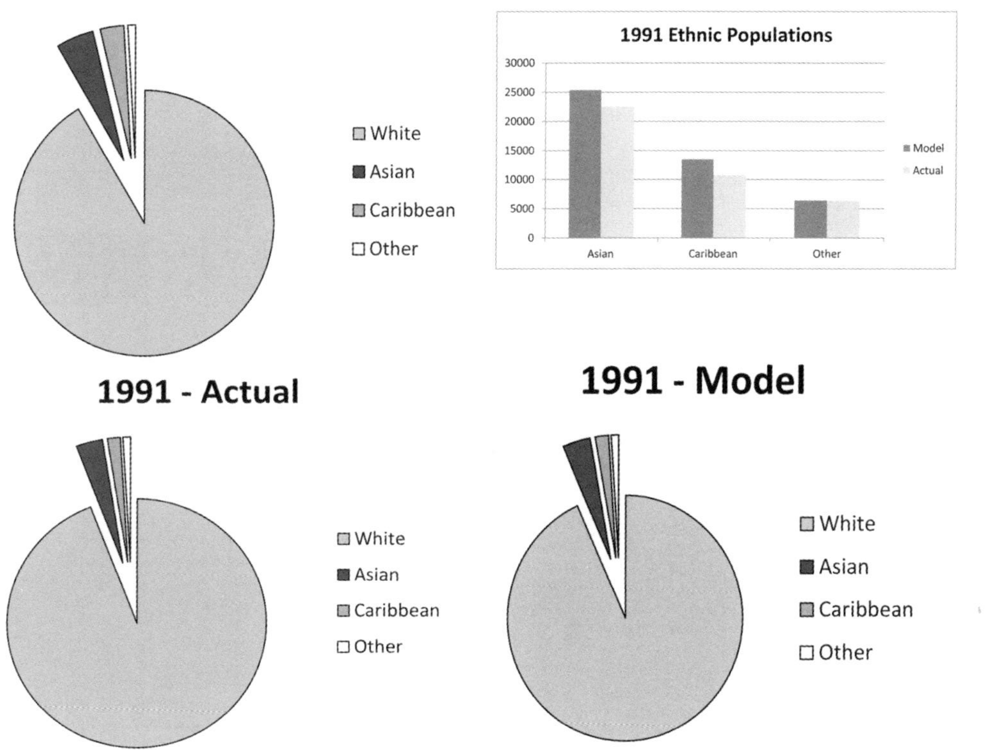

Figure 20.3   Demographic change by ethnic group

On the other hand, the patterns of occupational transition which are shown in Figure 20.4 are evidently very much less satisfactory. Whereas the actual trend is a substantial growth in professional and service occupations at the expense of manual work, the BackSim model shows almost the exact opposite. Once the model dynamics are deconstructed however these differences are quite intelligible in relation to the underlying causes. In the first place, the model assumes that new entrants to the labour market take the socio-economic status of their (male) parents. Thus ideas of social mobility are not incorporated into the model; whereas in practice of course a long-term shift in social mobility, linked to both an expansion in higher education and continued economic restructuring, has seen a general 'progression' from blue to white collar occupations. Whilst the possibilities for further microsimulation of social mobility and local labour markets has been demonstrated elsewhere (Lambert and Birkin 2012) the incorporation of more subtle mechanisms of this type into BackSim has yet to be effected.

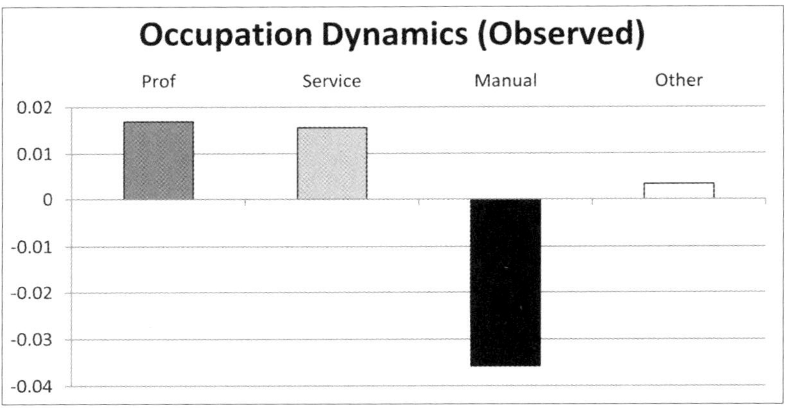

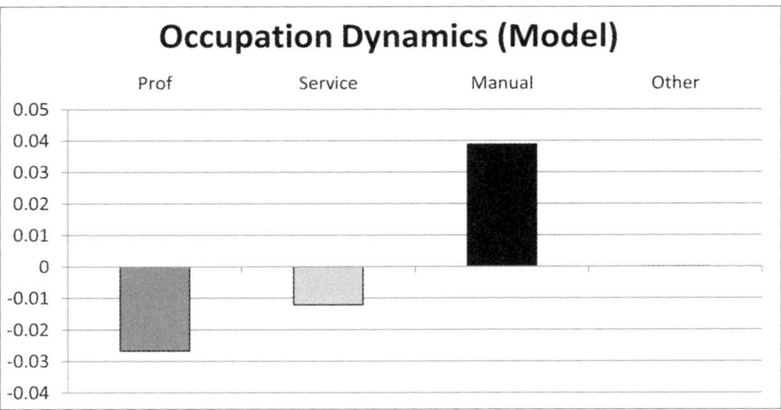

Figure 20.4   Demographic change by occupation

Discussion and Next Steps

This chapter is predicated on the notion that mathematical models and spatial simulation are potentially valuable activities, not just as thought experiments or pedagogic devices, but in the 'real world'. However some form of validation procedure is essential if models from regional science or other forms of spatial analysis are to be taken seriously in the process of planning and policy evaluation. We have used a reverse simulation procedure to begin an exploration of the properties of a dynamic population model for the city of Leeds.

The specific results from this exercise are interesting though by no means conclusive, as in some ways the models appearing to be performing effectively, but in other respects less well. Although the underlying dynamic framework for simulation is quite sophisticated, the mechanics of the process are still underspecified in a number of significant ways. Of particular note is the fact that certain ancillary processes such as labour market dynamics and ethno-demographics are less strongly represented than other social processes in the model. Another important difficulty is the treatment of the very significant student sub-populations in the city. More has been written elsewhere on the nature of this problem and a solution has been proposed which looks effective but is not easy to implement on a generic basis (Wu et al. 2008). An alternative investigation of the significance of this aspect of the dynamics would perhaps be to conduct similar experiments on a town or city with a much less concentrated student population.

A relatively straightforward but robust procedure for the implementation of the BackSim has been suggested. Whilst we feel confident that the procedure itself is sensible and reliable, it could perhaps be implemented in a more sophisticated way. In particular it would be interesting to explore a more refined implementation of the idea of household groups, perhaps using some kind of clustering or advanced classification system. Related work in the School of Geography at Leeds is well underway and could be incorporated at a later stage (Jordan et al. 2011).

One of the most important questions raised by the chapter concerns the relationship between calibration and validation. Many of the distortions in comparing modelled and actual data seem to relate to the calibration procedure in which model parameters have been estimated for a base year (2001) and then applied backwards on a linear, no-change basis. A more sophisticated procedure would be to at least consider trends in the key parameters, and could perhaps involve some form of calibration between actual and simulated data on a time series basis. One of our immediate plans is to attempt a calibration of this type and using a genetic algorithm to derive optimized parameter values for the key demographic processes. However the implications of any more refined strategy must be considered with care. If the ultimate objective of the exercise is to gain confidence in the predictive capability of a simulation, then model sparseness is a great virtue in reducing dependence on assumptions which are difficult to parameterize against an uncertain future.

Acknowledgements

The research reported in this chapter has been funded through the JISC Information Environments Programme, e-Infrastructure for Social Simulation; and by the ESRC National Centre for Research Methods.

References

Ballas, D., Clarke, G., Dorling, D., Eyre, H., Thomas, B. and Rossiter, D. 2005. SimBritain: a spatial microsimulation approach to population dynamics. *Population, Space and Place*, 11(1), 13–34.

Batey P. 2010. Regional Science and Regional Studies, unpublished address, RSABAIS, Glasgow.

Birkin, M., Procter, R., Allan, R., Bechhofer, S., Buchan, I., Goble, C., Hudson-Smith, A., Lambert, P., de Roure, D. and Sinnott, R. 2010. The Elements of a Computational Infrastructure for Social Simulation. *Philosophical Transactions of the Royal Society A*, 368 (1925), 3797–812.

British Society for Population Studies. 2012. Evidence to the House of Lords Committee on Public Service and Demographic Change, BSPS., August 2012. Online at: http://www2.lse.ac.uk/socialPolicy/BSPS/announcements.aspx, accessed 20 February 2013.

Epstein J. 2009. Modelling to contain pandemics. *Nature*, 460, 687.

Harland, K., Heppenstall, A., Birkin, M. and Smith, D. 2012. Creating realistic synthetic populations at varying spatial scales: a comparative critique of microsimulation techniques. *Journal of Artificial Societies and Social Simulation*, 15(1), 1.

Hirschfield A. 2010. Personal communication.

Jordan, R., Birkin, M. and Evans, A. 2011. Agent-based Simulation Modelling of Housing Choice and Urban Regeneration Policy, in Bosse, T., Geller, A. and Jonker, C. (eds), *Multi-Agent-Based Simulation XI, Lecture Notes in Artificial Intelligence*, 152–66. Berlin: Springer.

Lambert, P. and Birkin, M. 2012. Occupation, education and social inequalities: a case study linking survey data sources to an urban microsimulation analysis, in Pagliara, F., Simmonds, D., de Bok, M. and Wilson, A. (eds), *Employment Location in Cities and Regions, Advances in Spatial Science*. Berlin: Springer-Verlag.

Morrison, R. 2009. Rates of return in the Canada pension plan: sub-populations of special policy interest and preliminary after-tax results, in Zaidi, A., Harding, A. and Williamson, P. (eds), *New Frontiers in Microsimulation Modelling*. Farnham: Ashgate.

O'Sullivan, D. 2008. Geographical information science: agent-based models, *Progress in Human Geography*, 29, 749–56.

Willekens, F. 2009. Continuous-time microsimulation in longitudinal analysis, in Zaidi, A., Harding, A. and Williamson, P. (eds), *New Frontiers in Microsimulation Modelling*. Farnham: Ashgate.

Wu, B., Birkin, M. and Rees, P. 2008. A spatial microsimulation model with student agents. *Computers Environment and Urban Systems*, 32, 440–53.

Wu, B., Birkin, M. and Rees, P. 2010. A dynamic MSM with agent elements for spatial demographic forecasting. *Social Science Computer Review*, 29(1), 145–60.

Wu, B.M., Birkin, M.H. and Rees, P.H. 2009. A dynamic spatial microsimulation model of local populations, proceeding of 2nd General Conference of the International Microsimulation Association, 8–10 June, Ottawa, Canada.

Index

Page numbers in **bold** refer to figures and tables.